DIGITAL LIBRARIES IN KNOWLEDGE MANAGEMENT

Proceedings of the 7th MANLIBNET Annual National Convention held at Indian Institute of Management, Kozhikode During May5-7, 2005

M.G. Sreekumar
T. Sunitha
P. Sreejaya
Ashok Pathak

Ess Ess Publications

4837/24, Ansari Road
Darya Ganj
New Delhi-110 002
Phone: 23260807, 51563444
Fax: 011-51563334
E-mail: info@essessreference.com
url: www.essessreference.com

First Published **2006**

ISBN: 81-7000-442-X

Rs.1325/-

Published by:
Ess Ess Publications
4837/24, Ansari Road, Darya Ganj, New Delhi-110 002
Tel: 011-23260807, 51563444 Fax: 011-51563334
E-mail: info@essessreference.com
url: www.essessreference.com

Printed in India at:
Printline, New Delhi

Preface

Acquisition, preservation, retrieval and dissemination of scholarly information form the major business of academic and research libraries. Recent advances in Information and Communication Technology (ICT) makes possible the development and dissemination of information through various forms and means of media on a local, national and international level. ICT has produced marvels like the Internet, the World Wide Web, interactive multimedia, CD-ROMs, on-line, digital libraries, etc. These developments have a wider impact on library services.

The digital age has ushered significant changes in the information space in terms of operations, collection development strategies, services, and user preferences. Digital Libraries (DL) are structured storage environments of digital data with a consistent format for index and content abstraction. Open Digital Library (ODL) technologies, Open Archives Initiatives (OAI) and Open Access (OA) movements are fast gaining worldwide attention.

To achieve these broad objectives, Management Libraries Network (MANLIBNET) was initiated as a movement in 1998 by bringing together over 40 Library Professionals and Information Scientists at the first convention held in Ahmedabad jointly by the Indian Institute of Management (IIM Ahmedabad and Ahmedabad Management Association organized by late Shri Ashok jambhekar the then President of MANLIBNET, This was followed by a second, third, fourth , fifth and sixth in the year of 2000, 2001 , 2002 , 2003 and 2004 ; at the Institute of Management Technology, Ghaziabad, Indian Institute of Management, Lucknow, National Institute of Financial Management, Faridabad and XLRI, Jamshedpur, Indian Council of Social Science Research, Mumbai . The main objectives of MANLIBNET are to provide a common forum to the professions : and to develop understanding and co-operation particularly among management and business libraries.

The 7th MANLIBNET Annual National Convention was held at **Indian Institute of Management Kozhikode (IIMK)**, IIMK Campus PO, Kozhikode (Calicut), Kerala during **May 5-7, 2005 on the theme** 'Digital Libraries in Knowledge Management : Opportunities for Management Libraries' (http://intranet.iimk.ac.in/manlibnet05/ index.htm).

The Sub Themes of the Convention were the following:

* Knowledge Management and management of knowledge repositories ...leveraging on Digital Technologies
* Digital Libraries & Digital Archives: Design, development, organization, implementation, maintenance and the Digital Nervous System
* Digital Library Technologies: Architectures, Standards, Protocols, Resources & Formats
* Strategies for multi-media Digital Content development and providing intellectual access using COM/ DCOM
* Trends in Open Digital Libraries
* Strategies for multi-media Digital Collection building and management
* Design and implementation of cutting edge digital information services
* Open Access Initiatives for Digital Information Services
* Promoting and Supporting of Digital Information Services to user community

Another significant feature of the event was the Pre-Convention tutorial on Greenstone Digital Library Software on May 5th 2005.

The Convention was attended by over 50 top level management schools along with Universities, IITs, and other technical education institutions in the country. Knowledge Management leveraging on information science and technology was the ultimate objective of the Convention and all these related aspects were comprehensively reviewed and addressed and appropriate strategies resolved. This volume contains the proceedings of the Convention. The book carries 40 peer reviewed research papers contributed by over 65 authors from across the country.

Editors

Contents

1

CONVENTION THEME Digital Libraries in Knowledge Management: Opportunities for Management Libraries

M.G. Sreekumar
Librarian & Head, CDDL, IIM Kozhikode

Acquisition, preservation, retrieval and dissemination of scholarly information form the major business of academic and research libraries. Recent advances in Information and Communication Technology (ICT) makes possible the development and dissemination of information through various forms and means of media on a local, national and international level. ICT has produced marvels like the Internet, the World Wide Web, interactive multimedia, CD-ROMs, on-line, digital libraries, etc. These developments have a wider impact on library services.

The digital age has ushered significant changes in the information space in terms of operations, collection development strategies, services, and user preferences. Digital Libraries (DL) are structured storage environments of digital data with a consistent format for index and content abstraction.

Open Digital Library (ODL) technologies, Open Archives Initiatives (OAI) and Open Access (OA) movements are fast gaining worldwide attention.

Knowledge Management leveraging on information science and technology is the ultimate objective this Convention and all these related aspects will be comprehensively reviewed and addressed and appropriate strategies developed at the 7th **MANLIBNET Annual National Convention** being held at **Indian Institute of Management Kozhikode,** Kunnamangalam PO, Kozhikode (Calicut), Kerala from May 5 - 7, 2005.

Another attraction of the Convention is the Pre-Convention tutorial on Greenstone Digital Library Software.

Sub Themes

* Knowledge Management and management of knowledge repositories leleveraging on Digital Technologies
* Digital Libraries & Digital Archives: Design, development, organization, implementation, maintenance and the Digital Nervous System
* Digital Library Technologies: Architectures, Standards, Protocols, Resources & Formats
* Strategies for multi-media Digital Content development and providing intellectual access using COM/DCOM
* Trends in Open Digital Libraries
* Strategies for multi-media Digital Collection building and management
* Design and implementation of cutting edge digital information services
* Open Access Initiatives for Digital Information Services
* Promoting and Supporting of Digital Information Services to user community.

2

Technology Based Knowledge Management Developments: Threats and Opportunities for Libraries

T.A.V. Murthy
Director, INFLIBNET, Ahmedabad
(tav@inflibnet.ac.in)

ABSTRACT

Technology is still evolving at a rapid pace. While Libraries have embraced new technologies like digital reference services, the question is whether they will also adapt to the new modes of working which young people are now adopting. Until this day, we shed light on four emerging technologies that will affect library strategy. WIKIS - as collaborative working environments are increasing in popularity, while most Librarians probably dislike WIKIPEDIA, this tool might have possibilities for library as well. The day also covers access management: how to get rid of the simplistic IP range method of authentication and offer patrons anytime, any where access to digital collections. Portable devices are becoming even more powerful, a single note book can hold a complete Library of electronic books and journals, while mobile phones and PDAs might be an interesting platform to deliver new library services. And finally 2004 was the year of the blog, while some librarians have started their own blogs, the opportunities are much greater. Each of these technological masterpieces depends on myriad successes and failures, both mundane, and spectacular that have occurred through years of exploration and experiment. For a lot of us in the world of high technology, it is this real possibility of creating our own masterpieces, great or small, that keeps the knowledge industry vibrant and exciting. Having access to right information, at the right time without necessarily being an expert in all domains involved, would greatly improve organizational efficiency and effectiveness. In search of a way to work with knowledge as an asset, organization are transforming traditional knowledge from an abstract concept to tangible and manageable one and librarians play a vital role in this transformation. As epistemologists reason that as knowledge is 'justified belief', without advent of powerful and sophisticated hardware and software tools, the domain of knowledge management would only be subject of theory and philosophy. Knowledge Management processes perform well with sophisticated libraries when enabled by powerful technologies and tools like Inter-operable institutional repositories with OAI-PMH, Open access journals and open archives, open source digital library management software, web services, Nation wide networks between academic institutions etc. IT-Architecture is an increasingly common topic among K-industry experts. In the recent HBR article - GETTING - IT- RIGHT, the author names 3 critical steps to creating high quality IT environment: creating a long term plan in line with overall righteous goals, building a unifying technology platform that serves the overall needs of the organization and developing a high functioning culture that can anticipate and achieve strictly defined objectives.

3

Information Systems For Knowledge Enterprises

K.R. Srivathsan
Director
Indian Institute of Information Technology and Management Kerala (IIITMK)
(director@iiitmk.ac.in)

ABSTRACT

More and more institutions and organizations are increasingly employing advanced informations sytems like Digital Library, E-Publications, Learning Management Systems and such others. Emerging economy is more and more knowledge driven in all fields and walks of learning and economic activity. Broadband connectivity combined with emerging information systems paradigm, knowledge management and building the culture of learning organizations will change fundamentally the way we work and collaborate with other institutions. The librarians of tomorrow will have to learn to support actively the needs of information services and e-publications management of workgroups in different kinds of organizations. This has to be seen in the light of every institution's need to make every workgroup into knowledge enterprise that processes the received information, observations and requests and take knowledgeable actions and decisions aligned with its objectives and responsibilities.

The above scenario calls for understanding the basic paradigm shift in the emerging information services provided by the information systems managers and knowledge officers of tomorrow. The productivity and efficiency of institutions is critically depends on the quality of such services provided by the information officers to the workgroups in every organizations.

Extrapolating the Five Laws of Library Science enunciated by S.R. Ranganathan, we present how we may go about building the structure of future information, collaboration and computing services in the institutions of tomorrow. We show that there is acute and urgent need to ensure that the information archives and access like the Digital Library and Document Management Systems are provided as adjunct to any workgroup's dynamic and strategic information workflow requirements. Further the group also has to make itself accountable through its logs of the decision process, reports and conclusions. This leads to a reference information flow architecture for knowledge enterprises. Such architecture is readily extensible to virtual workgroups with members from different organizations. The example of the Police Portal for Community Interactions implemented by the IIITM-K is cited as a case study.

4

Knowledge Management in Libraries: Designing Proposal for Implementation

P.R. Goswami
Director, NASSDOC, New Delhi.

M.M.L Goyal
Librarian, ICFAI Business School, Gurgaon

ABSTRACT

Knowledge is an important source for competitive advantage. Knowledge management is management of knowledge people in organization. The paper presents guidelines for implementing a knowledge management project in a social sciences library.

0. Introduction

Knowledge Management (KM) is a buzzword. Private corporations all over the World are somewhat obsessed with this concept; and many of them are eager to imbibe it in their work culture. In 1991, Nonanka, a Japanese writer, created a stir when his paper '*The Knowledge Creating Company*' appeared in the *Harvard Business Review*. The paper began with a simple declarative sentence "In an economy where the only certainty in uncertainty, the one sure source of competitive advantage is knowledge". He candidly argued that because Japanese companies placed such a high value on 'Corporate Knowledge' or 'Intellectual Capital', a climate of continuous innovation existed. The Japanese are more inclined to value tacit knowledge or the knowledge that is intuitive, interpretive, ambiguous, non-linear and difficult to quantify. On the other hand, Americans put their faith in systematic, measurable explicit knowledge.

Before starting any KM initiative, one should understand that knowledge is wholly or completely a human function. Knowledge is not mechanical or developed in computers. In fact, computers are tools that can help a person with knowledge to create more knowledge. Because organizations employ people, knowledge management is, basically in one sense, people management. It is management of the knowledgeable people in the organization (and those associated with the organization) for the success of the organization.

The real question is whether it is feasible to implement KM project in a library or documentation center. The purpose of this paper is to present a set of introductory guidelines that can be followed for implementing a viable KM project in a library. Examples of KM initiatives have been given from a social science organizations' library.

1. Managerial Instincts

An important pre-requisite of a KM project is leadership. In fact, the projects that require changing the way in which the organization thinks, performs and measures its success require leadership. Leaders are essentially the persons others are willing to follow. A good leader always gives the followers something to believe in, something that has a good probability of working and ultimately adding to the wealth of the organization.

Another important trait of a KM project leader is to think how it will fit to the organization. To build a proposal one must work from a position that applies his or her knowledge of KM to meet the organizational goals. To start with, one must think of small changes. No organization is eager to undertake a major change in how it works. It is advisable to take up small projects and implement them successfully to create an example for others to assess and emulate. A KM project leader who is relatively new to the organization should wait to understand the climate. It is better to know more about the organization; learning what problems can be solved. Even when a KM project manager's job is to create a scheme, learning, talking and building networks within the organization are important KM strategies that can be accomplished by strategic waiting.

One should build his or her credibility in the organization for a KM project. The people working in the organization should not feel that KM is for aiding to the reduction of head count. It is important to show that KM is not about reduction but about building, creating and learning new ways for everyone to be successful.

A project leader should start the KM initiative with himself. Others may not follow the leader immediately, but they may follow later. Sometimes, the best project ideas start with problems that one need to solve and to start with. One can identify a problem and create a solution using KM principles. The problem may be universal in nature and the solution could provide valuable insight about KM to others operating in the vicinity.

Relationship building or networking is an essential component of a successful KM project. Networking for an organization includes internal and external connections. The same is true for individuals. If the library has not developed relationships with people and organizations inside and outside its walls, a KM project is likely face a rough weather. Learning how your library can help others as well as how your organization can benefit from others is part of a KM project

2. Social Science Library: Planning of a KM Project

In a Social Science institutions' library, one can think of KM projects that can lead to better organization and dissemination of knowledge artifacts to its clientele. National Social Science Documentation center (NASSDOC), which is a constituent unit of the Indian Council of Social Science Research (ICSSR) is primarily responsible for information support service to social science researchers. Major programmes of NASSDOC include:

i. Library and Reference service

ii. Literature search from electronic bibliographic databases on specific topics (on request from scholars)

iii. Bibliography on demand service for research scholars particularly these residing in small towns/remote areas

iv. Preparation of abstracts and indexes of major Indian Social Science periodicals and

v. Document delivery service.

In addition to this, NASSDOC also sponsor bibliographical and documentation projects and provides financial assistance to scholars for collection of research material from libraries and archives located in different metropolitan cities of India.

Keeping in view its organizational objectives NASSDOC has devised a plan to initiate the following KM initiatives.

a) Development of a knowledge base to assist PhD research scholars coming from small towns/remote areas who have limited exposure to basics of research metholodology. They also suffer from library anxiety and they are often hesitant to use information technology based library and documentation services. The knowledge base is to be eventually documented in the form of a 'manual'. The experience gained by the staff while interacting with research scholars is to be utilized for this purpose.

b) It has been experienced that majority of research scholars now work in the fields like regional economics, geography, social anthropology, governance, women's studies, environmental economics. Many of them look for micro-level data and information that are published in different government serials, newsletters of autonomous bodies and regulatory agencies. Therefore, it would be worthwhile to cull out data from different authentic sources (both published as well as unpublished) on different socio-economic variables and keep them region-wise under different folders. The source of data including methodology in the collection (survey, census or administrative record), concepts and definition used to describe the variables, limitations of data sets in terms of comparability are to be documented in the form of a 'users guide' for research scholars.

c) Results of the analysis of requests received for compilation of bibliographies and literature search from electronic databases can be documented properly to prepare a user responsive collection development policy. The endorsements made in the request form also provide an insight into information seeking behavior of the scholars. The professional staffs are required to develop a clear understanding of the collection in an information-seeking context. The matter is of critical importance in developing a KM initiative with the following questions:

   * Does a collection provide a major focus in information seeking?
   * How heavily the users rely on the collection for their information needs?
   * What do users do when the information resource sought is unavailable in the collection?

* How frequently do they resort to substitute resources in the same collection even when the substitutes are an imperfect match?

In collection development, the most important factor is reliability. A KM project involving collection development should develop a knowledge base to assess how reliable is the collection from the viewpoint of readers.

Needless to say, all these KM initiatives planned for the NASSDOC clients are aimed to transform tacit knowledge to explicit knowledge. Tacit knowledge is the KM term typically used to describe the knowledge that is in people's heads or in their own files as distinguished from explicit knowledge that exists in documents or databases.

3. KM in Practice: Structure and Content of Reference Sources (Census of India Data)

For developing skills of reference librarians, it is necessary to capture tacit knowledge pertaining to structure and content of certain esoteric sources of information. In a social science research library, Census of India data sources are used extensively; and reference librarians are required to develop knowledge management tools so that they can understand and interpret different categories of Census of India data sources. A descriptive account of census data sources would enable us to understand this phenomenon.

Census of India is the most prominent example of information generation and dissemination by a government agency in India. By measuring the scale of its operation and the magnitude of data collected through this operation, one can safely conclude that it is one of the largest administrative exercises in the world, and certainly so in the country itself. It is the source of maximum data on human population. Apart from total population count, the scope of the census extends to publication of data in its varied form which may include classification of person by sex and age, martial status, rural/

urban residence, educational standards, economic activity, etc.

As regards collection of data, census schedule or questionnaire is the main apparatus for collection of the data. The success of a census depends on the correct design and administration of the schedule. During the last four decades, the census organization has introduced several innovations in its schedule to reflect the changing socio economic milieu in the country. In this process, new schedules have been introduced and tabulation programmes have been expanded correspondingly. The number of volumes containing census data have also increased manifold during the last six decennial censuses (i.e. 1951, 1961, 1971, 1981, 1991 and 2001).

The policy regarding dissemination of Census of India data includes many aspects; in which form the data are to be published, how to organize the reports, what are the tables to be included and what sort of support is to be provided so that the users can identify and use the data. In India, census data are primarily, disseminated through printed tables that constitute the census volumes. These volumes are designed or planned by the census organization at center as well as in states depending on geographical coverage and demographic characteristics. The publication plan of census volumes is decided keeping in view the above two aspects and they are assigned series number and part number as shown below:

4. Classification of Census Volumes

Criteria for Classification of Census Volumes		Bibliographical Descriptor used for identification
A. Ad-hoc publications / basic tables / special purpose tables	a.1	Paper no./Occasional paper no. during a calendar year, e.g., paper No.1, 1981. Provision Population Totals
	a. 2	Census monographs during a particular census on subjects of topical interest.

B.	Geographic and administrative divisions covered, i.e. states, union territory, etc.	b.1	Series in Indo-Arabic numerals used as a descriptor, e.g. Series 1 India, Series 2 Andhra Pradesh, etc.
C.	Demographic variables	c.1	Part in Roman numbers used as a descriptor, e.g. Part 1 Administrative Report Part II General Population Tables, etc. These parts are further subdivided.
		c.2	Series in Roman alphabets has also been used to denote the demographic variables covered in a volume, e.g. A. Series General Population Tables. B. Series General Economic Tables etc.

The table provides a broad view of structure of census volumes. The volume containing basic data (i.e. primary census abstract, special purpose tables, research studies etc.) are released under the descriptor ' paper number' or 'occasional paper number' in a calendar year. The most important feature of a census volume is the coverage in terms of administrative region. As a first level classification, the mainstream census volumes are released in different series specified in Indo-Arabic numerals, each representing an administrative region as shown in the table. In the second level of classification, the census volumes are released in several parts containing data on a particular demographic feature. The part number are common for all series publications, all India as well as states. In addition to administrative/geographical divisions and demographic features, the census publications can also be grouped by the level of presentation of data. The volumes are published at three levels; i.e. all India tables, State and Union Territory tables, the District Census Handbooks. In order to provide an insight into the scope and coverage of different census tables, a tabulation plan is published before the census is undertaken.

For the purpose of dissemination of Census of India 2001 data, information and communication technology (ICT) has been used in a big way. In 1998, a website was created on the Internet to provide census data and metadata. And to make available thematic maps, a new GIS website has been created. (http: / /www.censusindiamaps.com) in addition to the existing website (http: / /www.censusindia.net) The GIS website allows the user to prepare maps up to Taluk or any sub district level. The software used for the management of this website is also user friendly. The census data pertaining to final population totals, urban agglomerations and certain other variables are available on CDs.

Knowledge management in a library has to do a lot with one's intuitive judgment. Intuition depends on the use of experience to recognize key patterns that indicate the dynamics of the situation. Because patterns can be subtle, people often cannot describe what they noticed or how they judged a situation as typical or untypical. Therefore intuition has a strange reputation. Skilled decision makers know that they can depend on their intuition but at the same time they feel uncomfortable trusting a source of power that seem so accidental.

It has been said that customer information is a great fit for any KM initiative for a library. One needs to know what information he has on members and how this can be used for improving the services. Because cultural realities can act as barriers on chablors for knowledge management, we have to understand our organizations' cultural realities and take them into account while finalizing any KM initiative.

One cannot dissuade the fact that librarian work with databases. Most of our professionals are equipped with a set of skills which enables them to get jobs. What has to be managed is their natural curiosity by leading them to the discussion groups, seminars and face-to-face knowledge sharing process.

There are several stages that information professionals can take to think beyond databases to something more useful. These include.

* Adding contextual information;- where was this information used. What factors need to be considered when using it.
* Giving details of originator; - allowing users of information to contact the contributors; e.q. Via e-mail, etc.
* Offering an expert' databases; pointers to people. Information on the location of experts and expertise; rather than the expertise itself.

If we take wider contextual view of knowledge, then it is really about getting the best out of your people. (i.e. your knowledge worker), their expertise and creativity. This requires higher skills of leadership. There is a shift of emphasis from knowledge management to knowledge creation and innovation.

References

1. Chait, Laurence P. Creating a successful knowledge management system. *Journal of Business Strategy.* March April 1999. p.23-26.
2. Day. Ronald E. Clearing up implicit knowledge: Implications for knowledge management, information science, psychology and social epistemology. *Journal of the American Society for Information Science and Technology* 56 (6), 2005. p. 630-635
3. Greco, Joann. Knowledge is power *Journal of Business Strategy*. March-April 1999. p. 19-22
4. Nordan, Ken. Knowledge management when your organization can not get a KM project started; take it personally. *Information Outlook.* 9(3), March 2005. p.17-20.

5

Digital Library Initiatives and Issues in India : Efforts on Scholarly Knowledge Management

M.G. Sreekumar and P. Sreejaya
Indian Institute of Management Kozhikode
(mgsree;sreejaya @ iimk.ac.in)

ABSTRACT

The academic and research libraries across the globe are striving hard to harness technology for achieving scholarly knowledge management, which is fast proliferating, distributed and scattered. Knowledge Management leveraging on information science (IS) and information technology (IT) is the recent trend and strategy seen in the advanced academic and corporate environment. Building world standard digital libraries, as powerhouses of knowledge, that are able to address the complex issues put forth by the technology push as well as the demand pull are fast catching up worldwide attention. Particularly, in India, Open Digital Library (ODL) initiatives are picking up unprecedented Institutional as well as professional group attention owing to a variety of excellent features offered by these DLs. During the past five years India has been responding to this global trend quite proactively and positively. One of the major reasons being, presently, more than 70 percentage of world's scholarly literature are born digital. Naturally when they are acquired by the libraries for patron's use they will have to be acquired in the digital form. A digital library is a collection of information that is both electronic (born digital) as well as digitized and it gives us powers we never had with traditional libraries. Digital libraries have attracted almost all the developed and developing countries due to its multifaceted features and the opportunities it extend to the information providers and information seekers. It offers new levels of access to broader audiences of users and new opportunities for library and information science field to advance both theory and practice. Creating effective digital libraries and providing cutting edge digital information services poses serious challenges for existing and future technologies. They include collection building, infrastructure, acceptability, access restrictions, readability, standardization, authentication, preservation, copyright, policy and strategic issues, user interface, funding etc. Yet the advantages outweigh most of the bottlenecks and hardships and therefore the importance of digital libraries have been recognized by all nations of the world. India has recognized the power of digital libraries and lots of initiatives are on the move for developing state-of-art digital libraries.

This paper discusses the various problems, challenges and issues involved in the design and development of world standard digital libraries, focused on the Indian context. It also highlights the initiatives taken by various Indian libraries / organizations towards the development of digital libraries.

Introduction

Knowledge Management leveraging on information science (IS) and information technology (IT) is the recent trend and strategy seen in the advanced academic and corporate environment. Libraries, especially academic and research libraries, are perceived to be knowledge repositories of scholarly content. Scholarly communication is a complex mechanism acted up on by many stakeholders. Scholarly communication refers to the formal and informal processes by which the research and scholarship of researchers, faculty and independent scholars (freelance researchers) are created, evaluated, edited, formatted, distributed, organized, made accessible, archived, used, and transformed. Publishing is the formal system whose key players include researchers, publishers (including scholarly societies), and libraries (1).

Over the past two decades dramatic changes have fundamentally reshaped the entire system of scholarly communication eco system. Recent advancements in technology and the advent of computers, Internet and communication technologies have revolutionised the scholarly communication scenario drastically. The first and foremost among these changes is the phenomenal increase in the body of published knowledge.

Data, Information and Knowledge

The role of pertinent and contextually relevant scholarly information in an academic or research environment is a complex issue which calls for an exclusive paper itself. Generally information involves data in context. Information is not separate from its context because the interpretation of incoming data streams is dependent not only on the perception of the receiver, but in the context of the moment. Information that is relevant becomes actionable knowledge during the duration of the specific context. This is the reasoning behind the design of specific subcomponents and companion-components to be introduced shortly. For a learning organization in particular, scholarly information is the critical piece that transforms fact into knowledge.

In the current practical setting the recorded knowledge reaches libraries by way of established scholarly publication types both in print as well as digital formats. There is an amazing penetration of scholarly digital information through a variety of forms such as books (published as such or issued as accompaniment), journals, portals, vortals, reports, CBTs,

WBTs, cases, databases etc. To make matters more complex the vast array of different file formats, standards and platforms in which documents are published, pose a multiplicity of threats to the information professional who is supposed to be the custodian and service provider of these information products once it has found its way into the library.

Digital Libraries

Digital Libraries (DL) are now emerging as a crucial component of global information infrastructure, adopting the latest information and communication technology. Digital Libraries are networked collections of digital texts, documents, images, sounds, data, software, and many more that are the core of today's Internet and tomorrow's universally accessible digital repositories of all human knowledge. According to the Digital Library Federation (DLF, USA - http://www.dlf.org), "Digital libraries are organizations that provide the resources, including the specialized staff, to select, structure, offer intellectual access to, interpret, distribute, preserve the integrity of, and ensure the persistence over time of collections of digital works so that they are readily and economically available for use by a defined community or set of communities".

In India currently the concept 'Digital Library' is being practiced by and large loosely or even confused by many information systems. It is therefore imperative that the concept is properly understood so that there is no ambiguity while we progress with the work of designing or developing a digital library which is fully justified in the technical sense of the word. It is important that embarking on a digital library project is something which will take away substantial amount of time, energy, manpower and of course the hard earned money being pumped into it–be it for system development or towards development and maintenance of the collection, in a meaningful way. There is consensus all over that there exists a very large quantum of digital information, scholarly as well as trade, which are scattered and distributed throughout the Net and also being stored in numerous other databases and repositories spread across the world. Also there is an unprecedented technology support and availability of infrastructure for digital libraries.

Features

Digital libraries have attracted almost all the developed and developing countries due to its features and the opportunities it extend to the information providers and information seekers. The digital library has the information in the electronic form and electronic media facilitates the access to information available in digital form at different places. It offers new levels of access to broader audiences of users and new opportunities for library and information science field to advance both theory and practice. They contain information collections predominantly in digital or electronic form. Electronic publications have some special problems of management as compared to printed document. They include infrastructure, acceptability, access restrictions, readability, standardization, authentication, preservation, copyright, user interface etc. But still the advantages are more and therefore the importance of digital libraries have been recognized by all nations of the world. India has indeed recognized the importance of digital libraries and lots of initiatives have been taken by various libraries / institutes / organizations.

Digital libraries do enable the creation of local content, strengthen the mechanisms and capacity of the library's information systems and services. They increase the portability, efficiency of access, flexibility, availability and preservation of content. Digital Libraries can help move the nation towards realizing the enormously powerful vision of 'anytime, anywhere' access to the best and the latest of human thought and culture, so that no classroom, individual or a society is isolated from knowledge resources. Digital library brings the library to the user, overcoming all geographical barriers.

DL Software

Undoubtedly it is essential to have a robust and flexible digital collections management and presentation software for creating and delivering digital collections. The preservation of digital objects is currently intimately tied to software that presents those objects. Complete preservation of complex digital objects, especially, is likely to require preservation of the software needed to use those objects. (2). The complexity of the situation is that digital library technologies and contents are not static. Continual evolution and investment are required to maintain the digital library. Commercial digital library products are comprehensive and extensible enough to support this evolution, but in many cases they are beyond the reach of most of the libraries in India. Some of the popular commercial DL software in the Indian libraries are VTLS (http://www.vtls.com) from the international market and ACADO (http://www.transversalnet.com/acado/index.htm) as an Indian initiative. The latter is definitely less costlier when compared but still striving its best to get a critical mass of users. The whole lot of associated issues include initial purchase fee, licensing fee, upgrade fee, annual maintenance contacts (AMCs) and so on. The best available choice for the librarian now is to turn to an Open Source Software (OSS). OSS has grown tremendously in scope and popularity over the last several years, and is now in widespread use. The growth of OSS has gained the attention of research librarians and created new opportunities for libraries (3). OSS is close to our hearts primarily for their free (or almost free) availability and the broad rights it awards to the consumer. According to Stallman and others at OSS, 'Free Software' uses the 'free' from 'freedom', not the one from 'free beer' (http://www.opensource.org/docs/definition_plain.html).

OSS is software for which the source code is available to the end-user. The source code can be modified by the end-user. The licensing conditions are intended to facilitate continued re-use and wide availability of the software in both commercial and non-commercial contexts. The cost of acquisition to the end-user is often minimal. According to the proponents of OSS, 'Open source is a development methodology; free software is a social movement'. There are number of other notable features to OSS. Firstly, it has no secrets and the innards are available for anyone to inspect. It is not privately controlled and hence likely to promote open rather than proprietary formats. It is typically maintained by communities rather than corporations and hence bug fixes and enhancement are often frequent and free. It is usually distributed free of charge (developers make their money from support, training, and specialist add-ons; not marketing). It is also essential to clear up some of the misunderstandings about OSS. Open source software may or may not cost money. The cost of ownership often bears little relation to the cost of acquiring a piece of software. 'Public domain' is something different. Open source software has a copyright holder and conditions of legal use. Open source software does not mandate exclusivity. One can use open source programs under Windows. Also one should not choose software solely on the basis of open source. Interoperability and open standards for data are equally important.

For the library fraternity there are other set of reasons too for preferring OSS over commercial software : preservation, privacy and auditing, community resources, and open standards. Since commercial software is usually distributed only as a binary that will run only on a single hardware platform (and often only under a single version of a particular operating system) commercial software is very difficult to preserve over the long run without developing hardware emulation (and possibly OS 'emulation', as well).

OSS, in contrast, can often be recompiled, or at least ported, to new hardware and operating systems. In order to get a picture about the availability of OSS for digital library applicartions, it is encouraged to visit the directories of OSS projects, such as GNU (http://www.gnu.org/) and Sourceforge (http://www.sourceforge.net/) which list over fifty-thousand projects, and the numbers continue to grow.

DL Objectives and Workflow

The primary objective of a digital library is to enhance the digital collection in a substantial way, by strategically sourcing digital materials, conforming to copyright permissions, in all possible standards/formats so that scalability and flexibility is guaranteed for the future and advanced information services are assured to the user community right from beginning. The digital library should also be able to integrate and aggregate the existing collections and services mentioned above with an outstanding client interface. This implies that the digital library system should also have a strong collection interface capable of embracing almost all the popular digital standards and formats and software platforms, in line with the underlying digital library technologies in vogue. This is crucial in the case of multimedia integration, which is again important as we planned to also host a digital audio and video library as part of the core library collection. Emphasis should also be given to maximise the efficiency and effectiveness of the information access and retrieval capabilities of the system by deploying cutting edge Resource Description Framework (RDF) standards for metadata and its encoding. The Internet also possesses, in addition to its mammoth proprietary information base, an invaluable wealth and a vast collection of public domain information products such as databases, books, journals, theses, technical reports, cases, standards, newsletters etc., scattered and distributed across the world. This treasure should also be explored to its maximum for collection building, based on the source and quality.

Standard workflow patterns are to be identified for the system which include 'content selection', 'content acquisition', 'content publishing', 'content indexing and storage', and 'content accessing and delivery'. The system should also concern about such related issues, viz., preservation, usage monitoring, access management, interoperability, administration and management etc. It was proposed to value add the digital catalogue of the library (OPAC), which acts as a stepping stone for effective information discovery in the library, by supplementing the bibliographic information with the scanned picture (.gif/.jpg) of the front cover and the contents page, so that users will be able to evaluate the book for further consultation while browsing the catalogue, right from their desktops. Dublin Core standards are the desired metadata format and XML, the desired encoding scheme (4).

Selection of the DL Software

The software selection based on set parameters is an uphill task, as the technology itself was still emerging only. In general, what is desirable is a system that is flexible enough to fit the current digital information system as above and to accommodate future migration. It should be robust in technical architecture as well as the content architecture. The system should address all major digital library related issues such as 'design criteria', 'collection building', 'content organisation', 'access', 'evaluation', 'policy and legal issues' including 'intellectual property rights'. That the system should be in a position to embrace almost all predominant and emerging digital object formats and capable of supporting the standard library technology platforms, should be the major focus. It should provide two important user interfaces: a public user interface for presentation and a metadata creation interface for administration. The system should also provide a powerful search engine and the interface should be easy to navigate and there should be provision for customisation.

There are many digital library softwares available, proprietary as well as open source, and most of them conform to international standards. As mentioned earlier, VTLS and ACADO are the commercial ones available and popular in the Indian market. Some of the popular Open Source Softwares for digital libraries, which are in use internationally, are 'DSpace', 'Dienst', 'Eprints', 'Fedora', 'Greenstone' etc. For want of control and clarity, Greentone, EPrints and DSpace are discussed in this paper.

Greenstone

The Greenstone (http://www.greenstone.org) Digital Library Software (GSDL) is a top of the line and internationally renowned Open Source Software system for developing digital libraries, promoted by the New Zealand Digital Library project research group at the University of Waikato, headed by Dr. Ian H. Witten, and is sponsored by the UNESCO. The software is issued under the terms of GNU General Public License. Greenstone provides a way of building, maintaining and distributing digital library collections, opening up new possibilities for organizing information and making it available over the Internet or on CD-ROM. One of the pioneering and laudable efforts of Greenstone is its commitment to lower the bar for construction of practical digital libraries, yet at the same time leave a great deal of flexibility in the hands of the user. Greenstone is being used by lot of libraries and institutions across the world and the feedback is encouraging. Couple of promotional articles appeared in D-Lib Magazine by the Greenstone team also were strong indicators for their continued interest and commitment to the software. Another word of inspiration is of Ian Witten's team itself, that 'we should now stop talking about digital libraries and start developing them'. Fig. 1 below shows the digital library site set up at IIM Kozhikode. The site is available at 'http://intranet.iimk.ac.in/cgi-bin/library'. Fig. 2 shows the system architecture of the IIMK digital library.

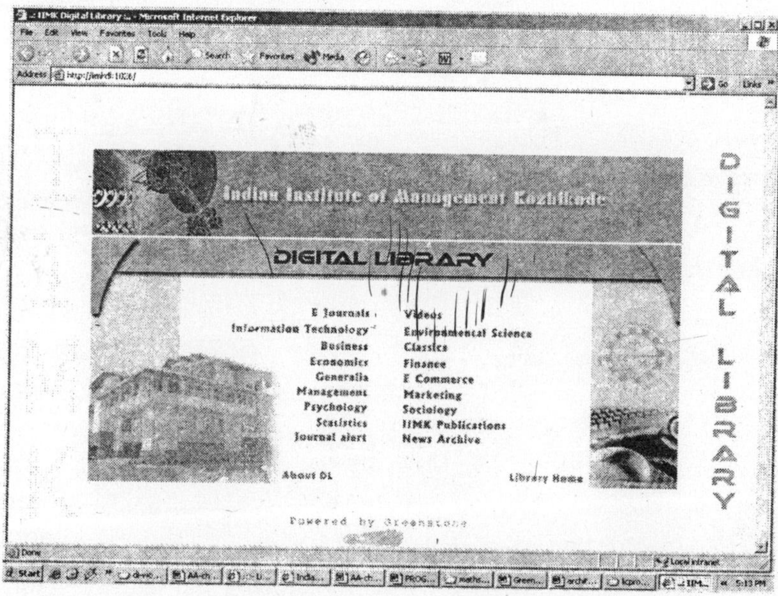

Fig. 1. IIMK Digital Library Home Page

Institutional Repository (IR) Softwares for DL applications

The current trend is to install, configure and customize softwares that are capable of performing as digital library as well as institutional repository functions.

An institutional repository, generally termed as E-prints archive, is a digital archive of the research output created by the scientists, faculty, research staff, and students of an institution and accessible over the Internet to end-users both within and outside of the institution, with few if any barriers to access. As a facility it consists of hardware, software and procedures to capture, organize, archive, disseminate and manage digital research resources of the institution. IRs

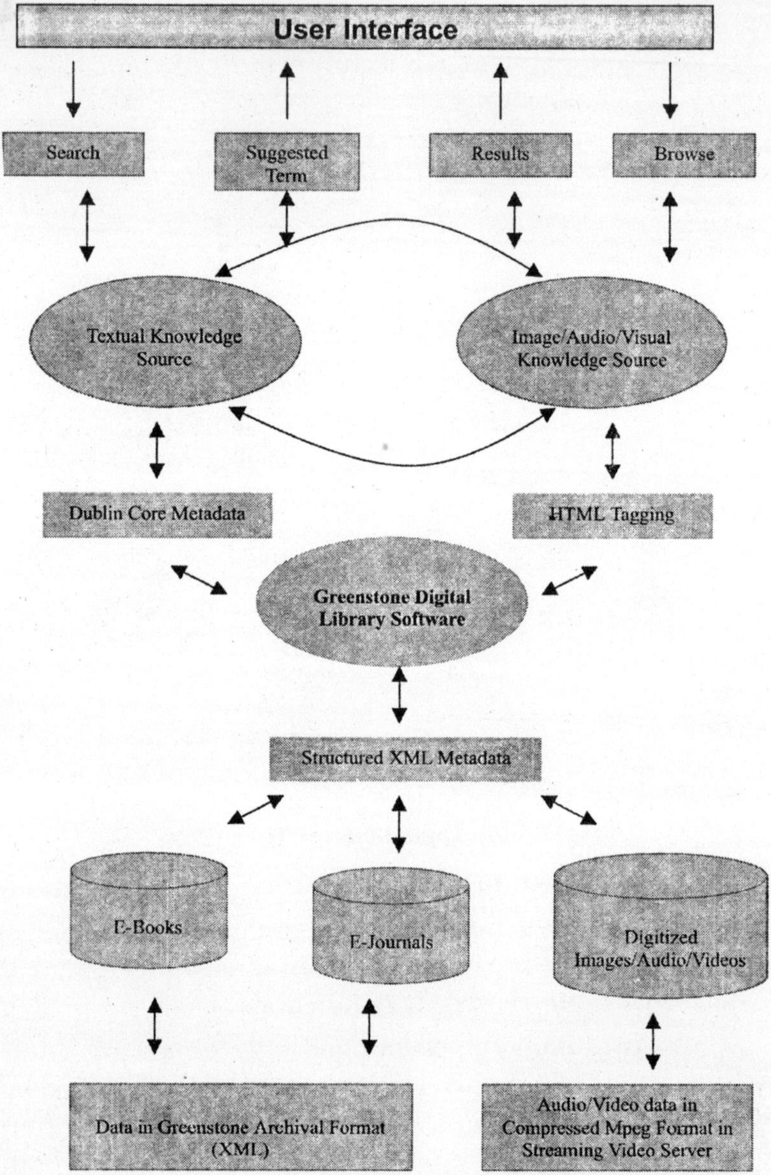

Fig. 2. System Architecture of IIMK Digital Library

provide a simple, web-based mechanism to researchers to deposit ('self-archive') and access their research publications. Further, by using the Open Archives Initiative (OAI) interoperability protocol, content in these repositories can be easily shared at metadata level to establish a single-point cross-indexing and search service at national level. The same protocol enables integration of content in these repositories with worldwide cross-archive search services.

As more and more research and educational material is 'born digital', institutions and organizations are increasingly realizing the need for a stable place in which such material may be stored and accessed long-term. Examples to this are EPrints software developed by the Southampton University, U.K. and the DSpace software of MIT, USA.

EPrints

The GNU EPrints is a free software which creates online archives. The default configuration is a repository of the research output of an academic institution. An EPrint archive can be adapted for many more purposes. It has been developed at the University of Southampton in relation to a variety of projects. The latest recommended version is 'eprints-2.3.11'. In India NCSI has been conducting workshops and training programmes for installing and customizing EPrints software. Details of the recently conducted programme is available at 'http://www.ncsi.iisc.ernet.in/indest-ncsi-ir/'. NCSI will provide a shell-script written by them for easy installation of EPrints on request. Fig. 3 below shows the system architecture of the Institutional Repository of IIM Kozhikode, and Fig.4 shows the archive's interface. The archive is available at 'http://eprints.iimk.ac.in'.

DSpace

DSpace (http://www.dspace.org) is a digital repository platform jointly developed by Hewlett-Packard and MIT Libraries collaborating over two years. DSpace provides the basic functionality required to operate an institutional digital repository, and is intended to serve as a base for future development to address long term preservation and access issues. On November 2002, the system was launched as a live service hosted by MIT Libraries, and the source code made publicly available according to the terms of the BSD open source license, with the intention of encouraging the formation of an open source community around DSpace (5). Initial developments in this area have been very promising. The software download, system documentation, installation, configuration and customization guide is available at 'http://dspace.org/technology/system-docs/install.html'.

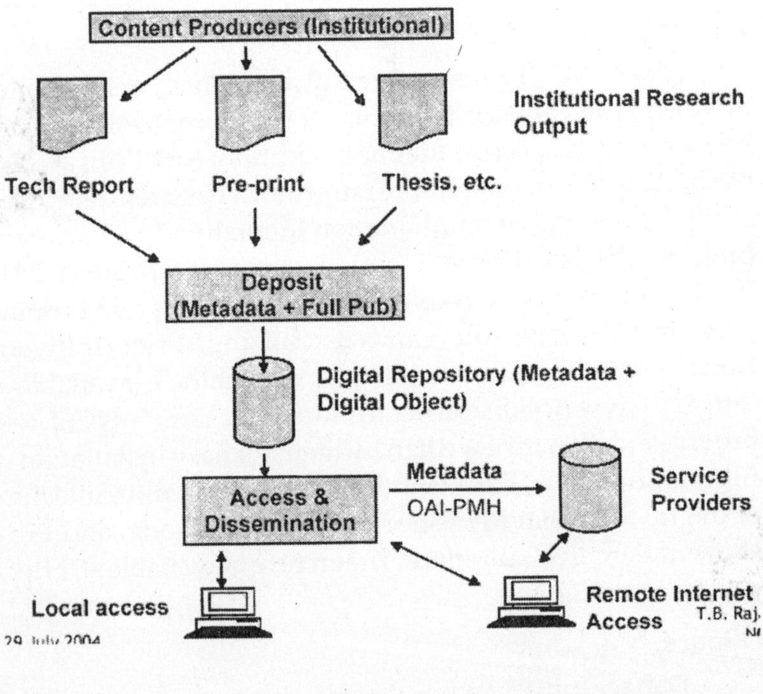

Fig. 3. Architecture of IIMK's Institutional Repository

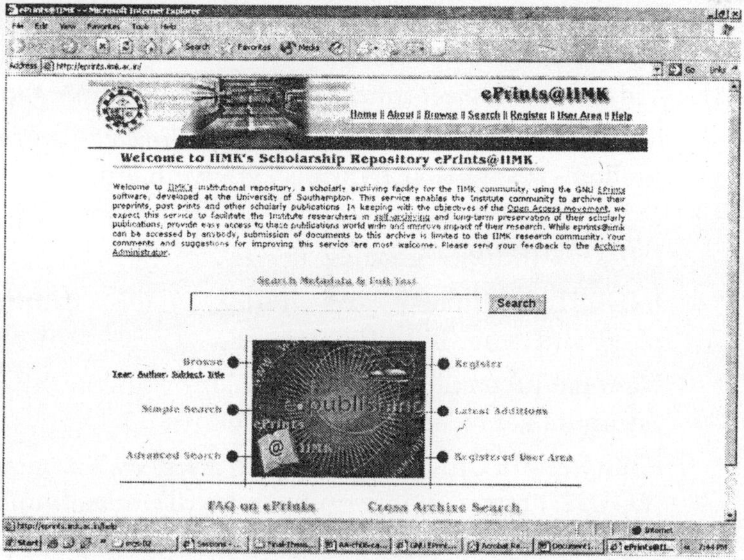

Fig. 4. Institutional Repository Home Page of IIMK

Digital library initiatives in India

During the past five years, India has seen several Digital Library initiatives at the institutional, organizational and at national levels. Some of them are quite successful while others are making significant progress.

Some of the major initiatives on Digital Libraries in India are furnished below:

* 'Archives of Indian Labour' at the V.V. Giri Institute of Labour (http://www.indialabourarchives.org/sources/jnu.htm)
* Indian Institute of Science NCSI (http://vidya-mapak.ncsi.iisc.ernet.in/cgi-bin/library)
* Indian Institute of Management Kozhikode (http://intranet.iimk.ac.in/cgi-bin/library)
* Search Digital Library SDL at DRTC Bangalore (https://drtc.isibang.ac.in/index.jsp)

* Nalanda Digital library, National Institute of Technology (NIT) Calicut (http://www.nalanda.nitc.ac.in)
* Vidyanidhi Project (http://www.vidyanidhi.org.in)
* Million Book Universal Digital library Project - Carnegie Mellon - IISc - ERNET (http://www.dli.ernet.in)
* Indira Gandhi Centre for the ARTS (IGNCA Digital Library) -(http://ignca.nic.in)
* INDEST, Ministry of HRD, GOI (http://paniit.iitd.ac.in/indest)
* National Tuberculosis Institute (NTI), Bangalore (http://ntiindia.kar.nic.in/)
* Rajiv Gandhi University of Health Sciences, Karnataka (RGUHS) http://www.rguhs.ac.in/dl/index.html)
* Traditional Knowledge Digital Library (TKDL) – (http://203.200.90.6/tkdl/langdefault/common/home.asp)
* Indian School of Business (http://www.isb.edu/lrc/index.html)
* Indian Institute of Technology, Kharagpur (http://www.library.iitkgp.ernet.in/usr/elib/digital.htm)
* Indian Institute of Technology, Mumbai (http://www.library.iitb.ac.in/ ~mnj/gsdl/cgi-bin/library)
* IITMK Trivandrum (http://www.iiitmk.ac.in/iiitmk/digitallibrary.htm)
* National Chemical Laboratory (NCL, CSIR) – Digital Repository – (http://dspace.ncl.res.in)
* University of Hyderabad (http://202.41.85.234:8000/cgi-bin/gw_42_6/chameleon

Digital library development issues in India

There are umpteen number of problems the Digital Library development teams face in India while they embark on the digital library development as well as during the progress phase. Some of the prominent and predominant among them include the following :

i. Lack of proper Information & Communication Technology (ICT) Infrastructure

Digital Libraries demand cutting edge IT and Communication infrastructure such as:

a) High end and powerful Servers; Structured LAN with Broadband Intranet facilities, ideally optical fibre based Gigabit networks;

b) Required number of Workstations capable of providing online information services, computing and multimedia applications;

c) Internet connectivity with sufficient bandwidth, capable of meeting the informational and computational requirement of the user community;

There are many more related facilities / services which are highly essential in an ideal digital library environment. It is observed that the ICT infrastructure in most of the Institutions / Organizations, barring exceptions, are not up to the desired level so as to run advanced digital library services to the optimum level.

ii. Lack of Proper Planning and Integration of Information Resources

Presently the library acquisitions in India are either paper based and electronic. In most of the libraries, paper based documents outnumber the electronic subscriptions and acquisitions. Some of the libraries need retro-conversion and digitization of library holdings too. Literature on related studies show that there is a severe lapse on the libraries with regard to proper planning of their information resources which are conducive for developing digital libraries. Also, the electronic resources penetrate to the libraries in a multiplicity of complex formats and with different access terms and conditions. These information resources are scattered and distributed across a wide variety of publication types and a vast number of publishers. There is a dire need for proper planning and a meticulously framed content integration model which is achieved and implemented through world standard digital library technologies.

iii. Rigidity in the publishers' policies and data formats

Having successfully installed and configured a digital library does not qualify a library to automatically populate all its digital collection into the digital library. One has to obtain publisher's consent and copyright permissions for the same. Digital library softwares usually accept and process all popular and standard digital formats such as HTML, Word, RTF, PPT, or PDF. Most of the publishers put their materials in their own proprietary e-book reader formats, from which the text extraction becomes almost impossible. A vast majority of the scholarly content rests in journal literature and due to copyright issues they cannot be easily (almost impossible) find its way into the local repositories of the digital library.

iv. Lack of ICT Strategies and Policies

A vast majority of the libraries in India do not have laid down policies on ICT panning and strategies to meet the challenges posed by the technology push, the information overload, as well as the demand pull from the users.

v. Lack of Technical Skills

The Human Resources available in the libraries need time-to-time professional enrichment inputs and rigorous training on the latest technologies which are playing around in the new information environment. The kind of training programmes being imparted in India at the moment are not able to meet the demand in terms of quantity as well as quality.

vi. Management Support

For the provision of world class information systems,

resources and services the libraries need the wholehearted support from the respective management. Institutional support in terms of proper funding, human resources and IT skills enrichment are prerequisites for the development and maintenance of state-of-art digital library systems and services.

There are many more pressing problems being faced by the libraries in India in its pursuit of building digital libraries.

vii. Copyright / IPR Issues

Issues of copyright, intellectual property, and fair use concerns are posing unprecedented array of problems to the libraries and librarians are struggling to cope with all these related issues in the new digital information environment.

Conclusion

This paper discussed the current trends in the recorded and explicit scholarly knowledge finding its way into our institutions and some of the proven methods of their efficient handling, effective access and management. Any forward looking enterprise or institution of these days need to be open to the changing information environment. Timely and strategically framed organizational transformation is a prerequisite for survival alone. For a learning organization in particular, scholarly information is the critical piece that transforms fact into knowledge. In the current practical institutional setting the recorded knowledge reaches our libraries by way of established scholarly publication types both in print as well as digital formats. There is an amazing penetration of scholarly digital information through a variety of forms and formats, standards and platforms, in which documents are published, which pose a multiplicity of threats to the information professional who is supposed to be the custodian and service provider of these information products. From the user perspective, what is important is the seamless access and uninterrupted services offered by the information system, no matter what kind of format and platform in which these information rests, whether sourced from internal repositories or from outside. It is heartening to note that Greenstone, DSpace and EPrint installations are picking up quite fast in India, and institutions like DRTC, INFLIBNET, NCSI, IIT's, IIMK and many others are giving wide popularity and training opportunities on these softwares.

References

1. Sosteric, Mike et al. 2001. Electronic first : The Upcoming Revolution in the Scholarly Communication System. The Journal of Electronic Publishing. Volume 7, Issue 2 ISSN 1080-2711 http://www.press.umich.edu/jep/07-02/sosteric.html
2. Stewart, Grainger. 2000 Emulation as a Digital Preservation Strategy *Dlib Magazine* 6 (10).
3. Frumkin, Jeremy (ED). 2002 Special Issue: Open Source Software *Information Technology and Libraries* 21*(1)*
4. Dublin Core Meta Data Initiative. http://www.dublincore.org (29 April 2005)
5. Tansley, Robert et al. 2003 'The DSpace Institutional Digital Repository System: Current Functionality'. [Proceedings of the 3rd ACM/IEEE-CS joint conference on Digital libraries. Houston, Texas. Pp.87 – 97].

Additional reading

1. GNU (GNU's Not Unix!) http://www.gnu.org/ (13, December, 2003)
2. INDEDEST Consortium (Indian Digital Library in Science, Engineering, and Technology) http://www.library.iitb.ac.in/indest/ (13, December, 2003)
3. Lesk, M. 1997 Practical Digital Libraries :Books, bytes, and bucks San Francisco: Morgan Kaufmann, 336pp
4. Magnussen, Amanda. 2003 Creating digital libraries: a model for digital library development [Proceedings of the 10th Asia Pacific Special Health and Law Librarians Conference , Adelaide 24–27 Aug 2003, Asia Pacific Special Health and Law Librarians]
5. Micah Altman. 2001 Open Source Software for Libraries: from Greenstone to the Virtual Data Center and Beyond *IASSIST QUARTERLY (IQ)(* 25). pp.5.

6. Open Source Initiative http://www.opensource.org/docs/definition_plain.html (13, December, 2003)

7. Schiller, Nancy. 1992 The emerging virtual research library [Association of Research Libraries. Office of Management Services. Washington, D.C.]

8. Schiller, Nancy and Barbara Von Wahlde. 1992a Toward a realization of the virtual library: first in a two-part series *ARL Newsletter*. (163): 3-4

9. Schiller, Nancy and Barbara Von Wahlde. 1992b Toward a realization of the virtual library: second in a two-part series *ARL Newsletter*. (164), 4-6.

10. Schauder, Don 1994 Development of the e-library concept, with special reference to Australian libraries *Australian Library Review*. 11 (1), 5-30.

11. SourceForge.net (world's largest Open Source software development website) http://www.sourceforge.net/ (13, December, 2003)

12. Transversal E Network (Pvt) Ltd., India http://www.transversalnet.com/acado/index.htm (13, December, 2003)

13. VTLS Inc., USA http://www.vtls.com (13, December, 2003)

14. Witten, Ian H. et al. 2001 Greenstone : Open-Source Digital Library Software *D-Lib Magazine*, 7 (10): 1-16.

15. Witten, Ian H. 2003 Examples of Practical Digital Libraries : Collections Built Internationally Using Greenstone *D-Lib Magazine* 9 (3): 1-15.

6

Gladiator: Cutting Edge Web Service Technology to the Indian Universities

TAV Murthy
Director

Manoj Kumar K
Scientist D (CS)

Ankit M Shah
Project Trainee
INFLIBNET centre Ahmedabad
(tav; manoj; ankit @ inflibnet.ac.in)

Keywords: Web services, Distributed Computing, Web Service security, Service oriented architecture, programmable web, Copy Cataloging, Resource sharing, Indian University Libraries, INFLIBNET, SOUL, UCMS XML, WSDL, SOAP, UDDI, DISCO

ABSTRACT

Innovations in Information Technology have brought radical changes in every possible field of life. Libraries being no exception, the world has seen digitization and automation of libraries as some of the inevitable changes that took place in recent years. With the penetration of Internet and application of distributed computing, the new era may soon witness striking changes in libraries the world over. Web Services, the fundamental building blocks in the move to distributed computing on the Internet that works on Open Protocols like XML, SOAP, UDDI, WSDL and TCP/IP, are widely seen as the next "Big Thing" in Information and Communication Technology. Web Services are program components that help to build scalable, loosely coupled, platform-independent applications which implements program logic and provides functionality for disparate applications. GLADIATOR is an attempt to bring Web Services to the Academic Community of India by sharing bibliographic resources between SOUL, a Library Automation Package, and UCMS (Union Catalogue Management System).

SOUL is state-of-the-art library automation software developed and distributed by INFLIBNET which is an Inter University Centre of UGC under Ministry of HRD. Already installed in over 500 universities all over India, SOUL today has helped these universities to manage their vast collections holdings and also controlling the huge amount of bibliographical data very efficiently. SOUL is a Client/Server based software having features that can suit any type of library with supports to all activities relating to Acquisition, Cataloguing, Circulation, Serials Control, web OPAC etc. UCMS is s management system for union databases of books, serials, thesis etc. GLADIATOR bridges SOUL and UCMS providing an integrated solution for automated data transfer between universities and the INFLIBNET UCMS server. GLADIATOR is a recursive acronym for Gladiator is Library Application for Data and Information's Automated Transfer on Requisition. It is an application for automated on demand data transfer between UCMS and University Libraries. It is also aimed to be a Security enhanced application which can act as a prototype for future Web Services. This paper describes Web Services, the Open Standards driving Web Services which includes like XML, SOAP, UDDI, WSDL and TCP/IP, architecture and design of GLADIATOR, Web Service security and the future of Web Services.

Introduction

Over the years technology has created many milestones

and new technologies have appeared with exiting prospects on Internet. Web Service is the latest driving force in service oriented architecture and serves as fundamental building blocks in the move to distributed computing on the Internet that works on Open Protocols. Each standards organization, marketing research firm, or vendor defines Web Services in a different way. Gartner[1], for instance, defines Web Services as "loosely coupled software components that interact with one another dynamically via standard Internet technologies." Forrester Research takes a more open approach to Web Services as "automated connections between people, systems and applications that expose elements of business functionality as a software service and create new business value."

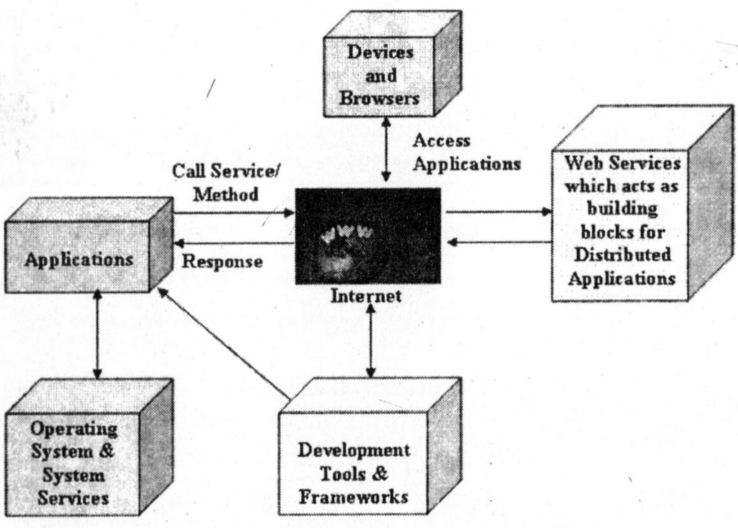

Fig. 1. Web Services and its interaction with applications and devices

A Web Service is used to integrate different applications that access data through the Internet as shown in Figure-1. To do this, Web Methods in a Web Service are called over the

Internet, which can then be accessed by applications developed on different platforms. Thus a Web Service is a reusable component. Before the dawn of Web Services, many technologies like COM (Component Object Model), DCOM (Distributed Component Object Model), CORBA (Common Object Broker Request Architecture), etc promised a lot towards distributed computing and making the applications truly language and platform independent. But, due to proprietary standards used by these technologies, communication between a client application and a component depends on various factors, such as programming language, hardware platform, operating system, vendor implementations and data encryption schemes. This means that to transfer data between two applications, a similar infrastructure is required at both ends. But, this is not possible for applications to interact over the Internet. This aroused necessity to develop components that can be accessed from various platforms. This is where Web Services comes into picture. Web Services allows developers to create platform independent distributed applications. Platform independence comes because of the use of Open Standards like XML, HTTP, SOAP, TCP/IP, WSDL and UDDI.

GLADIATOR is INFLIBNET's initiative to bring Web Services to the Academic Community of India. As stated earlier GLADIATOR is a bridge between SOUL and UCMS. At the INFLIBNET end there is UCMS, a gigantic collection of bibliographic data and the University Libraries end there is SOUL, a software that provide library automation. But, at both ends there is no facility for copy-cataloging, a feature that could save libraries and INFLIBNET a world lot of time. At present, the books and serials updates at University Libraries are copied manually at INFLIBNET. On the other end, even though the cataloged record already exists at INFLIBNET, the same has to be manually entered at University Libraries whenever needed. If Copy-Cataloging is provided then this tedious task of manually copying records that are already cataloged at the other end can be eliminated. This is the task of GLADIATOR.

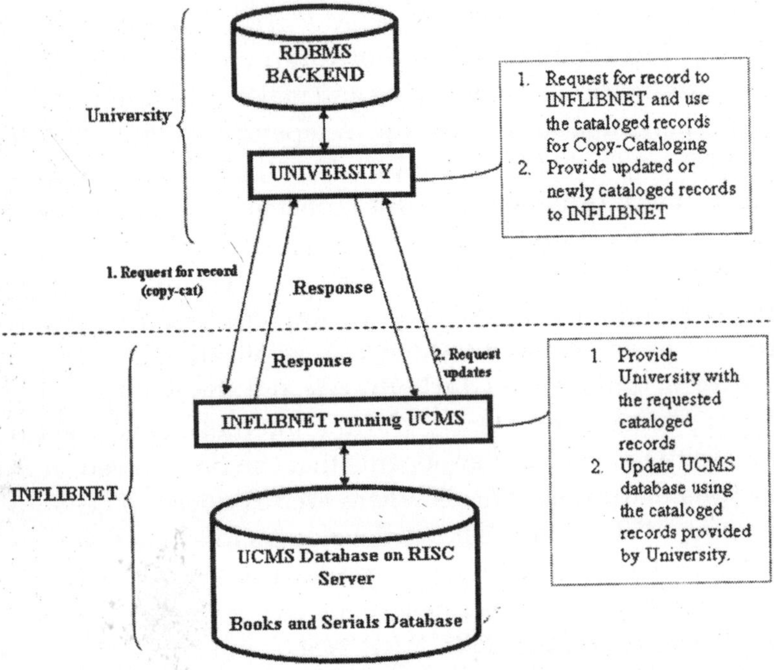

Fig. 2. Architecture of GLADIATOR

Fig. 2. Shows the overall architecture and design of GLADIATOR

GLADIATOR contains two packages:

1. INFLIBNET Interface Package
2. University Interface Package

It is expected to address two issues:

1. Copy Cataloging at University Libraries using cataloged records provided by UCMS database.
2. Updating the UCMS database using the newly cataloged records provided by University Libraries. At

present, this process is manual and time consuming. The Universities sends their updated or newly cataloged records to INFLIBNET that are then added to the UCMS database. Using this application the entire process will be automated and lot of tedious activity and time will be saved.

Figure-3 shows the interaction between Web Service and its client and the role of various protocols like WSDL, SOAP, UDDI, etc with reference to the GLADIATOR design model. Whereas the Figure-4 shows the layers in Web Service and Figure-5 shows the working of Web Services with reference to this layers.

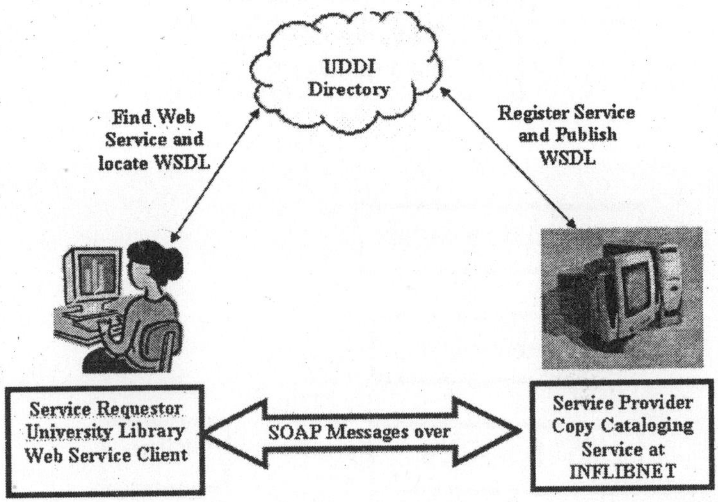

Fig. 3. Interaction between Web Service and its client.

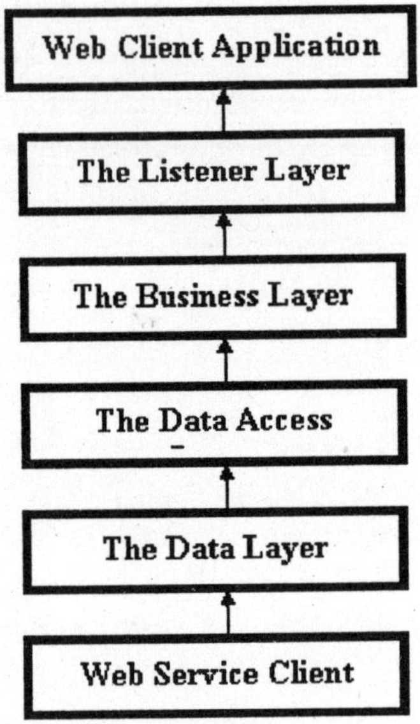

Fig. 4. Layered Web

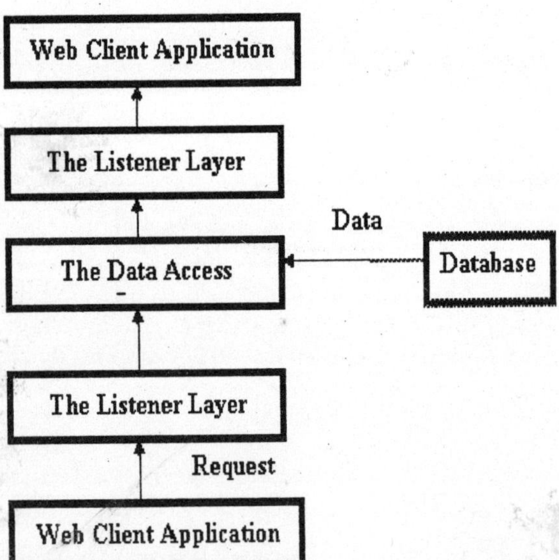

Fig. 5. Working Of Web Service Architecture

Technologies Used In Web Services

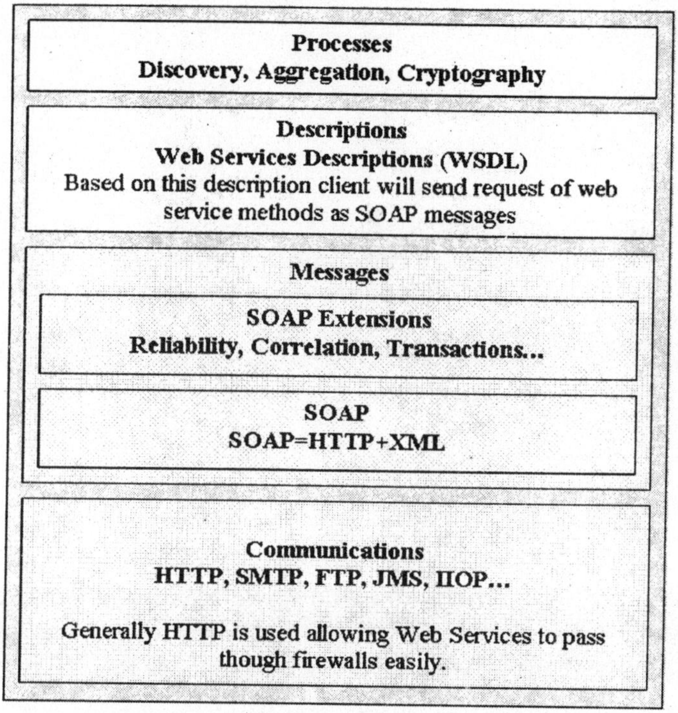

Fig. 6. Technology stack of Web Services

XML (eXtensible Markup Language)

XML[3] is a markup language used to describe data in a particular format. This data can be accessed by any application built on any platform. XML allows transfer of data in a format that is independent of the platform. Therefore, XML is a wildly used technology that transfers data across the Internet applications. XML documents store data in the form of text. This makes the XML document easily understood by applications built on different platforms. Moreover, content stored in an XML document is easily transferred over the network.

When a Web Service client application calls a Web Service, the client application passes arguments to the Web method. The Web Service processes the Web methods and returns a result to the client application. Because the client application can be built using any platform, the data returned by the Web Service is in the form of XML. Figure-7 shows XML data of GLADIATOR


```
  <?xml version="1.0" ?>
  <!--  Books detail    -->
- <Books>
    <ISBN>0-356-039781</ISBN>
    <Title>Computer-based information system</Title>
    <Author>Henley, J P</Author>
    <Publisher>London Macdonald and Co Ltd</Publisher>
    <Date_of_Publication>1972</Date_of_Publication>
  </Books>
```


Fig. 7. XML data of GLADIATOR

WSDL (Web Service Description Language)

WSDL is a markup language that defines a Web Service. WSDL[3] is an XML file that contains information about a Web Service. This information includes the Web Service called by a web site, the methods included in each of the Web Services, and the parameters that are required to pass to the Web methods. In addition WSDL includes information about the results returned when a request is processed by a Web Service.. For example, WSDL defines the type of the values returned by a Web method. Therefore, WSDL is a vocabulary defined for the creation of a Web Service that the developer may need to use while creating a Web Service.

In addition to storing information about the Web method, WSDL stores information about the format used by a user to access a Web Service and specifies the entire mechanism involved in the transfer of data form a Web Service client to the Web Service and vice versa. Figure-7 shows the general structure of SOAP message.

For example, a Web Service client application needs to call a Web method that validates the username and password entered by the user. The Web method is created in a Web Service. To call this Web method, the Web Service client sends a request to the Web Service. The request that is sent to the Web method is specified by WSDL. The request is sent to the Web Service in the form of XML, messages. In this case, WSDL stores the format in which the request is sent.

In addition, when a Web method is called, it is required to pass the username and password as parameters. The information about the type and the format of the parameters is stored in a WSDL file. When the request is processed and the result is returned, WSDL stores the format and other information about the result returned.

SOAP (Simple Object Access Protocol)

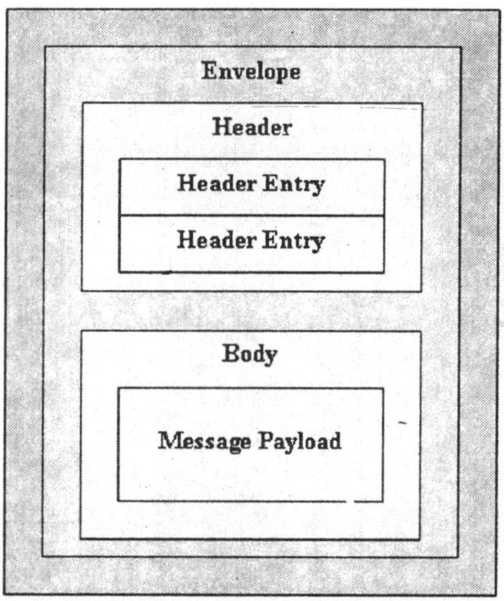

Fig. 8. SOAP Message Structure

To transfer data from a Web Service client to a Web Service and vice versa, the transfer protocol used is SOAP. SOAP is a protocol based on XML that is used by client application to access a Web Service. In addition to XML,

SOAP uses HTTP for the transfer of data.

Thus, SOAP = HTTP + XML

When a client sends a request, the request is in the form of a SOAP message. The SOAP message also includes the parameters and the method call statement. Based on this information in the SOAP message, the appropriate Web method is called. Figure-8 shows the structure of SOAP message.

SOAP is a standard protocol used for communication between a Web Service client and a Web Service. However, SOAP does not define syntax to be followed while transferring data. Instead, SOAP provides a mechanism for packaging data to be transferred across a network. In addition, SOAP is a transfer protocol based on simple Internet standards. The transfer of data using SOAP takes place in the form of a SOAP message. A SOAP package includes an envelop that encapsulates the data to be exchanged.

Figure-9 shows the SOAP request response for GetAll method of Copy Cataloging Web Service of GLADIATOR

SOAP Request

POST /CopyCatalogingUCMS/CopyCatUCMSService.asmx HTTP/1.1

Host: localhost

Content-Type: text/xml; charset=utf-8

Content-Length: length

SOAPAction: "http://tempuri.org/GetAll"

<?xml version="1.0" encoding="utf-8"?>

<soap:Envelope xmlns:xsi="http://www.w3.org/2001/XMLSchema-instance" xmlns:xsd="http://www.w3.org/2001/XMLSchema" xmlns:soap="http://schemas.xmlsoap.org/soap/envelope/">

<soap:Body>

<GetAll xmlns="http://tempuri.org/" />

```
</soap:Body>
</soap:Envelope>
SOAP response – Contd
HTTP/1.1 200 OK
Content-Type: text/xml; charset=utf-8
Content-Length: length
<?xml version="1.0" encoding="utf-8"?>
<soap:Envelope xmlns:xsi="http://www.w3.org/2001/XMLSchema-instance" xmlns:xsd="http://www.w3.org/2001/XMLSchema" xmlns:soap="http://schemas.xmlsoap.org/soap/envelope/">
<soap:Body>
<GetAllResponse xmlns="http://tempuri.org/">
<GetAllResult>
<xsd:schema>schema</xsd:schema>xml</GetAllResult>
</GetAllResponse>
</soap:Body>
</soap:Envelope>
```

Fig. 9. SOAP Request and Response for Get All method of GLADIATOR

UDDI (Universal Description, Discovery and Integration)

UDDI[3] provides a mechanism for Web Service providers to register their Web Services. When a Web Service is registered with a UDDI directory, an entry for the Web Service is created. A UDDI directory maintains an XML file for each Web Service registered with the UDDI directory. This XML file contains a pointer to the Web Service that is registered in the directory. In addition, the UUDI directory also contains pointers to the WSDL document for a Web Service. To do this, the Web Service provider needs to first describe the Web Service in a WSDL document. Once a WSDL document is created, the Web Service can be registered with the UDDI directory. This makes the Web Service easily accessible to the Web Service clients, as the client application can discover and identify a Web Service from a UDDI directory.

Consider the example of the Web Service used to perform user validation. Once the Web Service is created and described in a WSDL document, it can be registered with the UDDI directory. Then, any user who wants to use the Web method can search on the UDDI directory for the required Web method. The UDDI directory returns the list of Web Services that are registered with the UDDI directory. The user can then select the required Web method from the list of the available Web Services.

A UDDI directory contains white pages, yellow pages, and green pages. The white pages contain information about the organization that provides the Web Service. This information includes the name, address and other contact numbers of the Web Service provider company. The yellow pages in a UDDI directory contain information about the companies based on geographical taxonomies. The green pages provide the service interface for the client applications that access the Web Service.

DISCO

The DISCO protocol is used to discover Web Services located on a particular domain. Of all the protocols and formats of Web Services, this is the least concrete. Microsoft is the driving vendor behind this protocol but even so, its implementations differs from its documents.

The basic idea is to provide a single location for clients to locate all of the exposed Web Services in an enterprise. Therefore a company would have a DISCO file located on its web server. A potential client examines this DISCO file and learns where the WSDL files are located for every Web Service this company exposes. This is obviously useful, but when the

UDDI registry is introduced into the picture, the DISCO protocol's usefulness is brought into question. UDDI is a central repository for locating available Web Services on the Internet. In most cases, the UDDI registry will point to the specific WSDL document required to utilize the Web Service. This obviously cuts the DISCO protocol out of the picture.

The following figure shows a sample DISCO file.

```
<?xml version="1.0" ?>
<disco:discovery xmlns:disco=http://
schemas.xmlsoap.org /disco>
    <disco:contractRef ref="http://
    WebServerName/Username.asmx?WSDL"/>
    <disco:discoveryRef ref="FolderName/
    default.disco"/>
</disco:discovery>
```

Fig. 10. A sample DISCO File

Design of GLADIATOR

The application will provide the following functionalities:

On INFLIBNET Side

- *Copy cataloging*

University's web-service client will call the search function wrapped in SOAP messages using the signature provided by the WSDL file to search for specific records. The Web-service on INFLIBNET side will search for these records in the UCMS database on the RISC server. If records are found then it will send the records back as XML payload in SOAP response.

- *Updating the UCMS database*

The web-service client on the INFLIBNET side will request for updates as SOAP message. On receiving the newly added records from the university, it will add these records in the UCMS database.

On University Side

* *Copy cataloging*: University's web-service client will call the search function for specific records based on certain search criteria. The search will be in the form of a SOAP message using signature from the WSDL file. If it will receive the records from INFLIBNET then they can be copy cataloged as needed.
* *Updating the UCMS database*: The University's web-service will receive a request for updates. It will search its local database for newly added records and it will send these records back in XML format as payload of SOAP response message to the INFLIBNET web-service client.

Web Service Architecture

One of the salient features of Web Services is that both Client and the Web Service are unaware of the implementation details of each other. To consume a Web Service, the client first needs to locate it. The Web Service architecture helps client to first locate and then consume a Web Service. The four major components of Web Service Infrastructure are illustrated in Figure-11.

1. Web Service Directory

The directories are like Yellow Pages for Web Services. These directories provide a central place to store information about Web Services. The Universal Description, Discovery and Integration (UDDI) specification defines the guidelines for publishing information about Web Services. This information includes business, service and binding information and service specification. Client application uses a directory service to locate a service to use. Directory service returns a link to the selected service's discovery document.

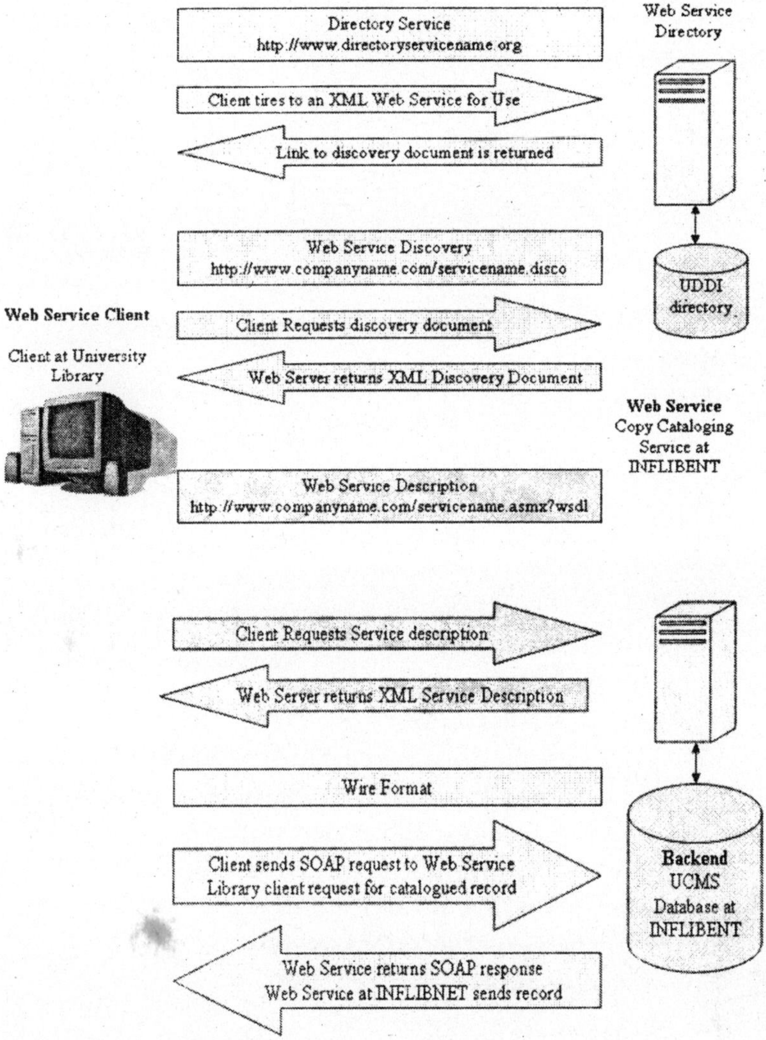

Fig. 11. Architecture of Web Services

Microsoft provides one such directory service, located at http://uddi.microsoft.com.

2. *Web Service Discovery*

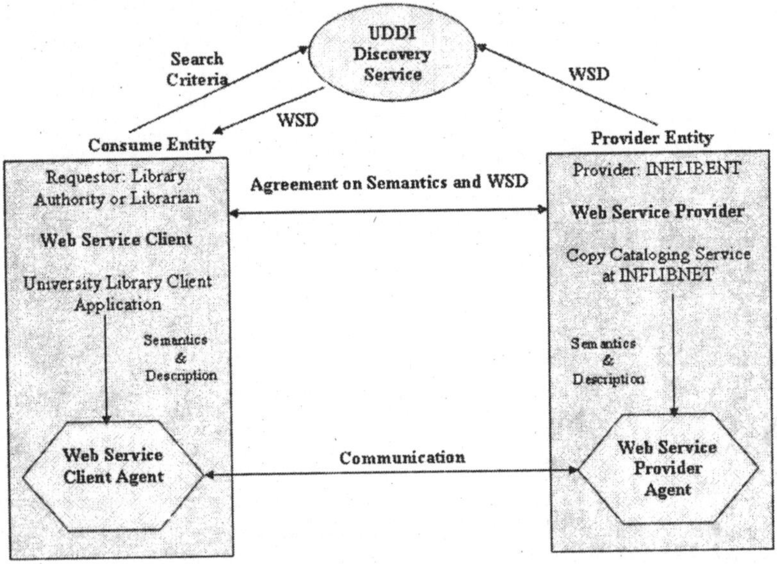

Fig. 12. Discovery Process

Clients locate the documents that describe a Web Service using WSDL. Client application uses the link returned by Directory service to request the service's discovery document. A document in XML format is returned which enable the client to know about the presence of a Web Service and the location of that particular service. The general discovery phase of Web Services is illustrated in Figure-12.

3. *Web Service Description*

Client application requests for the description of the desired service that will give information about the operations that can be performed on the Web Service. Web Service will return the service description in XML format. The description document specifies the format of messages that a Web Service can understand. For example, the document specifies the SOAP message schemas to be used to invoke method on a Web Service.

4. Web Service Wire Formats

Web Services uses open wire format to enable communication between disparate systems. Open wire formats are the protocols that can be understood by any system that is capable of supporting common Web Standards, such as HTTP and SOAP. Using the service description the client application makes a request to the Web Service. The response is sent back by the Web Service in XML format.

Creating Web Services

Web Services Using SOAP Toolkit

The Toolkit enables a developer to expose any standard COM or COM+ component as a SOAP-compatible Web Service. COM objects can be written in the language of developer's choice. No new skills are required to expose this Web Service to the world. Any client will be able to access and utilize the COM component via SOAP over HTTP. Clients can also consume Web Services using the SOAP Toolkit.

ASP.NET Web Services

ASP.NET is a set of components and services layered on top of the .NET Framework. Developers can use the extensive class library included with the Framework by developing Web Services using ASP.NET. It provides the functionalities for working with SOAP messages and WSDL files. Also, setting up and deploying Web Services is easy due to the runtime environment for hosting Web Services.

.NET Remoting Web Services

.NET Remoting it the Generation Next distributed computing technology. It is a successor of DCOM in the .NET Framework. .NET components can be exposed and utilized from a client machine like a local component using .NET

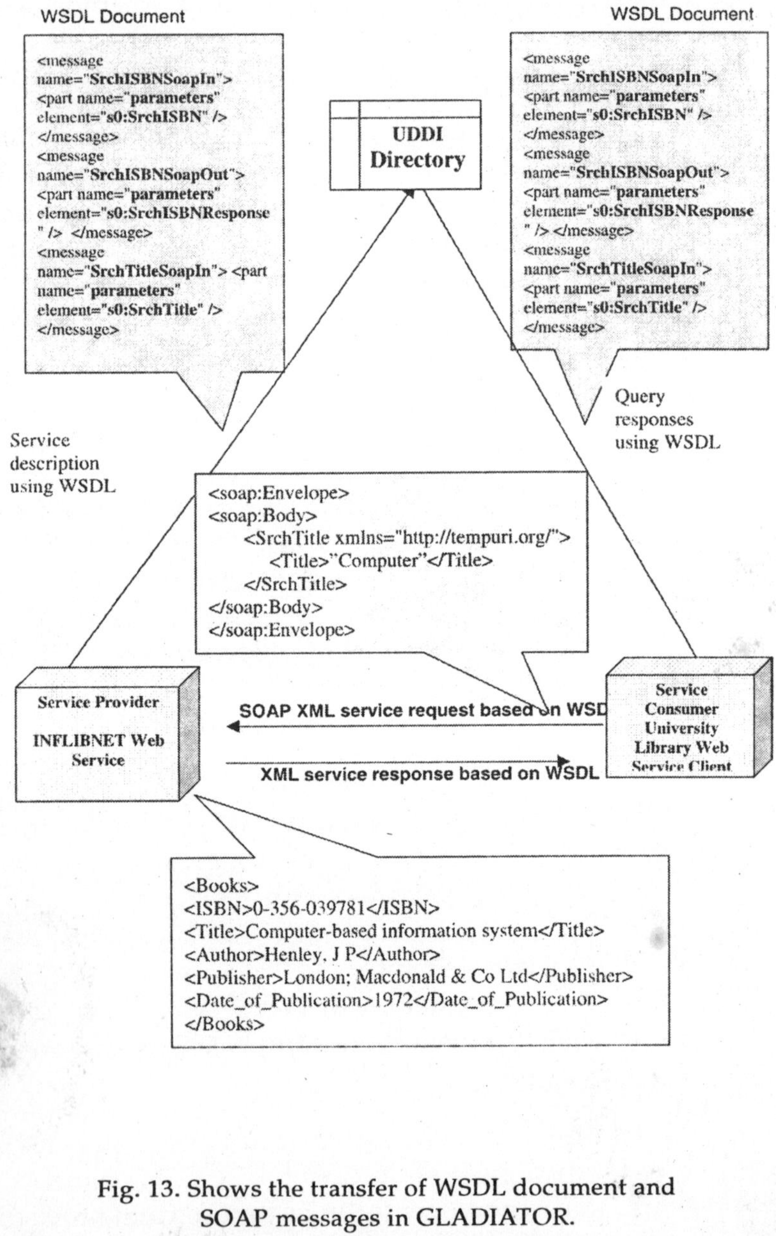

Fig. 13. Shows the transfer of WSDL document and SOAP messages in GLADIATOR.

Remoting. Though similar to ASP.NET Web Services, it provides services that can be performed on standard distributed object systems for Web Services.

Java and Web Services

The Java 2 Platform, Enterprise Edition platform provides the APIs and tools needed to design, develop, test, and deploy Web Services and clients that fully interoperate with other Web Services and clients running on any platform. To create Web Services and clients with the J2EE XML APIs, developer needs to pass parameter data to the method calls and process the data returned, or for document-oriented Web Services, and send documents containing the service data back and forth.

Benefits of Web Services

The most important benefits of Web Services are as follows[2]:

1. *Platform Independence*

Web Services can be accessed from any platform that can access Internet.

2. *Functionality Reuse*

Using Web Services developers can concentrate more on the business problem at hand rather than on coding a functionality which can be used from a third party. Again as the functionality accessed as Web Service is tried and tested by many, it guarantees robust performance and risk of failure of such components are relatively less

3. *High Level of Access and Availability*

Web Services uses Internet as its communication mechanism, which is build upon open standards like TCP/IP and HTTP. Using the Internet as communication backbone ensures that the Web Services will have very high level of access and availability.

4. *Enterprise Interoperability*

Business-to-Business (B2B) applications are on a rise. Web Services are easy to build and deploy. As they are built on open standards which are easy to understand and use, they provide ease of development. Web Services also provide the flexibility to change the functionalities as and when needed.

5. *Business Extension*

Web Services helps in business extension by allowing businesses to let third parties access their internal systems and functionalities via Web Services.

6. *Language Independence*

Accessing Web Services does not depend on the language or server used for its development. It thus provides language independence. For example a Web Service developed using C# and hosted on Windows platform can be accessed by a Java program running on UNIX.

7. *Security*

Though a lot of mist surrounds the security aspects of Web Services and a lot is to be done, but still Web Services today offers quite a secure communication mechanism. The technologies that were used the secure e-business applications can be used to secure Web Services as well. Already a lot of security features are provided by platforms like Java and .Net.

A discussion on Web Service Security will follow later.

Security

According to Business executives, Security[5] is the number one issue that will determining whether Web Services will reach its full potential or not. It is only factor that is holding the industry back from implementing Web Services. Web Services expose the entire business logic on the Internet and thus invite malicious codes and hackers. Web Services requires even more security than the in depth security implemented for web applications. With Web Services one need to protect both the server and the code.

The major issues relating to Web Service security are:

1. Authentication

A user may need to provide authentication information like username / password or X.509 certificate to the Web Service before he can make any transaction with it.

2. Authorization

Role based security needs to be provided by Web Services where the Web Service can control access to the services offered to determine which user can perform what function.

3. Confidentiality

The information exchanged between Web Service and its clients should be secret over a secure channel.

4. Integrity

It should be ensured that the information received by the client is exactly the same as transmitted by the receiver.

5. Non-repudiation

It is necessary to be able to prove that a client requested for a particular service and the Web Service processed the client's request. It can be done using digital signatures.

6. Availability

Web Services should be provided protection against Denial-of-Service attacks to ensure continuous availability.

Nascent Technologies for Web Service Security:

XML – Digital Signature

XML Signature, otherwise known as XML-DSIG, is a W3C Proposed Recommendation. XML-DSIG specifies the

XML syntax and processing rules for creating and representing digital signatures.

XML – Encryption

XML Encryption, otherwise known as XML-ENC, is a W3C Candidate Recommendation. XML-ENC defines a process for encrypting data and representing the result in XML. The data may be arbitrary data, an XML element, or XML element content. The result of encrypting data is an XML Encryption element, which contains or references the cipher data.

XML Key Management Specification

XML Key Management Specification, otherwise known as X-KMS, establishes a standard for XML based applications to use Public Key Infrastructure (PKI) when handling digitally signed or encrypted XML documents. XML Signature addresses message and user integrity, but not issues of trust, which key cryptography ensures.

Security Assertion Markup Language

Security Assertion Markup Language, otherwise known as SAML, aims to standardize the exchange of user identities and authorization by defining how this information is to be presented in XML documents, regardless of the underling security systems in place.

Future of Web Services

The advent of Web Services marks the beginning of a new era for developing Enterprise solutions. Web Services will change the way applications are built and the way business is conducted online. Though a lot is still required to be done to make the Web Service Dream come true, the future certainly looks bright.

Programmable Web

Programmable Web[2], a term found in many Microsoft's

press releases, simply means "Any Platform, Any Data, Any Format". The basic idea behind it is to enable the programmers to build an entire system by simply integrating the functionalities provided by Web Services across the Internet. This is a concept similar to Code Reuse as promised by Object Oriented Programming and Component based system that proliferated greatly in 1990s. Thus whenever a programmer needs a piece of functionality he can access one of the many Web Services spread all over the internet rather than writing the code himself or purchasing a component. This will help programmer concentrate more on the business problem rather than some time consuming code which can be developed better by some vendor who specializes in such applications. So what we are talking about is accessing Web Service functionalities across the Internet from any device connected to the Internet.

.Net My Services

Recently, Microsoft also announced .NET My Services[2], formerly codenamed "HailStorm" that represents a radical change in the way applications will use and access user information. It is a set of user-centric Web Services; including identification and authentication, email, instant messaging, automated alert, calendar, address book, and storage. Most of these services are provided separately today. The Cell phone's phone list may not match with the PDA's or the mobile phone may not be synchronized with Outlook. Microsoft Passport service provides Identification and Authentication facilities. Email might map to Hotmail or any other web-based email services. Instant messaging and automated alert should be familiar to you if you use MSN Messenger Service or AOL Instant Messenger. A calendar and address book are usually bundled together with the web-based email service. Consolidating these user-centric services and exposing them as Web Services would allow the user to publish and manage his own information.

Using .Net My Services, the user can have his information stored at a centralized location and protect that information through Microsoft's Passport Authentication Service. Disparate systems can access this data over the Internet using the standard SOAP protocol. A .NET My Services customer can also control access permission to the data to allow or restrict access to content. To show how useful this service can be consider the scenario in which the user has gone on a trip and wants the contact list from Outlook, or someone has met with an accident and someone wants to find out the location of the nearest hospital. The user is in control of what information is published and to whom the information will be displayed. The user would probably have it set up so that only he can access his address book, while the yellow pages Web Service that publishes the nearest hospital to his stranded location would be publicly accessible to all. Also, a user may have his email address entered at a number of different web sites. On changing his address he may need to update all this web sites manually. Using .Net My Services data store, the update will be reflected in all the applications and devices that are connected to it.

The potential for consumer-oriented and business-to-business Web Services like .NET My Services is great, although a lot is still desired in terms of security, privacy and confidentiality. But, it sure looks an innovation that is here to stay.

NB: Authors profusely thank Ms Ayesha S Shaikh, Project Trainee of Inflibnet, Nirma Institute of Technology, Ahmedabad for her valuable contribution to the GLADIATOR Project.

Reference

1. http://www.webservicesarchitect.com/content/articles/myerson01.asp
2. C# Web Services: Building Web Services with .Net Remoting and ASP.NET by Wrox Publication.

3. Microsoft C# Professional Projects by Geetanjali Arora, Balasubramaniam Aliaswamy, and Nitin Pandey with NIIT, PHI.
4. Professional ASP.NET Security by Wrox Publication.
5. Web Service and Interoperability: Security Challenges by S. K. Sharma, G. K. Sharma, and P. N. Shrivastava, 3rd International CALIBER 2005.
6. WS-Security Specification V1.0 – Chris Kaler (Editor). WS-Security, Version 1.0. An IBM, Microsoft and Verisoft joint specification. April 5, 2002. http://www-106.ibm.com/developerworks/webservices/library/ws-secure.
7. Web Service Description Language (WSDL) 1.1, http://www..w3.org/TR/wsdl
8. Extensible Markup Language (XML), http://www.w3.org/XML/
9. http://www.uddi.org/
10. msdn.microsoft.com/library/en-us/ cpguide/html/cpconEnablingDiscoveryForWebService.asp
11. SOAP Version 1.2 Part 1: Messaging Framework, http://www.w3.org/TR/soap12-part1/
12. http://www.w3.org/TR/ws-arch/
13. Developing XML Web Services and Server Components with Microsoft Visual Basic.Net and Microsoft Visual C#.Net, PHI.

7

Structural and Conceptual Changes in the Information Landscape : The New Challenges for Information Professionals

Saji Gopinath

Associate Professor, IIM Kozhikode

ABSTRACT

The information space has witnessed phenomenal changes in the last few years. The fast growth of information repositories and trend towards protocol standardisation had completely revised even the conceptual frame work of the ubiquitous platform of internet. In the application domain, need for systems that mine out knowledge from the distributed data and information resources, revealing the hidden footprints in the seemingly unrelated resources is on the rise. The developmental philosophy of the information/ knowledge repositories is moving from proprietary standards to the open standards, leading to several issues on the long term management of such systems. All these developments, happening at a rapid pace is posing newer challenges to the information professional involved in the design, development, deployment and management of the information repositories in the cyber space. This paper provides an overview of the developments happening in this area and focuses on the new issues emanating out of such changes. Rather than presenting a chronological review of the specific developments, the paper looks at the short and long term impact of philosophical and structural shifts happening in the information space and explore the methodologies for exploiting such changes. Specifically three aspects of structural and conceptual transformation are focussed in detail. On the conceptual front we focus on the transition of the internet from the "web" to "bow-tie architecture" and the subsequent death of "small world theory" in the design, deployment and access strategies of the information. On the structural front, the paper looks at the impact of "open standards" and "free ware" movement as against the dominance of proprietary domains. The strategic and tactical implications of this is analysed from the perspectives of the developer, user and the infomediaries. On the application front the paper focuses on the challenges of repositioning of information repositories as "knowledge estates". As the users are increasingly demanding the extracted knowledge from the information resources, the information landscape is witnessing radical changes forcing information science professionals to reposition as "estate managers" of knowledge space. Even though these three changes are happening independently, led by professionals from different domains, they pose several conflicts and dilemmas to the integrators. The paper provides an exploratory approach to understand and analyse these dilemmas which are being faced increasingly by the IS professionals.

Introduction

Ever since the academic community and business organisations started using the interlinkage of network of computers-popularly known as internet- for speedy and seamless transactions, several research studies have been conducted to understand the conceptual nature of the internet (http://www9.org). As Internet is self managed, under the loose framework prescribed by organisations like IANA and

InterNic, the multifold development of websites and information repositories were quite rapid in the recent past challenging the very nature of the Internet. The emergence of various access channels, servers with different processing capabilities and the positioning strategies adopted by the web developers, etc. had its impact on the structure of the Internet. The changing nature of the net is very significant for the information science professionals, who are engaged in the physical consolidation of distributed information repositories

The age old debate between data and information is currently being replaced by the conflict between the demand for information and knowledge. With the emergence of multidisciplinary applications, need for integrating the information points, and to mine out the knowledge contained them is on the rise. The corporate world is witnessing a phenomenal growth in Application Integrators while the Information users are increasingly demanding systems for seamlessly integrate incompatible- syntactically or semantically- information/data resources from the IS professionals. The role of IS professionals are thus changing from one of gatekeepers to that of knowledge estate managers

While rapid development is happening on the storage and access technologies of information, serious debates are also focusing on the economic relevance of such developments. With majority of information science projects are State funded, the commercial viability of the IS and IT projects is coming under close scrutiny of financial pundits and corporate strategists. The financial impact of adoption of open standards is being questioned widely due to the "strategic inefficiencies" resulting from such a move. With IT falling into infrastructure domain, the proponents of Open software movement argues strongly for its adoption indicating the "operational efficiencies" achieved by such a move. While long term sustainability of any venture is heavily dependent on the financial viability, the need for a clear understanding of this dilemma is very crucial for the Information Science Professionals.

This paper looks at these three themes. The structural and philosophical changes happening on the internet is discussed in the next section. The need and impact of transition from information space to knowledge estates is discussed in section 3. The section 4 reveals the ongoing discussion on the strategic and operational impact of the adoption of freeware standards in development. Each section discusses the relevance of the respective theme on the working of modern IS professional. Section 5 provides the summary and concluding remarks stressing the need for more focussed research on this area.

1.0 Theme 1: Structural Changes in the Information Space

The early studies on the internetworking of computers-internet- revealed a connected graph structure (www.www9.org/w9cdrom/160/160.html). With all the websites believed to be interconnected, the *small world theory*[1] (www.searchengineposition.com) was in vogue till recently. Small world theory, which estimates an average of 17 clicks (steps) for transiting from any webpage to another webpage is very relevant to information professionals in formulating search strategies as well as to provide accessibility to the information resources. The small world theory had conceptually modelled internet as a *web* (see fig 1) with seamless transition possible across the web sites

2.1 Small World Theory

Small world theory had its own impact on the design of digital libraries. With modern digital libraries providing seamless access to information distributed across the web, the digital library[2] developers have to create search and access strategies for providing faster information to the consumer, who is unaware of the underlying structure. With small world theory promising access to any resource in the world within 17 steps, the IS professional need to adopt only generic search strategies which skim from site to site in search of relevant information. The focus will be more on the faster point-to-point transition rather than on the structural aspect of the web. Most of the digital libraries (www.digtallibraries.com/design.html) are built assuming Small world theory as the underlying postulate.

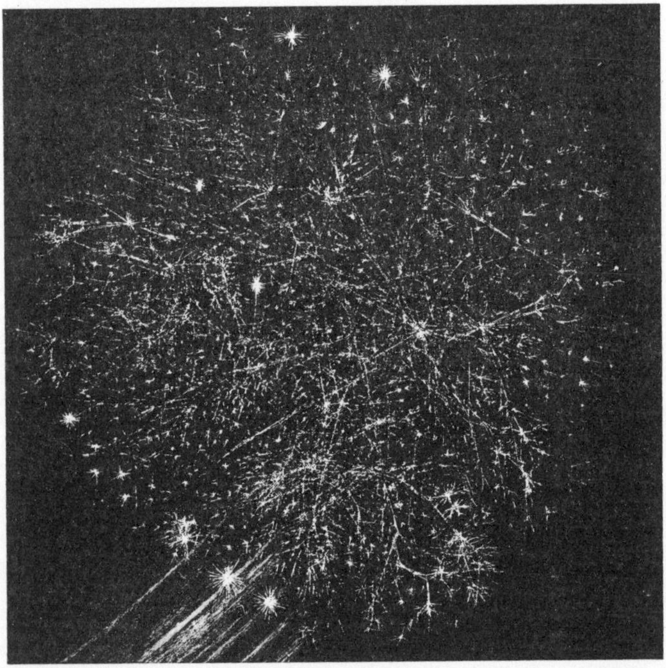

Fig 1: Conceptual structure of Internet (www.web-opte.org)

2.2 Bow Tie Theory and Emergence of Deep Web

Though unrelated, the newer revelations of the structure of the internet-challenging the very existence of the web structure- namely the bow tie structure as proposed by Border et.al (2000) and presence of deep web (http://library.albany.edu/internet/deepweb.html) has phenomenal impact on the search, access and positioning strategy development for IS professionals.

According to a recent research conducted by IBM, Compaq and Altavista, the Internet is like a bow-tie (see fig 2 below) with only around 56 million web pages (about 25% of total websites) are in the Strongly Connected Core that follows the Small world theory. In most of the other cases the probability of finding a path from one site to other, without accessing using an explicit URL address is almost zero. This finding has got significant relevance in the design of digital libraries as well as in adopting search strategies. If a website is hosted in a *tuber* or *tendril*, there is little chance of accessing their content using normal search strategies available with commercial virtual library software. With IS professionals adopting a vanilla approach for hosting the information repositories, there is a very high probability that a site with very useful content is residing in a remote corner of the bow-tie. Thus the IS professionals should restructure their search/

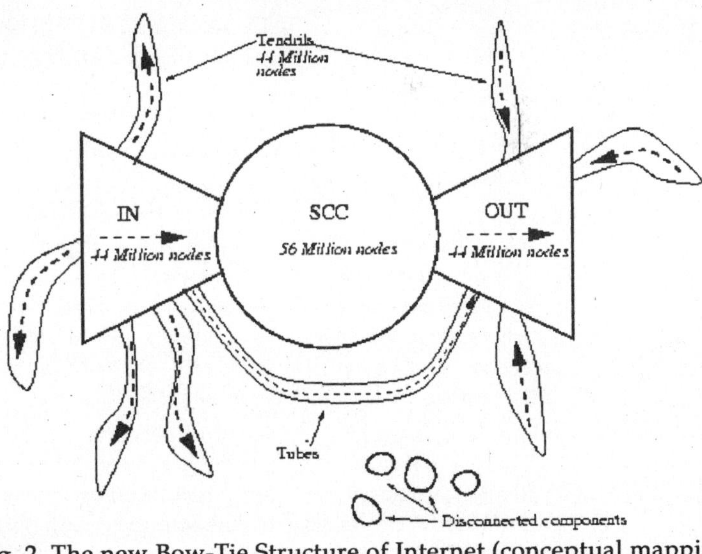

Fig. 2. The new Bow-Tie Structure of Internet (conceptual mapping)

access strategies as well as to adopt extreme programming measures to ensure that the content, when uploaded is residing on a site that forms the part of Strongly connected Core. The difference between Small world web structure and Bow-Tie structure is summarised in table 1

Table 1: The transition from Old Structure to New Structure of Internet

Item	Old Theory	New Theory
Conceptual Structure	Web	Bow-Tie
Interconnectivity	All nodes(web sites) are interconnected	Only the nodes in Strongly connected Core is connected. There are many IN –with connection to SCC and many OUT- connection from SCC sites. There are also Disconnected sites and interconnected tubers and tendrils
Accessibility	Any site can be accessed from any other site within a limited (usually less than 20) number of clicks or transitions	There is a high probability (almost 0.75) that there is no connection exists between any randomly selected pair of websites
Search Strategy design for a digital (virtual) library	Simple vanilla approach is enough as all sites are connected. The emphasis is on deep search within a site and meta data harvesting	Search strategy is quite complex. The exact position of the sites have to be obtained. While deep search within a site is necessary, newer strategies to locate the site is to be included
Hosting and Promotion	Simple. It is irrelevant where it is hosted as all sites are interconnected. The guiding factor is the bandwidth speed design simplicity for faster access	Need to be very choosy and careful. It is important that the information repository lies in a web site in SCC. Look for ward inward and outward references before hosting. The bandwidth speed, while is

		important is not as crucial as the position of the site in the Bow-tie
Challenge for	Need not have to bother about the structure of the web and exact position of hosting pointNeed for tracing the search path is not very useful as the benefit is marginal The need for Technology knowledge for IS professional is not crucial	Have to be extremely careful while choosing site for hosting the site as well as to adopt newer analytical techniques into search strategies Archiving the sites and deployment of high power robot programmes is very important to ensure better spanning of the Internet. The IS professional should be more knowledgeable in IT tools and Techniques as site design is very crucial in enhancing the effectiveness of the virtual library.

While Bow-Tie theory, discussed above throws open new challenges due to the changing nature of the interconnection between the sites, the methods of storage of information in the repositories is also creating new problems for the Information Science professionals. With the realisation that substantial (over 80%) of the information repositories are lying submerged in the Deep Web[3], which is seldom indexed by popular search engines, even if the site hosting such repositories form a part of SCC mentioned earlier, the IS professionals are forced to develop specific search strategies to get the information of the databases that form the part of the Deep Web. Due to commercial interests (discussed in section 4) the many players in the information industry had initially adopted proprietary standards for packaging and storing information. This has necessitated the need for understanding the syntax and semantics of such data sources to develop specific search strategies (www.completeplanet.com) to mine out the vast amount of data. While many IS professionals are working on developing specific search strategies for well known databases in medicine, science and humanities, a generic model is yet to emerge to solve this problem. In the absence of such a generic model, the amount of data accessible to a common digital/ virtual library design is only around 20% of that available in the net. This percentage will be further reduced substantially, when one considers the revelations of the Bow-tie theory explained earlier. Hence in order to make the searches effective, the IS profesional should not only concentrate on analytical techniques to spot the site lying on a distant-inaccessible- corner of the bow-tie but also should be capable of developing site specific search strategies to tap the data that lie invisible in the site. On the development front, they should be ensure that the site is hosted with in the SCC and the content should be following standard protocols so that it could be indexed and searched using common search engines.

2.0 Theme 2: Transition from Information to Knowledge

The changes in the structural nature of the web provides fresh challenges to the IS professionals in formulating search and positioning strategies. Along with this, the changes happening in the use of information is also throwing open a large number of new issues. It is widely recognised that a major advantage of digital form of accessing data is the flexibility of processing data and providing information relevant to the end user. For instance, while a physical data source like a text book can provide facts and figures, an e-book is capable of taking inputs from user and present the data in a way that useful and relevant to the user. Hence most of the digital data accessing devices are equipped with such information processing systems embedded in them. It could be a simple programme that categories the data or could be a very complex one that provide simulation capabilities. As shown in Figure 3 below, the cross references happening in research is on the rise. In other words the demand for content that spans multiple disciplines is on the increase creating new challenges for the managers of the data resources. Moreover the demand of the users for "knowledge" rather than for information is also on the rise.

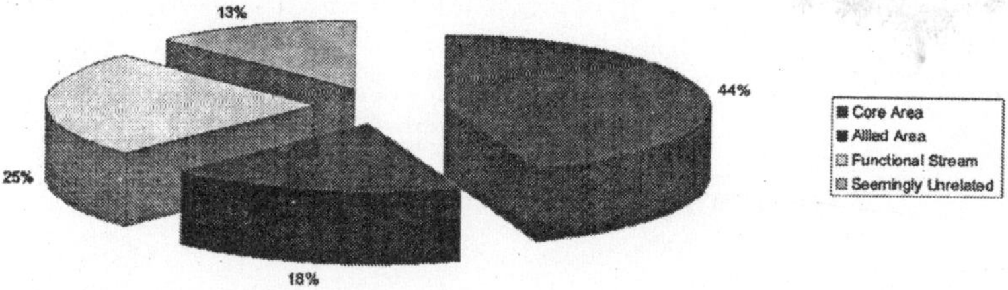

Fig. 3: Cross References in a typical research study

3.1 Information and Knowledge

Information is defined as processed data while Webster defines knowledge as *all that has been perceived or grasped by the mind.* While the proponents of Knowledge theories, are increasingly arguing for the transition of IS professionals to Knowledge Service professionals, there is also a strong counter argument that most of the disciplines at best require only processed data. Knowledge Management, the later argues, is more of canning the information for archival purposes and seldom include the feelingsand perceptions of the generators of information (www.know ledgemanagement. org). It is true that a large number of Knowledge management Systems are just a hype, an incremental improvement over the conventional Information Systems. However it also important to understand that for a large number of academic disciplines, mere information is not enough to do meaningful tasks. Gopinath and Sahadev (2004) had tried to resolve this paradox in the context of Executive Learning. Based on their research findings the various subjects of study could be plotted on a continuum based on the prescriptive and application complexity[4]. It is seen (see figure4) that as the implementation complexity increases, the need for "knowledge" component also increases proportionately. The modified knowledge requirement grid is given in Fig 4

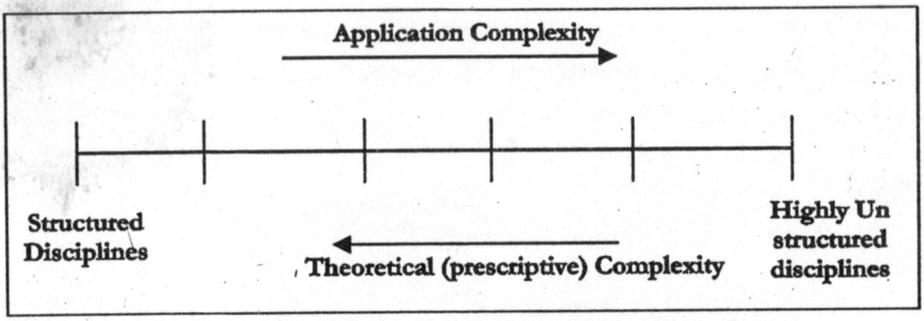

Fig. 4. Fuzzy Continuum of academic disciplines

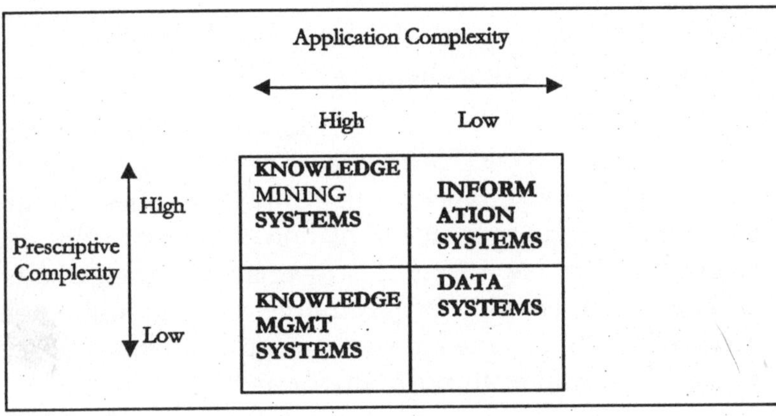

Fig. 5. Modified Knowledge Grid

From the Figure 4, it is clear that the level of Knowledge Management increases with level of Application complexity. For instance, in a discipline like Mathematics, which is having high level of theoretical (prescriptive) complexity (High level of AC as per Kolb's model (1995)) the users need more of Information Systems that simplify the data-the facts and figures- so that learning process will be effective. On the other hand, if a discipline like Management is considered, the theoretical complexity is low in comparison with application complexity (High level of AE-CE as per Kolb's model). In such disciplines, mere supply of information won't suffice the learning and more complex Knowledge management systems have to be developed. With the users adopting to multi-disciplinary learning, the complexity of learning process is increasing in both dimensions resulting in the need of yet another class of systems that provide high level of information derived through complex analytical models along with knowledge mined by creating seemingly unrelated patterns within the information and data elements.

As providers of the information resources and managers of data repositories, the modified Knowledge Management grid is posing some new challenges to the information scientists and professionals. With users moving into multi-disciplined studies, the data resources have to be converted into knowledge estates, where in the data, information, knowledge management and knowledge mining systems have to co-exist as per the user need. The IS professional, have to reposition themselves from their classical gate keeper role to the role of a facilitators, who could mine the knowledge out of the vast repositories of data that exist in distributed sources. This is no easy task given the syntactical and sematic differentials existing across the distributed data points. During the recent past several attempts have been done to create standard protocols for data (information) aggregation. However most of these are limited to the data packaging (web services for instance) and very little attempt is made to standardise the content, which is mandatory for the development of any knowledge management systems. For developing knowledge mining systems, IS professionals should acquire new skills in identifying the hidden patterns and be proficient in the domain of data mining and business intelligence. One of the major stumbling blocks is prevalence of multiple standards adopted in developing and storing the data repositories. Even though one can argue for standardisation and open software movements, there are serious financial flaws in such arguments. This form the third theme of this paper

3.0 Theme 3: Moving from Proprietary to Open Standards

A major chance that is happening in the Information landscape in the recent past is the emergence of Open Standards as against the proprietary standards for data creation and management. As shown in fig 5, the recent developments in Technologies are all XML based standards. Proponents of Open standards, argue that this development is very beneficial to ensure seamless integration of information/data repositories across the world.

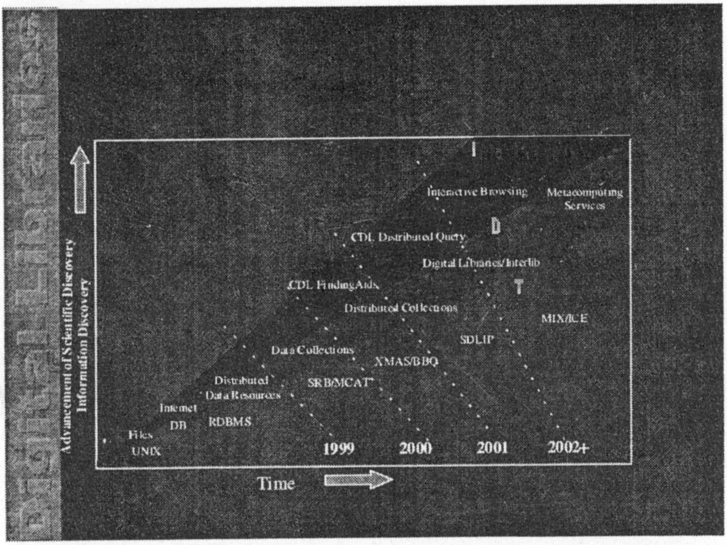

Fig. 6. Emergence of Technologies in the recent past

While, the open standards are necessary for integration and are having a social significance, it is important to understand the financial and strategic implications of this movement. Ever since the seminal article of Nicholas Carr (2003) had challenged the strategic advantages of the Information technology, the debate between the strategic and operational advantages of proprietary and open technologies are the focus of discussion in IT circles. The dilemma of the adoption of these technologies is summarised in figure 6

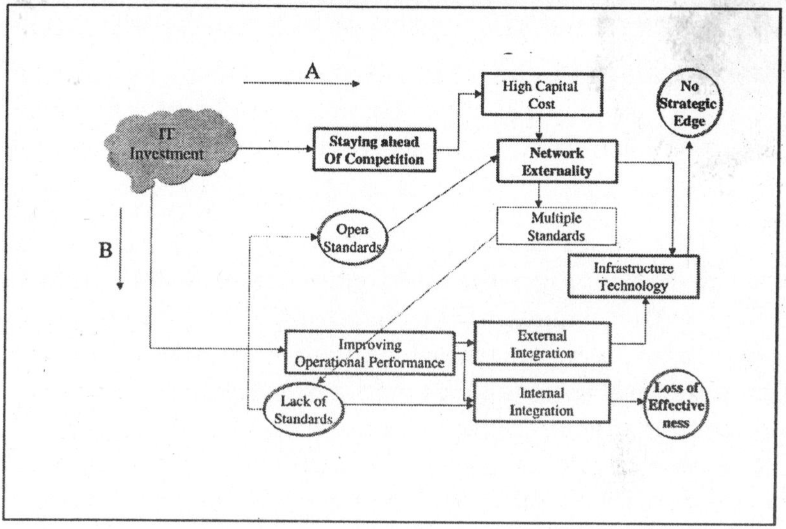

Fig. 7. Impact of Open Standards on Strategic relevance of IT investments

In the figure, the two paths (A and B) are shown. If Investment is made on developing Information resources, huge capital costs involved will force the investors to adopt proprietary standards so that the amount could be recovered through resulting network economics. However this leads to multiple standards. If one follow path B, the IT investment for increasing operating effectiveness, the prime objective will be to ensure internal and external integration, for which multiple standards form as stumbling block. The Open Standards movement have emanated out of this need. However this work against basic principles of network economics and would erode the strategic edge of the IT investment. This dilemma which Information technology industry is facing today, with resultant diminishing returns on IT investments (www.mckinsey.com) is yet to affect the IS domain, mainly due to the large level of State funding existing in the sector. However, over the period the State funding to digital library projects are on the decline and the financial viability of such projects are causing increasing concerns for the investors and IS managers. With corporate sector getting into Information Industry in a big way, the major challenge which IS professionals are going to face in the near future is to resolve the investment paradox of Information Technology.

4.0 Conclusion

This paper presents the structural and conceptual changes happening in the information landscape. The paper discusses the changes in the structure of IT infrastructure-the web- and explores how information professionals should re-orient themselves to get the best out of the changed scenario. As a second theme, the paper focus on the movement of users into Knowledge management domain and stresses the need for Information professionals to transform into Knowledge mining experts. The stumbling block in this transition, the paper argues, is the presence of multiple standards, which were introduced for commercial reasons. The Movement to Open Standards is not easy, with drying down of Government Funding in the Digital Library projects as Return on Investments in such projects may cause severe questions on the financial viability of such ventures. Solving this paradox will be the major challenge for the IS professionals in the near future.

References

The references of various websites are provided in the body of the text :

1. Carr, Nicholas.G (2003) *"IT Doesn't Matter"* Harvard business Review, May 2003
2. Gopinath.S, (2003) *"Pedagogical paradigms for E-learning"* Proceedings of International conference on E-learning, Chennai
3. Gopinath S and Sahadev S (2004), *" E- Learning : Assessment of pedagogical effectiveness in on-line management education"* Proceedings of CELDA 2004 Lisbon, Portugal
4. Kolb. D, Rubin. I, & Osland, J (1195) *"Organisational Behaviour : an experimental approach"* Edn 6, Prentice Hall

8

Knowledge Management Strategies For Effectively Managing Libraries

H. Anil Kumar
Chief Librarian
Nirma University, Ahmedabad
(anil@nim.ac.in)

ABSTRACT

This paper attempts to elicit the concept of Knowledge Management in the context of library management. The concept of Knowledge as related to data and information, tacit K, explicit K and the transformation processes of both these kinds of Knowledge are explained in the paper. The author tries to list the processes that a medium sized library requires and then provides a framework and direction to draw a Knowledge Map for libraries. This paper will prove to be useful for starters in KM, especially for library professionals with an orientation or curiosity to know about KM that has taken the corporate world by storm.

Introduction

Perhaps the most neglected area of library management, especially in developing countries like India, is human resource management. There are very few libraries that have customized training programs, reward systems for library staff, performance management or benchmarking, empowerment of staff, and leadership development programs. These terms are alien to library environment though many libraries, especially in business schools, would have ample resources in their own collections on these topics.

In fact we have seen professional management as a concept, taking off very slowly in the library environs. With much difficulty we understand that library management is management of resources, processes and functions of the library with a simple objective, i.e., to satisfy the customer. We find it very difficult to understand the simple concept of customer in the true 'business' sense. We also need to understand that to help the customer we begin by attempting to help the existing staff by managing the knowledge that is resident in employees and processes.

One of the strategies to manage a library effectively is to manage the knowledge that exists in the staff effectively. It is seen that on many occasions, in big libraries, it is very difficult to replace staff who retire and it often takes a lot of time before the library comes back to normal functioning. Even when senior staff members are on leave it is difficult to have a normal functioning library. Usually this is very true for providing services, as much effectively, that were being handled by the senior staff, in their absence.

The other case is that often we see staff members not sharing the knowledge even if the situation warrants. Reasons may be many ranging from personal conflicts to ineffective teams. But the fact remains that we have never attempted to look at the problem of under-utilization if not non-utilization of the knowledge available in the library. The point is that that the very knowledge that is useful for rendering smooth functioning of the library and to provide effective service to the customer is not being tapped.

It is also true that we see large libraries that are being (mis)managed more often than smaller and newer libraries. The reason being that the smaller and newer libraries do not have the scale to operate with, unlike larger libraries, in terms of resources (collection) and staff. Since older and larger libraries have a history or time that is associated with experience, and numbers in terms of staff; both contribute to the very relevance and need for Knowledge Management.

Knowledge Management – KM

Knowledge Management has been the most misused term in the recent times as far as the Industry is concerned in India. It is only now that many businesses are realizing the importance of KM and are attempting KM in the true sense. In the early years of KM in India (late nineties) we saw the IT sector lapping up the credit of introducing KM in India. In fact many companies thrived on the KM fad and went to the extent of making tall claims like 'knowledge company', 'knowledge managing company', 'knowledge based strategy' and so on. During this time we could also see another development and that is the rise of a new sector called – the Knowledge Industry and it included mainly the IT and Consulting sectors, and later on we witnessed the addition of pharma and biotech industry also to this group. The general corporate understanding was that Knowledge based industries would thrive if KM was implemented appropriately.

In late nineties proliferation of literature in KM was at its peak and every business newspaper and magazine carried an article on KM. Many books and articles were written on KM. In fact, if we survey the literature, we find few books that were not edited works. Most of the works varied in its defining KM but the common implication of these works (globally) was that Knowledge had to be treated as a resource like we treat human resources, finance, technology, and so on. In this regard Knowledge had to be managed professionally and hence required an inventory of where and what knowledge existed, a strategy to manage this knowledge, a map of actions to be carried out, a measurement mechanism, and an outcomes evaluation system to be designed. This required a design of a new system that could be termed as 'Knowledge Management.'

Data, Information and Knowledge

It is important to realize that knowledge is quite different from information though it stems from the same root. Information is converted to Knowledge when there is the process of comparison, or when we look at the outcomes or consequences or when we find a relation or attempt to match or when there is an exchange of information between two or more persons. Though information is the basis for knowledge it is also important to graduate our understanding to the most interesting aspect of KM and that is the existence of Knowledge in tacit form. It may be impossible to find information in a tacit form. Similar to this process of evolution or conversion of information to knowledge, data transforms into information through various means like contextualizing, abstracting or explaining, classifying, cataloguing, etc.

Now, for facilitating our understanding of KM in a library context, let us take for instance that,

1 In a library there are 20 shelves.

2 Each Shelf stores different books and is numbered 1, 2, 3, 4, 5, 6, 7, 20.

3 Shelf 1 has books on Computers, Shelf 2 has books on Philosophy, Shelf 3 has books on Religion, Shelf 3, 4 and 5 have books on Social Sciences and so on.

4 The library staff that shelves books on a daily basis knows that on Mondays Shelf 5 is the most used Shelf; they also know that Shelf 20 having books on History and Geography is the least used Shelf.

5 The reference librarian knows that students from vernacular medium use Shelf 6 the most as books on English Language as stacked there.

6 The Librarian knows that the Institute is working on a

project on High Tech Venture Creation.

These are simple statements that describe a few facts of a library. These may be true for many libraries with varying number of shelves, subjects covered, etc. Looking at the statements we can say that statements 1 and 2 are data. They are just representation of facts. 'Information' is that shelf 3 has books on religion. 'Information' is that Shelf 20 has books on history and geography. 'Knowledge' is that the shelving staff knows which shelves are used and which are unused. The reference librarian 'knows' that shelf 6 is most used by students of vernacular medium. The librarian 'knows' that the Institute is working on a project on High Tech Venture Creation.

This example helps us in firming up the understanding that Knowledge is based on information, and that information is based on Data. One can call this as the ladder of learning where each rung is accessible only by using its previous rung. In the ladder of learning, wisdom evolves from knowledge and is timeless. Another interesting fact is that the life or time validity of data is less than that of information and knowledge has a life more than that of information.

Explicit and Tacit Knowledge

Coming to the types of knowledge we understand that there are mainly two types of Knowledge that are identified as Explicit Knowledge and Tacit Knowledge.

Explicit K (Knowledge) is the knowledge that one can easily identify, capture, format, and retrieve. In the library context we could say some examples of Explicit K are:

1 User Guidelines
2 Classification Manual
3 Rules and regulations of Library
4 Purchase related documents
5 Library Committee minutes

Here we can clearly see that the examples depict the type of Knowledge that can be easily shared because of the convenience of being able to easily capture such knowledge and also equally easy to format and retrieve.

Tacit K (Knowledge) is the other type wherein knowledge is not easily identifiable, difficult to capture, format and retrieve. In the library context some illustrative examples could be:

1 Knowledge about a user that she/he does not like a particular publisher

2 One of the staff has a knack for class no.s.

3 One of the staff has the aptitude for design and colors

4 One of the staff has very good relations or knowledge of a user's research interests

Tacit K is something that cannot be easily captured or formatted or retrieved. But it is very important and will improve efficiency of output tremendously in case the tacit K is managed properly. The best way of managing tacit K is to develop systems where sharing is possible and promoted rather than capturing it. In simple terms it is easy to manage Explicit K and difficult to manage Tacit K.

Transformation of Tacit and Explicit K

Studies have shown that there is a sort of conversion that takes place between Tacit K and Explicit K and they keep interchanging in organizations. The famous Nonaka & Takeuchi work on KM shows that there are four main processes of transformation of one type of K to another. They are:

A Combination

B Internalization

C Socialization

D Externalization

Combination is when an attempt is made to combine a piece of Explicit K with another piece of Explicit K and the result is also again Explicit K. For instance a note by a shelving staff on reasons for additional book ends is combined with a note by reference librarian that indicates increase in requirement of books in a particular area we end up with a note that ascertains the requirement of books and shelves. This may happen due to adding a new course or increased intake of students, etc. The point is that the Explicit Knowledge of requirement of book ends documented by shelving staff is combined with another Explicit Knowledge in the form of another note that documents the requirement of additional books (and shelves) to again produce Explicit Knowledge that combines the both the documents.

Internalization happens when a new staff is given a staff manual on rules and regulations and the staff tries to assimilate the same in daily work. For instance a staff reads that rule no. 15 in the manual says that any book overdue would attract a fine of Re. 1/- per day and whenever he or she comes across this case then he or she would levy the fine accordingly. This is a simple illustration of internalizing explicit K (here the written rule).

Socialization happens when tacit K gets converted to tacit K. This generally happens face to face and when sharing of knowledge happens on a one-to-one or social basis. This is a good explanation of what happens when two staff socialize and attempt to understand each others problems. This appreciation leads to a new tacit understanding and improves efficiency of output. This is also a good example of a Library Trainee trying to understand some practical tips from senior staff during coffee or tea breaks.

Externalization happens when tacit K gets converted to explicit K. A simple example of this process is a staff writing a report on collection development in a library. The report will definitely include some portions that reflect his own tacit K. In fact writing a article on a topic like "Interpersonal problems at work" will have a lot of experiential K included and is a representation of Externalizing K for benefit of others.

Knowledge Map

The understanding these process is important so that we are able to manage the knowledge available effectively once we know what form of K is existing. The management of knowledge depends on the system that exists for the purpose and the system is effective only when the design is appropriate. When designing KM system for library, like for any other organization, we should try to understand the processes. Firstly list down all the main processes that you think exist in a library like Books Procuring, Book Processing, Periodicals, Databases, Other resources, Circulation, etc. Then breakdown these main processes into sub processes as indicated below:

Books Procuring

* Books on approval / recommendation
* Negotiation
* Duplicate checking
* Order placing
* Bill checking/GOC rate/Price verification

Processing

* Accessioning & Classification
* Data Entry
* Seal, bar-coding & Labeling
* Date slip & Seal
* New Arrival list
* Binding

Periodicals

* Accessioning
* Data Entry – Article indexing
* Renewal/ordering

* Binding
* Sending Remainder
* Articles Scanning/Photocopying
* New titles recommendation / quotation / circulation

Databases

* Updating information
* Renewing/ordering
* Reference Service (users)
* Installation & Technology
* Downloading articles from database - Major

Other Resources

* CD's
* Videocassettes/Audiocassettes
* Newspapers
* Photo Albums
* Annual Reports
* Project Reports
* Bound volumes
* Standards
* Catalogues
* Newspaper Clippings

Circulation

* Issue / Return / Renew
* Overdue checking
* Membership Queries/updating
* Reservation
* No Dues
* Maintenance of User Database

Automation

* Alice updating
* System Maintenance/Network checking
* Online searching/ down loading information
* Backup / Security
* Solving Hardware and Software Problems

User Services

* Reference queries
* Report generation (AFW)
* Inter Library Loan / DELNET
* Books in process Information
* Feedback
* No dues for members
* Book procurement
* Orientation
* Database Usage Sessions
* New Arrival List to all HODs
* Sending the articles to the faculties from the database

Statistics

* Issue / Return / Reservation
* Book Bank
* User Statistics
* Budget Statistics
* Library Resource Statistics
* ILL / DELNET Statistics
* Statistics for AICTE, Accreditation etc.

Website

* Content Management
* Site Maintenance

* Feedback

General

* Shift duty
* Shelving
* Books purchase (gifts, programs, etc)
* Correspondence
* Topical Display (Institute programs)
* Notice Board updating
* Newspaper/Journals scanning
* Visitors orientation / PR
* Education Abroad
* Memberships (Delnet, British, etc)
* Library Security

Now, after listing all the processes (the listed ones are indicative and can be modified, i.e., main and sub processes can be added or deleted) and we can go on to a point of ones own comfort we need to make a list 'what is the Knowledge required' to carry out these processes. The list will indicate whether K is explicit or tacit. Then prepare a list of people who complete or undertake these processes. This is what we can a Knowledge Map of the organization.

This is the most important document that is required for designing a KM system. This document will become the basis of designing a KM system that clearly indicates what K is available within your organization and what K you think is important for flowing across the organization. This will also help in our understanding the importance of people and processes from a Knowledge perspective. The important thing to keep in mind is that the base document - K Map will be dynamic and is a tool for development or evolvement of a knowledge organization rather than a rule book.

The KM system will extend beyond this K-map and go

on to include the indication of plans to fulfill the objectives, a time-frame to complete the processes, an outcomes measurement system and evaluation or feedback for the KM-System.

Conclusion

* Knowledge is an important asset for any organization and this is true for library also.
* The bigger the library and more the staff, KM is very useful but at the same time difficult. Knowledge is in the mind of the knower.
* Wherever the human component exists the system has to be dynamic and so is the case with KM system.
* Tacit Knowledge is difficult to handle so it is advisable to share rather than capture.
* A major barrier to knowledge sharing is in the minds of the staff and systems that are designed should keep this in mind.
* The success of a KM system depends on the leadership, as much on the entire team.

Further reading

1. Knowledge management in academic libraries: special tools and processes to support information professionals. By: Ron Jantz. Reference Services Review, 2001, vol. 29 (1), pp. 33-39
2. Making tacit knowledge explicit: the Ready Reference Database as codified knowledge. By: *Stover, Mar, Reference Services Review; Volume 32 No. 2; 2004, pp.* 164 — 173
3. SPECIAL ISSUE ON INFORMATION TECHNOLOGIES AND KNOWLEDGE MANAGEMENT. By: Sambamurthy, V.; Subramani, Mani. MIS Quarterly, Mar2005, Vol. 29 Issue 1

4. VICIOUS AND VIRTUOUS CIRCLES IN THE MANAGEMENT OF KNOWLEDGE: THE CASE OF INFOSYS TECHNOLOGIES. By: Garud, Raghu; Kumaraswamy, Arun. MIS Quarterly, Mar2005, Vol. 29 Issue 1
5. Five steps to a foundationwide KM strategy at the Annie E. Casey Foundation. By: Enright, Kathleen. KM Review, Jan/Feb2005, Vol. 7 Issue 6,
6. Why Does Knowledge Management Still Matter? By: Davenport, Rex. T+D, Feb2005, Vol. 59 Issue 2
7. Drivers of knowledge management in the corporate environment. By : M. du Plessis International Journal of Information Management, February 2005
8. Trust in Knowledge Management and Systems in Organizations. By: Jubert, Anne. KM Review, Jan/Feb2005, Vol. 7 Issue 6.
9. Working Knowledge: How organizations manage what they know / Thomas H. Davenport & Laurence Prusak; HBS press, Boston 1998
10. Knowledge Management: A review; DESIDOC Bulletin of Information Technology, July 2000
11. Knowledge Management: Enabling Business Growth / Ganesh Natarajan and Sandhya Shekhar; Tata McGraw-Hill Pub. Co. Ltd., New Delhi, 2000
12. The Knowledge Creating Company / Ikujiro Nonaka; Harvard Business Review on Knowledge Management; HBS Press, Boston, 1999
13. Knowledge Management Handbook / Jay Liebowitz; CRC Press, London, 1999
14. Leading With Knowledge: The Nature of Competition in the 21st Century / Richard C. Huseman and Jon P. Goodman; Sage Publications, London, 1999
15. Knowledge in Organizations: Access to Thinking at

Work/ John Sparrow; Sage Publications, London, 1998

16. The Knowing -Doing Gap: How Smart Companies Turn Knowledge into Action/ Jeffrey Pfeffer and Robert I Sutton; HBS Press, Boston, 1999
17. If only We Knew What We Know: The Transfer of Internal Knowledge and Best Practice/ Carla O'Dell; The Free Press, New York, 1998
18. What's Your Strategy for Managing Knowledge?/ Morten T. Hansen, Nitin Nohrit and Thomas Tierney; Harvard Business Review, March-April, 1999
19. Knowledge Management: Enabling Business Growth/ Ganesh Natarajan and Sandhya Shekhar; Tata McGraw-Hill Pub. Com. Ltd., New Delhi, 2000
20. Successful Knowledge Management Projects; Sloan Management Review, Winter, 1998

9

Library Capacity Building through E-Journal Consortia: The Indian Scenario

M.G. Sreekumar and T. Sunitha
Indian Institute of Management Kozhikode
(mgsree; sunitha @ iimk.ac.in)

ABSTRACT

The proliferation of E-publishing across the world have brought in a revolution in scholarly journal publication, subscription, access and delivery mechanism. E-journals are electronic equivalents of their print counter parts possessing many added features. E-journals offer a range of potential advantages to libraries and end-users: multiple simultaneous access to the same issue, remote access, in-built searching facilities, multi-media capabilities and reduced storage concerns. As a result of the above, libraries today buy licenses for an ever-increasing number of E-Journals from a range of different publishers and providers. At the same time the library budgets are dwindling and hence librarians are forced to work together for alternate strategies towards collection enrichment and sharing of resources. Consortium based library subscriptions to E-journals and electronic full-text Databases, are picking up good momentum in India. Over the past five years more than ten national level Consortia have come into existence and started playing around in the country. INDEST, CSIR Consortium, IIM Consortium, IBFLIBNET's Infonet,

FORSA etc. are successful ones to name a few. At the same time Library Consortia not free from problems. There are various issues relating to consortia like uninterrupted online access, perpetual access to back issues, pricing, licensing, copyright and archival solutions etc. These need to be strategically tackled and well addressed to get the best out of the consortia. This paper discusses the salient features of E-Journals, major E-Journal consortia initiatives in the country, benchmarks and models, advantages of consortia subscriptions and problems associated with consortia.

Introduction

Presently E-Journals have become the largest and fastest growing areas of the digital collections for most of our libraries. For instance, the E-Journals a few years ago numbered just few hundreds of titles, are now running in many thousands and the rate of growth is phenomenal as well as amazing. The advancements in digital technologies and the recent proliferation of E-Publishing across the world have brought in a revolution in journal publication, subscription, access and delivery mechanism. E-journals are the electronic equivalents of their print counter parts possessing numerous additional features. E-Journals often referred to interchangeably as "Electronic Serials", "Online Journals" and "Electronic Periodicals". Lancaster (1995) defines E-Journal as "a journal created for the electronic medium and available only in this medium" (1). Electronic serials may be defined very broadly as any journal, magazine or newsletter which is available over the internet.

Salient Features

E-journals are becoming increasingly in demand both as a means of rapid desktop access to current research materials and as a way to view past volumes. E-journals offer a range of potential advantages to libraries and end-users:

* Allows remote access

* Can be used simultaneously by more than one user
* Provide timely Access and at a 24 X 7 X 365 formula
* Supports different searching capabilities
* Accommodate unique features (e.g. Links to related items, reference linking)
* Save physical storage space
* Can support multimedia information

As a result of the above advantages, libraries today buy licenses for an ever-increasing number of Electronic Journals from a range of different publishers and providers, and use a diverse set of technologies for information delivery (2).

Subscription, Access and Pricing Models

A variety of subscriptions, access and pricing models are in vogue for E-journals. Electronic journals are literally the entire journal, along with the full content retained in print (if there exists a print version), available in digital format and accessible online throughout the world. An electronic journal is therefore a whole journal, and libraries can subscribe to electronic journals from publishers or through a second party (e.g. vendors) just like they subscribe to print journals. This distinction between publishers and second parties is an important one, as these are the major two ways libraries get electronic journals. Some companies (also known as aggregators) create collections of entire journals and sell access to these collections.

In summary, there are three major ways through which electronic journals could be sourced in libraries:

1. E-Journal sourced directly from publishers
2. E-Journal through second parties such as journal vendors and Gateways (Ingenta, J-Stor etc.), and
3. E-Journal through journal aggregators (Proquest, EBSCO etc.).

Access to E-Journals could be arranged from the respective publishers against User ID / Password or through IP authentication. For a wider audience (campus-wide, enterprise-wide), IP based access is mostly preferred. Some publishers even offer both the access options. These decisions are mainly based on the publisher's policy on online access and how much restricted the access to be.

There exist a number of pricing models for electronic journals such as the online only, online and print, print and online, flip-pricing, pay-per-hit, pay-per-view, pay-per-download, pay-per-print, deeply discounted pricing etc. Some of the other popular models include the FTE (Full Time Equivalence) based pricing", "core subscription plus pay-per-view", "usage based pricing", "licensee membership fees" etc. Based on the nature of the subscription / licensing arrangements and the availability of funds a number of models can coexist in a practical library setting (3).

It is disheartening to note that neither the libraries nor the publishers have sufficient experience towards fixing the cost of E-Journals. This is an area where libraries are being severely exploited and this need to be addressed on a war footing.

Need for E – Journal Consortia

Over the past 10 years there has been substantial increase in the production of E-Journals the world over. According to statistics, out of over 1,50,000 serials published the world over, more than 70,000 cover scholarly communications, and among these more than 20,000 titles are electronic journals and are accessible in the Internet. More than 2500 among these scholarly journals are free for all, which comprise a vast treasure of scholarly content from around the world (4).

At the same time, the user community also has been influenced by these technologies to such an extent that there has been demand from users for providing such electronic information services in the libraries. The situation prevailing in the current library scenario reveals that it has reached a critical mass both in terms of information products as well as the number of users. On the other side library budgets are shrinking. So librarians are prompted to work together for forming consortia for subscription to E-Journals.

The Technology paradigm

With the advent of the Internet, librarians realized the potential of Web technologies for the effective use of resource sharing. The key advantage is that the Internet can be used as the carrier network by all member libraries of a resource-sharing network. All that is needed is to have good Internet connectivity which is reliable and dependable. The common user interface provided by the Web browsers enables integration of access to shared resources (e.g. union catalogues) and also to local library collections and services. Integration of messaging and file transfer protocols in the Web enable easy support for inter-library loan and cataloguing efforts. Since Internet offers platform independent protocols and public domain tools, development of new applications and services and value addition to existing services becomes quite easy.

Consortia approach to E-Journal Subscriptions

A library consortium is a collective activity of a group of libraries towards a common goal of sharing resources (5). With the availability of the state-of-the art information technology solutions and the web revolution, libraries are now better off in terms of easy access to more information through meaningful co-operation among themselves.

The consortium approach is a win-win situation for all its stakeholders – users, publishers, and libraries – all alike. Users are the ultimate end beneficiaries of such initiatives.

For libraries (involved in the consortia), consortia offers several benefits including the following:

* Access to otherwise un-subscribed materials;
* Scope for electronic archives;
* Availability and monitoring of usage statistics;
* Getting deep discounts through joint pricing negotiations – hence lower unit cost of information;
* Reduced storage costs;
* Developing common resources databases;
* Effective document delivery systems;
* A single interface and access point;
* Enhanced search facilities;
* Better scope for developing a union catalogue among participating libraries, etc.

For publishers, the consortium offers reduced attrition; improved income stability; incremental revenue; and greater visibility of their products.

In addition, a wealth of relevant resources is freely available on the Web for libraries to incorporate into their e-collections and make them readily available to their users. In order to survive the array of challenges and also to have a meaningful presence in the digital era, libraries are rapidly adapting to the changing environments. Recently the concept of library resource sharing has been largely influenced by a variety of nation-wide techno-centric consortium approaches in pursuit of optimizing the libraries' resource base while achieving substantial savings through combined and coordinated bargains with publishers. There are several examples of web-based systems supporting resource sharing, collection development and professional enhancement. Applications include union catalogues, cataloguing, cooperative acquisition, inter-library loan, reference and referral services, retrospective conversion and so on. A few such international efforts include the following:

* Texas State Electronic Library (http://link.tsl.state.tx.us/)
* State Library of California (http://www.library.ca.gov/index.html)
* Consortium of University Research Libraries (CURL, http://www.curl.ac.uk)
* Consortium of Academic Libraries in Manchester (CALIM, http://rylibweb.man.ac.uk/calim)
* Colorado Library Information Network (http://www.aclin.org/)
* Washington Research Library Consortium (WRLC, http://www.wrlc.org)
* BIBSYS (Shared University, Research and National Library of Norway (http://www.bibsys.no/english.html)

Internet and the Web have given a strong impetus for consortia-based resource sharing of bibliographic databases and electronic journals. Database vendors like the *Institute for Scientific Information* and *Cambridge Scientific Abstracts* are promoting consortium approach to the use of their databases (e.g. *Web of Science*) among institutions with strong intranet and internet connectivity. Similar approach has been followed by journal publishers like *IEEE* and *Elsevier* in providing access to their electronic journals. This would not have been possible but for the availability of Internet. Internet has been used to provide nation-wide access to databases, for example the *ELSA (Electronic Library of South Africa)* in South Africa and *BIDS (Bath Information and Data Services)* in United Kingdom. Some of the popular international consortia arrangements which are in force are: *Ohio Link; HEAL Link; Virginia's VIVA; Georgia's Galileo; China's CALIS, and Hawaai Initiatives* for title-specific model.

Encouraged by the need to share the knowledge and experience of this emerging area, an International Coalition of Library Consortia (ICOLC) has been formed with Yale University Library as the coordinating center. ICOLC currently has a membership of 150 Library Consortia around the world. INDEST and FORSA consortia from India are the members of ICOLC (http://www.library.yale.edu/consortia/).

Consortia Initiatives in India

Some of the notable Indian initiatives on library resource sharing utilizing the internet technologies include:

* INDEST Consortium (http://paniit.iitd.ac.in/indest)
* UGC INFONET (http://web.inflibnet.ac.in/info/ugcinfonet/ugcinfonet.jsp)
* FORSA Consortium (Astronomy and Astrophysics Libraries) (http://www.iiap.res.in/library/forsa.html)
* DAE Library Consortium (http://www.tifr.res.in/~libws/)
* CSIR Library Consortium http://www.niscair.res.in/ActivitiesandServices/MajorProjects/majproj.htm#ejournalconsortia)
* ISRO Library Consortium
* IIM Library Consortium
* HELINET (Rajiv Gandhi University of Health Sciences, Karnataka) (http://www.rguhs.ac.in/hn/newhell.htm)
* ICICI Knowledge Park (http://www.iciciknowledgepark.com/)
* ICMR Library Consortium

Some of the prominent ongoing library consortia successfully operational in India are listed in Table 1.

Table 1. Major ongoing Library Consortia

Sl. No	Name	Participating Libraries	URL	Resources	Amount Rs. in Crores
1	UGC INFONET (INFLIBNET)	142 University Libraries	http://web.inflibnet.ac.in/info/ugcinfonet/ugcinfonet.jsp	1. 2000 E-Journals 2. Several Databases 3. JCCC	30
2	INDEST (MHRD)	120 (38 MHRD Institutes + 82 others)	http://paniit.iitd.ac.in/indest/	1. 10000 E-Journals 2. 16 Databases 3. JCCC	24
3	FORSA (Astronomy/ Astrophysics Libraries)	11	http://www.iiap.res.in/library/forsa.html	25 E-Journals, Nature Journals	Not provided
4	DAE	50	http://www.tifr.res.in/~libws/	1600 E-Journals	2
5	CSIR	40	http://www.niscair.res.in/ActivitiesandServices/MajorProjects/majproj.htm#ejournalconsortia	3100 E-Journals	25
6	ISRO	12	Not provided	1. 900 E-Journals 2. JCCC	Not provided
7	IIM	6	http://www.iimahd.ernet.in/ http://www.iimb.ernet.in/ http://www.iimcal.ac.in/ http://www.iimidr.ac.in/ http://www.iimk.ac.in/ http://www.iiml.ac.in/	1. 1050 E-Journals 2. 6000 Aggregated Titles 3. 12 databases 4. JCCC (4271 Journals)	5 (partly funded by INDEST)
8	HELINET (RGUHS, Karnataka)	26	http://www.rguhs.ac.in/hn/newhell.htm	1. 600 E-Journals 2. JCCC	2
9	ICICI Knowledge Park	7	http://www.iciciknowledgepark.com/	1. 500 E-Journals 2. JCCC	Not provided, funded by NISSAT
10	ICMR	24	http://www.jccc-icmr.informindia.co.in/about/about.asp	1. 693 E-Journals 2. JCCC (11800 Journals)	Not provided

1). A number of regional focused and city level consortia are slated to emerge having convinced at the success rates of the existing consortia in the country.

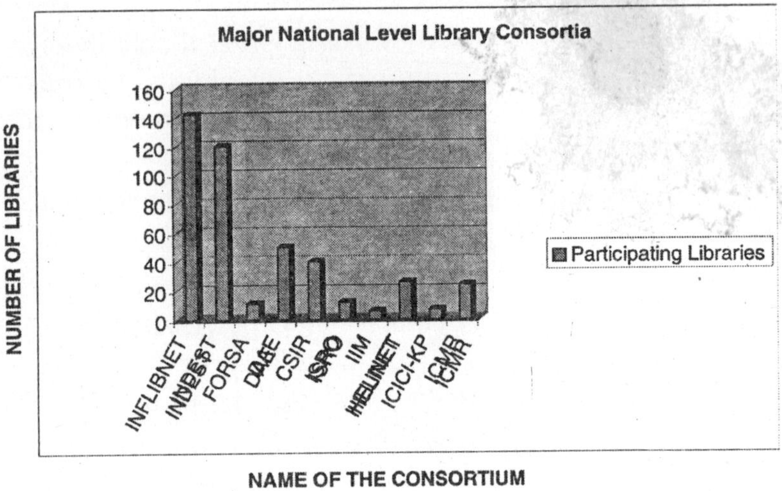

Fig.1. Membership base of major Library Consortia

INDEST Consortium is a welcome move from the Ministry of Human Resource Development of the Government of India and a number of other initiatives are taking place now in India all set to empower and enrich the libraries in the country. Similar is the case with the other library consortia in the country with regard to the increase in their electronic resources. It is heartening to note that the information resource enrichment being enjoyed by the participating libraries of the on going consortia in India is highly encouraging. The electronic journal base of major ongoing library consortia is illustrated in Fig. 2. This could be considered a role model for other libraries, parent organizations, and library networks in the country to emulate and accomplish.

Consortia Models

According to a study conducted during 2004 various consortia models are practiced in India and each of them have varied features (6).

They are:

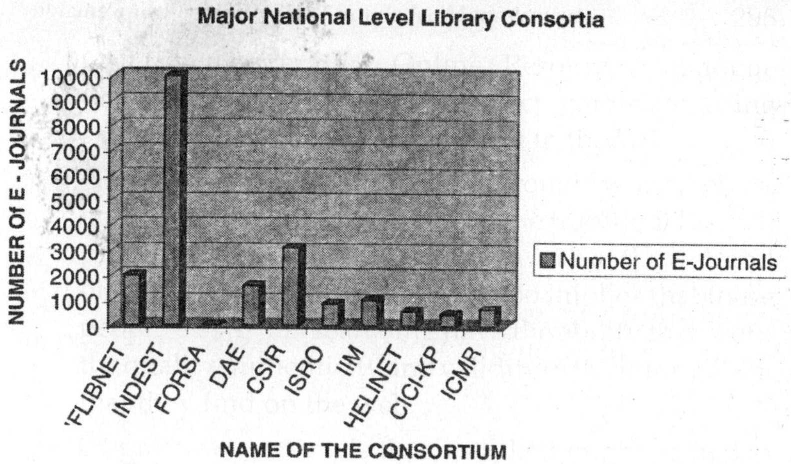

Fig.2. Journal Base of Major Library Consortia in India

i. Open consortia

This type of consortia is open ended and provides facility for the libraries to join and leave as they please. In this case, publishers define a minimum number of libraries for the consortium to take-off, at a specific rate per product. This type of consortia are generally driven by small homogeneous groups who have a need to cross-share the resources in a specific subject area. INDEST Consortium run by the Ministry of HRD, GOI, is an example to this.

ii. Closed Group Consortia

The closed group consortium stays exclusive with in a defined group. This type of consortia emerges either by coalition, affiliation and collaboration among them (CSIR, DAE, IIM Consortium).. Here the formation and operation of the consortia guidelines and its administration are fairly simple and easy.

iii. Centrally Funded Model

In this model, the very existence of the consortium will solely depend on the central funding agency. The strength of this model is that the financial responsibility of running the consortium is shouldered by the parent body. INDEST, UGC INFONET, CSIR, ICMR Consortia etc. are examples of this model.

iv. Shared-budget Model

In this model the participating libraries take the lead and form the consortium. IIM and FORSA are examples of this model. The operational aspects of the consortium especially the management of funds etc. are individually handled. Entering into an MoU for a better and strong footing is always recommended for this of this model.

v. National Consortium

This is a conceptual model or a framework as far as India is concerned, which is not being seriously attempted by any of the ongoing consortia in the country. There are some isolated efforts from UGC Infonet and INDEST in this regard, but they are yet to make any significant strides. National level licensing of information products could be achieved towards this end.

vi. Publisher Initiatives

In addition to the above, India has seen publisher initiated consortia models too, coming up in the recent years. The Emerald Full-Text Library published by the Emerald Publishing Group (formerly MCB University Press) is an example to this. Here, the publisher offered a deep discounted consortium price to the participating libraries on a national level. The pre-condition was that there should not be any drop in their print subscriptions. It is hoped that several such initiatives will be coming up from publishers' side in the near future.

Consortia Issues

The library consortium activity is a complex process, which involves the wholehearted support and concerted efforts of the librarians, their management and the publishers.

They form an important trio in the new scholarly information environment. There are umpteen number of issues relating to consortia like zeroing in and identifying the resources, uninterrupted online access, perpetual access to back issues, pricing, licensing, subscription payment, copyright and archival solutions etc. Planning and implementing the right kind of IT infrastructure is yet another pressing issue.

i. Resources Identification

Identifying the most suitable product which is agreed upon by all the members of the consortium is more or less a difficult proposition. This is mostly because each and every member will have their own wish list of information products and services, though the overlap between the products will be on the higher side in the case of an ideal homogeneous group.

ii. Technology Infrastructure

Long range planning and sourcing of the appropriate IT and Communication infrastructure conducive for proper delivery of information resources is pre-requisite for every participating library.

iii. Pricing Issues

As already discussed earlier, there is no standard practices or processes being followed by majority of the publishers of scholarly literature and hence this is a gray area all together. In most cases cost of the journals are out of reach of many of our libraries and only a consortia approach could provide some meaningful practical solution. Publishers are invited for negotiations and asked to offer their best prices to the consortia. Several methods of pricing are followed, but what is important is that finally the price offered by the publisher should be economically viable for the participating libraries. And it should also ensure uninterrupted and perpetual access to the resources.

iv. Access related issues

There are various access methods offered by publishers towards accessing their resources and it varies case to case. Access authentication could be User ID / Password based or IP based which are popular among them. Uninterrupted and hassle free access to the scholarly content is the ultimate objective of the consortium.

v. Licensing and Copyright issues

As against the print paradigm, the E-Journal subscriptions and access models allow only licensing of the content / product for a stipulated period of time which has several restrictions and bindings on the licensee. There are number of issues which are under debate between librarians, users and publishers which need international attention and solution.

vi. Archival Issues

This is an area which needs utmost attention and unfortunately this is yet to be attended to by the consortia in India. Long term preservation of the invaluable wealth of information being accumulated by the consortium is to be archived and preserved for posterity. As the technology is fast progressing and also getting obsolete almost at the same pace, it is high time that these costly information resources are care fully archived and preserved on a long tem basis.

i. Sustainability issues

Designing and launching a library consortium is perhaps the easier part when compared to its long term sustenance and longevity. The management and the members of the consortium have to strive hard in formulating and establishing robust models towards achieving the above goals.

ii. Usage and Usability Issues

The ROI (Return on Investment) of the consortium is measured in terms of the increased usage, usability of the costly information products which is ultimately reflected in the scientific productivity of the host institutes. It is the earnest efforts of the consortium, the management, the researchers and faculty and the librarians which determine the success or otherwise of any consortium.

Conclusion

We find that the library consortium activities in India are of recent origin and are fast evolving. At the time of writing this paper over 10 national level library consortia - though performance-wise at different levels of reach and richness - are live and operational in the country. As the consortium initiatives demand active involvement of the LIS professionals as well as the promoting / beneficiary institutions, it normally evolve and grow with hardships and bottlenecks. At times we find that the movement draws its strength even from its weaknesses, problems and from its own hard-learnt lessons. It is also to be noted that E-Journal subscription itself is a complex and complicated process, which adds up problems to the consortium activity in multiple ways. Naturally there will be a host of issues and problems that keep haunting libraries involved in consortia activities. At the same token and more importantly, the consortium approach brings in numerous benefits to the participating libraries - a steep increase in the resource base at a nominally higher investment burden; ensuring uninterrupted access to the array of E-Journals; enabling perpetual access to the previously subscribed scholarly content for future; increasing the institutional intellectual capability and scientific productivity; opportunities for long term preservation of scholarly materials through state-of-art archiving strategies; and above all, a tit-for-tat check and balance opportunity for libraries towards the monopoly and the upper hand being exercised by the commercial publishing community for long.

References

1. Lancaster F.W. 'The evolution of electronic publishing'. Library Trends, 43(4), 1995, pp. 518-27.
2. Terry, Ana Arias (2000). 'How today's technology affects libraries' collection choices'. Computers in Libraries Vol. 20, No. 6, pp. 51-55.
3. Sreekumar M.G. et al., "Digital subscriptions and content management in the internet era", Proceedings of the National Seminar on Information Access, Management and Exchange in the Information Age, University of Calicut 28-29 May 2002.
4. Goudar, IRN. and Poornima Narayana. 'Emerging pricing models for E-Journals Consortia and Indian initiatives'. Proceedings of the International Conference on Digital Libraries (ICDL 2004). New Delhi. 24-27 February 2004. 333-341.
5. Janakiraman, S., 'Thoughts on Library Consortium', Proceedings of the Round Table on Sharing of E-journals through Consortia in Indian Libraries, Bangalore. 28-29 November 2002.
6. Arora, Jagdish (et al.) 'Library Consortia and Resource Sharing Initiatives in India: A white paper'. HELINET Consortium. Rajiv Gandhi University of Health Sciences, Bangalore, May 1, 2004.

10

Approach for Accessing and Retrival of Digital Information System: A Model

Nataraj B.Vibhuti
Library-In-Charge
SAP Labs India Pvt. Ltd., Bangalore – 66
(nataraj.vibhuti@sap.com)

Introduction

In order to establish a good Digital information system, it must be properly equipped. So as to disseminate the desired information accessed, out of the digital storage media or digital databases.

The purpose of digitization is to collect, store, organize and disseminate information rapidly worldwide from one end to the other and vise-versa through the use of a computer and its network. This requires the Digital Librarian to be essentially a type of specialist librarian who has to manage and organize Digital information system, handle the specialized tasks of massive digitization, storage, access, digital knowledge mining, digital reference services, electronic information services, search co-ordination and manage the archive and its access.

The Digital Librarian in Digital information system acts as guardian of the global digital library and acts as a symbiotic human machine guru.

Need for digital information system

Necessity is the mother of invention. The emerging global Digital Information System generates the need to manage their digital knowledge resources. The huge Digital Information Systems are emerging as knowledge warehouses.

Need for Digital Information System is to;

* Manage the digital library sources.
* Organize digital knowledge and information.
* Disseminate digital information from the computer held digital information.
* Provide digital reference services and electronic information services.
* Provide knowledge mining from the emerging knowledge warehouses.
* Handle the tasks of massive digitization, digital storage process and digital preservation.
* Provide universal access and retrieval of digital knowledge, ultimately access to all.
* Cataloguing and classification of digital documents and digital knowledge.

Objectives

With the advent of digitization, individuals' expectations for access to information have increased dramatically. It is no longer considered practical or acceptable to travel to a specific location during certain hours to locate needed information. Library users are not satisfied to locate an item of interest that is housed at yet another physical location, request the item and then wait days or weeks for the item requested.

Users expect instant access to all the information resource they require, from any location, at any time and by any device. This is the objective of the Digital information system.

With Digital information system[1], the user can:

* Gain access to the holdings of libraries worldwide through automated catalogs.

* Locate both physical and digitized versions of scholarly articles and books.
* Optimize searches; simultaneously search the internet, commercial database and library collections.
* Save search results and conduct additional processing to narrow or qualify results.
* From search results, click through to access the digitized content or locate additional items of interest.

Approach for accessing and retrival of digital information system: a model

Digitization process

The concepts and technologies connected with digitization are complex. There is a basic process, which involves different sets of hardware and software technologies at each step. Determining the appropriate technology is directly linked to the anticipated use and purpose of the material being digitized.

The digitization process is showed in the below diagram:

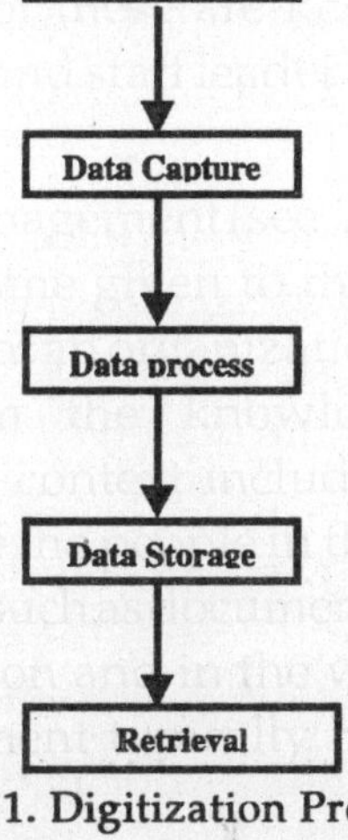

Fig. 1. Digitization Process

Access

Accessing the digital information from Digital information system can be done by the set of access tools used in novel ways to tackle the challenges and opportunities for information access technology and faster access.

Digital information system's set of access tools are like searching, retrieval, locating documents, browsing, navigation, archiving digital documents, content delivery, digital storage and preservation, multimedia indexing, representation, presentation, extraction, distribution, elicitation, e-messaging, storing, filtering, e-publishing, editing, annotating, interfacing online, off-ramps, processing data into digital information, dissemination of digital information, managing digital information, digital reference services, electronic information services, cataloguing and classification of digital documents.

Retrival

There are varieties of information retrieval techniques including metadata searching, full text document searching. In knowing what can or cannot be retrieved from the digital information sources, the Digital information system acts as an expertise in the acquisition of digital information.

A model approach for accessing and retrieving can be showen in fig. 2.

Above model shows the requirement of comprehensive knowledge of the retrieval engines and indexing structure, so that digital librarian can achive the goal of creating information queries with respect to the search system.

There are various tools available to use in Digital information system and they facilitate in accessing, searching, browsing, navigating, retrieving, indexing, storing, organizing and dissemination of digitized information.

There are some digital information sources and pools,

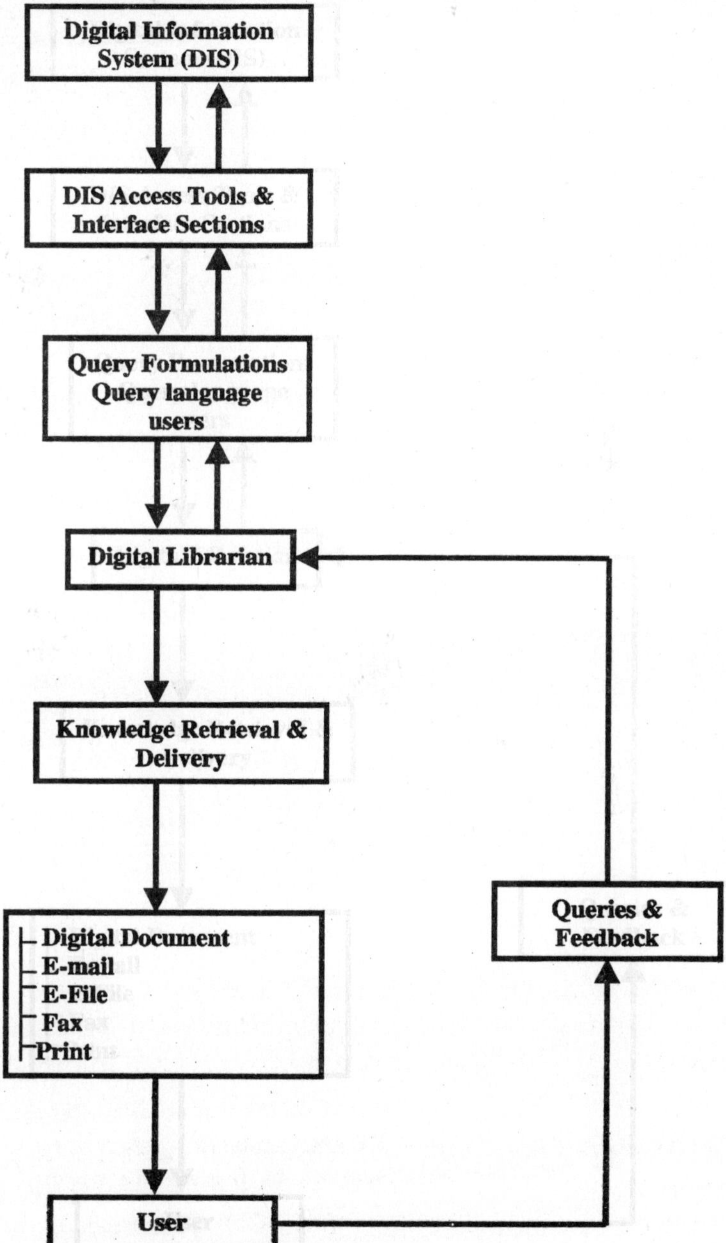

Fig. 2. Model for Accessing & retrieving

which are used as digital access tools, which ultimately aim to facilitate universal access to the users. They are:

* Online Public Access Catalogues (OPAC): meta-databases provide link to other databases/digital information sources: online databases like OCLC, MEDLINE.
* Internet based tools: e-mail networks, mailing lists, electronic conferences, World Wide Web, website homepages, Wide Area Information Services (WAIS),web browsers, etc.
* Digital networks/ networking: MEDLINE, NICNET, DELNET, AGRIS, all sorts of networks.
* Hypertext/ Hypermedia
* Multimedia networking protocols.
* Electronic publishing tools.
* Telephone/ Television.

Role of librarian in digital information system:

Role of Digital librarian[2] in Digital information system refers to the overall competencies (knowledge, know how skills and attitudes) necessary to create, store, analyze, organize, retrieve and disseminate digital information (text, images, sounds) in Digital information system.

Digital Librarian in Digital information system acts as

-a guardian of information superhighway.

(Infrastructure that provides band width-on demand and information on-demand services are called information superhighway)

-a guardian of the global digital library/ the universal digital library.

(Digital library will be a library without walls or national boundaries)

-a symbiotic human machine guru.

(Digital librarian and computers depend on each other for processing and dissemination of digital information and both are interrelated)

-an expert in navigation, browsing and filtering.

(To provide digital reference services and electronic information services from the digital information sources)

-an expert in multimedia search and indexing.

(Not just only standard indexing and retrieval, also sub-document indexing and summarization techniques more than that of paper documents)

-an expert in search and retrieval co-ordination.

(To achive the goal of creating information queries with respect to the search system)

-an intermediary between users and information.

(A fundamental role of a digital librarian in Digital Information System is to act as an intermediary who brings together user and information)

To provide effective service Digital librarian must develop competencies and skills to manage the digital libraries and digital knowledge in terms of digital knowledge management[3]. Following are the skills and competencies required for a digital librarian in the effective functioning if Digital Information System.

1] Internet, WWW:

* Browsing, filtering, retrieving, accessing, digital document analysis;
* Digital reference services, electronic information services;
* Creating home pages, content conversion, downloading techniques:

* Web publishing;
* Digital preservation and storage;
* Electronic messaging, connectivity skills.

2] Multimedia, digital technology, digital media processing:

* Advanced processing capabilities exploiting digital medium;
* Conferencing techniques including teleconferencing and radio conferencing;
* Searching and retrieval of text, images and other multimedi objects;
* Cataloguing and classification of digital documents, digital content.

3] Digital information system, online optical information:

* Development of digital information sources;
* Digitization of print collections;
* Development of machine-readable catalogue records;
* Conversion of print media into digital media;
* Knowledge in digital knowledge structures.

There are additional skills that the digital librarian should develop. They are in terms of knowledge networks[4]:

* *Internal networks:*
    * Personal networks;
    * Project teams, competence groups;
    * Internal digital knowledge resource;
    * Intranets.
* *External networks:*
    * External knowledge resources;
    * Customers, suppliers, partners;
    * External personal networks.

Conclusion

To conclude Digital Information System must equipped with fully advanced technology and must be kept on upgrading the systems for effective services to their community of users.

To provide effective service, Digital Information System should possess:

* Machine-readable data files;
* Components of the emerging National Information Infrastructure;
* Various online databases and CD-ROM information products.
* Computer information storage devices on which information resides.
* Computerized networked library system.

References

1. http://www.emerald-library.com
2. The role of Digital Librarian in the management of Digital Information System by V.Sreenivasulu: The Electronic Library; Vol.18 No.1 2000,Pp12-20.
3. Role of Librarian in Internet and WWW environment by K. Nageswara Rao and K.H.Babu: Information Science; Vol. 4 No.1 2001.
4. Digital Library technology trends by Sun Microsystems,Inc., USA; August 2002.

11

Library Consortia In India: A Successful Way

Rajesh Kumar
Librarian
Sri Sringeri Sharada Institute of Management
Vasant Vihar, New Delhi-57

ABSTRACT

A consortium of libraries is well known for sharing of resources all over the world. In this paper we discussed the historical background, concept, and purpose of digital library consortia. We also highlight present Scenario of Library Consortia in India. We discussed some well known consortia, consortia formation, consortia purchasing and types of Library Consortia of India.

Introduction

The Concept of library is not new, though many differences exist between the libraries of ancient India and modern India. As an observation the basic idea does not show any big difference. In the ancient period owing to the absence of printing, only hand written books or manuscripts comprised the library. In modern society situation has been changed. The basic function of a library is education. The significance of a library in modern society lies in educating the community in the wider sense of the term. Traditionally, the principle of resource-sharing has been adored in academic spheres where knowledge grows through the process of interchange. Resource-sharing, as a cost–effective alternative to collection building, is a recent idea. Librarians often had to rely upon personal networks for transacting materials on inter-library loan. The library network and library consortium are two common forms of implementation of the resource-sharing concept.

Library Consortia

For over a century, Libraries all over the world have come together to form consortia, formal or informal, for diverse purpose, but primarily to share resources. In 1880s, *Library Journal* published articles on library cooperation, which suggested that libraries should work together to share their collections. Triangle Research Libraries Network (USA) formed in 1933 by the University of North Carolina and Duke University is the earliest know consortium[1]. A study commissioned in 1972 by the United States Office of Education commission to conduct a nation-wide survey of academic consortia resulted in publication of the *Directory of Academic Library Consortia*[2] and the first book on library consortia by Ruth J. Patrick[3]. Apart from resources sharing, library automation was one of the major impetuses for development of more formal library consortia in the sixties. The Concept of Consortia is well thought out practical model by library profession for resource sharing. Libraries think about consortia as a means to derive the best possible purchase bargain with collective buying power, which is true, but is not an end in itself. A library consortium may have objectives beyond resource sharing or may limit itself to resource sharing projects and activities.

Historically, the common form of library co-operation was the sharing of union catalogue information, storage facilities, collection development was based on inter library loan services where co-operating libraries agree to enter into reciprocal borrowing and use of materials from other libraries. This form of Co-operation enabled libraries to borrow books and periodicals which were not available locally. The sending of requests and delivery of materials used postal Fax and courier services. However the real drive for co-operation was seen after 1980 only, when more and more libraries started getting automated and used computers for bibliographic processing activities and database searching. We define the library Consortia as-"*A library Cooperative constituted by a group of libraries, preferably with some homogeneous characteristics by subject, or institutional affiliation, or affiliation to funding authorities, who join together with the primary objective of providing expanded access to information resources needed by its user community through a process of pooling and sharing information and infrastructure resources with due adherence to copyright compliances.*"

Library Consortia – Purpose

The recent development of library consortia can be considered as a major step towards library cooperation. Impact of electronic resources on collection development; new development in e-journal licensing, various pricing models of consortia, the roles of librarians, and library consortia has brought revolutionary charges in the field of library and information science. On one hand funds crunch and on the other growing need for information to stay in the competition and knowledge-based economy placed the libraries at the cross roads of profession, feeling of being thrown out. Levels of technology deployment adequate for providing value added services and for efficient processing, retrieval and dissemination are necessary for continuous quality improvement. Competition among the teachers to give out to the students the appropriate and at the right time information from various sources including the peer source, among students for up to date information etc. requires each library to have a large information collection but this is possible if large amount of funds are available which are not simply there. The demands for new information and sources are unending because the changes are happening thick and fast.

No one library or more can ever think of becoming on their own sufficient. Hence it is necessary to enter into a collaborative arrangement where by while effecting saving, the resources base expands. The purpose of library consortia is to share human and information resources so that the collective strengths of the institutions facilitate the research and learning of the member's constituents. A consortium supports resource sharing and provides services to users through programmers in cooperative acquisition, access to electronic resources, access to physical collections, enhanced inter library loan and document delivery.

The Economic motivation continues to drive the consortia formation more than ever before, in the new world of electronic resources, where the risks are greater and scenario is still nebulous. Consortia or Consortium is new being overheard everywhere. Libraries have cooperated for centuries but the organization of libraries into consortia is a very recent development. Previous cooperative initiatives have been aimed at the sharing of scarce resources. Consortia formed by libraries with few common interests. Library Consortia are continuously supporting three principle causes-sharing existing collection through virtual library, reducing cost of operation of the member libraries and attempting to influence pricing policy. Copyright laws and bring down the unit cost of information. However the way these can be achieved and the degree to which these can be achieved depends on the type of the consortia and the power enjoyed by these consortia. It is high time to recognize the importance of sharing electronic resources. The Scope and activity of library consortia are not limited to licensing electronic Resources. It goes much beyond. It will eventually empower the users to access more information in the least possible time. Technology plays a major role in achieving this. In an ideal technology enabled library consortia environment, the entry point to the patrons of each member library is through a single web-enabled window system that is user-oriented and provides access to the entire collection of the consortium member- libraries. The system at the user end should offer services like patron identification and authentication, a comprehensive resource discover system, access to the entire e-journals collection and database. All these should be done through a single search and that should facilitate locating all the resources that are available across the member – libraries no matter where the search result comes from. In a technology-enabled library consortia environment, information is inherently a sharable resource as it is in electronic from. The interdependence of libraries in library consortia for access to the information makes mandatory the adoption of standards. Libraries need to establish cooperatively consortia for offering and sharing electronic resources. Many libraries, especially research libraries have their own network existing within their own locations. These networks can be expanded to enhance the access to the information resources through collaborative partnerships, in the form of consortia. It is essential to have some ideal consortia models for our libraries to adhere to for optimum utilization of their resources and services. Today Consortium's purpose is shifted from mere sharing of resources to sharing of expertise between libraries and also to explore the need for libraries to make the most effective use of their funds collectively. This is an essential future aspect to be considered seriously in the libraries. There are many objectives which are crucial to the consortia concept like collection development, purchasing techniques, electronic publishing, Co-operative organization, collective bargaining etc., need to be addressed in the proper perspective. There some objectives of Library consortia are given below:-

* A very small number of publishers currently offer consortia based purchased and access models.
* A Large number of small publishers represent a significant information resource base that users in

specialized fields have always depended on.

* Due to financial crunch many libraries do not subscribe to a large number of journals that their users need most. This is very true in Indian situation.
* A Well –balanced collection of a library should reflect a character that is publisher independent and user- need dependent.
* E-Journal subscriptions are priced by publishers almost at the same level as print subscriptions, and even more in some cases.
* Consortia development requires substantial initial funding on both infrastructure resources and information.

Consortia Formation

Every consortium evolves in its own mode and phase depending on the individuals and groups taking the initiatives. Whenever in the formation of Consortium there are some major steps to follow:-

* Enter an MOU describing briefly the purpose & plan for the Consortium
* Develop a constitution for the Consortium
* Designate a Consortium leader
* Obtain budgetary commitments from the funding agencies & members
* Create a website for the consortium
* Describe the rule of Resource Sharing agreements among members.

Consortia Purchasing

A number of publishers offer consortia.

(a) If their purchase power is big enough

(b) Access to the whole range of their Journals. Every member of the consortium will have electronic access not only to the journals currently subscribed to but all the journals. As we all know libraries currently subscribe only to those journals that they can afford on any specific time of date, and there will be a number of other journals of the specific publisher the library occasionally will have to interlend as well. Consortia purchasing offers for the single library the opportunity to get access to more journals than they currently have subscriptions to, thus eliminating the continuous cancellation operations.

Types of Library Consortia

There are several types of library consortia in India which are given below:-

(i) Open Consortia:-This types of consortia are open ended to provide flexibility for the libraries to join leave at their need, convenience and will. The publisher may define a minimum number of libraries for the consortium to take-off the ground. These types of consortia are generally driven by small homogeneous group who have a need to cross-share the resources in a specific subject area.

(ii) Closed Group Consortia: - The membership is defined by certain criteria and stays closed with in the defined group. These types of consortia emerge either by affiliation (CSIR, DAE Consortium) or by a strong bond of homogeneity and comradeship (IIM Consortium). Publishers generally prefer this model of consortia, as the negotiations are far easier.

(iii) Centrally Funded Model: - Funding models often decides the structure of a consortium. Central funding acts as a kind of e-subsidy and driving force for the consortium. Resource sharing policies and practices can be better administered provided the funding model also envisages an efficient management and co- ordination model.

(iv) Shared–Budget Model: - This is the only alternative where central funding is not coming. IIM and FORSA are examples of this model but the fund management does not have a central authority.

(v) National Consortium: - National Consortium is the similar to CALIS in China. A National consortium in spirit, similar to INDEST's national price negotiation, UGC's Britanica licensing for the entire education sector (Government funded) is a feasible idea. Developing country-archive infrastructure is an area that fits the role of a national consortium well.

Library Consortia in India

The Concept of library consortia has been floating around for quite some time in India and, Indian libraries are yet to move in the definite direction in this regards. Strong resource sharing activities among libraries, which are the prerequisite for right mindset towards consortia activities, have not been present in our country to the desired extent. Libraries today buy licenses for an ever-increasing number of information resources from arrange of different publishers and providers, and use a diverse set of technologies for information delivery. "Shared Subscription" or "Consortia-based subscription" to electronic resources through consortia of libraries is a feasible strategy to increase the access to electronic resources across Institutions at a lower cost. The Consortia-based subscription can be successfully deployed to meet the pressures such as diminishing budget, increased user's demand and rising cost of Journals. The librarians all over the world are forming consortia of all types and all levels with the objective to take advantage of current global network to promote better, faster and more cost effective ways of providing access to electronic information resources to the information seekers. The Progress of formation of library consortiums as visible organizations is quite slow in our country. This has happened in spite of the acute need of sharing of various resources among the Libraries. Experiences show that discussion of formation of consortiums takes place around the time when financial constraints are felt. Electronic information is quite expensive and in advanced countries, the libraries are attempting to normalize this high cost, through consortiums. In India too, the high cost of this very electronic information is forcing us towards consortiums. Consortia for shared access to electronic database have been talked about since late 90s.COMSAC (Consortium for Material Science and Aerospace Collection) is the first known formal consortia initiative led by the National Aerospace Laboratory (NAL) in 1998 for a few database. This consortium aborted in second year. The first limited purpose and successful, consortia-like model can be traced to Tata Institute of Fundamental Research (TIFR) in 2000, which used the consortia model offered by Springer for multi-site licensing and cross sharing of content among all the libraries falling under TIFR's affiliation. The reason for success was one central authority in command to negotiate a model on behalf of all. A few leading libraries, publishers and venders sustained the interests and momentum, leading to a few, open and non-formal consortia projects by the Forum for Research Sharing in Astronomy & Astrophysics (FORSA) and the (Indian Institute of Management) IIM Libraries for e-journals from Nature, Kluwer, Blackwell, Taylor, & Francis and other publishers. The Council of Scientific and Industrial Research (CSIR) can take credit being the first major and formal consortium at national level. Informatics India with initiation from three different educational institutes has successfully developed three consortium models. These are SNDT University consortia of Library and Information Science Abstracts (LISA) with other six Universities, Secondly, Forum for Resource Sharing in Astronomy and Astrophysics (FORSA) consortia of Kluwer E-Journal consortia program with five institutes and finally IIMs consortia of 33 Kluwer journals in management sciences. Some well known consortiums in India are given below:-

(1) Indian Digital Library of Engineering Science and Technology (INDEST) Consortium:-Indian Digital Library of Engineering Science and Technology Consortium can truly take credit as the first well planned and thoughtfully implemented national and multi-sector consortium with both funding and management commitment. The Ministry of HRD has set–up a "Consortia-based Subscription to Electronic Resources for Technical Education System in India" on the recommendation made by the Expert Group appointed by the ministry under the chairmanship of Prof. N. Balakrishnan. "Shared subscription "or "Consortia-based subscription" to electronic resources through consortia of libraries is a feasible strategy to increase the access to electronic resources across institutions at highly discounted rates of subscription. The Consortia- based subscription can be successfully deployed to meet the pressures such as diminishing budget, increased user's demand and rising cost of journals. The libraries all over the world are forming consortia of all types and at all levels with an objective to take advantage of current global network to promote better, faster and more cost-effective ways of providing electronic information resources to the information seekers. The library consortia , on the basis of sheer strength of numbers of institutions, offers healthy business growth opportunities to the electronic publishers and thus attracts the best possible price and terms of agreement in a win-win situation for both. The collective strength of consortia members facilitates the libraries to get the benefit of wider access to electronic resources at affordable cost and at the best terms and conditions.

The INDEST Consortium is the most ambitious initiative taken so far in the country. It would not only benefit 38 major technological institutions in the country (Including IITs,IISc,NITSs,RECs, IIITs, IIMs other), being an open-ended proposition, it also invites all AICTE- accredited and UGC-affiliated institutions to join hands with the leading

Engineering and Technological Institutions in India and share the benefits it offers in terms of lower subscription rates and better terms of agreement with the publishers. While the expenditure on electronic resources proposed for subscription under the consortium for selected institutions would be met from the funds made available by the MHRD, the consortium welcomes institutions to join the consortium on their own for sharing benefits it offers in terms of lower subscription rates and better terms of agreement with the publishers. Membership of the Consortium is open to any private or Government-funded Engineering/Technological/ Educational Institutions/Universities for one or more electronic resources. The members would be required to sign an agreement with the INDEST Consortium as well as with the publishers of electronic resources that they wish to subscribe. The Consortium would also charge a one-time entry fee of Rs. 1000/-.The Consortium offers the best possible price advantage ranging from 25% to 95% through its pricing agreements with publishers as well as terms of agreement for various electronic resources.

(2) UGC-Infonet E-Journals Consortium: - University Grant Commission has initiated a programme called UGC-Infonet E-Journals Consortium to provide online access to electronic journals and databases in all disciplines to the universities in India. All universities which come under the purview of UGC will be beneficiary members of the programme. The programme is being executed by Information and Library Network Centre, Ahmadabad, an autonomous institution under the UGC. Access to various electronic resources have formally commenced from January 1, 2004, initially for 30 universities. This is the largest consortium with a vision and plans to reach out to above280 universities and several thousand colleges affiliated to these universities, over a period of time. It is also the first consortium to address the infrastructure issues at the member library sites before planning the content licensing stage. It will go a long way in mitigating the severe shortage of periodicals faced by universities libraries for several years. The E-Journals programme is a cornerstone of the UGC-INFONET efforts, which aims at addressing the teaching, learning, research, connectivity and governance requirements of the universities.

(3) HELINET: - Health Sciences Library and Information Network (HELINET) is the first such initiative of a University consortium piloted by the Digital Library at the Rajiv Gandhi University of Health Science covering 25 medical libraries in the State of Karnataka.HELINET has also inspired other medical universities in the country. This consortium can be termed as a bold initiative with serious involvement and commitment by the Institutional and University managements and novel method of participative funding to self sustain the project.

(4) IIM Library Consortia: - The Indian Institutes of Management are premier national business management education institutions set up by the legislation of Government of India. They are independent societies governed by independent Board of Governors. Needs of resource sharing was realized by IIM Libraries a long back. Besides entering into the interlibrary loan practice, IIM Libraries also thought seriously of resource sharing in many other areas such as cooperative acquisition, cooperative processing and decentralized utilization. Encouraged by the success of such an arrangement, the librarians of IIMs felt emboldened to in initiate other major cost-effective and user-oriented initiatives. As a step towards it the IIMs have formed a Consortium. The concept of IIM Consortium has been floated a few years back. It was in the year 2000 that the librarians of all the 6 IIMs sat together to work out consortia-based subscription model for the otherwise very expensive electronic database. IIM Consortium is becoming a reality. The two areas were identified for partnership viz., (a) developing the collection on shared basis and (b) developing the services for exploiting such collection. IIM Library consortium has in the last one year successfully executed a few shared acquisition services Viz., Science Direct of Elsevier, John Wiley electronic journals and Kluwer electronic journals, Proquest and EBSCO services. More areas are identified for partnership.

(5) NISCAIR Consortium: - National Institute of Science communication & Information Resources (NISCAIR) is the nodal organization for developing a "Consortium for CSIR Laboratories for Accessing e–Journals". The activity shall range from creation to monitoring of the access facility of scientific periodicals published by leading international institutions. To start with, an agreement has been signed with, e-journal publisher, M/s Elsevier Science for a period of four years for 1200 journals. Under this scheme, CSIR scientists shall be able to access these journals and download material for their use. Such access to worldwide Journal resources will play a very vital role and strengthen research and development in CSIR laboratories, thus leading to knowledge generation useful for socio-economic development of the country. The objectives are:-

* To strengthen the pooling, sharing and electronically accessing the CSIR library resources.
* To provide access to world S&T literature to CSIR labs.
* To nucleate the culture of electronic access resulting into evolution of digital libraries.

(6) Tata Institute of Fundamentals Research Consortium: - The Tata Institute of Fundamental Research Library was established in 1945, almost simultaneously with its parent organization. Beginning with a small collection of books, it has now crossed more that 120,000 volumes. The first limited purpose and successful, consortia-like model can be traced to Tata Institute of Fundamental Research (TIFR) in 2000, which used the consortia model offered by Springer for

multi-site licensing and cross sharing of content among all the libraries falling under TIFR's affiliation

(7) CSIR CONSORTIA: - The Council of Scientific and Industrial Research (CSIR) can take the credit being the first major and formal consortium at national level. This well conceived pilot project with a limited central funding set a process and model for identification of resources and favorable licensing negotiation. The group firmed up its plans to launch the consortia with three major publishers- Elsevier, Kluwer, and Springer.

(8) Forum for Resource Sharing in Astronomy and Astrophysics: - Forum for resource sharing in Astronomy and Astrophysics (FORSA) came into existence in the year 1981, for sharing the resources available in astronomy libraries in the country. The following institutions are members of this forum:-

I. Indian Institute of Astrophysics, Bangalore

II. Inter-University Centre for Astronomy & Astrophysics, Pune

III. National Centre for Radio Astrophysics, Pune

IV. Nizamiah Observatory Department of Astronomy, Hyderabad

V. Physical Research Laboratory, Ahmedabad

VI. Raman Research Institute, Bangalore

VII. Tata Institute of Fundamental Research, Mumbai

VIII. Aryabhatta Research Institute of Observational Sciences, Nainital

FORSA has successfully completed 24 years and will add many more in the days to come.

All the above cited Consortia are well known consortia of India. There are some other consortia of India which are given below:-

* COMSAC (Consortium for Material Science and Aerospace Collection)
* DAE (Department of Automatic Energy)
* Indian Astrophysics Consortium

Conclusion

The Indian libraries face an enormous challenge in the area of Consortium formation and sustaining the activities. In India there is a big scope for Consortium. On the basis of the above discussion, it can be said that library Consortia may established and the member participating in library Consortia can work sincerely into the concept, then there is a big scope of saving funds, which are otherwise spent unnecessary when the journals and electronic Databases are subscribed in the capacity of an individual library where the scope of negotiation with vendor for price & benefits is very low in comparison to the group asking for. On the above discussion it can be said that the near future there is a big scope of library Consortia in India.

References

1. Sharon L. Bostick. The History and Development of Academic Library Consortia in the United States: An overview. Journal of Academic Librarianship, Volume 27, Number 1, pages 128-130.
2. Diana D. DeLanoy & Carlos A. Cuadra, *Directory of Academic Library Consortia* (Santa Monica, CA : System Development Corporation, 1972)
3. Ruth J. *Patrick Guidelines for Library Cooperation: Development of Academic Library Consortia (Santa Monica, CA: System Development Corporation, 1972).*
4. International Coalition of Library Consortia (ICOLC). Guidelines for Technical Issues in Request for Proposal (REP) requirements and Contract Negotiations. (January 1999). Http://library.uwsp.edu/aschmetz/Accessible/CIT2001/ICOLC.htm
5. Arora, Jagdish (et al.) Library Consortia and Resource Sharing Initiatives in India: A white paper: under preparation for Rajiv Gandhi University of Health Sciences, Bangalore, May 1, 2004.
6. Dai, L (et al.) China Academic Library and Information System : An

Academic Library Consortium in China, *Information Technologies and Libraries* 19(2) 2000: pages 66-67.

7. http://www.infolibrarian.com/cons.htm

8. Pandian,Paul.Standards for modern library Consortia : Librarians perspective, *Library Management: Trends and Opportunities*.New Delhi: Excel Books,2005.pp.126-140

9. http://www.library.iitb.ac.in/indest

10. http://www.ugc.in

12

Electronic Information Retrieval System Digital Library of National Institute of Pharmaceutical Education and Research

Shivendra Singh
Electronic Information Retrieval System

Anurag Sharma
Library & Information Services Division
National Institute of Pharmaceutical
Education & Research, Sector-67, Mohali-160062

ABSTRACT

WWW paradigm and digital data has revolutionized data dissemination among the library users. Paper proposes an electronic information retrieval system that enables the user to use electronic/digital, online information retrieval. The paper describes the uses and services of electronic information on the Electronic Information Retrieval System Centre, NIPER set up in the campus area network.

1. Introduction

In few years huge valuable collection of electronic resources have been subscribed and stored by the institute. This causes the difficulty of retrieving the objective information from the huge stored data. This requirement can be achieved through electronic publication or an electronic information retrieval system. The institute has setup an Electronic Information Retrieval System at NIPER on December 2001.

2. About NIPER

National Institute of Pharmaceutical Education and Research (NIPER) is the first national level institute in pharmaceutical sciences with a proclaimed objective of becoming a centre of excellence for advanced studies and research in pharmaceutical sciences. The Government of India has declared NIPER as an 'Institute of National Importance'. It is an autonomous body set up under the aegis of Ministry of Chemicals and Fertilizers, Government of India. The Institute is conceived to provide leadership in pharmaceutical sciences and related areas not only within the country, but also to the countries in South East Asia, South Asia and Africa. NIPER is a member of Association of Indian Universities and Association of Commonwealth Universities. The Institute is located about 250 Km north of Delhi at S.A.S. Nagar (Mohali), Punjab on a total area of 130 acres[1].

3. Library and Information Centre

The library at NIPER is being developed in a manner that it can eventually gain the status of National Library and Information Centre on Pharmaceutical Sciences. A beginning has been made with the subscription of 63 international and 47 national journals. The library has Chemical Abstracts from 1907 till date and Cumulative Indices up to eleventh bound volumes. A number of CD-ROM databases such as International Pharmaceutical Abstracts and Drug Information Full Text (1977-1997), Ekaswa, Syntheline, MFline & DRUGDEX are also available. The library is accessible to all the Pharmacy professionals from the country and abroad and provides information to the academia, researchers and the industry personnel. The library has obtained institutional membership of DELNET, Chandigarh Libraries Consortium,

British Library (Chandigarh), Current Science Association (Bangalore), and Association of Indian Universities (Delhi). At present library possesses 3331 books, 15, 518 bound volumes of journals, 204 theses and about 173 CD-ROMs.

4. Electronic Information Retrieval System

Electronic Information Retrieval Systems (EIRS) that manage full-text document databases with keyword or full text search. The Institute has set up an EIRS[2] (Fig.1) for the purpose of saving time of our faculty/scientist/students and staff. We are retrieving the information of patents, journal articles, books, and its parts, STN Search, Journals table of contents, List of Journals available in the different libraries from the Internet and others off-line databases. EIRS Centre stores all the data on Intranet server, which can be accessed by all users.

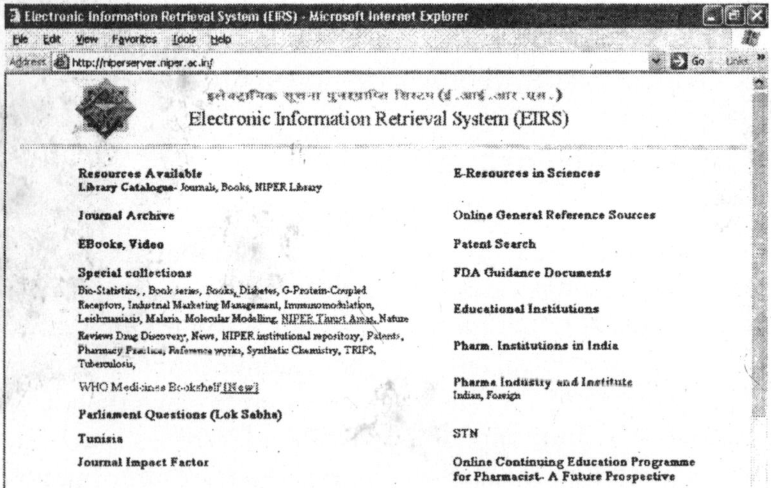

Fig. 1. Electronic Information Retrieval System (EIRS)

5. Users

Highly trained and experienced faculty have been

working at NIPER for almost ten years and several others are in the process of joining. The faculty is assisted by 70 supporting scientific and technical staff members. More than 200 students are living in the campus

6. Systems and Hardware/Network

WE have three servers for EIRS services. All the servers, computers and printers in the EIRS Centre are connected through a 10/100/1000 Mbps network.

6.1 Server I (for general HTML and others services)

Windows 2000 Server

Hardware Configuration of Server I

IBM X Series 225

Intel® XeonTM processors at 2.8GHz; high-performance 533MHz front-side bus speed

512MB standard/8GB max PC2100 DDR ChipkillTM memory

Five 36.4 GBUltra320 hot-swap hard disk drives

Gigabit Ethernet- Integrated

Hot-swap redundant power model

6.2 Sever II (for Greenstone Digital Library Software)

Windows 2000 Server

Hardware Configuration of Server II

Compaq Prolient 530 Server

2.4GHz 512K Xeon DP

I GB PC1600 DDR SDRAM

Integrated Dual Channel Wide

Ultra3 compatible SCSI Adapter

Raid 5 Hot swappable Controller

Embedded 10/100/1000

7 PCI-X (64bit/100MHz) available, 4 hot-plug

6.3 Server III (Library OPAC by Libsys)

Windows NT 4.0

Hardware Configuration of Server III

Dell Power Edge 2500-CPU

1133MHZ/ 36 GB

2 SCS HDD/ 512 MB RAM

Ethernet adapter/ RAID 1 configured/ WINNT Server/

DAT Drive/ DVD ROM

DELL Power Vault CD/E771a CD/Product DOC

CD/Server Assistant/ System Management

CD/ IE- CD Server Pack 69/WINNT 4.0.

The first server is Compaq machine where we have all offline databases which provide browsing facilities only. In the second sever is also in Compaq machine where we have installed digital library software (Greenstone Digital Library). The third server provides library OPAC services. The rest of the institute is also connected to the campus wide area network. Internet and EIRS services are provided to all users through a dedicated 256 Kbps Internet link. Users can use the EIRS resources of the institute from their residences by dialling through a modem. EIRS Centre also supports high speed colour and black & white laser printers, colour plotter and scanners

7. Software and DL Tools

GreenStone Digital Library

LibSys

WINISIS

STN Express

Adobe Acrobat

Adobe Photoshop

EndNote

8. Electronic Information Resources

8.1 Off Line Database

The NIPER Library is developed in a manner that it can eventually gain the status of National Library & Information Centre of Pharmaceutical Sciences. In addition to the 107 foreign and Indian print journals it subscribes to the following full text and Indexing and abstracting databases on CD-ROM pertaining to Pharmaceutical Management, Bioinformatics, Health Care, and Marketing of Products in Pharma sector, Trends in Global Pharmaceutical Market. Operations research, Patents field in India etc.

I. ***Global Pharma Trends:*** Is a comprehensive database on Trends in Pharmaceutical Industry and provides changing trends in a Worldwide Pharmaceutical Market share, Major Therapeutic Areas of Research Activities by Top companies.

II. ***Industrial Products Finder***: A database on Products and services and covers articles on industries, Industry Talks, Management techniques and Human Resource Management.

III. ***Marketing***: Mastering Business is an interactive Multimedia resource that uses video on business concepts, Marketing concepts, marketing strategy and consumer behaviour.

IV. ***Micromdex***: The database provides in-depth, referenced data on the dosing, pharmacokinetics, interactions, clinical applications, efficacy, etc for FDA approved, investigational, and international drugs.

V. ***Ekaswa Database***: A Database on Patent applications field in India.

VI. ***Mfline***: A database covering Pharmacological data.

VII. ***Synthline***: Database related to the synthesis of Marketed drugs.

VIII. ***International Pharmaceutical Abstracts on CDROM*:** The IPA is an abstracts database covering abstracts of the articles published in the field of Pharmaceutical and allied sciences like pharmaceutical technology, pharmacy practice, drug evaluation, Biopharmaceutics, Drug evaluation and Marketing, Pharmaceutical Induastries.

IX. **Intellectual Property Rights- Key to New Wealth:**

It consists of details on various facets of IP- Patents, designs, trademarks, copyrights, geographical indications, integrated circuits and trade secrets.

8.2 Online Database

I. ScienceDirect & BioMednet Reviews (License Agreements)

Institute subscribes selected collection of ScienceDirect and BioMed Reviews since 1995. It allows access to the full text journal articles published from 1995. We do not subscribe to the full ScienceDirect service.

II. ***STN Database (License Agreements)***

NIPER has subscribed the Scientific and Technical Information Network[3] (STN), a leading and comprehensive scientific online information service giving access to over 200 scientific and technical databases of chemistry, pharmaceutical sciences and biotechnology.

III. ***DELNET***

We are the regular members of the DELNET and access various services like Inter Library Loan, Union Catalogue and Bibliographic databases, Full text databases, Internet Resources, Resource Sharing

8.3 Inhouse Library Database

I. Thrust Areas of Research Database

Keeping in mind the national requirements, the following thrust areas have been identified for research at the

Institute Tuberculosis, Malaria, Diabetes, Leishmaniasis and Immunomodulation. EIRS has created Thrust areas of Research Database for the Institute thrust area's research activities[4] (fig. 2&3).

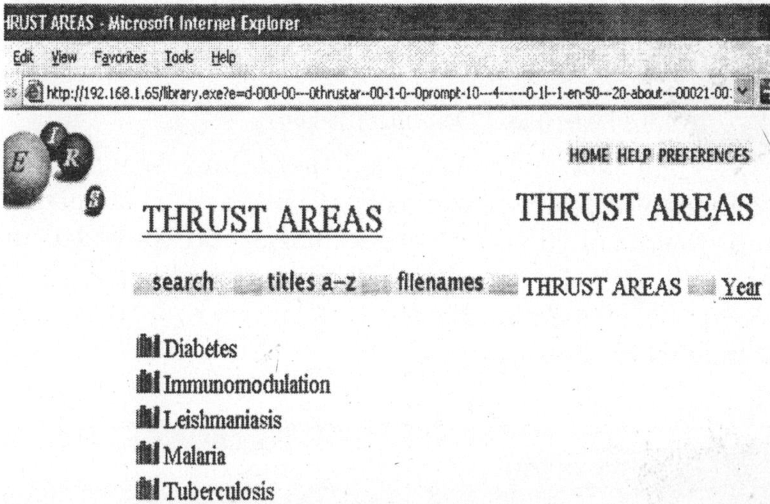

Fig. 2. NIPER Thrust Areas Database

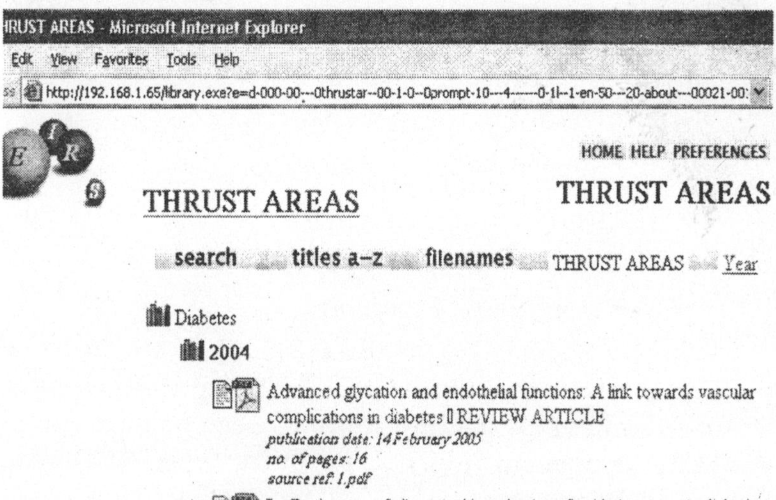

Fig. 3. NIPER Thrust Areas Database

II. Library Collection Online

At present library possesses 3331 books, 15518 bound volumes of journals, 204 theses. Libsys multi-user library management system software package is installed for providing library collection online search. The OPAC for searching the library's catalogue is available through intranet to all the in-house users.

III. Patent Search and Download Services

Here we have provided help and search and downloading search facilities of patens. We searches patents and download complete patent images and converted in single file and also make for offline uses for EIRS users. We continuously update our full text off line patent database (fig. 4) making over 400 patents accessible to our users till date.

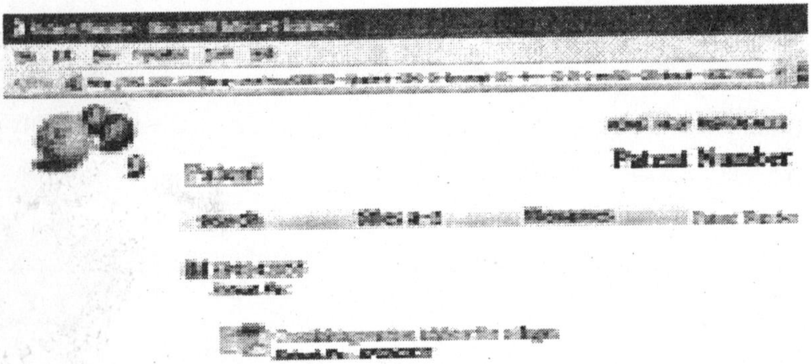

Fig. 4. Patent Database

IV. NIPER Institutional Repository

We have created a database (fig. 5) of our institute publications with the help of GSDL 2.52. At present we have 250 publications of leading journals searchable through Author, Department, Journal, Resource type, Title, Year, Subject and Keywords.

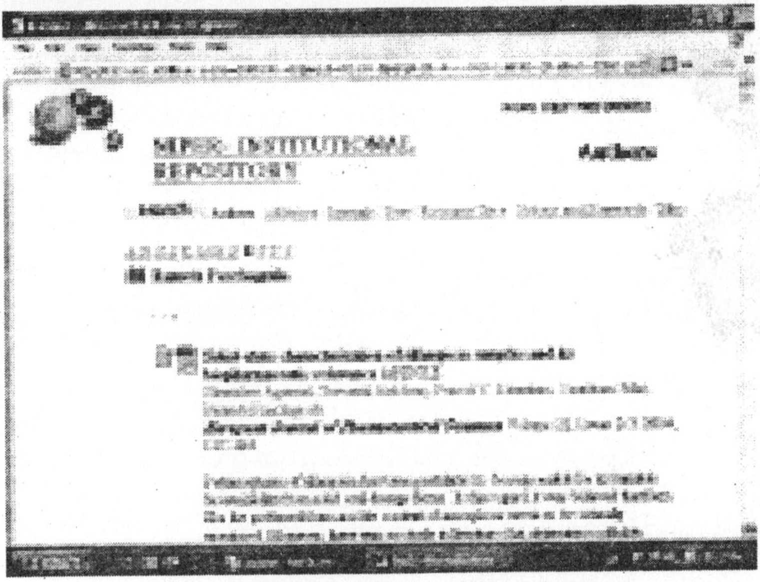

Fig. 5. NIPER Institutional Repository

V. Union Catalogue of Journals/Serials in Chandigarh Libraries

NIPER library is an active member of the Chandigarh Libraries Consortium, we have offline access to the Union Catalogue of about ten libraries in Chandigarh.

VI. E-mail address of Indian Pharmaceutical Industry

We have maintained a database of E-mail addresses of around 680 top pharmaceutical companies for our reference.

9. Cautions

The use of many electronic resources provided by the EIRS is governed by license agreements negotiated between the Institute and publishers or third parties. Such licensing agreements impose even greater restrictions on use than copyright law. In general, these legally binding contracts allow students, staff, faculty, and other authorized users to access these resources for non-commercial, educational, scholarly and research purposes. They generally prohibit large-scale systematic downloading of articles or other information, sharing of articles or other information with individuals at other institutions, and using such articles or information for commercial purposes. In addition, users should be aware that publishers may monitor use of electronic resources to ensure that the terms of their licensing agreements are enforced.

Do not share your access password with family, friends, or co-workers. Electronic resources are licensed for use by Institute, students, staff and faculty. Other users may access such resources only from a computer terminal in a campus library. Do not download entire issues of electronic journals or attempt to create large databases from bibliographic files. However, it is acceptable to download reasonable amounts of citations into bibliographic management software like Adobe Acrobat and EndNote. Do not share copies of material with friends at other institutions. Do not copy and use material without proper attribution. Do not share proprietary software (such as that needed to access the STN Express) with individuals at other institutions or companies.

10. Conclusion

Electronic Information Retrieval Systems and computers, networks are essential resources for supporting institute objectives. The resources should be valuable and professionally managed. It should be secured and accessible for all authorised users.

EIRS development, updating creating new database policies, standards, and guidelines should be defined. The policy should be known to all users like Director, Faculties, scientists, technical staffs and students. User database should be created for the faster user awareness, communication. All the software and hardware parts of related to EIRS services are available in desktop of End user. Database backup is one of the most important components of the EIRS. Time to time user's feedback is necessary for evaluating the services.

Respond to questions from users relating to appropriate use of system/network resources. Electronic information retrieval systems are fast, accessible and can easily be updated as required.

References

1. Decade of NIPER, 2004.
2. Minutes: an electronic Information Retrieval System. 13th Dec. 2001.
3. http://stnweb.cas.org/
4. http://www.niper.nic.in/admin.htm

13
Digital Information Services in an Undergraduate Management College

Meeta Rathod
Librarian, BRCM College of Business Administration, Surat

ABSTRACT

The present paper describes concept of the Need for Digital Information Services in Library of Business Management College. It also proposes how the Digital Information Services can be provided to the user community in the library of Business Management College. Further it highlights the functions and the services of library to be covered for the digitization process. This will help in Promoting and supporting the digital information services to the user community of management college library.

The library professionals play a very important role in improving the utilities of library resources in many innovative ways through information system. At the end, it highlights the characteristics that the librarians or the information professionals should possess to perform well in the digital era of knowledge management.

This is a kind of Conceptual Paper. The paper attempts to present fundamental steps for moving ahead towards the Digital Library from Conventional library of Business

Management College. This is being prepared with the personal experience of a librarian handling the Business Management College library, running undergraduate course of Bachelor of Business Administration affiliated to Veer Narmad South Gujarat University, Surat, Gujarat.

i. Introduction

The digital library provides digital information services in which most of the references are available and processed through Information Technology systems. The general functions of library such as acquisition, storage, access, retrieval, preservation and display are carried out through the use of digital technologies.

Automation of library functions along with digitization of its resources, thus the necessary steps towards fulfilling the present day concept of library.

ii. Need for Digital Information Services

Digital Information Services are those services that are delivered or catered to the users or information seekers digitally through Information Technology systems.

The need for Digital Information Services have been felt as in this age of Science and Technology the world surely stands on the threshold of a global Information and Digital Network. The Information is being generated and updated at a very fast rate.

Digital Information services are in the transitional stage moving from the local traditional collection to global resource sharing with the help of most advanced networking technologies.

iii. Digital Information Services in the Business Management College Library

Library is now better known as center of network of information sources for distribution rather than as a centralized repository of recorded knowledge.

The advancement of computer network has been accepted globally as the part of the library and Information center's infrastructure. Computer Network has significant impact on the way in which the library and the library professionals perceives and utilizes it.

In a bid to move towards a digital library from its conventional format, the areas enlisted hereunder needs to be addressed effectively. They are:

(A) Automation of basic library function.

(B) Networking of Computers through LAN.

(C) Access to Internet.

(D) Collection of Electronic Resources.

(E) Digitization of Information.

(F) Developing Institutional Digital Repository.

(G) Formation of Library Consortium.

(H) Creation of Library Home Page.

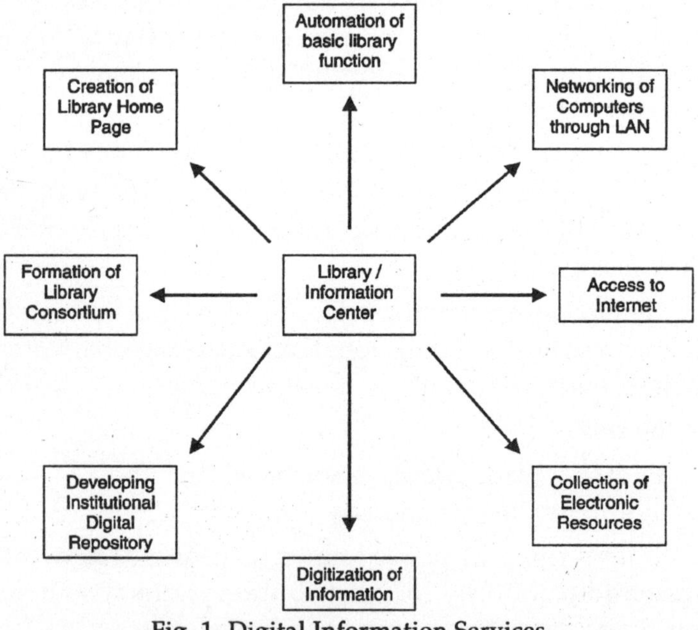

Fig. 1. Digital Information Services

The first and the foremost step towards the digitalization is Automation of basic library function. The next is networking of the computers through LAN. The first two steps mentioned above are already being implemented in our library, BRCM College of Business Administration. The other areas are being planned and they are in the pipeline.

(A) Automation of basic library function.

Library Automation is a first step towards the Digital Library. Automation is required for improving the efficiency of the services to be delivered at all levels. The hardware and the software and other related peripherals are being used for this purpose of Library Automation.

Library Functions of our library are being automated with the network version of SOUL software. Soul is the state-of-the-art library automation software designed and developed by the INFLIBNET.

(B) Networking of Computers through LAN.

In our college, the computer that resides at Library, Institute's Director's office, Faculty room and In charge of Computer laboratory's desk in the same premises are connected with each other through Peer-to-peer Local Area Network (LAN).

This networking is very important, as the main users of the library are Faculties and Students. These users can access to the information resources of library from any of the above-mentioned areas through the OPAC modules at their convenience.

(C) Access to Internet

Perhaps no other recent innovations have impacted the world, especially library profession to such a great extent as Internet. Innovative utilize of Internet Technologies facilitate us to reach at both information resources and users at local and global level much more easily and effectively.

At present this feature has been facilitated to four nodes —one each at Librarian's desk, Director's desk, Faculty room's terminal and at Administrative office for college staff only.

As the syllabus of Bachelor of Business Administration program of Veer Narmad South Gujarat University requires lot of literature search for the preparation of assignments in all subjects and summer/winter project reports. It is being observed that for the fulfillment of these purposes students have to do latest information search extensively both from print as well as electronic resources. The printed information looses its current relevance in short period of time, hence the users cannot depend entirely upon the printed documents. As the electronic resources are being updated regularly so they are becoming more useful for the study purpose.

The students can achieve their goals easily if they get free access to Internet during library hours in the college to carry out their academic work done efficiently and effectively.

(D) Collection of Electronic Resources

Since last 20 years tremendous changes have been observed in publishing world. This directly affects the information systems and services.

Information Technology has changed the mode of publication. Traditional sources such as paper copies now are substituted with the attractive electronic resources. There comes into existence the Electronic Publishing. Electronic publishing is the combination of Electronic Technology, Computer Technology, Communication Technology and Publishing. Electronic Publishing is economical and speedier. Use of Electronic Technology for publishing is not new concept but it is a new mode of delivery concept.

Electronic Publishing affects drastically to Producers, Publishers/Vendors, Library and Information Centers and Users/Clienteles. These publishing provide information to the user which is exhaustive, correctly, in time and pinpointed.

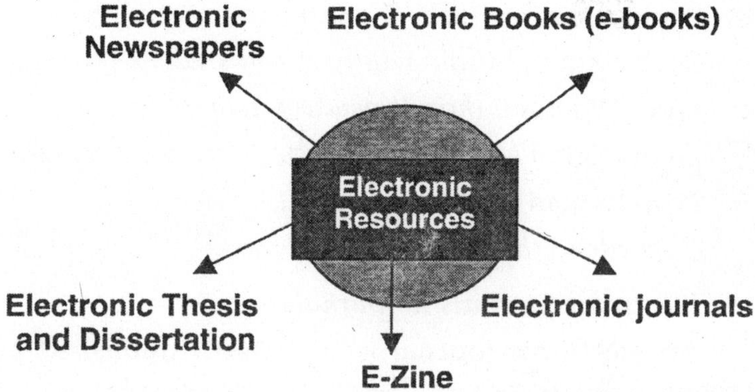

There are various kinds of electronic information sources being published like

· *Electronic Books (e-books)*

Electronic books are the electronic version of published works. E-books have easy search facility, contain hyper links and have multimedia capabilities.

Electronic books have electronic texts, which readers can see visually. Electronic text can be saved into a floppy disk, transferred into a CD Rom, downloaded from the internet and built into a palm sized digital reader. Business travelers can load e-books on their portable computers without adding weight or taking up space in their luggage. Some prominent e-book publishers and e-book sellers are described below.[1]

* netlibrary (*http://www.netlibrary.com/gateway.aspx*)
* kluweronline (*http://www.kluweronline.com/ebooks/sales*)
* SafariTech Books Online (*http://proquest.safaribooksonline.com/*)
* John Wiley (*http://www.wiley.com*)
* Questia (*http://www.questia.com*)
* E-Book Palace (*http://www.ebookpalace.com/*)

* BarnesandNoble.com (*http://www.barnesandnonle.com/*)
* Booklocker.com (*http://www.booklocker.com*)
* Book-Studio/Studio E (*http://www.studio-e-books.com*)
* Word Wrangler (*http://www.wordwrangler.com*)
* Palm Digital Media (*http://www.peanutpress.com*)
* Powells.com (*http://www.powells.com*)
* CyberRead (*http://www.cyberead.com*)

* ***Electronic journals (e-journals)***

An electronic journal is processed, published and distributed all over the world by electronic network. Electronic Journals are available on the on-line as well as in CD –ROM form.

DIALOG in 1980 started full text databases. Now, major publishers are using the Internet and the Web as a global way of providing their journals to International Community.

E-journals can be browsed and searched by

* Keywords
* Title of the article
* Abstracts
* Author's name
* Journal title
* Natural language searching

* *E-Zine*

E-Zine means electronic magazine and it is also called web-zine. Here the articles that are stored on a file server can be distributed or accessed via an internet for global search or an intranet for private circulation (eg. corporate monthly).

Eg. of e-zine is – *www.indiatoday.com.*

* *ETD – Electronic Thesis and Dissertation (ETD)*

An ETD is an electronic document that covers the

intellectual work or research of a researcher. Now-a-days Thesis is also submitted in an electronic medium that is called e-thesis.

Eg. of ETD is Saurashtra University, Rajkot(in PDF format).

Taking idea from the above concept we have also started collecting students project reports on CD's along with the hard copy from the current academic year.

* *Electronic Newspapers*

It is a self contained, reusable and refreshable version of a traditional newspaper, which acquires and holds information electronically. Information will be downloaded through an Internet connection.

The electronic resources have played a vital role in all the field of human life. These have rapidly changed the way of seeking and disseminating information. The speed of availability and the ease of accessibility of information make the users to use electronic resources more frequently.

Looking at the above advantageous aspects of electronic resources, in our library we have allocated separate budget for purchase of electronic information resources.

(E) Digitization of Information

Digitization of Information means process of converting paper documents such as text, graphics, etc into digital images, which can be made accessible over electronic network. There are two stages in digitization. The first stage is the conversion of physical medium into digital representation and the second stage is to extract this information from the digitized image.

Digital Resources can include a variety of materials such as –

i. complete contents of document in machine readable form,

ii. scanned images

iii. CD-ROMs
iv. database access through internet or other networks
v. metadata and digital audio/video clippings or full movies etc.

Digital materials include both information products and services. The tools, which can be used for such processes, are different types of scanners, digital cameras, video digitizers etc.

(F) *Developing Institutional Digital Repository (IDR)*

An Institutional Digital Repository is defined to be a web-based database of scholarly material, which is discipline based as opposed to a subject-based repository; cumulative and perpetual; open and interoperable; and thus collects, stores and disseminates knowledge.

Institutional Digital Repository is a digital collection of an Institute's intellectual material. Institutional Digital Repository centralize, preserve, and make accessible the knowledge generated by academic institutions. In India; IISC, DTRC, INFLIBNET and few other have explored the benefits of open source software for achieving the contents produced by their faculty members. A growing number of universities across the globe are running IDR projects using open source software, while many others are in the planning stages. Universities are developing institutional digital repositories of the research performed by their faculty and graduate students. The main purposes of Institutional repositories are to bring together and preserve the intellectual output of a university. Large numbers of open source software (Dspace, Eprint, Fedora, CDSware etc) are available and can be downloaded for running Institutional Digital Repositories. These softwares are Open Archives Initiative- Protocol for Metadata Harvesting complaint and require no royalty or fee.

This enables public access to scholarly journal articles

through the use of "pre-print" servers based on the Open Access Initiative(OAI)protocol. Authors can deposit their pre-prints (not yet published work) into such servers, providing readers worldwide with quick subscriptions to the source journals. These servers also act as informal vehicles for the disseminating of preliminary research results and non-peer reviewed literature.

The important factor for the development of Institutional Digital Repository is saving the high cost of scholarly journals, preservation and the need to facilitate open access to scholarly communication.

Institutional Digital Repository's are being discipline-based; represent the wide-range of research output produced by many institutions.

As we have seen the whole process of scholarly communication is currently undergoing a revolutionary change, we too have to think seriously and embark upon open access establish repositories.

At local level, we the librarians of Management Colleges should come forward to form an Institutional Digital Repository to enable the institutions to enhance its prestige by making visible the findings of its faculty's academic and research efforts. This will also help in reforming scholarly communication and in particular scholarly publishing.

An Institutional Digital Repository can be any collection of digital material hosted, owned or controlled, or disseminated by colleges irrespective of purpose or provenance.

Institutional Digital Repositories are entirely new field of information services for libraries. A fundamental principle for successful implementation of Institutional Digital Repository is that libraries should have trust-based and well co-ordinated relationship with faculty. The policies of Institutional Digital Repository should encourage faculty and their participation as simple and easy as possible. Faculty members being contributors to Institutional Digital Repository should feel that they are being helped and advanced through Institutional Digital Repository services.

(G) Formation of Library Consortium

Library Consortium is a collective action to provide better services by a group of libraries. This helps to cope up with the information crisis faced by individual library due to the information explosion in this era of knowledge management. This is being felt, as there is a constant increase in the number of journal titles, their price, conversion rate, and requirement of new infrastructural set up.

The academic and research community in the country mainly depends on the journals for their research work. The consortia have made available for the libraries what they could not achieved even spending their 75-80% of the library budgets on journals and e-resources.

This has lead to the formation of more than ten consortium in India in last 3-4 years with the facility to access more than 40000 e-journals under two major consortium viz, UGC-Infonet E-journals consortium (for university under UGC) and INDEST, (the consortium of IITs, IISc, IIMs and the Engineering Colleges funded by MHRD and AICTE). Scientists, research scholars, and faculty members of the member institutions can access these journals without any fee.[2]

A single library howsoever rich in its data collection and the other aspects cannot fully cater the needs of the information demanded by the information seekers or clienteles.

To overcome these limitations the concept of library consortium has come into existence for quite some time. There are many library consortiums are working at present at national and international level. Taking inspiration from such consortiums we, the libraries of management colleges are planning to come together and form a library consortium at local level to give better services to their users.

The above aspect is very important as this will definitely help the small college library to enrich their collection, for providing advanced user services, to emerge out of economic constraints in relation with library affairs, for dealing efficiently with the publishers or vendors of e-journals, to avoid duplication, to avoid misuse of funds, to avoid unnecessary blockage of space etc.

(H) Creation of Library Home Page

A Web Page or Web Site containing information of a library is "Library Home Page". The present time and the time to come is an era of digital communication. Now the time has come when most of the libraries are either computerized or going to be computerized, fully or partially. After automation of library, the database of information regarding the library is available in the computer unit has to be uploaded on the net for the accessibility.

The Contents of the planned Library Home page are shown below.

1. Home (First Page)
   * Introduction of College
   * Introduction of library
   * General Information
2. Aim/Goal
   * To facilitate the users.
   * To improve efficiency of services
   * To train to acquaint with digital information resources as students belong to under graduate course.
3. Staff

* Name: Meeta Rathod
* Designation: Librarian
* Qualification: B.Sc. M.L.I.Sc.
* E-mail ID: *mudita96@yahoo.co.in*

4. Time

   Monday to Friday : 7:30 am to 1:30 pm

   Saturday : 7:30 am to 10:30 am

5. Calendar

   Information regarding the holidays declared by the university should be available on Homepage.

6. Facilities (in house)
   * Audio Video Laboratory
   * Reading Room

7. Services (to the users)
   * Current Awareness Services (CAS)
   * Selective Dissemination of Information (SDI)
   * Newsletters
   * Clippings

8. Membership Forms

   Different types of forms have been designed for different categories of users.

9. Books

   Online Public Access Catalogue (OPAC)

10. Journals/Periodicals

    Online Public Access Catalogue (OPAC)

11. Project Reports/Assignments

    Online Public Access Catalogue (OPAC)

12. News papers

    Details of newspapers.

13. Queries

    This is important. Here users can type their problem/ suggestion / question with their E-mail ID.

14. Contact

    Name : Meeta Rathod

    E-mail ID: *mudita96@yahoo.co.in*

Role of Library professionals in this digital era of knowledge management

The development of any profession depends entirely upon the continuous learning of professionals of its field. Librarian as an information manager is a imperative individual in management system of an organization that is responsible for his own library management. In the info-tech-age, information is considered as the key resource for the economic, socio-cultural and political development of the nation. Importance of a library professional in digital age is very vital.

The growth of information technology has challenged this role and resulted in considerable instability and uncertainty among library and information professionals. They have been forced to redefine and restructure library resources and services and in the process, the library itself.

When we look at the library professionals we can see that there are two distinguished groups. One group consists of the conventional librarians who have passive approach towards the profession. The other group of library professionals of special or corporate or industrial library enriched with the high tech knowledge of Information technology providing the amazing and advanced services to their clientele.

I strongly feel that these two groups should join their hand together in the conferences, seminars, conventions like the present convention. They should share their knowledge with each other for the uplifting of their library as well as librarianship as a whole.

Conclusion

The conversion of Conventional library into Digital library or electronic library or Virtual library is the demand of this era of knowledge management. The areas, which have been identified by the study, have significant impact in the direction of moving towards the digitization of information process.

The paper tries to convey that how the small library of business management college running undergraduate course can digitize its information recourses. Paper also highlights how effectively and efficiently information services can be delivered to the user community. The major areas of information services for digitization are identified and discussed.

The Library professionals play a vital role in it. The mindset of library professionals has to be changed. To get acquaint with the modern technology they should regularly participate in the conferences, conventions, seminars, work shops, training programs, etc., at local as well as at national levels. The refresher courses for academic librarians run by Academic Staff College and sponsored by UGC are equally helpful in getting the knowledge about the new tools and techniques developed in the field of library and information science.

With structured planning and thereafter by its proper implementation the target can be achieved.

References

1. Ahmad, Shamim (1993) *"Computer in Library Management"*, A. P. H. Publishing Corporation, New Delhi, 1993.
2. Chaudhary, S. K. (2002) *"Modern Library Strategies"*, A. P. H. Publishing Corporation, New Delhi, 2002.
3. Dhiman, Anilkumar (2004) *"Acquisition, Preservation and Retrieval of*

Digital Resources: Role of Library Consortia" Seminar Papers of All India Library Conference, Vadodara, 2004.

4. Gaur, Ramesh, C. and others (ed.) (2003) *"Business and Management Libraries: Opportunities and Challenges in the 21st Century"*, Excel Books, New Delhi, 2003.
5. Gayatri, D. and Sridhar Kumar, M. (2004). *"Consortium of Journals"*, SRELS Journal of Information Management, Vol.41, No. 3, September 2004.
6. Ghosh, T. B. (2004) *"E-Books: It's Accessibility, Problems, and Prospects in the Context to Science and Technology Libraries in India."* Seminar Papers 50th All India Conference on Knowledge Organization in Digital Environment in Libraries (KODEL): Introspect and Prospects, 1-4 Dec., 2004, Vadodara.
7. Gopal, Krishan (2001) *"Intellectual Freedom in Digital Libraries"*, Authorspress, Delhi, 2001.
8. Prem Chand and others. (2004) *"A Policy For Institutional Repositories and Open Archives Initiative – Protocol For Metadata Harvesting"* Seminar Papers 50th All India Conference on Knowledge Organization in Digital Environment in Libraries(KODEL): Introspect and Prospects, 1-4 Dec., 2004, Vadodara.
9. Maruthupandian,B., Moorthy, R. and others, *" Impact of E- Documents in the Modern Information Era"*.
9. Sahu, Hemant Kumar. (2004) *"Human Resource Development: Knowledge, Skills and Qualities"*. Seminar Papers 50th All India Conference on Knowledge Organization in Digital Environment in Libraries (KODEL): Introspect and Prospects, 1-4 Dec., 2004, Vadodara.
10. Tiwari, Aravind. (2002) *" Evaluation of Electronic Libraries"*, A. P. H. Publishing Corporation, New Delhi, 2002.
11. Walia, P. K. (2004) *"Challenges and competencies For Library and Information Professionals in The Digital Environment"*, Seminar Papers 50th All India Conference on Knowledge Organization in Digital Environment in Libraries (KODEL): Introspect and Prospects, 1-4 Dec., 2004, Vadodara.
12. www.da-iict.org
13. www.mica-india.net
14. www.prl.ernet.in
15. www.ipr.res.in
16. www.iimahd.ernet.in
17. http://www.soros.org/openaccess/software/
18. http://www.arl.org/newsltr

14
Knowledge Management: Strategy, Technology and Application

Biswajit Saha
Indian Institute of Management Calcutta
Kolkata-700104
(biswajit@iimcal.ac.in)

KEYWORDS / DESCRIPTORS: Knowledge management (KM), Knowledge assets, Knowledge workers, Knowledge Application management, Knowledge Dissemination management, Knowledge Innovation management.

ABSTRACT

Knowledge is the totality of ideas, conserved through human civilization (Dr.S.R. Ranganathan) and Knowledge Management (KM) is a process, which converts the internal and external information of the organization into actionable knowledge. KM has emerged as a key concern of organizations. Better management of knowledge within the organization leads to improved innovation and competitive advantage. It works for converting intellectual assets of workers and staff members in the organization into higher productive forces - competition power and new value. Knowledge management requires linkage of information with information, information with activities and information with man - so as to realize the sharing of knowledge (including tacit and explicit knowledge). Developing an effective KM system requires a well-balanced approach. Technology is a required foundation for managing knowledge-assets and bringing people together in dispersed organizations. The true drivers of KM are people, policies, organizational culture, appropriate strategies and leadership. Unless deeper issues of organizational culture and human resource management are addressed, together with a good understanding of the dynamics of knowledge evolution and growth in organizations, technology alone cannot deliver the goods. This paper presents an overview of KM, various strategies of KM, and also narrates the technological aspect of KM with the factors to be considered for an effective KM. This paper discusses how KM should be applied in Library and Information Centers and the role of library & information professionals in KM process.

1. Introduction

Present society is metamorphosed into knowledge society taking it as a global phenomenon transacting at local and across the geographical boundaries and territories. Knowledge is applicable as a building block from the individuals to the groups and organizations. The more we use and share the knowledge, the more it is spread and authenticated among the individuals and the value intensive organizations where information / knowledge is accounted to its necessary parameters [1]. The knowledge workers have become multidisciplinary in their work culture. The concept of information scientists, information officer, librarians, library officer have got trivia to upkeep its myth for longer journey of information age in the present cutting edge of information technology.

One of the key objectives of a KM system is to insulate an organization's intellectual capital from degeneration. It is seen that knowledge capital is often lost through employee attrition, high turnover rates, cost saving measures and improper documentation. The knowledge workers represent the most significant edge in the market place. In fact, application of KM mainly in the corporate sector, but it also apt and applicable to non-corporate sector too.

2. Definition and Concept of Knowledge Management (KM)

Tom Davenport and Laurence Prusak define knowledge as 'a fluid mix of framed experience, values, contextual information, and expert insight that provides a framework for evaluating and incorporating new experiences and information. It originates and is applied in the minds of knowers. In organizations, it often becomes embedded not only in documents or repositories but also in organizational routines, processes, practices, and norms' [2].

KM is the name given to the set of systematic and disciplined actions that an organization can take to obtain the greatest value from the knowledge available to it. "Knowledge" in this context includes both the experience and understanding of the people in the organization and the information artifacts, such as documents and reports, available within the organization and in the world outside. KM is first and foremost a management discipline that treats intellectual capital as a managed asset. The primary tools applied in the practice of KM are organizational dynamics, process engineering and technology. These work in concert to streamline, and enhance the capture and flow of an organization's data, information, and knowledge and to deliver it to individuals and groups engaged in accomplishing specific tasks. These individuals or knowledge workers are unequivocally the most vital resources in the 21st century organizations.

1.1 Tacit and Explicit Knowledge

Tacit knowledge is what the knower knows, which is derived from experience and embodies beliefs and values. It can not be articulated or externalized. It is actionable knowledge and most important basis for the generation of new knowledge, that is, according to Nonaka: "the key to knowledge creation lies in the mobilization and conversion of tacit knowledge."

Explicit knowledge is represented by some artifact, such as a document or a video, which has typically been created with the goal of communicating with another person. It can be codified. Both forms of knowledge are important for organizational effectiveness.

3. Strategies for the KM

i) Strategy of knowledge Creation

This strategy includes organizational learning, basic and applied research development and motivation of employees to innovate and capture lessons learned to obtain better new knowledge, which will improve competitiveness. Knowledge also is obtained through formal channels like conferences, through the Internet, newspapers, and journals as well as informal channels such as social gatherings, museums and movies etc. [3].

ii) Strategy of capturing relevant knowledge external to the organization:

It emphasizes systematically seeking outside resources in order to gather information that can help the organization. These external ventures include study missions to better understand the performance and distinctive skills of other organization, benchmarking of best practices in the industry and attending conferences and forum [4].

iii) Encourage team mixing and job rotation to maximize knowledge transfer across boundaries:

One of the most effective ways to transfer knowledge in an organization is to transfer the individual or teams possessing the knowledge whether it is technical, interpersonal or managerial knowledge. People transfer is powerful because the person having the knowledge has the capacity to assure that knowledge has indeed been transmitted. Another benefit of team mixing and job rotation is the freshness of the approaches and perception that the new person brings to the situation [4].

iv) Knowledge transfer strategy:

This strategy includes obtaining, organizing, restructuring or memorizing, repackaging for developing and distributing knowledge to points of actin, where it will be used to perform works. This also includes knowledge sharing and adopting best practice [3].

v) Developing knowledge base around the values and learning needs of the organization:

Information must be coded and stored in a way that makes sense to individual and the organization. The knowledge stored should be easily accessible across the functional boundaries. It should be structured and organized so that the users can find concise information in quick fashion. The knowledge stored should be updated so that it remains accurate and valid.

vi) Intellectual- assets management strategy:

It gives emphasis on enterprise level management of specific intellectual assets such as patents, technologies, customer relation etc. Management task is to renew, organize, evaluate, protect and increase the availability and marketing of these assets.

4. Supporting technologies and applications for KM

There are a number of technology components around which a KM system can be built. These technologies are chiefly software are Internet-centric. A few also developed for use on local area network or LAN with or without Internet or Intranet. The role of technology in KM is to broaden the reach and enhances the speed of knowledge transfer. In fact, technology helps KM in storing, retrieving searching, networking, collaborating and communicating of knowledge.

Amrit Tiwana has given stress on communication, storage and retrieval technologies in KM. According to Tiwana while communications technology does provide for transfer and exchange of structured and formalized knowledge, it also provides and outlet for knowledge that cannot or has not yet been structured yet can be immediately applied. According to Tiwana there are seven layer in the system architecture of KM. Which are as follows [5].

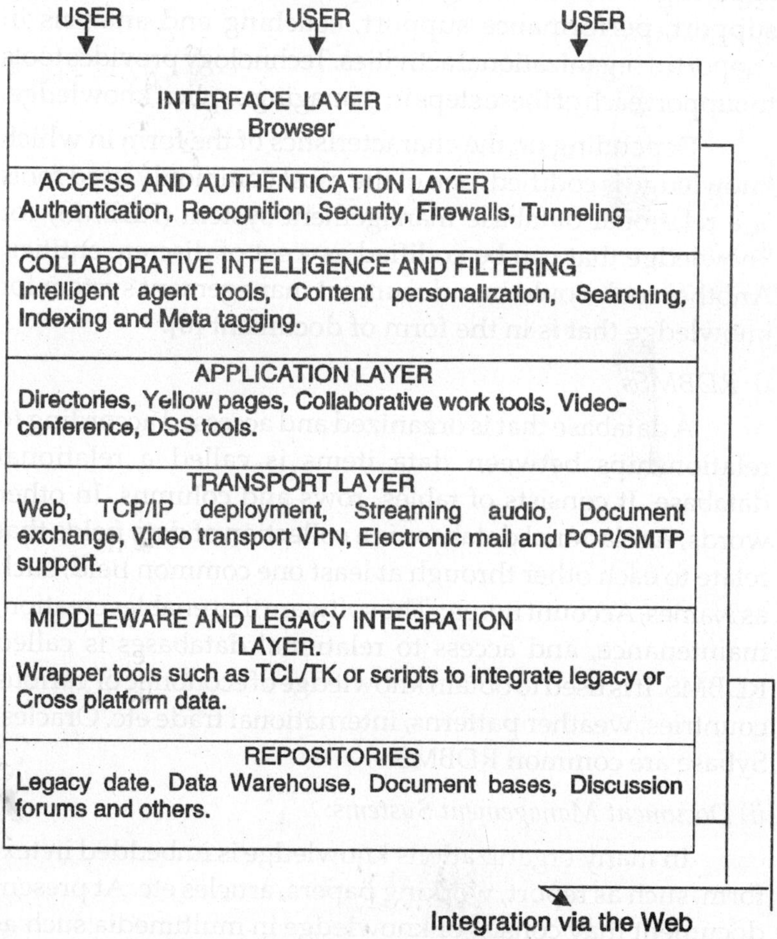

4.1 *Technology for Managing and Organizing Explicit Knowledge*

Organizing and managing explicit knowledge includes generation, creation, or acquisition of knowledge; codification and organization of that knowledge for easy access; publishing or communicating the availability of that knowledge; searching for and accessing that knowledge; and using or applying that knowledge for problem solving, decision support, performance support, coaching and analysis in support of organizational activities. Technology provides tools to support each of these steps in managing explicit knowledge.

Depending on the characteristics of the form in which knowledge is codified, one of the most commonly used tools is a relational database management system (RDBMS) for knowledge that can be codified as a set of discrete entities. Another tool would be a document management system for knowledge that is in the form of document [6].

i) RDBMSs

A database that is organized and accessed according to relationships between data items is called a relational database. It consists of tables, rows and columns. In other words, A relational database is a collection of data fields that relate to each other through at least one common field, such as Names, Account no. etc. The software that enables creation, maintenance, and access to relational databases is called RDBMS. It is used to obtain knowledge of economic of various countries, weather patterns, international trade etc. Oracles, Sybase are common RDBMS.

ii) Document Management Systems:

In many organizations knowledge is imbedded in text form, such as report, working papers, articles etc. At present document may consist of knowledge in multimedia such as text, graphics, audio and video. DMS support production, storage search of and retrieval of these mixed media documents.

4.2 Technology for Accessing and Managing Explicit Knowledge:

i) Internet:

Web provides the common base that allows data exchange across all platforms. Therefore, the web plays a vital role in KM. Tiwana explains the role of Internet as follows:

* Internet provides a cost effective global network backbone.
* Internet connects user anyplace and anywhere, as long as they have access to the Web.
* Distributed resources and databases can be interconnected cost effectively and reliably, using virtual networks tunneled with the Internet.
* The inherent nature of Internet offers unprecedented redundancy and robustness.
* Internet provides cheaper, faster and directly usable global competitive intelligence.

ii) Search Engines:

Various search engines are very effective and powerful tools in the context of KM. Indexing and retrieval capabilities of a KM system determine the ease with which a user can find relevant knowledge or points to knowledge in the system. These rely on text indexing and retrieval technologies adopted by web based search engines and in Information Retrieval and Document Management systems. There are four types of navigation strategies that are deployed by web based search engines. Such as: Meta Searching, Hierarchical Searching, Attribute Searching and Content Searching

iii) Intranet:

Internet technology used within an organization, with

restricted access from outside, is called an Intranet. Those within an organization can access sites outside the Intranet, but access from outside an organization to an Intranet is usually restricted. If the knowledge within an Intranet is proprietary, the appropriate security measures must be implemented, such Firewalls.

iv) Workflow Tools:

These information technology based tools allow documents and other forms of information to be routed among individuals and applications according to predefined processes. This may include routing a new document to various members of work team or sending a draft document to individuals for review and approval. These tools enable provision of information required to support each step of the business processes. These processes may be predefined and never varying, or they may vary depending on specified rules. Workflow tolls allow setting up the workflow environment in terms of users, types of information, processes, timing constraints, alternatives etc.

4.3 Technology for Using or Applying Knowledge

Sometimes it is very troublesome and time consuming to find useful data or information from enormous data. There are various tools available to find useful information, which are as follows:

i) Performance Support Systems (PSS):

Performance support systems are software products aimed at assisting individuals or groups in carrying out specific tasks quickly without requiring special training on to use them. These systems may incorporate multimedia delivery and use techniques such as expert systems and natural language recognition.

i) Decisions Support Systems:

DSS are software products that transform data into

useful information such as statistical models and trend analysis, which are used by management in making business decisions. DSS can access data stored in large databases and can analyze the data to produce graphs, charts, and simple reports, which management can access from desktop computers. These systems may retrieve data from internal and external sources.

iii) Data Mining:

Data mining is considered to be a step within the knowledge discovery in database (KDD) process, through which an organization's data assets are processed and analyzed to gain insights for business decisions. Data mining refers to using sophisticated data search capabilities that use statistical algorithms to discover patterns and correlation in vast amount of data.

iv) Data Warehousing:

Many organizations have several databases existing throughout their hierarchy. A data warehouse attempts to unify all these databases. The technology aggregates the data from different databases and cleans the data in the process in an attempt to increase the quality of the data. But, the disadvantage is that it does not deliver data in real time.

4.4 Technological Support For Managing Tacit Knowledge

Of late, the most prominent use of IT is to enable effective working of communities of practice. The choice of technology tools depends upon the desired characteristics of the networking. Meeting face to face is an effective means to share knowledge. Communicating using paper mail also to be used extensively. Use of fax increased the speed of paper communication. Telephonic conversation also effective means of sharing knowledge. But all these means of communications are synchronous. IT provides others a lot of means for effective communications across geographical boundaries. Which are as follows:

i) E-mail:

It enables a community of practice to share knowledge asynchronously. Individual from a community can share knowledge with other community by sending a message to all of them. Using distribution lists eliminates the need for everyone to remember the names of all those in the community and ensures that everyone gets the message. With the increasing access to email via the Internet, a community of practice can be spread across the world.

ii) Video Conferencing:

It allows two way or multi way calling with live video, essentially a telephone system with an additional visual component. Cost and compatibility issues limited early use of video systems to scheduled conference meeting rooms. Video is advantageous when visual information is being discussed. This is an effective means for sharing knowledge.

iii) Virtual Meeting:

Web conferencing allows virtual meetings where people from different locations connect, conduct meeting and share knowledge as if everyone was in the same room. Applications such as presentation graphics, spreadsheets, word processing can be shared in real time.

iv) Document Collaboration:

Web based real time distributed collaboration lets team members to work together with many other participants with documents or information in real time. Everyone can view the information in real time and can take control to edit or paste information in real time.

5. Various factors for determining Knowledge management technology

Various technologies required for KM is already exist in most of the organizations. The critical part is to determine the best mix of available tools and integrating them in one's project's KM architecture. The following factors are vital while determining the mix:

i) Choose IT components to find, create, assemble, and apply knowledge:

Since content comes from a variety of sources both within and out side the organization, the optimal choice of components must help to create, assemble, find, and apply knowledge in cost effective and timely manner.

ii) Pick one: Web or Notes:

Customized implementations of proprietary technology might seem to be easier to implement than the Web based intranets with equivalent functionality; using open standards such as intranets holds more long term promise both in terms of cost containment and incremental development. Choosing the Web option over other options can potentially lead to tighter integration of commercially available complements and push delivery mechanisms.

iii) Identify and understand components of the collaborative intelligence layer:

Artificial intelligence, date warehouses, genetic algorithms, neural networks, expert reasoning systems, rule bases, and case based reasoning are some of the technologies that provide intelligence to the KM system. Understand how these tools and technologies work and when their use is appropriate.

iv) Optimize knowledge object granularity:

Granularity of knowledge (represented in terms of knowledge objects or elements that are specified in descending order as knowledge domains, regions, sections, segments, elements, fragments, and atoms) objects refers to the level of detail in which they are stored in the KM system. Avoid overpopulating knowledge repositories of the organization. At the same time, too little detail might make content useless or unactionable, The key lies in striking the right balance between too much and too little detail.

v) Create knowledge tags and attributes:

Domain, form, type, product/service, time and location tags automatically classify content along several dimensions. Using standardized tags allows for uniformity in retrieval and storage of content. Defining such tags up front also helps one to determine the right mix of components for searching, indexing and retrieval.

6. Knowledge Management in Library & Information Centers (LICs)

Knowledge Management in LICs should be as follows [7]:

Knowledge Innovation Management

Knowledge innovation management in LICs refers to the management of the production, diffusion and transfer of knowledge as well as of the network systems constructed by related institutions and organizations. It includes three aspects, namely, theoretical innovation management of knowledge, technical innovation management and organizational innovation management.

Theoretical innovation management is to enrich and enlarge the theoretical and practical research fields of library science and information science through pursuing the latest development trends in library science the world over. Technical innovation management is to manage the network systems constructed by institutions and organizations that relate to the full course of technical innovation. In their evolution from conventional libraries to electronic libraries, or digital libraries, Libraries should make technical breakthroughs and progress and build up technical facilities to support knowledge management. Organizational innovation management is to create a set of effective organizational management systems adaptable to the requirements in the electronic library era to support and strengthen knowledge management activities, by optimizing the functional departments and operation procedures of libraries.

In these systems, it firstly requires that leaders who take charge of knowledge management activities should undertake to formulate the management plans and coordinate all knowledge management related activities. Secondly, it requires establishment of special leading groups of knowledge flow for accomplishing all tasks relating to knowledge management activities. Electronic resources committees are established composed of various types of specialists to take charge of evaluating, procuring and creating the electronic resources on the one hand, and coordinating activities of business departments and spurring them on to close cooperation in such fields as procurement and organization of the electronic information resources as well as providing services on the other hand.

Knowledge Dissemination Management

Knowledge dissemination is of equal importance as compared to knowledge innovation. Knowledge creators do not have much time and energy to look for knowledge users. Though there are a multitude of knowledge users, it is very difficult to acquire knowledge that already exists in the minds of knowledge creators as restricted by various objective and subjective conditions. Therefore, LICs may play the part of knowledge tosser, use diverse media and channels to disseminate various new knowledge. The Internet, with its mass information and extensive contents, will provide people with the main approach to searching knowledge and acquiring information. But now there emerge absurd, salacious, false and uncivil information resulting from seeking for commercial profits and political objectives on the Net. Therefore, it is necessary to strengthen knowledge dissemination management in libraries as follows:

1. Uninterruptedly strengthening the creation of libraries' own document resources and deepening the development of document information resources;
2. Continuously raising the quality of libraries' staffs and strengthening continuous engineering education of working staffs;
3. Giving full play to the special role of the expert system in knowledge dissemination;
4. Making a comprehensive utilization of all media to ensure security of operation of networks, and prevent online criminal activities and online dissemination of inappropriate information.

Knowledge Application Management

Libraries should also attach importance to provision of services for people to acquire knowledge and achieve maximum functions and efficiency of knowledge information. Therefore, knowledge services based on high-speed information networks should be carried out by:

1. Setting up virtual libraries or information centers for enterprises, governments, public organizations and scientific research institutions. It is difficult for an enterprise or a social organization to put sufficient manpower, material and financial resources on information gathering, organizing and developing. It is also impossible and unnecessary to spend a large amount of funds on information resources for their own use. Libraries can create virtual libraries or information centers for these organs separately according to their respective information requirements by using abundant information resources on the high-speed information networks.

2. Setting up digitized knowledge services which is, at present, actually a development trend of libraries. This presupposes: creating step by step the users-oriented information service systems such as information dissemination, information search and special supply of information; quickening the creation of digitized libraries; studying the methods, means and techniques of information distribution and search with the Internet as the base and WEB technique as the core.
3. Digitizing LICs' resources. The electronic libraries or digitized libraries are the technical modes and development trends of libraries in the knowledge economy era. The knowledge services of libraries in the future will start with creation of databases comprising electronic journals and books in different languages that have discipline features and can operate on high-speed information networks. Great efforts should be made to transform all existing large non-electronic information resources into electronic information and integrate them into electronic libraries.

Human Resources Management

Human resources management takes it as its basic starting point to train high quality specialized talents and to revitalize the library undertaking. In practice, we should pay full attention to diversity and variation of library staffs' requirements, strengthened management of different library staffs by applying contingency management approach. That is, to some people, rigid management method is applied, rigorous supervision and control imposed, and quantity and quality requirements of work according to regulations and procedures are made clear. And, to the rest of people, more flexible management method is applied to let them participate in decision-making and consultation and undertake more jobs so as to bring their management abilities into full play and realize organizational and personal objectives. Doing well in continuous engineering education of specialized staffs, which should not only focus on the theory of library science and related disciplines, but also cover the latest technical knowledge. And strengthening professional ethics education

7. KM and Library and Information Professionals (LIPs)

To improve services to users, enable users to share and learn the created knowledge and capture relevant information the role of LIPs includes: (i) facilitation of the reuse and consolidation of knowledge operations, (ii) standardization of existing knowledge in the form of procedures (iii) acquisition of new knowledge from external sources (iv) generation of new knowledge within the organization and (v) transforming individual knowledge in to collective knowledge. As 'knowledge is the full utilization of information and data coupled with the potential of people's skill, competencies, ideas, intuitions, and commitments and motivation' and knowledge is constantly being created by people and becomes a powerful commodity and a combination of people and technology, it is essential to orderly articulate, capture store, access and share the knowledge for reuse. In LICs knowledge is captured in various forms and developed into a comprehensive collection of current as well as old documents in physical, electronic or digital forms such as OPACs, various subject databases, research publications: thesis, dissertations etc. The knowledge thus generated needs to be organized for storage and retrieval. Electronically stored knowledge represented as knowledge repository. The efficient query language for database searching, navigation system or rule based system needs to be developed to retrieve the knowledge from knowledge repository and making it available and accessible to users. LIPs role includes the identification and analysis of available and required knowledge, its planning and control to fulfill organizational objectives and to meet the need of users and patrons. They may apply their skills for indexing, abstracting or classification to select the requisite information from the ocean of knowledge or apply metadata techniques to retrieve the data from the online sources of information. The role of traditional librarianship is changing into 'cybrarianship' to include the tasks of scanning, filtering, selecting, organizing, and packaging, repackaging the flood of information [8]. The acquisition task in LICs is becoming easy and prompt with the emergence of online acquisition reference sources as well as vendors (e-commerce). Electronic document delivery services, fax, e-mails etc are encouraging LIPs to procure quality learning resources. Various standard and integrated library management softwares are available in the market to help LIPs in acquisition, organization and dissemination of information and knowledge. Thus, the role of LIPs is being changed as knowledge workers from mere repositories of information to channels facilitating the process of knowledge generation, organization and dissemination.

8. Conclusions

KM as it is practiced today, is a system of technologies focused upon the delivery of strategically useful knowledge and expertise, the availability of which facilitates effective collaboration and timely decision making.

KM should be well understood as strategic process, as it involves the planning, implementation and outcome. There is confusion that KM is basically a technological process but in practice it is seen that it is more strategy oriented towards the goal of organization, whether it is an academic, R&D or commercial organization. Technology only plays a supportive role in KM, as the main bottlenecks are culture, quality and utility of knowledge. Developing KM system requires a well-balanced approach. Technology is a required foundation for managing knowledge assets and bringing people together in dispersed organizations. But the focus of KM is not just on the effective use of available technology but on creating a synergy between the human capital and information technology tools.

References

1. Mahapatra (Gayatri) and Das (Bhagwan). Towards Knowledge Management: An Emerging Paradigm. SRELS Journal of Information Management. Vol.39 (4), December 2002, p339
2. Ojha (Abhoy). Individual and Organizational Learning Issues Relevant to Knowledge Management in Organizations. IIMB Working Paper 175, September 2001, p1.
3. Sajpal (Upasna). Knowledge Management. ILA Bulletin. Vol.XXXIV (1-2); 1998; p21
4. Dhar (Upinder) etc. Local Champions To Global Masters: Mobilizing For Growth. Indore, Excel Books, 2002, p.248-250.
5. Tiwana (Amrit). The Knowledge Management Toolkit: Practical Techniques for Building a Knowledge Management System. Upper Saddle River, NJ, USA, Prentice Hall, 2000.
6. Srikantaiah (T.K) and Koenig (Michael E.D) ed. Knowledge Management for Information Professional. Medford, American Society for Information Science, 2000, p.270-274.
7. Shanhong (Tang). Knowledge Management in Libraries in the 21st Century. 66th IFLA Council and General Conference, Jerusalem, August 13-18, 2000. (Web document: http://www.ifla.org)
8. Raina (Roshan) etc. Changing role of LIS Professionals in the Knowledge Management Life Cycle. Second National Convention of MANLIBNET on Challenges 2000: Challenges and Opportunities for Management Librarians in the New Millennium. Ghaziabad, IMT, Feb.3-5, 2000, p.17.

15

Music Library Management in Knowledge Society

Nithin. L.
Library Trainee in J.R.D Tata Memorial Library
Indian Institute of Science, Bangalore

ABSTRACT

This paper begins by providing a brief overview of Knowledge management. Focuses on the field of Music Librarianship with an Indian perspective. Attempts to narrate different facets of Music Library. Discusses about the problems faced in Music librarianship. Presents a brief picture of Music Information retrieval. This paper also tries to throw some light on the vast field of Music metadata. This paper also argues why there is not even a single library in India which is dedicated for people or users interested in the field.

0. Prologue

What is Music? The word is such a vague term covering everything from the whistle of a janitor to the beauty of Beethoven's symphony.

The American Heritage Dictionary describes music as "the art of organizing tones to produce a coherent sequence of sounds intended to elicit an aesthetic response in a listener".

Music is the (a) art of arranging the sound of voice(s) or instrument(s) or both in a pleasing sequence or combination, (b) compositions made by doing this (c) (books, sheets of papers, etc. containing) written or printed signs representing such compositions.

But in this part of the world we have no arrangements for organizing musical resources. Is it that, we lack in the knowledge of music or don't we have good musicians. Whatever it is we are lagging behind in archiving musical resources.

Archiving musical resources is totally a neglected field of area in our country.

1. A peek into knowledge management

A widely accepted 'working definition' of knowledge management applied in worldwide organizations is as follows "knowledge management caters to the critical issues of organizational adaptation, survival and competence in face of increasingly discontinuous environmental change.... essentially, it embodies organizational processes that seek synergistic combination of data and information processing capacity of information technologies and the creative and innovative capacity of human beings".

In simpler terms, knowledge management seeks to make the best use of the knowledge that is available to an organization, creating new knowledge in the process.

Knowledge management is seen as a means of achieving organizational goals. It consists of the systematic processes that are put into place to identity, create, capture, share, and leverage the knowledge that is needed for an organization to succeed. Putting it simply, knowledge management aims to 1. Determine what knowledge an organization needs to be successful; 2. capture and store explicit knowledge until required for reuse; and 3. manage and exploit the unspoken knowledge that resides within people.

Knowledge management initiatives use four primary processes to achieve the above said aims:

1. identification/discovery
2. creation/acquisition

3. capture/storage /codification/retrieval
4. sharing/transfer/flow

The knowledge management is holistic, with all processes and programs having as organizational focus rather than section/department/business unit focus, and incorporating the external environment in which the organization operates. It is also open and visible – knowing what everyone does and why. The knowledge management environment is a sharing culture, value based and people focused, motivated, proactive, resourced and supported, and technology enabled.

When working in a knowledge management environment, the information professional has three primary roles and responsibilities:

1. To provide information products and services that continually and consistently match the requirements of the organization;
2. To educate information users to ensure that they can access and use the information products and services effectively to maximize the quality and consistency of organizational knowledge; and
3. To facilitate the sharing and transfer of knowledge.

This brief overview of the knowledge management/ society, it gives us an idea on how to organize, build, or archive information resources of any form (print or electronic). Adaptation of different features of knowledge management can be successfully utilized in the libraries. A library that comprises musical materials can effectively adapt knowledge management to fulfill the needs of its users [4].

1.1 Why Music Library?

A 'music library' may be distinct entity or a segment of a larger library. 'Music Library' is the library which concentrates in musical materials: books, scores, and recordings exist in various formats–libraries may have books in electronic form, scores on microfilm or paper and recordings on disc, tape or in any digital form. Music libraries may also have holding of a museum character, such as actual instruments and items associated with composers or other personalities. Like all libraries, music libraries are supportive. They serve the needs of the researchers; students' performers, music lovers and those in the music business. But they also have direct relationship with music itself. They act as an intermediary between music and music lovers. So, we can say music library refers to the special library or collections of documents, dealing specially with music available for reading, study, research and reference or any other purpose. So the question now is "WHY NOT A MUSIC LIBRARY?" Why don't we have library which caters to the needs of all the people who are in the music industry and all the musicians who wants to learn or research about the older artists. So, its time we thought think about it seriously and find ways to build a library which fulfills the needs of all the people who wants to know more about the subject music [7].

2. Different facets of music library

Music is complex and multifaceted in nature, presenting several challenges to information organizers. A musical work contains a particular musical idea, this musical idea can be expressed through music notation as a printed score; it can be coupled with textual material that becomes an inherent part of the musical work, such as a song and opera; it can be expressed in sound by performance; and a performance can captured visually. Music information, therefore, can be represented as a notation based, text based, audio based or visually based. Each representational form can be considered a type of music information. It is common for a digital music resource to contain all of these forms of music information with the additional interactive capabilities. Either it is uncommon for users to search for a musical work in any or all of these form.

2.1 What's special in music librarianship?

The traditional responsibilities of the librarians are at the heart of most music librarian's activities: organizing, cataloguing, and maintaining collections, providing instructions in use of the library, answering reference inquiries, selecting music, book, journals, recordings, microforms and sometimes manuscripts and other rare materials for acquisition. Music librarians recommend means of preservation and housing of materials in their custody and use electronic bibliographic and reference resources to their full potential.

Beyond these typical responsibilities, the activities of music librarians will reflect the nature of the institution where they are employed and their personal interests, for example: they can plan exhibits and concerts, and collaborate with the other institutions in organizing lectures, classes or other public programs. Librarians who work for music publishers might have editorial duties or manage the inventory of rental music. Those employed by the music dealers acquire materials from numerous publishers worldwide for retail sale to over-the-counter and mail- order customers. Librarians can take active role in music bibliographies, pursuing research, or writing reviews of new publications [6].

2.2 Collection development problem:

A music librarian is confronted with the different kinds of materials besides print media such as discs, tapes, cassettes and now also internet materials, all of which he/she is expected to house and make available to their users. Still to this extent it is common problem as of any other librarian of modern library. The actual problems lie on the fact that "musical materials" contain music in any form but not textual matter. Print media also consists of musical scores as well as musical literature.

These musical materials can not be always regarded as a homogeneous whole, where the music on one of a record may have no connection whatsoever with that on the other side. One record looks very much like another only close inspection of the label will distinguish each form its neighbor. Moreover there is no way to have the deeper idea about the quality of the content otherwise heard or seen using any playing equipment. Thus both user and staffs are almost entirely dependent on the catalogue for knowing what they want. Library has to provide and maintain also various playing equipments.

2.3 *Shortage of selection aids:*

There is a shortage of good selection aids on the realm of music scores and books about music and also various recording published throughout the world, in various forms. There is no equivalent of 'Books in Print' or BNB, neither there is a comprehensive list of music imprint at international level. For western music, somehow one can get help form 'Notes'-quarterly journal of MLA, which includes lists of music received as well as annual surveys of choral music and organ music, published during the year. There are also some good selection aids for western music like RILM (Repertoire International Des musicales), etc. there is MLO (Music Online project), a UK higher education funded project, for selection of music online.

Indian music has as many varieties as India has varieties in languages. Every region again has music and their recordings as well as scores and writings about music. But no aid at all to bibliographically to control them, some publisher's list are the only the tool for music librarian in India. The patron is not familiar with the range of publication and cannot offer much guidance to the staff in choosing important new works.

2.4 Classification and shelf arrangement problem:

Sound recordings and scores have been artificially grouped in many libraries because of their physical characteristics. Various formats of recordings are also grouped separately. This separation and a general reluctance to organize their library value has affected their classification and resulted in frequent use in house schemes. There is no such classification scheme which can be used for Indian music. Another challenge is presented by the need to assign dates to early music scores (undated by their publishers omitted printing dates from music imprints).

2.5 Problem of cataloguing and indexing:

Cataloguing of music scores and recordings presents some unique challenges. Critical to music cataloguing is absolute identification of the aural phenomenon "the music" within the text of the catalogue information. Although there are a number of standards and rules for cataloguing and indexing these materials, but no one of them is beyond of question. They are not helpful at all for cataloging Indian music. As the musical recordings are totally equipment dependent (i.e. the content of these materials are hidden, which is to be heard or seen through other media), so it is necessary to describe the contents in full and in greater specificity in the catalogue and to give more comprehensive references. Again, we know that references and added entries, annotations and explanatory matter should be within definite limit for the sake of the convenience of the users as well as to maintain the catalogue in a convenient size. Thus the cataloguer is constantly faced with decisions which can never safely be taken in a mechanical fashion. One typical problem arises in music cataloguing with the subject headings these are generally "form" headings (e.g. Flute and piano music, vocal music, sonata, etc), but sometimes they relate to the topic of the text.

Librarians can take an active role in music scholarship by compiling bibliographies, pursuing research or writing reviews of new publications. They often teach music bibliography and other classroom subjects within their area of specialization. As members of professional organizations, they may serve on local, national or international committees devoted to issues such as electronic information storage and retrieval cataloguing standards, education for librarianship, preservation and library management. Within the library, it might be their responsibility to organize training programs for staff, researchers of interns. Librarians of public music libraries have more responsibilities. They have the duties to entertain users of all level as well as to help users in knowing and studying music.

As different types of music libraries have different types of function to perform, so the librarians of one kind of libraries can not get more help from the librarians of other kinds of libraries. All have to take their own decisions regarding the policy of work.

2.6 Qualities of a Music librarian:

A music librarian is a librarian qualified to specialize in music. As music library may acquire music of any style or language or medium or era, so a broad musical background is essential. A music librarian should have as broad an education as possible in both music and liberal arts. Training in music must be the equivalent of at least substantial undergraduate work. Music librarian need to be familiar with the relationship of music to other disciplines. Music and the literature about it are published throughout the world in varieties of languages. Basic cataloging and bibliographic research require a working knowledge of German, and at least one Roman language in addition to the knowledge of English, Hindi, Urdu and regional languages, in Indian respect.

3. Music Information Retrieval (MIR)

Considering the sheer magnitude of available music facing MIR researchers: 10,000 new albums are released and 10,000 works registered for copyright each year (Uitdenbogerd and Zobel, 1999). Notwithstanding the intrinsic intellectual merits of MIR research problems, the successful development of robust, large scale MIR systems will also have important social and commercial implications. According to Wordspot (2001), an internet consulting company that tracks queries submitted to internet search engines, the search for music-specifically, the now- ubiquitous MP3 format – has displaced the search for sex- related materials as the most popular retrieval request. Yet at this moment, not one of the so- called "MP3 search engines" is doing anything more than indexing the textual metadata supplied by the creators of the files. It is not an exaggeration to claim that a successful, commercially based, MIR system has the potential to generate vast revenue. In the U.S alone, 1.08 billion units of recorded music (e.g., CDs, cassettes, music videos and so forth, valued at $ 14.3 billion, were shipped to retailers in 2000 (Recording Industry Association of America, 2001). Vevendi Universal, parent company of Universal Music Group, recently bought MP3.com, a popular Internet based distributor of MP3 files, for $372 million (Welte, 2001). Beyond the commercial implications, the emergence of robust MIR systems will create significant added value to the huge collections of underused music currently warehoused in the world's libraries by making the entire corpus of music readily accessible. This accessibility will be highly beneficial to musicians, scholars, students, and members of the general public alike.

A growing international music information retrieval research community is being formed, drawing upon multidisciplinary expertise from library science, information science, musicology, music theory, audio engineering, computer science, law and business.

Problems are not unique to music, but are found with much greater frequency in music catalogues, thereby creating a complex music metadata environment. A new data model developed by IFLA (International Federation of Library Associations) task force helped clarify the confusion and confirmed the conceptual model used in music cataloguing. The IFLA model identified four states of a resource as outlined in the FRBR (Functional Requirements of the Bibliographic Recorded) (IFLA, 1998). These include the *work*, and the *expression*, the *manifestation* and the *item*. It is generally agreed that the *work* and *expression* exit in an abstract state, while the *manifestation* and the *item* exist in a tangible state.

Current issues and problems confronted when organizing music resources fall into two categories: creating music metadata and using music metadata. The bottom line is that music metadata is only as useful as the capabilities of the integrated library system (ILS) or database that contains it. Database structures, encoding syntax and collection and display of retrieval sets all play an important role in the success of a metadata system to meet user needs.

In most library systems, retrieval of a musical work through a library catalogue is only possible by accessing a metadata record that describes the resource in terms of the physical item and the musical content. Since the metadata is textual, it is not derived from the musical content itself; it is transcribed from the bibliographic information associated with the musical work and its specific manifestation. This textual substitute for the musical resource includes information about the musical content, such as title, composer, conductor, key duration, publisher, etc. A text based metadata system for music requires a two step process to retrieve the desired music; first, a text search of the catalogue to find the surrogate record. This requires the searcher to have some factual information about the musical work. Once the metadata record is retrieved, a second search must be performed to physically locate and access the resource. Today's web based catalogues can provide direct linkage from the metadata record to the musical resource if the resource is available online digital form [2].

4. Future perspectives on music access and retrieval

The 'best practice' music metadata system would have to provide information about and access to textual metadata, audio files, image files, and encoded notation. In addition, it must be capable of synchronicity to provide access to time – based information and ideally it would have a non textual means of access. The ideal music metadata system, therefore, would incorporate description, access and retrieval techniques developed in the music library community, the computer science community and the scholarly music community.

While libraries use textual metadata for resource discovery and retrieval, the retrieval, the comparatively new interdisciplinary area of music information retrieval is conducting research on retrieval using the music content rather than a description of the content. In order to understand the many difficulties and possibilities for music content retrieval, it is necessary to understand the inherent facets of music. Many of the excellent music information retrieval literature review article, illustrates that music contains up to seven facets that are inherent of a musical work or phrase. These are pitch, duration, harmony, timbre, editorial content, textual content and bibliographic information. Each of these facets may be represented in a variety of different ways. Music information retrieval researchers are developing methods to retrieve music information directly on the musical content using each of these music facets in either notated or aural form. If a system is designed using each of the seven facets for retrieval, and multiple representational possibilities for each facet are accommodated, the complexity of designing a music information retrieval system becomes obvious.

Music information retrieval falls into two groups: analytic/production music information retrieval information systems and locating music information systems. Again the distinction focuses on the intended use. Analytic/production MIR system strive for the most complete representation of the music, including the symbolic notation and other editorial content. These systems are designed for use by musicologist, music theorists, music engravers and composers in the creation, analysis and production of music. Locating MIR systems are designed for the identification, location and retrieval of a musical work and can be notation based and / or audio based. Some locating systems do not provide a complete representation of the music (e.g.: an incipit is a truncated form of a melody). This incompleteness helps the less musically sophisticated user because the user does not have to input a complete music query. Other MIR locating systems are "full text" in the sense that the music incipit is not truncated. The primary goal for users of the MIR locating systems is to locate and use the musical work retrieved, not to manipulate the various facets of the music in the musical content [3].

5. Conclusion

The complexities of music information organization and retrieval are compounded by the many metadata options available today. It is possible that a music-specific metadata scheme will be developed in the future, but it is just as possible that the music community will continue to use a variety of existing metadata schemes and adapt them to their music needs. Advanced computing has opened new doors for the scholarly music and library communities: it has also presented many challenges for librarians. Interestingly, the traditional methods of organizing music resources, i.e. AACR2R and MARC, are still flourishing. The rich descriptive detail offered by these standards is still useful in the new digital environment as several digital music library projects have shown. The new technology allows information specialists to push the boundaries of the music catalogue in new directions and offers opportunities to collaborate creatively with the music and computer researchers. A coupling of textual metadata with music content retrieval techniques would provide greater precision in the search and retrieval process and offer imaginative search options for music users to explore.

References

1. Nandi, Ratna. (2004). Music Librarianship: A neglected area of Librarianship in India. *IASLIC Bulletin 49(1), p.51-56.*
2. 2.Downie, Stephen J. (2004). Music Information Retrieval. *Annual review of Information Science and Technology.*
3. Vellucci, Sherry L. (2004). Music Metadata. IYLIM 2003/2004.
4. Henczel, Sue. (2004). Supporting the KM environment: The Roles, Responsibilities, and Rights of Information Professionals. *Information Outlook 56(1), p14-19.*
5. http://www.bambooweb.com/articles/k/n knowledge_management.html
6. http://www.musiclibraryassoc.org
7. http://www.cliea.it/music/iaml

16

Competencies and Challenges for Information Professionals in Promoting and Supporting of Digital Information Services to user Community in Bangladesh

Md. Shiful Islam
Lecturer,
University of Dhaka, Bangladesh
(shifuldu@yahoo.com)

ABSTRACT

The paper specifies the skills and capabilities of information professional in digital library or digital environment. There are a number of skills required of a modern information professional such as vision, professional skills, communication skills, presentation skills, negotiation skills, subject skills, technical and IT skills, project management skills and a number of capabilities i.e. the ability to work with a variety of people, capability to work under pressure, ability to learn new and new things etc. The objective of the study is to explore the present scenario of information professionals of Bangladesh in digital era. It also discusses the role and service abilities of library and information professionals in digital library or information institution in Bangladesh. The author has attempted to explain the challenges for information professionals in promoting and supporting of information services to user community in Bangladesh. The study expands the functions of information professionals to work as information expert, technologist, communicator, instructor, negotiator, planner, evaluator, manager and above all project manager. Some suitable suggestions have been made for professional enhancement in digital era of Bangladesh.

1. Prelude

In the present age of information superhighway, libraries and information institutions are facing a threat from the internet and vast web of electronic resources. Emergence of Information Communication Technology (ICT) has greatly influenced on each and every facet of information activities and information services. 'In order to cope with the changing roles, functions and responsibility as envisaged in the electronic information age, library and information professionals would have to learn new information technology and management skills. In the emerging scenario, dominated by digital and network resources, the involvement of library and information professionals in organizing library services will increase manifold.[1] So digital librarianship requires a number of skills, tools and techniques, which are also required to manage traditional librarianship. But these need to be modified or sharpened to meet the requirements of digital library world. In digital librarianship, there will be also required new sets of skills, tools and techniques. Ideally, it is difficult to identify the essential skills required to manage a dynamic field like digital libraries. I have made an attempt to identify some essential skills and competencies that are specifically required to build and manage digital libraries. 'These skills may be categorized into four groups: Information Communication Technology (ICT) skills, Information skills,

Management skills and Research and Project Management skills.[2]

2. Objectives of the study

The main objectives of the present study are to:

a) identify the skills and competencies of library and information professionals.

b) explore the responsibility and role of information professionals in digital library.

c) explain the challenges for the information professional in digital environment.

d) suggest some suitable recommendations for the advancement of the profession.

3. Methodology

A pre-tested questionnaire (Appendix-1) was prepared and used to collect information on the existing knowledge, skills and roles of information professional in their respective fields. Copies of the questionnaire were distributed among the information professionals of different information institutions in Bangladesh. Moreover, some other necessary information has been collected from the primary and secondary sources of information.

4. Information communication technology skills

The combination of computer and telecommunication technologies make the foundation of digital librarianship. So the professional of digital libraries must have a basic understanding of these technologies. Now a day, digital library professionals may need to design web pages containing information about and links to various services. They may not actually do the design and development work themselves but would invite others. A clear conception will be required to judge and appreciate the problems and to make optimum use of the products and services. Information communication technology skills required by the information professionals in a digital library is as follows:

* Fundamental networking skills.
* Web programming skills by HTML, ASP, PHP, or any web programming Language.
* Basic understanding for digitization.
* Sound knowledge for digital library architecture, systems and software.
* New digital library product and service design skills.
* Document and information management skills.
* Assessment, selection and application of current and emerging information tools and creation information access and delivery solutions.
* Application expertise in databases, indexing metadata, information analysis and synthesis to improve information retrieval and use in the organization.
* Protection the information privacy of clients and maintenance awareness of new challenges to privacy.
* Maintenance current awareness of emerging technologies that may not be currently relevant but may become relevant tools of future information resources.

5. Information skills

Advanced information professional may have sophisticated approaches to the organization of information resources, searching and retrieving information. These are variety of skills to build good information retrieval systems and user interfaces, and a number of tools and techniques that are used for the purpose. Information professionals should acquire these skills and should also be familiar with the various information retrieval tools and techniques for building better digital libraries.

'This is an era that has changed significantly in a digital library environment-human intermediaries have been replaced by e-mail or web-based reference question forms, and in many cases trained reference librariarins have been replaced by subject experts.[3] So it is obvious that information professionals must be able to provide fast and efficient proactive and reactive digital information services. Therefore the information professionals must have the following information skills:

5.1 *Skills of Information Organization:*

The information professionals should know how to manage information organizations ranging in size from one employee to several hundred employees. These organizations may be in any environment from corporate, educations, public, government to non-profit. They should align the information organization, assess and communicate the value of the information organizations, establish effective management, operational and financial management processes, contribute effectively to senior management strategies and decisions regarding information applications, build and lead effective information services team and champions the professionals, advise the organization on copyright and intellectual property issues.

5.2 *Skills of Information Resources:*

Information professionals should have expertise in total management of information resources, including identifying, selecting, evaluating, securing and providing access to pertinent information resources. These resources may be in any media or format. Information professional recognize the importance of people as a key information resource. As information resource manager, they should be able to manage the full cycle of information, build a dynamic collection of information and information resources, demonstrate expert knowledge of the content and format of information resources, provide access to the best available externally published and internally created information resources, negotiate the purchase and licensing of needed information products and services and develop information policies for the organization.

5.3 Skills of Information Services:

The information professionals should know how to manage the entire life cycle of information services. So they should be able to develop and maintain a portfolio of cost-effective, client-valued information services, conduct market research of the information behavior and problems of current and potential client groups, research, analyze and synthesize information into accurate answers or actionable information for clients, employ evidence-based management to demonstrate the value of and continually improve information sources and services.

6. Management skills

Information professional must have a number of management skills including personnel and financial management and marketing. Because these skills are equally important in digital libraries, many of them need to be modified in the content of the needs and characteristics of digital environment. Digital libraries require to cope with a business model where client- service and satisfaction are the main goals and in many cases they need to meet these goals by reduced budgets. So the marketing of digital information services will form a significant part of the work of information professionals of digital library. Moreover, customer or user care and strategic decision making in a competitive environment, are also very useful for digital information professionals. Thus the information professionals of digital library should have the following management skills:

* Common management skills i.e. leadership qualities, interpersonal communication skills, vision, strategic decision making qualities etc.
* Skills of personnel and financial management.
* Skills of marketing.

* Customer/user care, relations and management skills.

7. Research and project management skills

Raising funds for the digitization projects may be major challenges for information professionals of digital library. They need to acquire some research and project management skills in order to be able to raise or allocate sufficient funds and successfully accomplish the project.

The information professional in a digital library should have the following skills:

* Skills of research design and management skills of fund raising.
* Skills of publication and reporting.
* Skills of learning new things and adopting new environment quickly.
* Skills of undertaking the project.

8. Information professional scenario in Bangladesh

The libraries working with computers and communication technologies are the initial stage of digitization/digital process. The special libraries and information centers are the pioneer in digitization of library in Bangladesh.[4] However, let us take a glance at the information professionals of Bangladesh:

Table 1: Some selected libraries, the inception year of computers, name of the software and the competencies of the information professionals

Name of the library	Inception year of using computer	No. of computers	Name of the software used	Knowledge and experiences on software and hardware of the inf. professionals	All of the lib. staff have the ability to operate the computer
Dhaka University Library	1998	30	GLAS	Yes	No
Bangladesh University of Engineering and Technology Library	1987	41	In house package software	Few of them	No
East West University Library	1997	12	EWULIBMIS (In house Package)	Yes	Yes
North South University Library	1996	40	Locally Developed Software	Yes	Yes
Bangladesh Central Public Library	1991	12	--------------	No	No
National Library of Bangladesh	1997	06	CDS/ISIS	No	No
BIDS Library & Documentation Center	1996	08	CDS/ISIS	Few of them	No
British Council Library	1997	20	LIBSYS	Yes	Yes
BANSDOC Library	1993	05	CDS/ISIS	Few of them	No
DISC (ICDDR, B)	1991	15	CDS/ISIS	Yes	Yes

Source: questionnaire & observation report

Table 2. Educational, professional qualification, training and consciousness of information professionals on digital library.

SL. No	Name of the library	Highest qualifications of the librarian	Special training on digital librarianship	Concepts of digital library	Conscious of the benefit of digital library
01	Dhaka University Library	Ph. D. in Library & Information Science	No	Yes	Yes
02	Bangladesh University of Engineering and Technology Library	M.A. in Library and Information Science	No	Yes	Yes
03	East West University Library	M.A. in Library and Information Science	No	Yes	Yes
04	North South University Library	Ph. D. in Library & Information Science	Yes, There is a training program entitled ' Digital and online librarianship'	Yes	Yes
05	Bangladesh Central Public Library	M.A. in Library and Information Science	No	No	No
06	National Library of Bangladesh	M.A. in Library and Information Science	No	No	No
07	BIDS Library & Documentation Center	M.A. in Library and Information Science	No	Yes	Yes
08	British Council Library	M.A. in Library and Information Science	No	Yes	Yes
09	BANSDOC Library	M.A. in Library and Information Science	No	Yes	Yes
10	DISC (ICDDR, B)	M.A. in Library and Information Science	No	Yes	Yes

Source: questionnaire & observation report

The above table shows that the information professional of 50% of the libraries have the knowledge and experiences on hardware and software, 30% of libraries have few information professionals who are equipped with knowledge and experiences of them, 20% of libraries have no such knowledge and experiences. Only 40% of libraries have all the information professionals who can operate the computer properly and 60% of libraries where all of them are not able to operate the computer but most of them can operate the computer.

It is evident from the table that only the Librarians of Dhaka University Library and the North South University Library have Ph.D. in Library and Information Science. It is also observed that the North South is conducting a training program on " Digital and Online Librarianship". The

Table 3. Measurement of competencies of information professionals in Bangladesh

SL. No	Name of the library	ICT skills	Information skills	Management skills	Research and project manageme nt skills
01	Dhaka University Library	√	√	√	X
02	Bangladesh University of Engineering and Technology Library	√	√	√	X
03	East West University Library	√	√	√	X
04	North South University Library	√	√	√	X
05	Bangladesh Central Public Library	X	√	√	X
06	National Library of Bangladesh	X	√	√	X
07	BIDS Library & Documentation Center	X	√	√	X
08	British Council Library	√	√	√	X
09	BANSDOC Library	√	√	√	X
10	DISC (ICDDR, B)	√	√	√	√

Source: questionnaire & observation report

information professionals of 80% of libraries have the concept of digital library and 20% of library professionals have no ideas about digital libraries.

The above table indicates that 70% of libraries have the information professional with ICT skills and 30% of libraries have no staff with such skills. It is also worth noting that 100% of libraries have the information professionals with information and management skills and 90% of libraries have no staff with research and project management skills and 10% of libraries have the staff with research and project management skills.

Table 4. Performance of the information professionals in the basic functional unit of digital libraries

SL. No	Name of the library	Capable of online acquisition	Capable of online processing	Capable of online circulation	Capable of online reference services
01	Dhaka University Library	No	Most of them are capable	Most of them are capable	No
02	Bangladesh University of Engineering and Technology Library	No	Few of them are capable	Few of them are capable	No
03	East West University Library	Yes	Yes	Yes	Yes
04	North South University Library	Yes	Yes	Yes	Yes
05	Bangladesh Central Public Library	No	No	No	No
06	National Library of Bangladesh	No	No	No	No
07	BIDS Library & Documentation Center	Yes	Yes	Yes	No
08	British Council Library	Yes	Yes	Yes	Yes
09	BANSDOC Library	Yes	Yes	No	No
10	DISC (ICDDR, B)	Yes	Yes	Yes	Yes

Source: questionnaire & observation report

The above table reveals that 60% of libraries have the information professionals who are capable of performing online acquisition and 40% of them are not able to do that. It is also observed that 60% of libraries have the staff who are fully capable of accomplishing the online processing and 20% of libraries have no such staff and 10% of libraries where most of them are able to do and 10% of libraries have few of the information professionals are able to perform the online processing. Moreover, 50% of libraries have the staff with the capability of performing the activities of online circulation and 30% of libraries have no such staff and 10% of libraries where most of them are able and another 10% of libraries where few of them are capable of performing the online circulation activities. It is also to be noted that 60% of libraries have the information professionals who are able to provide online reference services and 40% of libraries have no information professionals with such capability.

Table 5. Capability of providing digital/online service of the information professionals

SL. No.	Services	Total libraries	No. of libraries where the information professionals are capable of providing the services	Percentage
01	Web based information services	10	06	60
02	Selective Dissemination of Information (SDI) services	"	10	100
03	Current Awareness Services (CAS)	"	10	100
04	Inter-library loan services through networking	"	04	40
05	Online indexing and abstracting services	"	05	50
06	Reprographic services	"	08	80
07	Online bibliographical services	"	06	60

Source: questionnaire & observation report

The above table shows that 100% of libraries have the information professionals who are able to provide Current Awareness Services (CAS) and Selective Dissemination of Information (SDI) services and 60% of libraries have the staff who are capable of offering web based information and online bibliographic information services and 80% of libraries with the staff who can provide reprographic services, 40% of libraries equipped with the information professionals who are capable of rendering inter-library loan services through networking and 50% of libraries have the staff who are able to provide online indexing and abstracting services.

9. Challenges for information professionals in digital library

The information professional in the digital and networked library is to face the situation effectively as:

Information expert[5]**:** The information professional who has a fundamental understanding of information resources, including identifying, selecting, evaluating, securing and providing access to relevant information resources. Information professionals should have expertise in total management information.

Technologist[6]: The information professional must work as a technologist who is aware of new and emerging technologies and understand a library's technology infrastructure and various services and resources and collect data regarding the use of those services.

Communicator[7]: They should be communicators who have the ability to communicate effectively not only face to face but also non-face to face computer mediated forms of communications i.e. online chat, email etc.

Instructor[8]: They should be instructors who can instruct users and other library staff on a number of network-based services and resources (e.g., computer use, Web searching, online data base use) as well as aspects of information literacy.

Manager[9]: They should also be managers who can manage varied and numerous projects, and delegate responsibility to others.

Negotiator[10]: They should be negotiators who are able to engage in informed contract negotiations with a number of content and resource providers such as database vendors/ aggregators and systems providers.

Planner[11]: They should be planners who think strategically, strives toward a vision, and can develop and implement strategic planning initiatives, Librarians also need to engage in strategic planning activities that extend beyond the library to the large communities that they serve, such as a university, city, country etc.

Evaluator[12]: They should be evaluators who know the various assessment techniques available to them, the ways in which to use these techniques, as to benefit the library's understanding of their services/resources, data analysis of the evaluation project collection activities, the interpretation of the results of such assessment approaches, and ways in which to feed the results of the evaluation projects into the library's provision of services and resources and planning activities.

10. Recommendations for the professional development in Bangladesh

The information professionals in Bangladesh should constantly scan the horizon for new technologies, or new business models, which will impact the way in which the profession develops. They should also follow the following ways to keep abreast of future changes:

10.1 Reading National and foreign Journals: It is not enough to simply read the journals library and information science but also important to regularly read the key computing journals and the key journals that discuss the organization in which the information professional operates.

10.2 Attending Conferences: Attendance is recommended at conferences (whether Local or international) that are not purely focused on the information profession, but cover the organization in which the information professional is employed.

10.3 Joining Training Courses: There are many opportunities in Bangladesh, for training which the information professional could, and should seize. These range from traditional databases skills to training courses on project management, communications skills and courses in information technology. It is in the best interest of information professionals to adopt a proactive approach to manage their own continuing professional development.

10.4 Capitalization on new opportunities: The information professional in Bangladesh should adopt them to seek out challenges and capitalize on new opportunities.

10.5 Effective Communication: They should communicate effectively and present ideas clearly, negotiates confidently and persuasively.

10.6 Mutual respect and trust: They must build an environment of mutual respect and trust in order to develop their profession.

10.7 Team approach: The information professionals in Bangladesh should employ a team approach, recognize the balance of collaborating, leading plans, priorities and focuses on what is critical, demonstrate personal career planning, think creatively and innovatively, recognize the value of professional networking and personal career, planning remain flexible and positive in a time of continuing change, motivate himself and others.

11. Conclusion

Information professionals have been used directly as all the persons or people or staff who are working in various libraries or information institutions and professional competencies consist of information professional knowledge of information resources and the ability to use this knowledge as a basis for providing the highest quality information services. Information professionals harness the current and appropriate technology tools to deliver the best services, provide the most relevant and accessible resources, develop and deliver teaching tools to maximize clients use of information, and capitalize on the library and information environment of the 21st century.[13] Maximum libraries of Bangladesh are passing through an exciting phase of transformation under the impact of information technology. It is imperative to equip information professional with all the required knowledge, skills, competencies and capabilities to handle the information communication technology and other changes in the field with greater motivation and commitment. Enthusiasm for ICT applications among the information professionals can be infused only through training programme. They should also be offered adequate opportunity for continuing professional enhancement. The libraries should motivate their information professionals to attend various conferences, seminars, symposia and workshops so that they interact with different expert professional and get latest information in the professional and update their competencies. Most of the information professionals in major libraries of Bangladesh are facing so many problems. If they follow the above suggestions strictly, their problems will be solved.

References

1. *Walia, P.K.* Challenges and competencies for Library and Informational Professionals in the Digital Environment. Paper presented and published in the 50th All India Library Conference Seminar Papers on "Knowledge Organization in Digital Environment in Libraries (KODEL):Introspect and Prospects". Vadodara, December 1-4,2004. Edited by Dr (Mrs.) Ashu Shokeen, Dr. M. Madhusudhan and Sh. D.V. Singh. p547
2. *Chowdhury, G.G. & Chowdhury, S.* Introduction to digital libraries, London: Facet Publishing, 2003, Pp 285-291.
3. *IBID*, Pp 288-289.
4. *Uddin, H. & Islam, S.* Digital Library: Concepts, Issues and Implications in Bangladesh. Paper presented and published as abstract in the 50th All India Library Conference Seminar Papers on "Knowledge Organization in Digital Environment in Libraries (KODEL):Introspect and Prospects". Vadodara, December 1-4,2004.

Edited by Dr (Mrs.) Ashu Shokeen, Dr. M. Madhusudhan and Sh. D.V. Singh. p 283

5. *Walia, P.K.*2004. p548
6. *IBID*, p 549
7. *IBID*, p 552

APPENDIX-1

Questionnaire for the survey of the competencies and challenges for the information professionals in promoting and supporting of digital information services to user community in Bangladesh.

(Please tick (✓) marks where necessary). **Confidential**

1. Name of the library:
2. Inception year of using computers:
3. Highest qualifications of the librarian/head of the library:
4. Have any special training on digital librarianship?

   Yes ☐ No ☐

   if Yes, Name of the training program:
5. Professional competences of the present staff of the library:

   i) Information communication technology skills

   ii) Information skills

   iii) Management skills

   iv) Research and project management skills

6. Are the information professionals competent enough to place the acquisition order online?

   Yes ☐ No ☐

   Others (please specify):

7. Are they capable of performing the processing activities (classification and cataloguing) of the library by using software?

   Yes ☐ No ☐

8. Are they able to handle all the digital activities of circulation section?

   Yes ☐ No ☐

   Others (please specify):

9. Are the information professionals capable of providing reference services automatically?

   Yes ☐ No ☐

10. Are all the information professionals able to operate computer properly?

    Yes ☐ No ☐

11. How many computers are being used by the information professional of the library?

    No. of computers:

12. The information professionals are skilled enough to provide the following services (Please give the tick marks):

    i) Current awareness services
    ii) Selective dissemination information services
    iii) Inter-library loan services through networking
    iv) Online indexing and abstracting services
    v) Web-based information services

vi) Online bibliographical services.

vii) Reprographic services etc

13. Have they minimum experiences on computer software and hardware?

    Yes ☐ No ☐

    Others (please specify):

14. Name of the software used by the information professional in the library:

Questionnaire filled by:

Date:

17

Computerisation of Library Functions and Services at IMCC, Pune

Meenal Oak
Librarian, IMCC, Pune

ABSTRACT

The paper discusses the computerisation of library functions and services at IMCC, PUNE on the following topics

* Selection of integrated Library software package
* Migration of libraries earlier database from FoxPro 2.5 to MS- SQL system
* LAN configuration and setup at library
* Internet services
* Bar coding of library documents and reader's ticket
* Training of library staff
* Role of the librarian as a subject expert and as a coordinator in the development of library software system

Introduction

The institute popularly known as IMCC, was established in 1983 by Maharashtra Education Society Pune, one of the oldest educational institution in Maharashtra. The great revolutionary freedom fighter Late Shri Vasudev Balwant Phadke, Late Shri L N Indapurkar and Late Shri Prabhker Bhave have a lions share in establishing M E Society.

The institute provides quality education at the post graduation level , in the field of Management and computers. The institute is recognized by University of Pune under section 85 of Maharashtra Universities Act , 1994 .

Computerisation of library operations

Now a days, use of computers in all walks of life is a common activity.

Computerisation of library operations is basically concern with the use of computers and computer based products and services in library work.

To cope up with the demands of rapidly changing requirements of its users, today libraries have no option excepting computerisation and digitization. Computerisation of library function and services is the first step in the development of a digital library. [1]

IMCC library collection and services upto 1996

The IMCC Library has grown steadily from the year 1996. It was a very small library with a small cabin for collection and a small reading hall. The collection was only near about 1000 volumes and 5 or 6 periodicals subscribed by the institutional library. The collection was not classified properly , that is half of the collection having DDC numbers and half of the collection was without any classification number. Library catalogue was also not there. The library was functioning with the help of one professional and one peon, both were working on part time basis. The library working schedule was only for 3 hours and that was 5.30 pm to 8.30 pm

IMCC library development : a study from 1996

The existed IMCC library system was studied by observing library functions and services as well as the needs and requirements of IMCC Library were identified through the discussions with faculty members and students of IMCC. Following things were realised

- * Lack of information sources
- * Lack of information retrieval tools
- * Lack of discipline among students, regarding their library behaviour, for e.g. students were using the library reading hall as a common room for their discussion, not giving library fine etc.
- * Lack of space

After identifying lacunas, the Library development process started as per the developmental plan.

IMCC library: a review

Work for the development of IMCC library.

CRITERIA	UPTO 1996 (1987-1995)	FROM 1996-2003
Courses available in IMCC	MCM ,DCM MPM ,MMS ,DTL ,DBM	MCA ,MCM ,DCM MPM ,MMS ,DTL ,DBM
No.Of Students	200	600
Library Time	5.30 p.m to 8.15 p.m (2.85 hours daily)	8.00 a.m to 9.00 p.m (13 Hours Daily)
Library Collection	1000 Books ---- ---- 6 Periodicals&journals --- 3 Newspapers ---- Selected Project reports.	7488 Books 400 Donated books 400 Hall Reading copies 49 nationaljournals&periodicals 06 Int journals &Periodicals 06 News papers Video cassettes Selected project reports.
Library Service	Issuing for 3 hours -Hall reading • Books • Journals • Project report For 3 hours	Issuing of books, journals,project reports, cd's for 11.30 hours. -Hall reading • Books • Journals Project report • SDI Service • CAS • Reference & Referral service for 11.30 hours
Library Catalogue	No separate library catalogue or any other retrieval tools for collection.	Separate catalogue in the form of cardex + computerized databases of books, cd's project report for the retrieval of document.

After achieving this stage, the requirement of computerisation of library functions and services was realised. The proposal for the procurement of readymade software was forwarded to the Director, IMCC. It was decided to develop "In house library software" for the computerisation of library functions and services. After 6/8 months it was realised that it is not possible for the Head of computer dept, to develop a library software , because of his very heavy workload. Therefore a committee was constituted for Library Computerisation project.

Role of librarian in computerisation

For getting success in any project, planning is must. Planning of each and every activity under the project helps to achieve the success at the desired level. Librarian has to act as a subject expert and as a coordinator in the library computerisation project. He/ she should chalk out the Library Computerisation Plan. While planning Librarian should consider the opinions of technical subject experts (APPENDIX-1). Therefore the Library Computerisation plan was prepared by considering following elements

Budgeting [2]

Cost of Library software

Cost of Hardware including components of networking, other components

Such as Bar code reader , printer , Digital Camera etc.

Site Preparation Plan

Space for server machine

Space for client machine

Plan to fix Network Cable, Hubs

Plan for Equipment Furniture

Plan for required furniture

Plan for Development and Implementation of Library Software

Time frame considered to develop the Library software System Modules

Time frame for Implementation process

Plan for Monitoring progress of Implementation

Staff Training Plan

Maintenance Plan

4Major categories were considered under this as follows:

Library software Maintainance

Network Maintainance

Hardware and other equipment Maintainance

Human Resource Maintainance

As a project coordinator Librarian should coordinate each and every activity under the project and take care that the project will be completed in stipulated time period.

Therefore the plan was prepared and submitted to the management of the organization for approval.

Purchase of library software

The Director IMCC, Librarian IMCC (Subject Expert), HOD Computer. Dept.(In house Technical Expert), Chairman of M .E. Society, Life-members of M E society were the Committee members. The important points raised in favour of development of library software by giving contract to the software company were:

a. Cost effectiveness.

b. Software along with a source code.

c. Applicability of Software in M E society's other branches.

After a long discussion, the committee decided to develop library software by giving contract to a software company and the library automation process at IMCC was intiated. Quotations were invited and the following software companies provided the quotations for developing Library Software System.

1. Priyamvad corportion
2. Apt's solution.
3. PC House.

Preliminary study

It was decided to observe the demonstration of software packages developed by these software companies. Questionnaire was also prepared and circulated among the users of these software packages. (Sample Questionnaire – APPENDIX-2). The report regarding Customer feedback was submitted, and the committee meeting was held on 6TH October 2003 where all the representatives of the software companies were invited for discussion. After detailed discussion, it was asked them to submit the revised quotations by following the software requirement specifications provided by IMCC. Based on the information received from the users of these software companies, the committee came to the conclusion that "Priyamvad Corporation" was the one which could develop the library software as per the library requirements. The final order was placed in 9th October 2003

Study and analysis of library requirements

As it was not readymade library software, it was necessary to study the IMCC library requirements for developing library software system. It mainly includes background study regarding the objectives and major functions being used in different sections of the library.

In house feasibility study was conducted for identifying the key areas of computerisation. Therefore Acquisition, Cataloguing, Circulation, Serial control, User OPAC, these areas were studied and the scope of each area was decided as follows

SOFTWARE REQUIREMENT SPECIFICATIONS

Acquisition

Acquisition system should cover the entire range of

activities from the time of making proposal to the accessioning of item.

Document Purchase/Selection File is to be created consisting list of required titles for the LIBRARY having following fields.

- Type (Type of document i .e .Book ,CD ,VCD ,Journal , Video Cass,, Project Report)
- Title of the Document
- Author of the Document
- Price
- Date (Date of Communication)
- Status
- Remarks
- Dealer

(A) Accessioning : Consisting different files for (having separate Serial Numbers)

1. Acc. Register for Books purchased by Library.
2. Acc. Register for Donated Books.
3. Acc. Register for Xeroxed Copies.
4. Acc. Register for Project Reports.
5. Acc. Register for CD'S.
6. Acc. Register for Video Cass.

   Fields for every file will be given.

**** After Document Entry Bar Code Label for document is to be generated.**

Reports required from Acquisition Module:

1. Creating Purchase order for document.
2. No. of Titles available per subject.
3. No of Volumes /Copies available per subject.
4. No of Titles available per Course.

5. No of volumes available per Course.
6. No of Title purchased during one academic Year/ Financial Year.
7. No of Title purchased per subject during the academic Year/Financial Year.
8. No of Volumes purchased during the academic Year/ Financial Year.
9. No of Volumes purchased during the academic Year/ Financial Year.
10. List of Hall Reading copies.
11. List of Reference Books.

Cataloguing

The scope of cataloguing module was decided by following Classified Catalogue code format having

Main Entry

Author Entry

Class Index Entry

* Title Entry is to be created for each document.
* Facility for printing each entry for manual Catalogue.

Serials Control

Consisted of Registration of journals & Periodicals having following elements

Class No

Type Journal / Periodical

Volume No.

Issue No.

Monthly Table for Registration.

Article Index

Name of the Publisher

Publisher Address

Agents Name

Address of the Agent

Demand Draft No.

Date of Demand Draft

Date of Reminder

Remarks

(**) System should generate the list of periodicals which are overdue.

Reports Required from Periodicals Section :

- Reminders to Publisher / Agent.
- Letter for Subscription.
- Letter for Subscription Renewal.
- List of Journals Subscribed
- List of Periodicals Subscribed

Circulation

The book circulation issue and receiving entries are to be grabbed using bar code reader.

Member File

Having information about each and every library user consisting of 3 different categories Students, IMCC Staff & Visiting Faculty Members having following

elements of information

Category

Name

Address

Phone No.

E-mail

Fax No.

Course

Roll No.

Photo

While registration Member photo Image is to grabbed using Web Camera and reader card should be printed along with Photo and Bar Code. Issuing system should generated Flash Message for the records of the persons having library material due. System automatically calculate the delay period in terms of days & rupees.

Reports required from Circulation Module :

Reminders to the Users.

Generation of Fine Receipts.

Library Notices (A per the provided format)

Library Budget Module :

Scope of the Library Budget module was considered as

No of courses

Budgeted amount per courses

-for Books

-for Journals

-for AV Material

Reports

Report of Library Budget.

User OPAC

A search Engine is to be built to access library information using browses through Institute's Network. A member should be given facility to reserve the document through such Search Engine.

Platforms are available with Institute:

* Oracle 8i Enterprise Server

Developer 6i

JAVA JDL 1.3.1

* SQL Server 7.0 Visual Basic

The suggested software may be build using any of the above platform.

Developing Library Software

The detail technical discussion regarding the development of library modules held from 13 Oct to 17 Oct 2003 for 3-4 hours daily between librarian IMCC & the project engineer of Priyamvad corporation , responsible for the development of library software.

Installation of acquisition module

Acquisition module was installed at IMCC library on 29 Oct 2003.

Migration of Database From FoxPro 2.5 to MS-SQL systems

Before migrating the database it was necessary to verify the present data as per library material available in the library. It took 30-40 days for verifying the data collection at IMCC library. Thus the library collection database was verified & corrected & the database from FoxPro 2.5 was migrated to MS-SQL systems.

Installation of information search module (USER OPAC)

This module was installed on 7 Nov 2003. Library Web OPAC is available on institutional intranet.

This allows a user to

* Browse the library collection by Author, Title.
* To reserve the items.
* To read the library notices.
* Facility to give Top 10 rating to the books studied by them. This allows library staff to-
* Display / Broadcast the library notices through web OPAC.
* To send reminders.

* To render computerised SDI service.

Installing of IMCC Library LAN

A separate LAN was installed in the IMCC library in Jan 2004 . Under this a library server & 4 Machines have been connected via the library LAN . The library LAN is connected to the institutional intranet , thus providing accessibility of library resources to all the campus including Faculty cabins.

Installation of circulation module

Before installing circulation module , one Bar code reader , one printer and digital Web camera were ordered . The following models were selected by discussing with in house technical expert.

ITEM	MODEL	QUANTITY
Barcode Reader	PSCQS1000Laser Scanner (Trigger less scanner with stand)	1
Digital Camera	Kodak Easy share Cx-6200 Digital camera	1
Printer	HP Laser 1010 printer	1

The printer, Barcode reader, Digital camera received on 5 Jan 2004, after testing the equipments are connected to library computers. In the meantime circulation module was installed. The students and faculty member details were entered in the respective master files.

Barcode label Pasting

The next step in library automation was pasting of barcode labels on each & every document, as well as on borrower's ticket also. The library staff members were deputed on the job of barcode label pasting.

Installation of library budget module

This module was comparatively small. The library has provided format for library budget as well as format for stock

Taking report was also provided to the software company.

Installation of cataloguing module

The library uses classified catalogue code for cataloging of documents; therefore format of classified catalogue entries was provided to the software company for developing cataloging module.

Installation of serials control module

The periodicals module apart from periodical master also includes Article index which is connected to the information search module(library web OPAC)and thus facilitates to render computerized SDI to the library users

Staff training (Jan 2004)

An advanced level training for using the use of library software was organised in the 2nd week of Jan 2004 for the library staff of IMCC by Priyamvad software and at the institutional level also, hands on training was organized for the library staff.

Human resource is the most important resource of any organization. In any academic library generally people are not ready to accept the technological changes , so it is the responsibility of the librarian to dicuess each and every step of computerisation with the library staff for getting their valuable cooperation , and give hand's on training to them.

Software configuration

Back End Database: Microsoft SQL server 7.0

Front End: Visual basic

Intranet application

Application Server : Tomcat 4.0

Application Development Language : Java Server Pages (JSP)

Conclusion

After the computerization of library functions and services, library is rendering the services more effectively. Our users are very happy by using the computerised services. All our efforts are directed towards improving the library services.

References

1 Faruqi, K K (2004), " Benefits of Library Automation ", Library and information studies in Cyber Age: Essays in honour of Professor J L Sardana. Authors Press, new Delhi ,

2 William, Saffady (1994) . Introduction to Automation . American Library Association , Chicago.

3 Dhanasegaran, G (2004) . "Computerisation of Library Operations : Recent Trends ", Organisation, Processing and Use of information in the Digital Era . ESS ESS publications, New Delhi,

4 Kocher, K N. (1997). Library Automation . APH Publishing corporation, New Delhi

5 Phadke , D N (1999) . In search of excellence. Multi-tech Publishing , Mumbai

6 Gaur, Ramesh (2003). Reengineering Library and Information Services. Allied Publishers, Mumbai

APPENDIX 1

FLOW CHART DIAGRAM SHOWING THE ROLE OF A LIBRARIAN AS A SUBJECT EXPERT AND AS A COORDINATOR IN THE DEVELOPMENT OF LIBRARY SOFTWARE SYSTEM

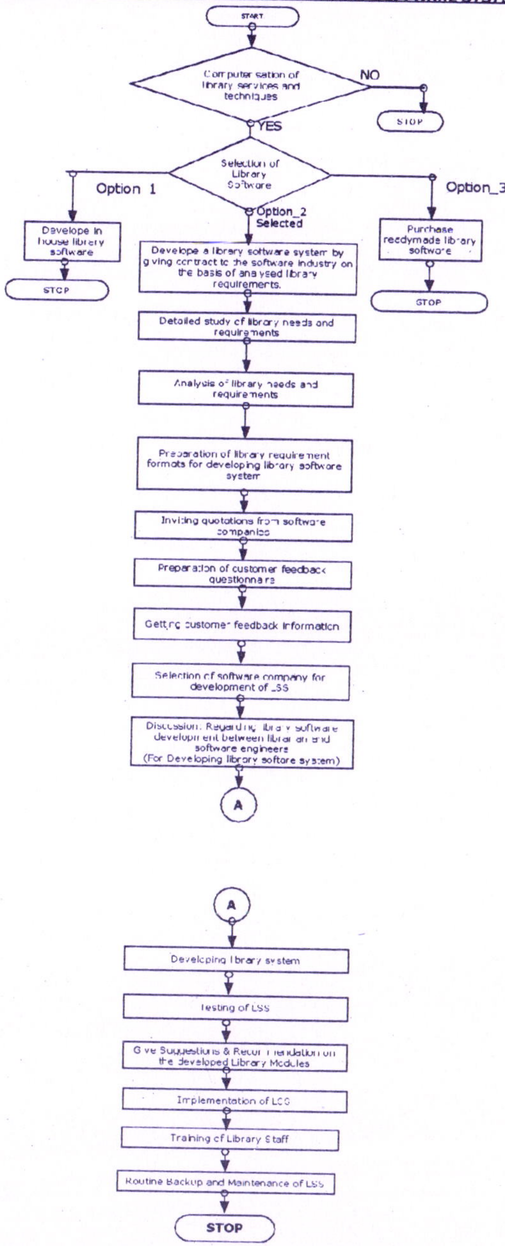

APPENDIX 2

Sample of Customer Feedback Form

1. Scope of the system.
2. Goals (Objectives) of the system.
3. Architecture of the system.
   * Front End
   * O.S.
   * Database
   * Implementation Details (Information module)
4. Software Development cost
   * With source code-
   * Without source code-

2. Hardware configuration (M/C configuration) Requirement.
3. Time Frame Involved.
4. Systems Maintenance & Support.
5. Training support.
6. Warranty.
7. Systems Reliability, Q.A.& Testing comments.

18

Knowledge Sharing: A Key for KM Success

Appasaheb Naika

Senior Executive (Asst. Librarian), Mahindra-British Telecom Ltd.,Oberoi Estate Gardens, Wing-1,Andheri-East, Mumbai-72,

Ramesh Paloti

Librarian,Bhavan's College Munshi Nagar, Andheri-West, Mumbai-58

ABSTRACT

Today's turbulent business environments, the conventional base of competitive strategy are increasingly being eroded. In such environment the ability to posses and disseminate knowledge is an essential prerequisite to success. This paper provides an understanding of an emerging paradigm of business where knowledge and knowledge sharing has become the singular basis not only for competitive success but also for corporate survival. It also describes how business organizations can use knowledge and knowledge sharing tools as strategic enabler to transform their operation paradigm. Beginning with discussion on the radical changes taking place in knowledge sharing (KS) platforms with the help of information technology and its vast application to business activities. It also depicts that even though most of the business organizations aware of this competitive strategy and its benefits there are still lot of hurdles to share the knowledge. To overcome these knowledge sharing (KS) barriers lot of researches and efforts have been on the screen to arise as successful organization. This paper basically concentrates on KS and its various kinds of platforms. We also emphasized on the KS tools, which are inseparable part of the KM.

1. Introduction

In a growing global economy managing knowledge effectively has become a source of competitive advantage. Companies are adopting integrated approaches to identify, manage, share and capitalize on the know-how, experience and intellectual capital of employees (Steyn, 2002; Todd, 1999; Katz, 1998; Martensson, 2000). During the past decade, many companies invested heavily in electronic knowledge management (KM) systems hoping to increase their ability to manage the vast array of knowledge hidden within the many nooks and crannies of organizational life (Eginton, 1998; Sbarcea, 1998). However, experienced users of electronic KM systems now realize that managing knowledge is a much more complicated process than previously recognized.

It's an open secrete that today's business organizations greatly depend upon maximizing resources, eliminating redundancy and automating process to meet the business goals. Further it's also clear that Knowledge Sharing [KS] has become as essential part of Knowledge Management [KM]. The effective use of knowledge is a key ingredient in all successful organizations, no matter what business they are doing, what services they may provide. Using knowledge correctly in an organization requires an understanding that the mere availability of simple, disconnected bits of information is not knowledge and can't adequately address these enterprise imperatives. While KM must focus on supporting the sharing of knowledge between individuals, this can't be done in isolation. Instead KM projects must recognize the importance of providing effective platforms for this dissemination of knowledge.

2. Why Knowledge sharing (KS)

The ultimate goal of KS is to distribute the right content to right people at right time. The system therefore must enable us quickly and effectively to find relevant information & expertise and that can aid into decision-making & problem solving. Hence, the tacit knowledge resides in the minds of individuals, in their skills, experiences, value judgments. Individuals are often the most difficult source to document because they feel that sharing what they know will make them expandable or that their knowledge on any given subject is what makes them unique. Another biggest challenge for KS is each time employees leave their job, they carry what they know with them. If they share tacit knowledge among employees it ensures that pertinent employees knowledge stay around long after the employees leave the company.

3. Platforms of KS

Knowledge sharing (KS) has become an essential part of knowledge management (KM). The ultimate goal of KS is to distribute the right content to the right people at right time. To accomplish this goal each and every organization are using many distributing channels, here we are mentioning some most popular platforms of KS, which are being widely used by many organizations.

3.1 Team Meetings

Meetings are the one of the best ways and means of KS, where the people come together formally in order to discuss about the problems, projects, experiences, opinions and take decisions. In such meetings people express their opinions, expertise and their knowledge about particular subject or topic, which enhances the knowledge of other participants and leads to knowledge sharing.

3.2 Video Screening Sessions

This is one of the most effective means of KS. It' s an act

of sharing a film / movie / television program. The program usually contains case studies, past experiences, best practices and methods etc to achieve the objectives, goals and meet the deadlines.

3.3 Training

Training sessions / training programs are the process of learning the skills, procedures, activities for a particular job or task. Training programs allow the trainees to interact with each other, interact with trainers/experts. In such programs trainer shares his knowledge with the trainees and trains them to do/lead particular job.

3.4 Workshops / Seminars / Conferences

Seminars/conferences allows the people to discuss their views. Usually the people at seminars have common work or interest. With the advancement of technology " video conferencing" a system that enables people in different parts of the world/region can meet by watching and listening to each other using video screens.

Apart from the above there are other ways through which people can share their knowledge – to name some a) Talks/Speech from experts, eminent personalities b) News Bulletins c) New events/happenings d) Open houses etc.

4. Knowledge Sharing Tools

Once knowledge shared properly by using effective platforms now its time to store this knowledge for future use, reuse and refinement. The tools mentioned here are widely used by one other organizations.

4.1 Enterprise Resource Planning (ERP)

The Enterprise Resource Planning facilitates the configurable information systems packages that integrate information and information based processes within and across functional areas in an organization. The ERP is one such program, which allows the effective deployment and mobilization of knowledge resources available across the organization.

4.2 Collaborative Tools

Collaborative Tools (groupware) are more popular within/outside the organization for people to share information and work together. These collaborative tools are computer based, which allows virtual on-line meeting and data sharing. These tools bring geographical dispersed teams together for virtual meetings across great distances. Groupware is an effective tool for knowledge dissemination because it allows people/employees to have access to all current as well as past information, regardless of their physical location. Collaborative tools give tremendous results in saving time and cost, faster and better decision making and improved communication flow across the organization.

4.2.2 Content Management

There are many tools that are designed for knowledge sharing and leveraging. Content Management is one such tool, which helps in creating, reviewing, approving and otherwise managing the complex, hyperlinked relationships of huge websites. By automating the publication process lot of problems can be solved.

4.2.3 Document Management Tools

These are used to create discrete document. These tools revolve around the ability for an author to build a single document or set of documents from a variety of source material. Policy documents are a classic case because they often have to be customized for different reasons.

4.2.4 Portals

Today's corporate portals have greatly been helping the companies to search, browse and personalization of information. Intranets in general and portals in particular started with the objective of giving employees access to any and all information they needed a self-help approach. It helps to publish all types of documents ranging from human resources policies to product manuals. Compared to conventional ways of storing text documents, documents published via the internet are accessible through a more user-friendly interface (a web browsers), they are easy to index and search, and different documents can be linked with just a click of the mouse.

It also allows for interaction using electronic forms. These forms can speed up tasks such as getting reimbursed for petty cash, ordering suppliers, signing up for a health care plan.

4.2.5 Data Warehousing

According to Bill Inmon, known as the father of data warehousing, a data warehouse is a subject-oriented, integrated, time-varient, nonvolatile collection of data in support of management decisions.

4.2.6 Web logs

Web logs have exploded in popularity over the last year. At their most simple form, a web log (also commonly known as 'blog'), is an online dairy created by one or more writers. They typify the new class of 'personal publishing' tools that some see as a 'disruptive' threat to existing publishing tools.

A web log provides a simple interface for writing a new entry, typically via an online form. This is published to the site, with standard page layout and formatting automatically added. What the reader sees is then an online diary, with the most recent posts first, and a archive of past writings.

There are now tens of thousands of web logs in existence, written by a wide range of people (including my web log column too), covering every possible topic. A quick search for KM will reveal dozens of web logs specifically addressing this subject.

From a KM at perspective, web logs harness the power of conversation narrative to convey messages in a very honest and powerful way. With web logs being written in a first-person format, the voice of the author comes through clearly, thereby supporting the message with the reputation of the author.

As such individuals, communities and companies to share knowledge across traditional boundaries are increasingly using web logs.

6.1.7 K-Logs

Web logs become particularly interesting when they are used within an organization. Where they are known as 'knowledge logs' or 'k-logs'. This has been an approach evangelized primarily by John Robb. The proponents of this approach see k-logs as a way of breaking down the barriers within the organization and facilitating a more efficient flow of information and knowledge for Ex:- Key individuals with a knowledge and respect can use web logs to record progress on strategic projects or issues. By building on the reputation of the writer, web logs harness recognized benefits of 'story telling' techniques.

Web logs can also be used by project teams to both communicate to the wider organization and to keep track of who is doing what within the team. In this way, the web log acts as wise for the projects and an archive of past decisions.

4.2.8 WIKIS

Wikis are a surprising new approach to publishing on line information. They are essential an ultra light weight content management system., developed primarily in the open source world. A wikis impose no controls over who can create or edit pages. Making it very simple to update content supports the ongoing growth of content and not imposing any restrictions encourages multiple people to add content to a single page.

It is this easy of editing and natural support for collaborative work which makes wikis an ideal tool for communities of practice or team level knowledge sharing.

Knowledge sharing a key to success

KS a Key to Success

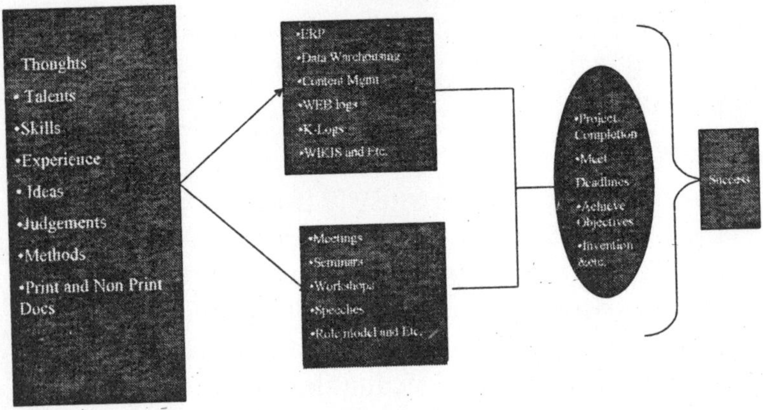

Fig. 1.

5. Barriers to KS

5.1 Belief in the concept " Knowledge is Power"

Of course "Knowledge is Power" forever, but today's enterprise, which believes and encourages much teamwork, collective knowledge and relay research rather than individual, solo researches. It is only a handful of people who have knowledge for which they can hold their peers for rewards. It might be the owner manager of a company not wanting to have trade secrets, it may be a particular specialist who has been in the organization many years and built up his/her own unique way of achieving success.

5.2 Don't advice me attitude

This is more common in people. People think that they know everything and feel pride in not having to seek advice from others and in wanting to discover new ways for themselves.

5.3 Non awareness of importance of knowledge

An individual may have knowledge used in one situation but be unaware that other people at other times and places might face similar situations and problems.

5.4 I can't trust you

Sometimes lack of faith in others also becomes a barrier to share the knowledge. Some people feel that if they share some of their knowledge others may use it out of context, may mis-apply or pass it off as their own without giving acknowledgement or recognition to them as the source.

5.5 I don't have time

This is the major reason given by most of the organizations, as time is barrier to knowledge sharing. There is lot of competition, there is pressure on productivity on deadlines, and it's a general rule to collar you for the next task. Under such circumstances how can you possibly find time to add your lessons learnt to the knowledge database or have a knowledge sharing session with your colleagues.

Other barriers cited by experts include functional silos, individualism, poor means of knowledge capture, inadequate technology, internal competition, top-down decision making and so on.

KS Barriers Way to Failures

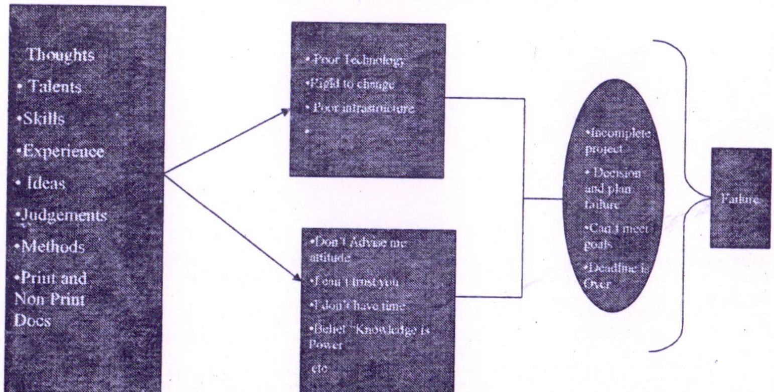

Fig. 2

6. How to overcome these barriers

6.1 Change organization culture

Changing culture is not easy as we say. Culture can be changed over the time. Culture of an organization has commonly held beliefs, attitudes, and values. The culture has the collective programming of the mind that distinguishes one group from another. And in other ways that also encompasses rituals, artifacts, and other trappings of the work environment. Using some of the activities can change such kind of cultures.

6.1.1 A culture audit

A culture audit is helpful in tracing out the distinguish between what is articulated as the desired culture and what is done by providing questionnaires, interviewing the people and team sessions a cross section will definitely help in understanding the culture of an organization.

It is also common that you may meet several subcultures that conflict with overarching goals. Here, you should clearly identify which values and behaviors conflict with better knowledge sharing and perhaps (more importantly) which people should be the target for change. In such cases challenge the improper behavior if you identify people hoarding knowledge unnecessarily.

6.1.2 Total involvement

Some of the best knowledge sharing cultures are where everybody (even novices & newcomers) believes that their knowledge is respected, valued and used to inform decision.

6.1.3 Use role models

Identify those people who are willing to share, whose behaviors are an example to others. Involve them with other groups.

6.1.4 Team building

Conduct organizational development sessions in that sessions allocate time to understand and improve internal processes, give behavioral training, the team building sessions should address the means of achieving successful or individual expertise.

6.1.5 Reward system

Align rewards and recognition to support appropriate behaviors. There should be reward system on team effectiveness rather only on seniority or individual expertise.

6.1.6 Change people

By consulting, by adopting knowledge shares, industrial psychologists and behavioral experts on board and develop a quality leadership in people that will enable all the other culture change techniques to achieve their aims.

6.2 Challenging through competition

Human beings are at the same time social co-operative beings and have a competition streak. We all like to do better than our peers and excel in something. Yet, in today's complex world, we need help from them to achieve our aims. In an organization lack of competition- both for individuals and teams – leads to complacency. But competition must be done in a healthy manner.

6.2.1 Bench marking

Continuous comparison of internal processes, methodologies and functions with other organizations and potential companies. Encourage the people to strive for improvements through learning from each other.

6.2.2 Healthy Competitions

There should be a continuous healthy competitions as competitions should not be against other people or teams, but setting and reaching goals, challenging targets or competition against external competitors.

6.3 *Commitment*

With commitment the organization will change its culture and develops competitive people. Organizations need to create a commitment to culture, to change, to challenge. to compete and co-operate. If, as is often the case, time pressure leads to poor knowledge sharing, then there must be a commitment to allow time for it to happen. There should be enough budgets for projects and resources.

7. Benefits of KS

7.1 *Expertise can be shared:*

KS makes the captured expertise available to all people serving in an organization uniformly. Thus organizations can leverage their knowledge and make it much more broadly and consistently available to their customers, partners and end-users.

7.2 *Turnover and job changes don't cripple the system:*

A KM is to capture knowledge and make it accessible to all service and support agents. Thus, knowledge no longer stays with those who hold or discover it; it becomes an organization asset available to all who need it. This addresses two essential problems; the challenge of making the job more effective and satisfying so that key people stay with the company; and it addresses the problem of how to keep the knowledge in the company if a key person does leave. Therefore it can reduce turnover and minimizing the impact when it does occur.

7.3 *Reduces Cycle time:*

KM reduces time to market for new markets

7.4 *Reduces costs:*

Km reduces the costs of repeated mistakes or re-inventing the wheel

7.5 More efficient use / reuse of Knowledge assets:

KM organizes Knowledge in a form that allows it to be used and reused.

7.6 Enhances functional effectiveness:

Reduced response time to customers.

7.7 Increases Value of existing products and services:

KM initiatives allow to knowledge to be used to improve existing products and services to significantly differentiate on offering from competition.

7.8 Creates new knowledge –intensive products, processes and services

By managing its products more effectively a company can save millions as well as generate more in licensing revenues.

8. Conclusion

One of the greatest challenges of the KM Practitioner is to find the ways of organizing the vast KM resources out there and deriving value form each resource. The findings of this paper demonstrate that there are various set of platforms to encourage people to share their insights, thoughts, which are valuable assets for companies. What draws people to share their knowledge in various organizations would be different, but ultimately matches the company's core values as well as the look and feel of the other organizational processes.

All organization should focus on supporting the knowledge sharing (KS) between individuals The KS tools can therefore seen as providing a foundation for knowledge management initiatives. Besides this different kind of valuable technologies like weblogs, wikis etc. can be used to support the KM goals.

References

1. Robertson, James. Intranets and Knowledge Sharing: KM column May 2004. Retrieved from http://www.steptwo.com.au on 20th July 2004; pp. 4-6
2. Liu, F.T. and Others. How to Implement Knowledge Management in your company: Competing in the knowledge based economy: Retrieved from http://www.ikma.org.sg/docs/How%20to%20Implement%20km% 20in%20your%20company%20R1%5B1%SD.12.pdf on 20th July 2004
3. Skyrme, David J. The 3Cs of Knowledge Sharing: Culture, Co-opetition and Commitment, Aug. 2002: retrieved from http://www.skyrme.com/updates/u64_f1.htm on July 2004; pp. 1-6
4. Pasquariella, Susan; Knowledge Management and KS : An Interactive Session. April 2003:Retrieved from http://www.unfpa.org/knowledgesharing/docs/km_ks_02_may_03.ppt . pp. 6,9 and 12
5. Bhosle, Hemali; " Knowledge Management" Paper presented atTracmail India Ltd; 24th April 2001 pp. 10,12 and 13
6. Appasaheb Naikal & Ramesh Paloti; Role of libraries in knowledge management; IASLIC national conference D Dun 2003pp.
7. Bukowitz, Wendi; & Williams, Ruth; The knowledge management field books; Pearson Education Limited., 1999 pp.
8. Kimball, R & Ross, Margy; The data warehouse toolkit; John Wiley & Sons, Inc. New York, 2004 pp. 7-14
9. Chua, Alton; A framework for implementing knowledge management projects; Information and knowledge management society, 22 Aug. 2003: Retrieved from http://www.ikms.org.sg/docs/altonchua.pdf on 20th July 2004.
10. Davenport, T.H., & Prusak, L. (1998) *Working knowledge: how organizations manage what they know.* Boston, Massachusetts: Harvard Business School Press.

19

Managing Change in the New Knowledge Economy with Redefined Competency - With Special Reference to Academic Libraries

Saramma Shaji
Librarian
Ethiraj College for Women

ABSTRACT

The knowledge economy is a new fangled concept that has come into view worldwide in recent years. As a sub-discipline of the knowledge economy, knowledge management is a wholly new concept and the method of management. It alters intellectual assets of workers and staff members in the organization into elevated productive forces-competition supremacy and new worth. Knowledge management requires linkage of information with information, information with activities and information with man–so as to realize the sharing of knowledge including tacit and explicit knowledge.

The information rumble is plunging exultantly towards the 21st century, with the libraries and information centre finding them engrossed, ahead of times in the frantic rapidity and surrounded by the technological innovations. The future is well defined with the librarians taking up a role that of a knowledge manager. The paper discusses the need for a redefined competency in user education information technology and knowledge management.

Introduction

"If you want to innovate, to change an enterprise or society it takes people's will to do what's not expected"[1]

The academic libraries have a considerable part to play in the verve of the universities. They have been looked upon as a vital factor contributing to research and academic studies. Physically they have often been sited in the centre of the campus and echoed as the heart of the university. The have also been a much valued source for other parts of society. Loud and sonorous is the bang of technology, paving way to embed artificial hearts and influence the human genes. What implants would reinstate the prospective academic library is a matter of great conjecture.

Events within and outside higher education are altering[2]. Development in computers, microelectronics, and communication technologies has primarily changed the library and information milieu. Gone are the days of stand-alone libraries in which a library was judged less by the superiority of its resources and services than by the number of documents it had available. Traditional libraries were dominated by print publications and the access mechanisms were also by and large manual. There has been a paradigm shift from stand-alone libraries to library and information networks, available via the Internet.

The knowledge workers would be the most sought after professionals. Who would be the new breed of knowledge workers, holding the reins of the knowledge of the universe? There is no doubt that they would be the information specialists-the librarians. Through the years they have developed a knowledge and methodology in collection management, quality assessment and retrieval that are decisive whether we are dealing with printed or digital information

Even though students, teachers researchers veer in a digital world with fast t access to the core body of the knowledge form their personal computer, they still would visit the library. Why? Because the library is committed to solve their information needs and personal communication would be the best way.

The state of affairs demands an amalgam or multifunctional library, in years, to come. For all these reasons, the library of the future will need to heighten on core competency in user education, information technology and knowledge management

User Education

"It is easier to act yourself into a new way of thinking than to think yourself into a new way of acting" [3]

User education is an incessant process, which has to be performed for all user groups. To make sure that users are ready with accomplished methods of accessing, evaluating information from a range of sources and synthesizing the information into a stable whole, training could be organized around level of difficulty of information and or users educational background.

The central and essential roles for librarians as teachers cannot be over accentuate. Librarians' need to cuddle and extensive concept offer user education in which they see themselves are dynamically contributing to the educational programs of the organization.

The new paradigm of the teaching library, librarian as a teacher is one in which librarians actively finds users in a variety of settings. They need to provide instructions about information resources. Aiding them in acquiring skills in locating, evaluating and using a variety of methods of information would be expected from the future librarians. They would create almost a library without walls with presentations such as interactive networks, multimedia and compiler instructed instructions and at different locations such as labs workrooms and classroom.

There is an exemplar shift from a parent-child relationship between information provider and user to an adult-adult relationship[4]. While novel formats and mechanisms are being developed to deal with this rapidly changing environment the existing gap between the generation and utility of information is further broadened in the current situation.

The major aim of user education would be to strengthen the use of a range of library resources, which will ease academics to perk up their teaching and research. This will help students to learn more and achieve better results in their work. Content for library instruction will vary from general orientation on information resources to instruction in the intricacies of using, and even developing sophisticated electronic databases to assisting faculty in incorporating multimedia resources into their courses. The goal of user education should be to develop the quality of users research output and unsure life long learning.

Some Specific Components of user Education[5]

* The Librarian would have a broader role than the passive nature of reference desk service in which professionals wait for the user to determine he/she has a question and then to ask it.
* Library personnel would need to lend a hand to the faculty to search information relevant to their work using networked resources and through other latest methods in information.
* Librarians need to introduce new students, to the

complexities of university library facilities, some of whc come from school systems where there are generally no school librarians or well-established libraries.

* Librarians need to familiarize users who have little or no information seeking skills at all with a broad range of library resources in order to develop library skills
* Librarians need to educate users on how to find materials manually or electronically using on line public access catalogues and CD –ROMs

Traditionally, librarians instructed the end-users in the use of print publications, but equilibrium between print and digital documents will be an indispensable norm in the near future. In this context, training and refraining the end-users in the use of IT-based resources and services, such as e-mail, fttp, telnet www, mailing lists.

Information Technology

"For more than 500 years, the bulk of human knowledge and information has been stored as paper documents...Paper will be with us indefinitely, but its importance as a means of finding, preserving and distributing information is already diminishing"[6]

Driven by computers, satellites laser beams and an optic fiber, the information rumble is plunging exultantly towards the 21st century. The stage has come when traditional type of library is fast becoming obsolete and meaningless, incompetent of managing mass of knowledge. Changing technologies and formats are also recasting the roles of librarians who collect, organize and conserve information resources.

Electronic collections will necessitate new procedures for selecting and cataloguing, and librarians will confront critical new preservation and archiving challenges. Some everyday jobs associated with print publications will disappear, allowing more time to be forwarded to the instructional aspects of the librarians' changing role.

The need of the hour is creation of online library catalogs and the automation of circulation and technical services. The scholarly materials have moved beyond reference databases and catalog into full text journals and e-books. The combination of librarianship and IT knowledge gives greater insight potential areas of development than mere computer knowledge.

Online Information Resource.[7]

Electronic Books become an interactive notebook with hyperlinks to the text and to electronic sources elsewhere on the Internet, the feature, unfeasible to execute in a printed version. The e-book can be incessantly updated. Electronic publishing will become commonplace at many places as faculty and researchers who sere on editorial boards seek ways to shift existing journals into this format while others to seek to establish new and competitive electronic publications.

Online Library for Distance Education Students[8]

The amalgamation of new types of educational technologies allows supple learning, augmented potential for interaction and access to a wide clientele and the global market. The expansion of distance education worldwide is amazing as technological development, globalization, bring changes to the educational environment that alter the traditional educational system and structure. Involvement is building information literacy skills are one important role even in the online environment, including building information literacy skills into the teaching material at the design stage.

Librarians can contribute enthusiastically by providing distance learners with various forms of information literacy instruction for effectual use of library and information resources and services and ensure that students are made aware of their significant role and importance to their learning.

The Era of Digital Libraries

The most precious contribution of information technology is the birth of digital libraries.

What is a Digital Library?

Digital library is commonly viewed as an electronic throughput replacing conventional archival and print media by electronic version. It is a comprehensive logic of greater information exchange and value added professional elevations. It is a collection of all kinds that are indexed efficiently. It comprises of formal/ informal communications text/image/.video repositories across languages and culture. A digital library comprises of widely distributed resources, maintained autonomously by different organizations having no adherence to uniform interface.[9]

Fundamentals of Digital Libraries

* A local computer based library system
* Need to procure sufficient PC's having Local area networked connections
* Capability to provide e-mail services, access to servers, and to distant databases etc.
* Facility of Internet Browsing
* Co-coordinated system functions to administer the entry and to retrieve data.

Digital Library Features[10]

* The digital library facilitates access to very large information collections
* Provides access to primary information
* Supports multimedia information
* Network accessibility
* user friendly interface
* hyper media and hypertext features

* support traditional system
* integrate personal, group, enterprise public digital libraries.

World Wide Web a promise or a pitfall? -Issues of Concern

Libraries provide us with a clear example of both the promise and the pitfalls of technology, the problems solved, and the problem created. The incorrect impression among al too many political and academic leaders that all someone has to do are search the web for any information one needs. A vast amount of information is indeed; available on the web today, but it is not a coherent collection of information.[11]

The amount of intellectual, scholarly and aesthetic information available on the web is truly nominal when evaluated with what is available in a good library.

The web is not catalogued, no one has an idea what is there, or how this information fits into a larger classification of knowledge.

The non existence of copyrighted material on the web also portrays a major inadequacy. Most of the materials that is past and that precedes copyright haven't been digitized and there are no methodical efforts going on to address this.

Some individual libraries have programs to digitize some of this material and include it in their own collections; these efforts represent a duplicative and non-comprehensive approach.

[12]Web lacks standards and methods to authorize or authenticate information. There is no librarian making informed decisions about the quality or appropriateness of the information and then adding this to a logical collection. With the web, everything is equally valid (or not) and there are no filters. However, the web is an outstanding example of the power of digital technology to provide widespread access to information.

Libraries would need to be part of the fabric of the new electronic infrastructure that is emerging. Currently, scholars trying to thoroughly research an area have to a library to the traditional search process and then do an electronic search of the web and other electronic resources.

This also involves that these people doing this searching have the aptitude to distinguish the quality, authenticity and validity of the information that they find on the web. Of greatest concern, is that a student might go just to the Web, either assuming that the information available there is absolute and accurate, or assuming that the Web alone provides an ample search.

There is a lot of reason to believe that students today and in the future will fall into this catch, because their favored method of working is to do everything online. In an ideal world, an appropriate professional needs a search engine that concentrates exclusively on Websites, data sets, video clips and other source material deemed to have academic value. These materials need to be collected and brought together, though the use of a common interface.

The hundreds of thousands of websites that presently feed our current search engines need to be filtered, identifying those that have legitimate valued and including them for preservation in much the same way that a traditional library collection is assembled

A sophisticated search engine would provide complex Boolean logic and search algorithms that are the equivalent of modern library search engines. Over the long term this process should develop a collection with the same degree of reasonable completeness associated with a good library.

Knowledge Management

T.S Eliot wrote years before in the poem Rock

Where is the Life we have lost in living?

Where is the wisdom we have lost in knowledge?

Where is the knowledge we have lost in information?

Data, Information knowledge-Strategies within Knowledge Management

Data are simple, discrete, facts and figures, such as names, characteristics, and amounts. Information is a bit more complex, for it organizes data for a meaningful purpose. Data might be a table of circulation statistics, but once those statistics are arranged, charted, annotated, or organized in a meaningful way to describe say trends in library use, you have information.

A progression towards knowledge management[13]

As we go down the memory lane "collection development" was the most important word in any library. The librarian was busy in just building up the collection. That era was called as the collection development era, the post sputnik era way back in the year 1950 to 1975. This era saw the libraries spending time in acquiring materials to build the collections as fast as possible.

Collection development to collection management

The period between 1975 and 2000 saw a sea change in the functions of the library. This period saw the IT revolution, soaring prices of journals, less flow of money, as a result of which the libraries started to think management over development.

Collection management to knowledge management –A paradigm shift

Collection management had to be comprehensive to cover new forms and arrangement of information resources in the digital age. A collection, while still crucially significant to a research library, is too stagnant and too inadequate a concept to fully describe the range of information resources now offered to users. As we all know by now, digital information resources accessible to our users may or may not be actually possessed by or housed in our libraries. In a new-fangled information universe characterized by numerous and altering formats and by networked access, does the word "collection" really express what research librarians do today? Are the databases and electronic texts we lease and the Internet sites we link to really our "collections"? And beyond digital surrogates for print formats –online reference tools, full text electronic articles, and e-books – do World Wide Web sites, preprint archives, learning objects, and the burgeoning electronic texts we rent and the Internet sites we connect to really our "collections"? These changes made the way to stagger on to a new concept of knowledge management.

What Is Knowledge Management?

In recent years, a new phrase - knowledge management - has entered the lexicon[14]. According to the experts in this field knowledge management is the process of transforming information and intellectual assets into enduring value. It connects people with the knowledge that they need to take action, when they need it. In the corporate sector, managing knowledge is considered key to achieving breakthrough competitive advantage.

We all know by now, digital information resources offered by our libraries to our users may or may not be actually owned by or housed in our libraries. In a new information universe characterized by multiple and changing formats and by networked access, does the term "collection" really convey what research librarians do today? Our academic libraries have focused quite effectively on collecting, organizing and making explicit information/knowledge available. Knowledge management means managing two types of knowledge namely tacit and explicit.

Tacit knowledge is personal, or in some cases organizational, and includes skills, heuristics or rules of thumb, habits, culture, undocumented history, and ways of thinking. Tacit knowledge is present in a person or an organization, but it is not written down or documented, and it is often difficult to express or describe.

Explicit knowledge, on the other hand, is knowledge that has been explained, recorded, or documented an explicit knowledge artifact, for example a final report of a project, may embed knowledge in a document, but this is not really knowledge per se by many definitions, since knowledge only really happens "in the minds of knower."

Understanding the importance of expertise and tacit knowledge and understanding the personal, social, and dynamic nature of knowledge underlies many of the strategies of knowledge management.

The academic community has been collecting tacit information for years. It has been known as marginalia or annotation, it has taken the form of bookmarks (either physical or electronic), and it most recently has manifested itself in the form of hot-links that connect related Web sites. This tacit information is what one person argued was as valuable as the scribbling and notes that one once found on the backs of the physical cards one used in a library card catalog[15].

However, for the most part, these have been "tools" or "aids" that are created by the individual and this information is not systematized, and certainly not available to a broader community.

We have already encountered the challenges associated with determining whether linkages are authoritative and legitimate in scholarly inquiry, and unleashing all of these other types of tacit knowledge seems massive, unwieldy, and overwhelming.

Why would one even think of such absurdity? The answer lies in the potential increased productivity and innovation that might arise if this information were somehow integrated into the processes of scholarly inquiry.

Knowledge management in an academic setting must encompass the community of scholars in a given discipline and must be able to integrate publications, data sets, tools for manipulating such data, connections to databases of pictures and images, and much more

KNOWLEDGE OF THE UNIVERSE[16]

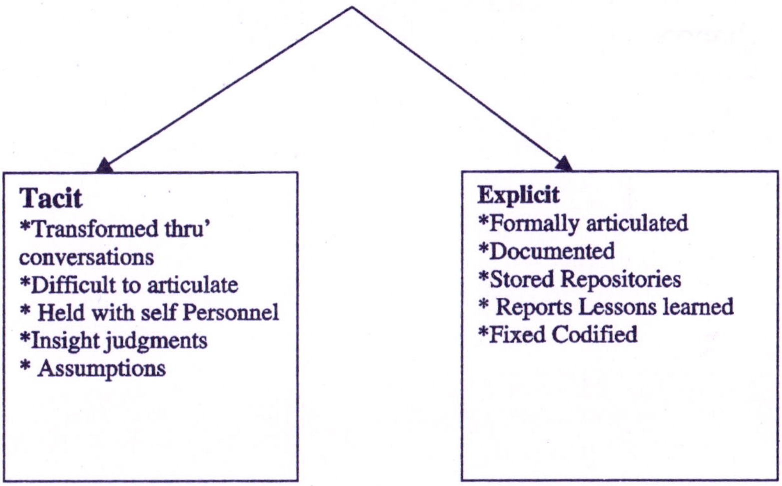

The academic librarians, whether we work in administration, collection management, reference, or technical services, must take on new roles as knowledge managers. In this, new role we will be

* [17]Knowledge management developers, working more closely with faculty and students to design, organize, and maintain a broader range of digital assets;
* Knowledge management integrators, having a more active role in the educational and research mission of university, integrating information resources and services in course and research projects;
* Knowledge management educators; teaching and training students and faculty information literacy and how to organize, preserve, and share their own information resources;

* Knowledge management researcher: applying library and information science and new digital technology to create new organizational (metadata), retrieval, and storage (preservation) options.

Conclusion: The need for a vision

Academic librarians' roles have been altered due to changes in the society, many new developments and transfiguring educational environment, introduced by information and communication technologies. They play imperative roles in the changing new environment. To carry on as an institution and to uphold its values of access to high-quality information, service, and preservation, the library must consider how to remain trusted and essential in a fast-evolving environment – while controlling costs.

Librarians need to team up closely not only as a profession (as they always have) but with partners in other areas of higher education and cognate fields such as computer science, information architecture, and instructional design. Their leadership must create a coherent environment for engaging with erudite information in all its forms.

While professional values have become largely institutionalized in the traditional library, this is not the case in the networked digital environment. For this reason it is crucial that librarians work to make their values explicit and realize them in a new environment.

References

1. Tariq Ashraf (2003). The Changing Role of .Information Professional Universtity News 41(19), 10-15p
2. Association of College and Research Libraries. (1998). ACRL guidelines for distance
3. learning library services. College & Research Libraries News, 59(8), 689-694.
4. Breivik, P.S.(1991) A signal for the need to restructure the learning process. NASSP Bulletin 75(535),1-7.

5. Bruce, C. (1997). The seven faces of information literacy. Adelaide: Aslib.

6. Carr, J.A. and Zeichner,K. (1987). Academic libraries and teacher education reform: the education ofprofessional teacher. In Libraries and the search for academic excellence. Proceedings of the Arden House Symposium. New York: Arden House.

7. Caspers, J. ; Fritts, J. and Gover, H. Beyond the rhetoric: a study of the impact of the ACRL guidelines for distance learning library services on selected distance learning library services on selected distance learning programs in higher education. Journal of Library Administration 31(3/4), 127 – 148.

8. Campbell, Jerry D. "The Case for Creating a Scholar's Portal to the Web: A White Paper." http://www.arl.org/newsltr/211/portal.html

9. LaBranche, Gary A. "Knowledge Management: The Killer App for the 21st Century." http://www.asaenet.org/sections/membership/article/1,2261,50864,00.html

10. Christina Vasanthi. (2001)The Changing Environment of Academic Lirbaries.: End User and Planning strategies for Libraries In India 4(1) Library Philosophy and Practice

11. Bertnes, Pal.(2000). A New Role for Academic Libraries in Scientific Information. Liber Germany

12. Hawkins, Brian.(2000).Libraries, Knowledge Management, and Higher Education in an Electronic Environment. Proceedings ALIA

13. Newton, Robert & Dixon, David. (1999) New Roles for Information Professionsals: User Education as a core professional competency within the new information Evironment 40(3) 151-160 Journal Of Education For Library and Information Science

14. Branin, Joseph.(2003) Knowledge Management in Academic Libraries. Journal of Academic Librarianship.

15. Blair, David C. (2002). "Knowledge Management: Hype, Hope, or Help?"

16. Journal of the American Society for Information Science and Technology.53(12): 1019-1028.

Footnotes

[1]Jean Reboud in The Discussion Series The Academic Library: Changing Roles of Information Professionals log on to http//www.cetus.org

2 Ralph Wolf in the Discussion Series The Academic Library : Changing Roles of Information Professionals log on to http// www.cetus.org

[2] Michael Pascale in the Discussion Series The Academic Library: changing roles of information professionals log on to http//www.cetus.org

[3] Christina Vasanthi(2001).The Changing Environment of Academic Libraries.: End User and Planning strategies for Libraries In India 4(1) Library Philosophy and Practice.

[4] Babakisi T. Fidzani(1995) User Education in Academic Libraries a study of Trends and Developments Conference Proceedings IFLA

[5] Bill gates in the Discussion Series Academic Library and the information professional: changing roles http//www.cetus.org

[6] Tariq Ashraf (2003). The Changing Role of .Information Professional University News 41(19), 10-15p

[7] Tariq Ashraf (2003). The Changing Role of .Information Professional University News 41(19), 10-15p

[8] Gopalakrishnan (2000). Digital Libraries-an overview. Hi-tech Library – Modern Reader. Ist Edition Tamil Nadu Library Association , Chennai pg 78-83

[9] Gopalakrishnan(2000). Digital Libraries-an overview. Hi-tech Library – Modern Reader. Ist Edition Tamil Nadu Library Association , Chennai pg 78-83

[10] Hawkins, Brian. (2000).Libraries, Knowledge Management, and Higher Education in an Electronic Environment. Proceedings ALIA

[11] Hawkins, Brian.(2000).Libraries, Knowledge Management, and Higher Education in an Electronic Environment. Proceedings ALIA

[12] Branin, Joseph.(2003) Knowledge Management in Academic Libraries. Journal of Academic Librarianship.

[13] Hawkins, Brian.(2000).Libraries, Knowledge Management, and Higher Education in an Electronic Environment. Proceedings ALIA

[14] Branin, Joseph.(2003) Knowledge Management in Academic Libraries. Journal of Academic Librarianship.

[15] Claire Mc Inerye JASIST 2002

[16] Branin, Joseph.(2003) Knowledge Management in Academic Libraries. Journal of Academic Librarianship.

20
Managing Knowledge for Knowledge Society: A Proving Ground for Digital Libraries

V. Ravi Nandhan
Project Assistant, NCSI

N. Girish Kumar
Library Trainees, JRD Tata Memorial Library

A.S. Gangadharesha
Indian Institute of Science, Bangalore-560 012

ABSTRACT

Information Explosion is the biggest problem faced by the end user in today's world. The abundant Information sources that lies in various forms each and everywhere has led to Information Management with newer techniques and a challenge for the Library Professionals. Knowledge Management would be of a much greater challenge in the Knowledge society. It is a chance to prove the potentiality of the Digital Libraries in managing Knowledge. This paper discusses how the knowledge is created, the types of knowledge and knowledge workers in the knowledge society. Later it tells about the digital library being a suitable solution for managing knowledge. Also the ongoing projects to digitize explicit knowledge are discussed.

1. Introduction

It has taken decades to arrive at the information and knowledge from the agriculture society. The fast development of the Information and Communication Technologies (ICT) has brought change in the whole community. New innovations have changed the work environment and the way of living in this society. Knowledge society provides great opportunity for employment with new technologies for education and training and easier access to public services. People in knowledge society will be knowledge workers rather than skilled or semi skilled. Knowledge workers have to be aware of the latest trends and technologies in the concerned areas, these workers need to have overall understanding of the entire process of the organization the active involvement.

ICT has touched all the fields directly or indirectly in today's world. We are able to enjoy the facilities that are available in most of the fields, which were once a tedious job, but now they are as a move click. Few of the examples where we are forming as a knowledge society in India are E-Governance: Almost all the states in India are planning to move to E-governance, wide spread use of Telecommunication i.e. mobile phone, EduSat programme, Smart cards etc.

1. What is Knowledge?

The Study of knowledge management should begin with the study of knowledge itself. Knowledge is the awareness of what one knows through study, reasoning express or association, or through various other types of learning. It is "acquaintance with or understanding of a science, art or technique"[5]. The oxford English Dictionary presents the word "Knowledge"[6] as meaning, "acknowledging... recognizing... inquiring... being aware... understanding... cognizance... intelligence...information acquired through study, and learning".

2. Forms of Knowledge:

Knowledge is created in the human brain, experience and comprise of ideas. When proceed and applied it becomes reusable knowledge. Knowledge can be broadly divided in to two forms.

2.1 Tacit Knowledge

Tacit knowledge is knowledge that an individual is unable to articulate and thereby convert into information. Tacit knowledge is more useful to an organizational system if it can be transferred to others so they too can use it.

2.2 Explicit Knowledge

Explicit knowledge that individuals are able to express fairly easily using languages or other forms of communication.

3. Knowledge Management:

Knowledge Management is not just like a Data Management and Information Management. Organizational Knowledge management has been characterized as consisting of three overlapping process; knowledge *creation*, knowledge *codification* and knowledge *application*. Knowledge creation refers to the development of new knowledge through the inter play of tacit and explicit knowledge at different ontological levels. Most knowledge creation occurs with in the content of social systems such as problem solving groups and project teams. Some new knowledge is explicated and formalised during the knowledge codification phase. Codification of complex knowledge frequently relies on information technology. Expert systems, decision support systems, document management systems, and relation database tools represents some of the technological solutions development primarily to support this phase of knowledge management. An important aspect of knowledge management is enhancing the organisation/institute knowledge application process. Knowledge to organizational value when it is used to produce effective performance. Creation, Codification and storage of new knowledge without its application lead to its under-utilization as a driver performance. Knowledge application is the phase in which existing knowledge is brought to bear on the problem at hand. Value of knowledge is created only when knowledge distributed throughout an organisation is located and transferred from its previous site and applied when it is needed[1].

Knowledge Management has many difficulties that is organizing and disseminating it to right users at right time. It is a challenge for the professional to put the knowledge in the right place (Database) and retrieve it easily when ever it is required. The most important part of knowledge management is the update of knowledge.

4. Why KM:

Effective knowledge management helps the entire community in different forms these are:

* Faster delivery of information to users.
* Effective organization of information/knowledge
* Sharing knowledge
* Special information services to users
* Ease of access across/different plat forms.

5. Knowledge Worker:

In the Knowledge society large number of knowledge workers will be available rather than skilled or semi skilled workers. Knowledge workers work with efficiency and usually in multilevel jobs. Library and Information Professionals will be best suitable for knowledge management as the concept of organization and retrieval of information is of high need in this field. Librarians have good skills in organizing and codifying information sources and making these accessible to users. Knowledge workers use their intellect to convert their ideas into products, services or processes. From a practical knowledge workers can be useful to consider two distinct types of knowledge workers, namely *core knowledge workers* and *non core knowledge workers.*

***Core knowledge** workers* one those in specific knowledge management roles. Examples include Librarians, Knowledge Managers, Information/Knowledge Officers, Content Managers and Knowledge Analysts. *Non core knowledge workers* include other than above workers/professionals.

6. What are the Technologies for KM?

KM is not the same data or information management, data and information retrieval can be important components of it. Data, text, images, schematics, video, audio, web pages, compound and multimedia documents can all be important ancillaries of KM. Consequently technology that can physically mange this wide variety of information media. Oracle's 9i Database Management System that appeared recently is a good example of the technology that can mange this wide variety of informative media that may be necessary for KM other database vendors like IBM and Informix, have similar technology.

We will need to access these wide varieties of media in a variety of places and through a variety of networks, storage systems, user platforms and interfaces. Consequently, we will need communication networks that can handle this variety. We need cheap high bandwidth communication channels, and a common multimedia communication protocol that will allow a wide Variety of systems to communicate with each other[3].

7. Digital Libraries for KM:

Digital Libraries concepts tell us that it has some means of digital object collection. There is no sensible definition for digital libraries. Digital libraries are still in mid-stage but rapidly developing to serve the user community in a better way. Digital libraries are in one type, a solution for the KM, provided that a digital library is built for serving the knowledge society and capable of handling and managing knowledge.

None of the digital libraries that exist today is a complete one. Today's digital libraries have to set of rule for the collection and they do not cross the limit as it may lead to confusion or it may be irrelevant, for example: a music library comprises move on music. A photo collection has only concerted images. Today's digital libraries mostly do not support multiform access too. In knowledge society the quality and the services offered by the services provider is expected in full, that is, a user may need an information source to be opened on a personal computer (eg: PDF or Word) and if he likes to carry it with him he may ask for the same source to be made compatible over his mobile phone or PDA for accessing with e-books or any other software that his device support. In such cover the library must be always ready to satisfy the needs of the patrons.

8. Moving Explicit Knowledge to Digital world:

The world is all set to move the explicit knowledge to the digital world and serve the Knowledge society with ease of access. Moving the explicit knowledge like books, thesis and other sources will enable a user to access the digital content from anywhere in the world. There are many ongoing projects, which are dedicated to move the knowledge to the digital world. A few of the examples are Internet archive, Project Gutenberg, Vidyanidhi, Million Books Project, ePrints@IISc, etc.

8.1. The Internet Archive

The Internet Archive is a public nonprofit organization that was founded to build an 'Internet library,' with the purpose of offering permanent access for researchers, historians, and scholars to historical collections that exist in digital format. Founded in 1996 and located in the Presidio of San Francisco, the Archive has been receiving data donations from Alexa Internet and others. In late 1999, the organization started to grow to include more well rounded collections. Now the Internet Archive includes texts, audio, moving images and software as well as archived web pages in our collections.

8.2. Project Gutenberg

Project Gutenberg (www.gutenberg.org) is the first and largest single collection of free electronic books, or eBooks. Michael Hart, founder of Project Gutenberg, invented eBooks in 1971 and continues to inspire the creation of eBooks and related technologies today. Project Gutenberg is the oldest producer of free electronic books (eBooks or etexts) on the Internet. Project Gutenberg collection of more than 15.000 eBooks was produced by hundreds of volunteers. Most of the Project Gutenberg eBooks are older literary works that are in the public domain in the United States. All may be freely downloaded and read, and redistributed for non-commercial use[9].

8.3. Vidyanidhi

Vidyanidhi (Meaning 'Treasure of Knowledge' in Sanskrit) (www.vidyanidhi.org.in) is India's premier Digital library initiative to facilitate the creation, archiving and accessing of doctoral theses. Vidyanidhi is an information infrastructure, a digital library, a portal of resources, tools and facilities for doctoral research in India. Vidyanidhi is envisioned to evolve as a national repository and a consortium for e-theses through participation and partnership with universities, academic institutions and other stakeholders. Vidyanidhi enhances access to Indian theses and enlarges the reach and audience for Indian doctoral research works.

Vidyanidhi began as a pilot project in the year 2000 with support from NISSAT, DSIR, Govt. of India and demonstrated the feasibility of e-Theses programme in India. With support from the Ford Foundation and also from Microsoft India, Vidyanidhi is evolving as a National Initiative. Vidyanidhi is a member of the Networked Digital Library of Theses and Dissertations (NDLTD), a global initiative with more than 170 members from different countries of the world. Vidyanidhi is also part of UNESCO (http://www.unesco.org/webworld/etd and http://etdguide.org) efforts in this direction. Unesco supports ETD initiatives worldwide. Vidyanidhi Visions are to evolve as a National repository and a collaborative consortium of participating universities and academic institutions and to evolve as an online resource and a technical mechanism for the creation, submission, archiving, and accessing of Indian theses[10].

8.4. Million Books Project (2001-2007):

The Million Books Project (MBP) aims to digitize at least one million books and offer them free-to-read on the Internet. In addition to providing the world's largest collection of e-books, the project will provide a rich test bed for many different areas of research and innovation. Project partners include government and academic institutions in India and China, academic libraries in the United States, and OCLC. Most of the scanning will be done in India and China. To date, three grants have been received from the National Science Foundation for equipment and planning. Use Internet Explorer to access the Million Book Project/Universal Library sites:

1. Million Book Project [The Universal Library, China site], available http://www.ulib.org.cn
2. Million Book Project [Digital Library of India], available http://www.dli.ernet.in
3. Million Book Project [The Universal Library, U.S. site], available http://www.ulib.org

8.4.1. Million Book Project in India

The mission is to create a portal for the Digital Library of India, which will foster creativity and free access to all human knowledge. As a first step in realizing this mission, it is proposed to create the Digital Library with a free-to-read, searchable collection of one million books, predominantly in Indian languages, available to everyone over the Internet. This portal will also become an aggregator of all the knowledge and digital contents created by other digital library initiatives in India. Very soon we expect that this portal would provide a gateway to Indian Digital Libraries in science, arts, culture, music, movies, traditional medicine, palm leaves and many more. The result will be a unique resource accessible to anyone in the world 24x7, without regard to socioeconomic background or nationality. Digital Library of India hosted by Indian Institute of Science, Carnegie Mellon University and Ernet (India) for the office of the Principal Scientific Advisor to the Government of India, Ministry of Communication and Technology and 21 participating centers.

Funding for the Million-Book Project is coming from multiple sources: The Office of the Principal Scientific Advisor to the Government of India is funding the project in the Indian Institute of Science. The Ministry of Communication and Information Technology (MCIT) is funding the project at various partner centers of the Digital Library of India. Various Centers have also pledged their local resources to make the Digital Library of India a reality. National Science Foundation is providing funding for Scanners and Software research and development.

8.5. ePrints@iisc:

ePrints@IISc repository collects, preserves and disseminates in digital format the research output created by the IISc research community. It enables the Institute community to deposit their preprints, postprints and other scholarly publications using a web interface, and organizes these publications for easy retrieval. While eprints@iisc can be accessed by anybody, submission of documents to this repository is limited to the IISc research community. ePrints@IISc repository is running on EPrints open archive software(www.eprints.org), a freely distributable archive system available from eprints.org. ePrints@IISc complies with the Open Archives Initiative (OAI) framework allowing publications to be easily indexed by web search engines and other indexing services. Other institutions are invited (and encouraged) to set up their own open archives for author self-archiving, using the freely-distributable eprints.org software used at this site[11].

Other that these there are so many universities and institutes across the world who is trying to digitize the Knowledge in their Institutions. Some of the examples are, Dspace, ACM Digital Library and Digital Library of IISc.

9. Conclusion

Managing Information in this information era is the challenge that is being faced in today's information world. Managing knowledge world is a much greater challenge in the knowledge society. Digital libraries can prove the capabilities to manage knowledge in the knowledge society by proper planning towards management of knowledge. Knowledge management tools and techniques promotes the use of knowledge in a much faster and easier way. The development of digital libraries helps managing knowledge in a easier way and enhance the use of knowledge as it is faster than any other means.

10. References

1. ALAVI (Maryama) and TIWANA(Amrit): Knowledge Integration in Virtual Teams: The potential role of KMS. Journal of the American Society for Information Science and Technology. Vol. 53(12), 2002, p.1029-1039.

2. BHATTACHARYA (Partha) and CHAUDHURY (Pravin kumar): Knowledge Management and it's untilisation: an overview. 2nd International CALIBER 2004. New Delhi. February 2004, p.591-599.

3. BLAIR (David C): Knowledge Management: Hype, Hop or Help? . Journal of the American Society for Information Science and Technology. Vol. 53(12), 2002, p.1019-1028.

4. Gopinath (M.V): Knowledge Management Principles. SRELS journal of Information Management. Vol.40 (2), 2003, p. 87-92.

5. Merriam Webster's Collegiate Dictionary. http://www..m-w.com/egi-bin/dictionary.

6. Oxford English Dictionary. http:// dictionary.oed.com.

7. Singh(D.K) and Sing(B.K). Knowledge Management and Librarianship. IASLIC Bulletin. Vol49 (2), 2004, p. 75-79.

8. SOUNDARA RAJAN (V): Librarian in the Knowledge Era. SRELS journal of Information Management. Vol.37(3), 2000, p. 157-164.

9. www.gutenberg.org

10. www.vidyanidhi.org.in

11. www.eprints.org

21

Digital Reference Services in the Virtual World

Gangadharesha A.S.
Tejaswini T
Surulinathi M.
Library Trainees, J. R. D. Tata Memorial Library

Ravinandhan, V.
Information Professional, National Centre for Science Information
Indian Institute of Science, Bangalore-12

Key words: Digital Reference Services, Virtual Communication Tools, and Information Services.

ABSTRACT

Due to the advent of Internet, information and communication technologies (ICTs) changed the mission and role of libraries and role of library professionals significantly. From the point of view of librarians and user community rate of change of technology and generation of information is breathtaking. Librarians are moving dramatically into different roles as new services are implemented. At present time 'virtual library', 'digital library' are considered as the ultimate flower of ICTs, If so, online information's services are considered as the beautiful future bud under digital libraries, because any libraries ultimate mission will be satisfaction of their patrons, by providing right information to right user at all time. In this digital world Digital Reference service (DRS) is also one of the products of ICTs which is metamorphosed product of traditional reference can be implemented in libraries. This article deals more on DRS and give an introduction to application of Virtual communication tools, technologies like E-mail, Mailing lists, News groups, Bulletin boards, Web forms, Library Web blocs, Instant Messaging, Chat or conferencing, Internet telephony, are discussed to provide digital reference services.

0. Introductions

Reference Services, since its inception in 1878 by Melwil Dewey has played a pivotal role in answering reference queries and providing factual information to the users. The service has been modified from time to suit the user needs; started as a bridge between reader and static library collections, it was broadened and included different types of reference services such as initiation of freshmen, ready reference, long range of reference or documentation, referral, CAS, and SDI. Traditional reference and information services have focused on providing access to information resources available in the library but online reference services or DRS expand that concept to include access to citations concerning resources in other places. Thus DRS is an expanded metamorphosed integrated approach of reference service in the digital environment.

With advent of Internet and its associated web technologies have influenced and changed the way libraries providing information services to their patrons and the way patrons choose to access information significantly. Due to this fast advancement of technology affected library system as a whole, meanwhile the nature of reference services has changed significantly not only in its mission of providing right information to right user but also it has added several new dimensions and opened new avenues to their task. In the present scenario reference librarians, while assisting users in the library, now have an additional set of remote users, who access the reference service online, who are more demanding? Due to technological penetration to remote areas library user community increased by understanding information demand form users a large number of web based reference services have appeared over the past few years while Commercial companies provide most of these services on the web, some libraries and library consortia have also introduced web based reference and information services, such personalized online services are termed as DRS. This paper discusses the concept of DRS, tools and technologies involved and the role of Digital reference in the present era.

1.Concept of Digital Reference Services

The terms "Virtual reference", "Digital reference", "E-reference", "Internet information services" "Live reference" and "real time reference" are used interchangeably to describe reference services that utilize computer and internet technology in some way. Digital reference is significantly influencing the delivery of high-quality library services. Virtual reference service or DRS (Digital Reference Service) are simply defined as the "provision of real time personnel assistance to the users via web based interactive software methods (may be chat reference, e-mail, web forms etc.) On demand". Digital reference, or "AskA", services are Internet-based question-and-answer services that connect users with experts and subject expertise. Digital reference services use the Internet to connect *people* with *people* who can answer questions and support the development of skills. OCLC defined DRS as "Using computer and communications technology to provide reference service to patrons anytime anywhere". Further it states that "types of digital reference include: 1. Asynchronous digital reference, such as e-mail and web form questions in which the patrons submits a question and the librarian responds at a later time. 2. Synchronous digital reference service such as chat and voice IP, in which the patrons and librarian communicate real time. (1).

2. Need For Digital Reference Services.

* To provide a variety of information to users for diverse information needs of instructional, research, learning and reference activities.
* Due to multidisciplinary aspects of almost all the subjects in the universe of knowledge, subjects concepts are interlinking with other subjects, due to this dynamic nature demands the user to communicate with experts for his/her information needs.
* To provide and maintain an appropriate collection of reference resources both print and collection.
* To educate users concerning about resources and research techniques in order to help the users to become information literate.
* To exploit the resources and technology to facilitate the patron needs of information as much as possible.
* To attract the user community.
* Change in information seeking behavior of user and they have not recognized that wanting is not the same as getting.
* Complex user groups and divergent needs.
* Complex technologies and technical information oddities and strengths of technological tools that makes any service global than local.
* Marketing of wares and services based on quality, core and concern of the customer.
* It is a challenging opportunity to reestablish our identity and enhance our role and status that we deserve.

3. Planning And Pre-Requisites For Digital Reference Services

* Physical service location: the service may be offer at library (central library if it is consortia based) that has a proximity to print and electronic resources.

* Virtual reference location i.e. the server space Internet service provider. Etc.
* Hardware and software requirements PC/Workstation, printer, scanner, mail client, web form, chat software, authentication software, video-conferencing package, and Internet telephony software with microphone for computer and additional video and audio equipment and associated furniture.
* Programming and web expertise i.e. web design database management etc.
* Quality control in offering the services i.e. web design, database management etc.
* Staff with skills to offer the service: digital reference librarian.

A digital reference transaction will usually include the following elements.

* The user.
* The interface (communication tools like web form, e-mail, chat, video)
* The electronic resources (Including electronic or CD-based resources, web resources local digitized material) as well as print resources.
* Information professionals.

4. Digital Communication Tools

Virtual communication tools are widely used in libraries communicating with users, and they provide an important channel for many information workers to communicate with their colleagues, the professionals and with other professionals over the network. Virtual communication tools are of two main types.

4.1. Asynchronous tools

That enables people to communicate at a time that suits

them. Individuals post a message that is held by the system. This message can be read and responded to as and when the recipient comes online. Asynchronous communications take place over time rather than at the same time.

Example: - E-mail, mailing lists, news groups, bulletin boards, web forms.

4.2. Synchronous Tools

That enable people to communicate when they log onto the same system at the same time i.e. they are immediate and live communications unlike with face-to-face communication, a transcript or record of the communication process is available in most systems. Example: - Instant messaging, chat or conferencing, Internet telephony, video conferencing etc.

4.1.1 E-Mail Reference Service

Many libraries offering e-mail as a reference services or as a support mechanism within information literacy programmes. User sends the library e-mail with a reference query the library professional may reply by e-mail, phone, fax, or letters etc. Turnaround times for answers typically range from 24-48 hours depending on individual library policy and question volume. Advantage of e-mail reference is that the users doesn't need to come into the library and can ask the question at a time which is convenient for them. One of the drawbacks is that e-mail is not immediate and immediacy is what expects in this digital world.

4.2.2. Mailing Lists

As well as sending mails to individuals is concerned, it is possible to send them to groups using mailing lists, which are also called discussion lists or list -servs. The process is managed by a hosting service that maintains a list of all the different discussion lists and the people who subscribe to them. It is run using a mail server, which is a piece of software that stores a mailing list of E-mail addresses to individuals.

Two common mail server programmes are LIST SERVER and MAIL BASE. Mail list can be used in a variety of ways and in general they provide a forum for a) Requests for factual information. b) Requests for advice and opinions or experience c) Information about new websites, products, and publications. d) List of new arrivals of books and journals to the library. e) Conference and meeting announcements. Examples like

* NCSI, L IS-Forum at http://ncsi.iisc.ernet.in/mailman/listinfo/lis-forum
* JISC mail at www.jiscmail.ac.uk and
* CILIP (Chartered Institute of Library and Information Professionals) at www.cilip.org.uk

4.2.2. *News Groups*

News groups or Usenet's are similar to discussion lists in that they provide an opportunity to share news with like minded people. A user or an individual will send a message to a central source, which then copies it to individuals and/or other news groups. In this way messages can be sent all around the world extremely quickly up-to-date information, provide access to huge audience and extensive range of news groups that meet both serious and frivolous interests of both user and information professionals.

4.2.3. *Bulletin Boards*

Many library and information services provide bulletin board within their websites as a means of enabling their users to discuss ideas and share information. They provide a facility for discussion under various topic headings and not in real time. They allow individuals to respond to topics or threads in the group, or to begin a new topic or threading by posting a comment or question. Any messages sent to a discussion group are permanently visible to everyone who has access to it.

4.2.4. Web forms

Increasingly, libraries are moving to web forms that individuals must fill in online to ask their question or to provide information. Web forms have a number of e-learning and library applications, common uses include: a) Reference services b) Administration of services such as mentoring programmes c) As a tool for obtaining information from participants on e-learning programmes. Web forms are often used as a means of providing reference service within a library or information unit. Examples of libraries with web forms for reference services include: 1. *Ask the librarian* offered by the Madden library at California State University. 2. *Ask us virtual reference service* offered by University of Michigan Library staff.

4.6.6 Library Web Blog

In simple terms, a blog is a web site, where you write stuff on an ongoing basis, up to date happenings in the field of library service, new services added to library. New stuff shows up at the top, so your visitors of the library can read what's new. Then they comment on it or link to it or email you. Since Blogger was launched, almost five years ago, blogs have reshaped the web, impacted politics, shaken up journalism, and enabled millions of people to have a voice and connect with others. And we're pretty sure the whole deal is just getting started. A blog is a personal diary. A daily pulpit. A collaborative space. A political soapbox. A breaking-news outlet. A collection of links. Your own private thoughts. Memos to the world. Your blog is whatever you want it to be. There are millions of them, in all shapes and sizes, and there are no real rules.

Librarians have had to learn how to do a lot with just a little in order to promote awareness of their programs and services. They have seized the opportunities to market libraries in the real world via traditional media: newspapers, corporate newsletters, radio, and TV. Many libraries produce brochures, pathfinders, and their own newsletters. So it is no surprise to see librarians stepping up to the plate and spreading the word online with blogs. Savvy librarians have identified blogs as another means to market libraries and their services.

Example: Library Weblogs at http://www.libdex.com/weblogs.html

2.3. 2.4. Synchronous Virtual Reference tools: -

1.1.1. Instant Messaging: - Instant messaging enables you to send and display a message on someone's screen in a matter of seconds. It will allow librarians to communicate in real time with users through a series of messages sent back and forth. For librarians and user community is concerned, this may sound like a nightmare scenario, although it does offer the opportunity to provide immediate access to help and support. Examples of instant messaging software include ICQ ('I Seek You') available from www.icq.com and AOL Instant messenger available from www.newaol.com/aim.

1.1.2. Chat or Conferencing: - Chatting online can be helpful for people with hearing of speaking impairments. Chat or conferencing software enables users and the information workers to hold a 'live' discussion by sending each other short written messages. Chat is a very popular means of communication over the Internet. As reference service is concerned chat is not a perfect medium because librarian cannot able to answer for many long queries, everything he/she has to type each and every word and letter, and another disadvantage is the difficulty to multitask during a chat reference session, this makes chat reference not only much slower than other means of traditional reference but also requires additional reference librarian staff during busy hours. Staff training plays a key role in making sure that staff is comfortable with short telegraphic messages and proficiency over language is most essential.

1.1.3. Internet Telephony: Synchronous communications now includes Internet telephony, which is the ability to make phone calls via the Internet. The advantage of Internet telephony is that it enables individuals to make long-distance phone calls through the computer and the Internet without paying expensive long-distance phone charges. It's more economic and can be implemented to serve the remote user (Foreigner) of the library, its can serve as a cheap platform between the user and librarian.

2. Reference and Information Services on the Web.

A number of reference and information services are now available on the web. These services are now available on the web. Dotcom companies, libraries and specialized institutions, offer these services. These services use the web only for communication between the user and the system/ answer provider, while the information service is provided by human expert. Here user needs to conduct a search for a reference query. Such services provide free access to various online reference services, and allow users either to select a specific source or conduct a search on a range of reference services. Some of the examples are: -

* Internet Public Library http://www.ipl.org (13)
* Info pleasehttp://www.infoplease.com (14)
* Britannica http://www.britannica.com (15)
* Bartleby Reference http://www.bartleby.com/ reference (16)
* Internet library for Librarians http:// www.itcompany.com/inforetriever/ (17)
* Media eater Reference desk http://www.mediaeater. com/easy-access/ref.html. (18)
* Reference desk http://www.referencedesk.org/ (19)
* Xrefer http://www.xrefer.com/ (20)
* RCLS DeskRef http://www.ansernet.rcls.org/ deskref/ (21)

* Digital Librarian: Reference http://www.digital-librarian.com/ref (22)
* Ask Me http://www.askme.com (23)
* Virtual Reference Desk http://www.vrd.org (24)
* Allexperts.com http://www.allexperts.com (25)
* British Colombia Virtual Reference Desk http://www.bcpl.gov.bc.ca/vrd (26)
* Ask Jeeves http://www.askjeeves.co.uk(27)
* http://www.libraryworld.co.uk (28)
* Infolibrarian.com http://www.infolibrarian.com (29)

While most of these web-based reference services are free, some others need to pay nominal fees.

Current Project on Digital Reference Services.

Some research projects aimed at providing reference and information services as part of the digital library services have begun. Some of the well-known examples are: -

Collaborative Digital Reference Service (CDRS)

(http://www.libraryspot.com/spotlight/cdrs.htm) (30)

This is the most prominent project launched by the library of congress and its partner libraries to fulfill the goal of providing professional reference service at anytime, anywhere. The CDRS is a library-to-library network for asking and answering reference questions.

Automatic Reference Librarians for the World Wide Web.

Etioni and Weld reported on the project 'Automatic Reference Librarians For the World Wide Web', a DLI-2 funded project at the University of Washington. The central objective of this project, according to them "is to create software agents that possess intelligence- a limited understanding of complex technical topics, but a very sophisticated understanding of how and where to find high-quality information on the World Wide Web" (8). In the project the automatic reference librarian program explores web directories to find searchable sites. Thus, each searchable site gets a wrapper containing some assigned topics that are used for matching the topics of user queries.

Virtual Reference Desk

The Virtual Information Desk (VRD) is a project sponsored by the United States Department of Education, dedicated to the advancement of digital reference and the successful creation and operation of human-mediated, Internet-based information services to user community.

Conclusion

Librarianship now called information management emerged as a profession only in the 19th century. As a profession we have espoused continuous change and progress in techniques, future vision, philosophy and outlook to cater to the expanding information needs of the society. Technological revolution brings new challenges opportunities, a new 'golden age' for professionals. We have to employ healthy marketing of our wares and services based on quality, core and concern of the customers. In the present digital world library with both print based and digital collections not is a complete one, without provision for personal assistance in the digital form. DRS holds enormous potential for revolutionizing the way users find and use reference services, by utilizing virtual communication tools to their online information services. Intact, the awareness of Internet and associated web technological development and relevant skills to handle them are becoming very important for all library professionals.

Virtual communication tools have helped to accelerate and facilitate opportunities for information exchange, sharing of ideas and support within the library and information activities in general and reference service in particular. Virtual communication tools offer new approaches to delivering library instruction, training programmes and also for professional communications. Modern Libraries are concerned they can't utilize all the above virtual communication tools for propagating and implementing digital reference services, hence the libraries can examine the possibilities of introducing the DRS by utilizing any above mentioned virtual reference tools. At the same time one should not fear that the new emerging technology based services will replace the traditional services completely rather these services are emerging as supplementary services to improve the information dissemination amongst the user community.

3. Reference

1. http://www.oclc.org/questionpoint/about/default.htm
2. Chowdhary, Gobinda G. "Digital libraries and reference services: present and future". Journal of documentation, 2002, 58(3), Pp 258-283.
3. Allan, Barbara. E learning and teaching in library and information services. Facet publishing, London; 2002.
4. Chowdhury, Gobinda G and Chowdhury, Sudatta. "Information sources and searching on the World Wide Web". Library Association publishing, 2001.
5. IFLA digital reference guidelines. http://www.ifla.org/VII/s36/pubs/drg03.htm
6. Murthy, T. A. V. and Vijaya, Kumar. "Virtual reference desk in University libraries of India: planning, management and evaluation". SIS-2005. 27-29 January 2005. India: Andhra University, Visakapatnam. Pp. 239-243.
7. Sloan, B (2001). "Electronic reference services: some suggested guidelines" Reference and users services quarterly. 38(1), 77-81, summer 1998.
8. Etioni, O. and Weld. "Digital libraries research". Available at http://www.cs.washington.edu/research/diglib.
9. Vijaya Kumar, Manju and Vijaya Kumar, J. K. "Digital reference service: Libraries online 24/7". SIS-2005. 27-29 January 2005. India: Andhra University, Visakapatnam. Pp 212-218.

10. Virtual Reference desk. Available at www.vrd.org/about.html
11. Walia, P. K. "Trends and issues in digital reference services". SIS-2005. 27-29 January 2005. India: Andhra University, Visakapatnam. Pp 219-224.
12. Sharma, Sumati. Ashok Kumar and Singh, Mohinder. "Digital reference service". Desidoc Bulletin of Information Technology. Vol. 24(6). Pp 11-18.
13. Internet Public Library http://www.ipl.org/ref
14. Info please (http://www.infoplease.com)
15. Britannica (http://www.britannica.com)
16. Bartleby Reference (http://www.bartleby.com/reference)
17. Internet library for Librarians (http://www.itcompany.com/inforetriever/).
18. Media eater Reference desk (http://www.mediaeater.com/ref.html).
19. Reference desk (http://www.referencedesk.org/)
20. Xrefer (http://www.xrefer.com/)
21. RCLS DeskRef (http://www.ansernet.rcls.org/deskref/)
22. Digital Librarian: Reference (http://www.digital-librarian.com/ref)
23. (http://www.eduref.org/)
24. Ask Me (http://www.askme.com)
25. Virtual Reference Desk (http://www.vrd.org)
26. Allexperts.com (http://www.allexperts.com)
27. British Colombia Virtual Reference Desk (http://www.bcpl.gov.bc.ca/VRD/subject_list.php)
28. Ask Jeeves (http://www.askjeeves.co.uk)
29. http://www.libraryworld.co.uk
30. Infolibrarian.com (http://www.infolibrarian.com)
31. http://www.libraryspot.com/spotlight/cdrs.htm

22

Problems and Perspectives of Knowledge Management in Libraries

G. Thamaraiselvi
Librarian, National Institute of Technology Tiruchirappalli- 620 015, Tamil Nadu

A. Kaliammal
Librarian (i/c), Bharathidasan University Tiruchirappalli – 620 024, Tamil Nadu.

KEYWORDS: Knowledge Management, KM, Information Technology, Internet, Knowledge innovation, human resource management.

ABSTRACT

The knowledge economy is a new concept that has appeared worldwide in recent years. As a sub-discipline of the knowledge economy, knowledge management is a completely new concept and method of management. It works for converting intellectual assets of workers and staff members in the organization into higher productive forces - competition power and new value. Knowledge management requires linkage of information with information, information with activities and information with man - so as to realize the sharing of knowledge. One of the aims of knowledge management in libraries is to promote the knowledge exchange among library staffs, strengthen innovation consciousness and abilities, and arise the library staffs' enthusiasm and abilities for learning, making the knowledge most efficiently applied to business activities of the library, and rebuilding the library into a learning organization. This paper first gives a brief definition of what is meant by "knowledge", then outlines some of the major problems associated with it, and gives an overview of a new approach to managing it. Also it explains about the concepts and tools of the knowledge management. This paper also discusses the main problems in Knowledge management and provides few solutions to overcome the problems and realizing the benefits of knowledge management.

1. Introduction

The knowledge economy is a new concept that has appeared worldwide in recent years. As a sub-discipline of the knowledge economy, knowledge management is a completely new concept and method of management. It works for converting intellectual assets of workers and staff members in the organization into higher productive forces - competition power and new value. Knowledge management requires linkage of information with information, information with activities and information with man - so as to realize the sharing of knowledge. The conventional functions of a library are to collect, process, disseminate, store and utilize document information to provide service for the society. Since knowledge has become the driving force for social development, the attention of the society to information and knowledge is rising and people's demands for information and knowledge are increasing step by step. This has provided a good environment for library development.

Clearly, the knowledge that supports an organization's processes and decision-making capability is an absolutely vital resource, but it is a resource that usually suffers from under management. This is a major cause of sub-optimal performance and is a source of risk. The two major reasons for this situation are:

* a poor understanding of what knowledge is;
* the lack of an approach to managing it to best advantage.

2. Definition of "knowledge" and knowledge management

"The management process of, ensuring that the organization's knowledge needs are met; and exploiting the organization's existing knowledge assets is known as Knowledge Management.

Knowledge management is the process of transforming information and intellectual assets into enduring value. It connects people with the knowledge that they need to take action, when they need it. In the corporate sector, managing knowledge is considered key to achieving breakthrough competitive advantage.

Knowledge management is not only about managing the knowledge assets but managing the processes that act upon the assets. These processes include: developing knowledge; preserving knowledge; using knowledge, and sharing knowledge.

Therefore, Knowledge management involves the identification and analysis of available and required knowledge assets and knowledge asset related processes, and the subsequent planning and control of actions to develop both the assets and the processes so as to fulfill the organizational objectives.

3. The major aspects of knowledge management:

The Major Aspects of Knowledge Management Are:

* the identification of knowledge needs and assets, knowledge problems and opportunities;
* the design, development and implementation of knowledge management strategies and solutions.
* Knowledge management is concerned with managing the underlying knowledge development cycle to:

* meet existing and emerging needs;
* develop new opportunities.

4. Concept of 'thinking organization' in knowledge management

The concept of the "Thinking Organization" embodies a vision of the standards that represent the best in knowledge management. The Thinking Organization:

* Promotes and supports thinking through the use of models, methods, ools and techniques that assist with group and individual thinking;
* Encourages and rewards thinking through its structure, processes and culture;
* Continually strives for the best in knowledge management.

The Thinking Organization operates a strategy for meeting its knowledge needs and exploiting its knowledge assets. Knowledge management is embedded in the organization as an ongoing management process.

5. Problems with knowledge

The major issue about knowledge is that it is:

* vital to the continued operation and development of organizations and their plans;
* expensive to acquire and valuable once you have acquired it;
* but intractable: difficult to understand, assess, obtain, retain, share and protect: difficult to manage.

Specific Characteristic Problems Associated With Knowledge:

* Knowledge bottleneck: a particular skill or expertise is in short supply causing a bottleneck that restricts the operations that compete for that supply;

* Corporate amnesia: organizations fail to retain knowledge acquired and lessons learned in the past. The people who had the knowledge leave and no retrievable record remains;
* Sub-optimal decision-making: the best knowledge available fails to be applied correctly leading to sub-optimal decision-making;
* Wasted resources: since the organization does not really know what knowledge resources it has it fails to capitalize on potential new initiatives.

In business terms:

* some knowledge resources are under-utilized or wasted completely;
* some knowledge resources are over-stretched;
* the organization is exposed to many kinds of risk;
* the growth and development of the organization is restricted.

Despite the vital nature and value of knowledge, its apparent intractability has meant that it has not, in the past, received the direct attention of management that it deserves and needs. Knowledge has usually been only indirectly managed through human resources and information technology initiatives.

6. The objective of knowledge management in libraries

The Objective of Knowledge Management in Libraries is to Promote Knowledge Innovation. Knowledge innovation is the core of the knowledge economy society. As bases for collection, processing, storage and distribution of knowledge and information, libraries represent an indispensable link in the scientific system chain, an important link in the knowledge innovation. Secondly, libraries take part in scientific research process directly. The library work is a component of knowledge innovation. Thirdly, libraries must pay attention to diffusion and conversion of knowledge. They act as bridges for turning the results of knowledge innovation into realistic productive forces. Knowledge management in libraries is to promote relationship in and between libraries, between library and user, to strengthen knowledge internetworking and to quicken knowledge flow. In the knowledge economy era, libraries will carry out researches on development and application of information resources, construction of virtual libraries, protection of intellectual property rights in the electronic era etc., thus founding the base for knowledge innovation.

7. Tools for knowledge management

Information Technology is a Tool for Knowledge Management in Libraries. Knowledge acquisition is the starting point of knowledge management in libraries. The application of information technologies enlarges the scope of knowledge acquisition, raises knowledge acquisition speed and reduces knowledge acquisition cost. It is impossible to accomplish such important tasks by using man's brains only in the modern society in which the knowledge changes with each passing day. It will be possible to link closely knowledge sources and knowledge workers by computer networks, thus constructing knowledge networks in libraries based on realization of single-point informatization.

The knowledge acquired must be accumulated and converged into knowledge warehouses of libraries. The priority of information technologies in the field of knowledge storage not only finds expression in quantity, but also in retrieval, sorting and security of the knowledge. It functions as a source and tool for knowledge innovation.

8. Contents of knowledge management in libraries

As a completely new method of management, knowledge management in libraries leaves much to be desired in its theoretical system. Knowledge management in libraries should include such respects as follows:

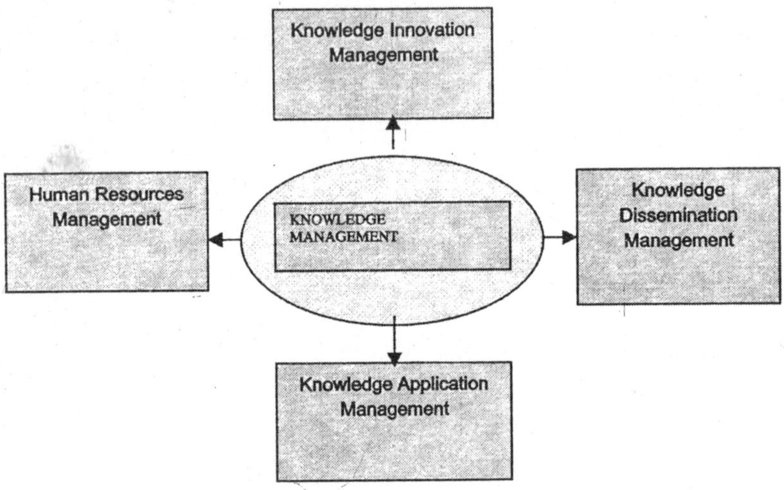

8.1. Knowledge innovation management

Knowledge innovation management in libraries refers to the management of the production, diffusion and transfer of knowledge as well as of the network systems constructed by related institutions and organizations. It includes three aspects, namely, theoretical innovation management of knowledge, technical innovation management and organizational innovation management.

8.2. Knowledge dissemination management

Knowledge dissemination is of equal importance as compared to knowledge innovation. Knowledge creators do not have much time and energy to look for knowledge users. Though there are a multitude of knowledge users, it is very difficult to acquire knowledge that already exists in the minds of knowledge creators as restricted by various objective and subjective conditions. Therefore, libraries may play the part of knowledge tosser; use diverse media and channels to disseminate various new knowledge services as follows:

1. Uninterruptedly strengthening the creation of libraries' own document resources and deepening the development of document information resources;
2. Continuously raising the quality of libraries' staffs and strengthening continuous engineering education of working staffs;
3. Giving full play to the special role of the expert system in knowledge dissemination;
4. Making a comprehensive utilization of all media to ensure security of operation of networks, and prevent online criminal activities and online dissemination of inappropriate information.

8.3. Knowledge application management in library and information services

The knowledge services based on high-speed information networks should be carried out by:

1. ***Setting up virtual libraries*** or information centers for enterprises, governments, public organizations and scientific research institutions. It is difficult for an enterprise or a social organization to put sufficient manpower, material and financial resources on information gathering, organizing and developing. It is also impossible and unnecessary to spend a large amount of funds on information resources for their own use. Libraries can create virtual libraries or information centers for these organs separately according to their respective information requirements by using abundant information resources on the high-speed information networks.
2. ***Setting up digitized knowledge*** services, presupposes: creating step by step the users-oriented information service systems such as information dissemination, information search and special supply of information;

quickening the creation of digitized libraries; studying the methods, means and techniques of information distribution and search with the Internet as the base and WEB technique as the core.

3. ***Digitizing libraries' resources***. The electronic libraries or digitized libraries are the technical modes and development trends of libraries in the knowledge economy era. The knowledge services of libraries in the future will start with creation of databases comprising electronic journals and books in different languages that have discipline features and can operate on high-speed information networks.

8.4. Human resources management in km

Human resources management takes it as its basic starting point to train high quality specialized talents and to revitalize the library undertaking. In practice, we should pay full attention to diversity and variation of library staffs' requirements, strengthened management of different library staffs by applying contingency management approach. Doing well in continuous engineering education of specialized staff, not only focus on the theory of library science and related disciplines, but also cover the latest technical knowledge.

9. Technologies for realizing knowledge management in libraries:

One of the aims of knowledge management in libraries is to promote the knowledge exchange among library staffs, strengthen innovation consciousness and abilities, arise the library staffs' enthusiasm and abilities for learning, making the knowledge most efficiently applied to business activities of the library, and rebuilding the library into a learning organization. Therefore, the main train of thought in realizing knowledge management of libraries is a rational design of the organizational structure and business procedures of libraries, and cultural fostering, as well as modernized information support, thus creating an environment and incentive mechanism for innovation, exchange, study and application of the knowledge.

9.1. Introducing the CKO system

The Chief Information Officer (CIO) is a conspicuously high management position that has emerged successively in the government departments and large organizations in Western countries since the 1980s. The Chief Knowledge Officer (CKO) is the highest-ranking person in charge of knowledge management, which has evolved from CIO along with the transition of information research management into knowledge management. The CKO system represents the latest development trends of the information management system of the organizations, and marks the transition of information management from the stage of information resources management to that of knowledge management.

9.2. Realizing seamless combination of library business management with knowledge management:

Knowledge management integrates itself with the whole process of knowledge exchange, sharing, innovation and application of the organization, and becomes the key driving force for the knowledge innovation, exchange and application of the organization. The implementation of knowledge management will inevitably give rise to organization of library business process. This reorganization will also be the process of further combination of library business management with knowledge management.

9.3. Rebuilding the library culture by using the theory of knowledge management

Knowledge management will inject new blood into the library culture. The main contents include: mutual trust, open exchange, studying, sharing and developing knowledge operation mechanism of libraries, enjoying the knowledge management process . In a word, to make full use of knowledge, it is necessary to foster a new type of library culture suitable to its requirement. This is high level requirement of realizing technology of knowledge management.

10. Current challenges and possible solutions

1. The rise of electronic information resources freely accessible through the Internet has disrupted the relatively efficient system in a number of ways.
2. There is no clear and defined role for libraries with regard to the selection, preservation and provision of access in regard to the digital resources accessible through the net. Additionally, students and faculty have a need to learn how to evaluate these new information resources, and it is far more difficult to do so on the Web than it has been in a traditional library.
3. With a traditional library, the very fact that a book or a journal was held by a library represented a conscious set of decisions about the validity of the information, and implied a filtering process that suggested a reasonable level of legitimacy. This is not true when one surfs the Web.
4. Another problem is that of scale, as some libraries, academic departments, and even individual scholars are creating their own collections of Web sites, selecting and describing network resources they find useful and credible. In some cases these resources are even added to centralized databases, but the combination of the growth of the web, and the lack of scalability of these individual, highly labor intensive approaches do not make such efforts a viable or affordable means of addressing this important challenge.
5. There is some hope on the horizon in dealing with some of these issues, as there are some newly emerging, shared (and hence leveraged) cataloging resources such as

OCLC's Cooperative Online Resource Catalogue (CORC) project, and the subject gateways being established by the ROADS project in the UK.

6. Currently, scholars trying to thoroughly research an area have to go to a library to do the traditional search process and then do an electronic search of the web and other electronic resources. This also implies that these people doing this searching have the ability to discern the quality, authenticity and validity of the information that they find on the web.

7. Of greatest concern, is that a student might go just to the Web, either assuming that the information available there is complete and accurate, or assuming that the Web alone provides an adequate search. There is plenty of reason to believe that students today and in the future will fall into this trap, because their preferred method of working is to do everything online.

8. Another problem with the Web today is the nature of the various search engines such as Yahoo! and Altavista. While such services offer far wider coverage than any traditional cataloging approach can possibly match, they do so with far less quality, filtering and a very different, often less powerful, level of description. A search using one of these engines may yield a half million or more hits. These search engines are also tainted by a bias in the selection process rooted in their commercial advertising relationships, rather than solely on the search parameters.

9. Most users don't use or know how to use their advanced features and the more sophisticated search algorithms embedded in these highly used applications. Consequently, they search virtually the entire web. In summary, in the current environment and with the current tools, we are left with incomplete information,

little if any organization, and rudimentary, inefficient and often inaccurate searching.

10. The current electronic environment, however, does offer the advantage of being able to provide an interesting set of "reference" services, such as those found on Amazon.com, offering reviews and related or recommended materials in association with the material for which the user was searching. These services are increasingly being perceived as a value to scholars, and academic libraries need to think through the relationship between their own service offerings and these other commercial services.

10.1. Knowledge management solutions and strategies

Knowledge management solutions and strategies encompass:

* **People aspects:** Training, development, recruitment, motivation, retention, organization, job design, cultural change and encouraging thinking and participation;
* **Process aspects:** Process innovation, re-engineering; both for radical and continuous improvement;
* **Technology Aspects:** Information and decision support systems, knowledge-based systems and data mining systems.

Knowledge management in an academic setting must encompass the community of scholars in a given discipline and must be able to integrate publications, data sets, tools for manipulating such data, connections to databases of pictures and images, and much more.

11. Conclusion

As information and knowledge has become an important productive factor for the modern economic system, the society will inevitably require intensified management of information and knowledge. How to manage knowledge will become an important subject facing libraries in the near future.

Knowledge management in libraries should be focused on effective research and development of knowledge, creation of knowledge bases, exchange and sharing of knowledge between library staffs including its users, training of library staff, speeding up explicit processing of the implicit knowledge and realizing of its sharing. Economic environment and information environment is changing quickly today. Since Knowledge management has become a powerful tool for promoting innovation and realizing reengineering the various walks of life, it occupies very outstanding position in the creation of the knowledge innovation systems of a country. Hence it is very essential to focus on Knowledge Management systems in Libraries by which the timely information service can be provided to the user society.

References

1. Wang Yunhua. Knowledge Economy and the Development of the Library, Library Work & Research. 1999(6), 17-19
2. Cao Yi. The Reorientation of Libraries in the Knowledge Economy Era, Library Work & Research, 1999(3), 24-26
3. Wang Delu. The Collection and Processing of Knowledge. February 4,199. http://www.bsti.ac.cn/bsti_kmchina/gei/048_001.htm
4. Sheng Xiaoping. Knowledge Management of Libraries in the 21st Century, Library Magazine, 1999 (8), 29-32
5. Chen Rui. Thoughts and Technologies of Knowledge Management, Information Knowledge in Libraries, 1999 (1), 10-13
6. Thomas H Davenport. The Future of Knowledge Management. http://www.cio.com/archive/010196-dovenpor-content.html
7. becker, A., Bernardi, A., Hinkelmann, K., Kühn, O., & Sintek, M. (1997). Towards a Well-Founded Technology for Organizational Memories, in B.R. Gaines, & R. Uthurusamy (Eds.), Artificial Intelligence in Knowledge Management, Papers from the 1997 AAAI Spring Symposium, Menlo Park, AAAI Press.
8. Benus, B. (1993). Organisational modelling and Knowledge Management, Department of Social Science Informatics, University of Amsterdam, Amsterdam.
9. Dieng, R., Corby, O., Giboin, A., & Ribière, M. (1998). Methods and

Tools for Corporate Knowledge Management. Proceedings of the 11th Banff Workshop on Knowledge Acquisition, Modelling and Management, KAW'98, Banff, Alberta, Canada.

10. Kaplan, Robert S.; Norton, David P. (1996). Balanced Scorecard: Translating Strategy into; Harvard Business School Press Book; Product Number: 6513.

11. Kingston, J.K.C., Lydiard T., & Griffith, A., (1997). Multi-Perspective Modelling of Air Campaign Planning; Proceedings of the International Joint Conference on Artificial Intelligence (IJCAI '97), Nagoya, Japan.

23

Knowledge Management: Strategies for Managing the Knowledge in the Digital Age

Mahesh G T
Assistant Librarian
Alliance Business Academy, Bangalore
(maheshkirangt@yahoo.co.in)

ABSTRACT

Today, Digital technology is unquestionably one of the major drivers of competitiveness in knowledge management .All civilizations are knowledge societies, they have used knowledge formally and informally in economic growth and in social development. In today's knowledge age intellect and creative, innovative and inventive ideas have been recognized and leveraged to become a primary source of advantage and wealth.

Essence of this emphasis on knowledge lies in the management of information. The Information Communication Technology (ICT) revolution at the end of 20th century has revamped the ways in which information can be created, harvested, assembled, combined, manipulated, enhanced and channeled in the digital manner. This has increased the efficiency and effectiveness of using knowledge for economic growth and development to the extent that it is becoming the leading factor for adding value and for wealth creation in the market economy. All aspects of human lives have been profoundly affected, be it agriculture, health or environment. Legal issues of protection of information of bio-diversity and genetic pool, intellectual property and indigenous knowledge are major concerns today. The provision of information resources and services is now readily available online via digital libraries furnished by a wide variety of information providers. Information is no longer just text and pictures, and is now available in a wide variety of multimedia formats. Digital libraries represent a new form of information technology in which content management, service delivery and social impact matter as much as technological advancement. In addition, for digital library researchers there is a need to transform information access to knowledge creation and management.

Taking a critical view of the mainstream characterization of KM technologies, this article provides a framework for configuring a firm's organizational and technical resources and capabilities to leverage its codified knowledge. And highlights the 'critical gaps' between technology inputs, related knowledge processes, and business performance outcomes. Drawing upon the above issues, the article develops pragmatic understanding for leveraging the power of disruptive technologies through disruptive business value propositions and customer value propositions embedded in organizational business processes and enterprise business models. And also it's an attempt to discuss a strategic roadmap for Knowledge Management and management of knowledge repositories leveraging on Digital Technologies. Whatever the information that I have discussed and mentioned here are based on the digital implications and in the digital context.

Introduction

Knowledge is like the sound of the tree that falls in the forest when no one is there, it doesn't exist unless people interact with it. Nurturing innovation and rewarding the sharing of ideas fertilizes seedling ideas. Setting up processes to highlight what's worthy and weed out useless undergrowth help grow healthy trees.

"Knowledge is information that changes something or somebody — either by becoming grounds for actions, or by making an individual (or an institution) capable of different or more effective action."

"Knowledge Management is the broad process of locating, organizing, transferring, and using the information and expertise within an organization. The overall knowledge management process is supported by four key enablers: leadership, culture, technology, and measurement."

Knowledge Management is a case of the blind men and the elephant. KM refers to one or more of these activities:

* creating and populating a repository of in-house knowledge
* measuring the dollar-value of chunks of knowledge
* facilitating the transfer of knowledge
* creating a knowledge sharing environment
* building a corporate culture focused on innovation and knowledge creation

Digital libraries can be an extremely effective method of extending the services of a traditional library by enabling activities such as access to materials outside the physical confines of the library. The true benefit of a digital library, however, comes not from the replication and enhancement of traditional library functions, but rather in the ability to make possible tasks that would not be possible outside the electronic environment, such as the hyper textual linking of related texts, full text searching of holdings, and the integration of knowledge management, data visualization, and geographic information tools with the texts in the digital library. One of the challenges in building this type of system is the ability to apply these sorts of tools in a scalable manner to a large number of documents tagged according to different levels of specificity, tagging conventions, and document type definitions (DTDs).

To address this challenge, one has to develop a generalizable toolset to manage XML and SGML documents of varying DTDs for the effective execution of the Digital Library. These tools extract structural and descriptive metadata from the chosen documents, deliver well formed document fragments on demand to a text display system, and can be extended with other modules that support the sort of advanced applications required to unlock the potential of a digital library.

What Is Knowledge Management?

"Knowledge Management caters to the critical issues of organizational adaptation, survival, and competence in face of increasingly discontinuous environmental change.... Essentially, it embodies organizational processes that seek synergistic combination of data and information processing capacity of information technologies, and the creative and innovative capacity of human beings."

Knowledge management as a business activity with two primary aspects:

* Treating the knowledge component of business activities as an explicit concern of business reflected in strategy, policy, and practice at all levels of the organization.
* Making a direct connection between an organization's intellectual assets — both explicit [recorded] and tacit [personal know-how] — and positive business results.(Rebecca O. Barclay. & Philip C. Murray,2004)

In practice, knowledge management often encompasses identifying and mapping intellectual assets within the organization, generating new knowledge for competitive advantage within the organization, making vast amounts of corporate information accessible, sharing of best practices, and technology that enables all of the above — including groupware and intranets.

Knowledge management overview

The goal of this paper is to provide an in-depth knowledge and overview of technologies that can be applied to knowledge management and to assess their actual or potential contribution to the basic processes of knowledge creation and sharing within organizations. The aim is to identify trends and new developments that seem to be significant and to relate them to technology research in the field, rather than to provide a comprehensive review of available products.

"Technologists never evangelize without a disclaimer: "Technology is just an enabler." True enough — and the disclaimer discloses part of the problem: Enabling what? One flaw in knowledge management is that it often neglects to ask what knowledge to manage and toward what end. Knowledge management activities are all over the map: Building databases, measuring intellectual capital, establishing corporate libraries, building intranets, sharing best practices, installing groupware, leading training programs, leading cultural change, fostering collaboration, creating virtual organizations — all of these are knowledge management, and every functional and staff leader can lay claim to it. (Tom Stewart,2002).

Knowledge management (see, for example, Davenport and Prusak) is the name given to the set of systematic and disciplined actions that an organization can take to obtain the greatest value from the knowledge available to it. "Knowledge" in this context includes both the experience and understanding of the people in the organization and the information artifacts, such as documents and reports, available within the organization and in the world outside. Effective knowledge management typically requires an appropriate combination of organizational, social, and managerial initiatives along with, in many cases, deployment of appropriate technology. It is the technology and its applicability that is the focus of this paper.

To structure the discussion of technologies, it is helpful to classify the technologies by reference to the notions of tacit and explicit knowledge introduced by Polanyi in the 1950s and used by Nonaka to formulate a theory of organizational learning that focuses on the conversion of knowledge between tacit and explicit forms. Tacit knowledge is what the knower knows, which is derived from experience and embodies beliefs and values. Tacit knowledge is actionable knowledge, and therefore the most valuable. Furthermore, tacit knowledge is the most important basis for the generation of new knowledge, that is, according to Nonaka: "the key to knowledge creation lies in the mobilization and conversion of tacit knowledge." Explicit knowledge is represented by some artifact, such as a document or a video, which has typically been created with the goal of communicating with another person. Both forms of knowledge are important for organizational effectiveness.

These ideas lead us to focus on the processes by which knowledge is transformed between its tacit and explicit forms, as shown in Figure 1. Organizational learning takes place as individuals participate in these processes, since by doing so their knowledge is shared, articulated, and made available to others. Creation of new knowledge takes place through the processes of combination and internalization. As shown in Figure 1, the processes by which knowledge is transformed within and between forms usable by people are

* ***Socialization (tacit to tacit):*** Socialization includes the shared formation and communication of tacit knowledge between people, e.g., in meetings. Knowledge sharing is often done without ever producing explicit knowledge and, to be most effective, should take place between people who have a common

culture and can work together effectively (see Davenport and Prusak, p.96). Thus tacit knowledge sharing is connected to ideas of communities and collaboration. A typical activity in which tacit knowledge sharing can take place is a team meeting during which experiences are described and discussed.

* *Externalization (tacit to explicit):* By its nature, tacit knowledge is difficult to convert into explicit knowledge. Through conceptualization, elicitation, and ultimately articulation, typically in collaboration with others, some proportion of a person's tacit knowledge may be captured in explicit form. Typical activities in which the conversion takes place are in dialog among team members, in responding to questions, or through the elicitation of stories.

* *Combination: (explicit to explicit):* Explicit knowledge can be shared in meetings, via documents, e-mails, etc., or through education and training. The use of technology to manage and search collections of explicit knowledge is well established. However, there is a further opportunity to foster knowledge creation, namely to enrich the collected information in some way, such as by reconfiguring it, so that it is more usable. An example is to use text classification to assign documents automatically to a subject schema. A typical activity here might be to put a document into a shared database.

* *Internalization (explicit to tacit):* In order to act on information, individuals have to understand and internalize it, which involves creating their own tacit knowledge. By reading documents, they can to some extent re-experience what others previously learned. By reading documents from many sources, they have the opportunity to create new knowledge by combining their existing tacit knowledge with the knowledge of others. However, this process is becoming more

challenging because individuals have to deal with ever-larger amounts of information.

Conversion of knowledge between tacit and explicit forms (Figure 1)

Tacit to TacitSocialization (Meetings and discussions)	Tacit to Explicit Externalization (dialog within team and discussion forum)
Explicit to TacitInternalization (from secondary sources)	Explicit to Explicit Combination (e-mail, meetings)

These processes do not occur in isolation, but work together in different combinations in typical business situations. For example, knowledge creation results from interaction of persons and tacit and explicit knowledge. Through interaction with others, tacit knowledge is externalized and shared. Although individuals, such as employees, for example, experience each of these processes from a knowledge management and therefore an organizational perspective, the greatest value occurs from their combination since, as already noted, new knowledge is thereby created, disseminated, and internalized by other employees who can therefore act on it and thus form new experiences and tacit knowledge that can in turn be shared with others and so on. Since all the processes of Figure 1 are important, it seems likely that knowledge management solutions should support all of them, although we must recognize that the balance between them in a particular organization will depend on the knowledge management strategy used.

Table 1 shows some examples of technologies that may be applied to facilitate the knowledge conversion processes of Figure 1. These technologies and others are discussed in this paper. The individual technologies are not in themselves knowledge management solutions. Instead, when brought to market they are typically embedded in a smaller number of solutions packages, each of which is designed to be adaptable to solve a range of business problems. Examples are portals, collaboration software, and distance learning software. Each of these can and does include several different technologies.

Examples of technologies (Digital Library) that can support or enhance the transformation of knowledge (Table 1)

Tacit to Tacit
Tacit to Explicit
E-meetings
Answering questions
Synchronous collaboration (chat)
Annotation
Explicit to Tacit
Explicit to Explicit
Visualization
Text search
Browsable video/audio of presentations
Document categorization
(Digital Library)

The approach to the technology of knowledge management in this paper emphasizes human knowledge. Sometimes in computer science "knowledge management" is interpreted to mean the acquisition and use of knowledge by computers, but that is not the meaning used here. In any case, automatic extraction of deep knowledge (i.e., in a form that captures the majority of the meaning) from documents is an elusive goal. Today the level of automatic extraction is deemed to be rather shallow because only a subset of the meaning, sometimes a very limited one, can be captured, ranging from recognition of entities such as proper names or noun phrases to automatic extraction of ontological relations of various kinds and there is no system that can reason (in the sense of deducing something new from what it already knows) over the extracted knowledge in a way that even approaches the capabilities of a human. As an example of the current state of the art in applications for extracting knowledge automatically shows a system for analyzing reports of appellate court decisions to find the precedents they may affect. Court opinions are analyzed to find language that refers to other cases that the opinion may modify or invalidate. For the foreseeable future, knowledge management in business will be about human knowledge in its various forms.

The use of Digital Library technology in knowledge management is not new, and considerable experience has been built up by the early pioneers. Even before the availability of solutions such as Lotus Notes on which many contemporary knowledge management solutions are based, companies were deploying intranets, such as EPRINET, based on early generations of networking and computer technology that improved access to knowledge "on line." Collaboration and knowledge sharing solutions also arose from the development of on-line conferencing and forums using mainframe computer technology. Today, of course, intranets and the Internet are ubiquitous, and we are rapidly approaching the situation where all the written information needed by a person to do his or her job is available on line.

The Objective of Knowledge Management in Libraries is to Promote Knowledge Innovation. Knowledge innovation is the core of the knowledge economy society. As bases for collection, processing, storage and distribution of knowledge and information, Digital Libraries represent an indispensable link in the scientific system chain, an important link in the knowledge innovation. Secondly, Digital Libraries take part in scientific research process directly. The library work is a component of knowledge innovation. Thirdly, libraries must pay attention to diffusion and conversion of knowledge. They act as bridges for turning the results of knowledge innovation into realistic productive forces. Knowledge management in libraries is to promote relationship in and between libraries, between library and user, to strengthen knowledge internetworking and to quicken knowledge flow. In the knowledge economy era, libraries will carry out researches on development and application of information resources, construction of virtual libraries, protection of intellectual property rights in the electronic era etc., thus founding the base for knowledge innovation

The management of explicit knowledge basically utilizes the primary resources

Repositories of explicit knowledge;

* Refineries for accumulating, refining, managing, and distributing that knowledge;
* Organization roles to execute and manage the refining process; and
* Information technologies to support those repositories and processes.

The Knowledge Repository

The design of a knowledge repository reflects the two basic components of knowledge as an object: *structure* and *content*. Knowledge structures provide the context for interpreting accumulated content. If the repository is conceived as a "knowledge platform", then many different views of the content may be derived from a particular repository structure. A high degree of viewing flexibility enables users to alter and combine views dynamically and interactively and to more easily apply the knowledge to new contexts and circumstances. At this point, knowledge-as-object becomes knowledge-as-process.

The basic structural element is the *knowledge unit*, a formally defined, atomic packet of knowledge content that can be labeled, indexed, stored, retrieved and manipulated. The format, size and content of knowledge units may vary depending on the type of explicit knowledge being stored and the context of their use. The repository structure also includes the schemes for linking and cross-referencing knowledge units. These links may represent conceptual associations, ordered sequences, causality or other relationships depending on the type of knowledge being stored.

To reflect the full range of explicit organizational knowledge, repositories should strive to record significant and meaningful concepts, categories, and definitions, (declarative knowledge), processes, actions and sequences of events (procedural knowledge), rationale for actions or conclusions (causal knowledge), circumstances and intentions under which the knowledge was developed and is to be applied (specific contextual knowledge), and the linkages among them. The repository should be indexed according to those concepts and categories, providing access paths that are meaningful to the organization. It should accommodate changes or additions to that knowledge (e.g., by linking annotations) as subsequent authors and creators adapt the knowledge for use in additional contexts.

The Knowledge Refinery in the Digital Library

The refinery represents the process for creating and distributing the knowledge contained in the repository. This process includes five stages:

* ***Acquisition.*** Information and knowledge is either

created within the organization or can be acquired from many different internal and external sources.

* *Refining.* Captured knowledge, before being added to the repository, is subjected to value-adding processes (refining) such as cleansing, labeling, indexing, sorting, abstracting, standardizing, integrating, and re-categorizing.
* ***Storage and Retrieval.*** This stage bridges upstream repository creation to downstream knowledge distribution.
* ***Distribution.*** This stage represents the mechanisms used to make repository content accessible.
* ***Presentation.*** The value of knowledge is pervasively influenced by the context of its use. Capabilities should be provided for flexibly arranging, selecting, and integrating the knowledge content.

The Role of Information Technologies in the Digital Scenario

The information technology infrastructure should provide a seamless "pipeline" for the flow of explicit knowledge through the 5 stages of the refining process to enable

* capturing knowledge,
* defining, storing, categorizing, indexing and linking digital objects corresponding to knowledge units,
* searching for ("pulling") and subscribing to ("pushing") relevant content,
* presenting content with sufficient flexibility to render it meaningful and applicable across multiple contexts of use.

Information technologies such as the World Wide Web and Digital Library software's offer a potentially useful environment within which to build a multimedia repository for rich, explicit knowledge. Input is captured by forms for assigning various labels, categories, and indices to each unit of knowledge. The structure is flexible enough to create knowledge units, indexed and linked using categories that reflect the structure of the contextual knowledge and the content of factual knowledge of the organization, displayed as flexible subsets via dynamically customizable views.

Effective use of information technology to communicate knowledge requires an organization to share an interpretive context. The more that communicators share similar knowledge, background and experience, the more effectively knowledge can be communicated via electronically mediated channels. At one extreme, the dissemination of explicit, factual knowledge within a stable community having a high degree of shared contextual knowledge can be accomplished through access to a central electronic repository. However, when interpretive context is moderately shared, or the knowledge exchanged is less explicit, or the community is loosely affiliated, then more interactive modes such as electronic mail or discussion databases are appropriate. When context is not well shared and knowledge is primarily tacit, communication and narrated experience is best supported with the richest and most interactive modes such as video conferencing or face-to-face conversation.

Business strategies related to knowledge management

As you explore other explanations of knowledge management — Bo Newman's Knowledge Management Forum is a good starting point — we would detect connections with several well-known management strategies, practices, and business issues, including

* Change management
* Best practices
* Risk management
* Benchmarking

A significant element of the business community also views knowledge management as a natural extension of "business process reengineering," a fact underscored by the recent announcement that John Wiley's *Business Change and Reengineering* will become *Knowledge and Process Management* in March, 2001. See (http://www.mgmt.utoronto.ca/~wensle/journal1.htm)

The need to manage knowledge seems obvious, and discussions of intellectual capital have proliferated, but few businesses have acted on that understanding. Where companies have take action — and a growing number are doing so — implementations of "knowledge management" may range from technology-driven methods of accessing, controlling, and delivering information to massive efforts to change corporate culture.

Why we need knowledge management now

Why do we need to manage knowledge?

* Service areas are increasingly competitive and the rate of innovation is rising.
* Reductions in staffing create a need to replace informal knowledge with formal methods.
* Competitive pressures reduce the size of the work force that holds valuable business knowledge.
* The amount of time available to experience and acquire knowledge has diminished.
* Early retirements and increasing mobility of the work force lead to loss of knowledge.
* Changes in strategic direction may result in the loss of knowledge in a specific area.(Ms. Macintosh's observations,2004)
* Most of our work is information based.
* Organizations compete on the basis of knowledge.
* Products and services are increasingly complex,

endowing them with a significant information component.

* The need for life-long learning is an inescapable reality.

In brief, knowledge and information have become the medium in which business problems occur. As a result, managing knowledge represents the primary opportunity for achieving substantial savings, significant improvements in human performance, and competitive advantage.

Benefits

The nature of the benefits from managing explicit knowledge depends on the type of application. Electronic publishing and other low interactivity, high-structure applications tend to provide a significant cost saving or increased efficiency. Publishing electronically is much less expensive than the distribution of paper. In the case of distributed learning, distributing pre-packaged knowledge (e.g., electronic textbooks and course notes) electronically can save significant travel expenses. In contrast, the more interactive or emergent-content applications tend to provide support for solving problems, innovating, and leveraging opportunities. The greatest impact, however, comes from combining the two. For example, Buckman Labs is adding a distance learning capability to its other applications, rounding out its portfolio where Digital Library at the back end as rich source. They are poised to reap the greatest benefit by integrating the capabilities of all applications. The emergent knowledge developed through the forum can be archived not only for searching by individuals in the field, but edited and repackaged for use as training materials within the distance learning application. Thus training will have more of a real-world feel and focus. Actual problems can be presented to students who, after deliberating on their own, can view how they were actually dealt with at the time. And formal training can now take place in the field, giving the students the ability to directly apply or integrate the training materials with their own day-to-day problems. In this way, those materials become more relevant and interwoven into the student's tacit experience and the learning more meaningful and lasting. By integrating the interactive, emergent forums with the structured content and distribution of formal training, a continual cycle of knowledge creation and application can be created. Tacit knowledge is made explicit via the forums, formally transferred via distance learning, and tacitly reapplied in context. That new tacit knowledge is now available for sharing with others via the same cycle. At each turn of the cycle, the knowledge of the organization increases, providing potentially greater competitive advantage.

The value of Knowledge Management relates directly to the effectiveness with which the managed knowledge enables the members of the organization to deal with today's situations and effectively envision and create their future. Without on-demand access to managed knowledge, every situation is addressed based on what the individual or group brings to the situation with them. With on-demand access to managed knowledge, every situation is addressed with the sum total of everything anyone in the organization has ever learned about a situation of a similar nature.

To summarize these findings, organizations that managed knowledge effectively

* Understood their strategic knowledge requirements
* Devised a knowledge strategy appropriate to the firm's business strategy;
* Implemented an organizational and technical architecture appropriate to the knowledge processing needs of the organization; enabling them to
* Apply maximum effort and commitment to creating, explicating, sharing, applying, and improving their knowledge.

Hurdles to adoption of knowledge management solutions

There have been many roadblocks to adoption of formal knowledge management activities. In general, managing knowledge has been perceived as an unmanageable kind of problem — an implicitly human, individual activity — that was intractable with traditional management methods and technology.

But it isn't necessary to throw up one's hands in despair. We do know a lot about how people learn. We know more and more about how organizations develop and use knowledge. And computer technology — itself a cause of the problem — can provide new tools to make it all work.

We don't need another "paradigm shift", but we do have to accept that the nature of business itself has changed, in at least two important ways:

1. Knowledge work is fundamentally different in character from physical labor.
2. The knowledge worker is almost completely immersed in a computing environment. This new reality dramatically alters the methods by which we must manage, learn, represent knowledge, interact, solve problems, and act.

You can't solve the problems of Information Age business or gain a competitive advantage simply by throwing more information and people at the problems. And you can't solve knowledge-based problems with approaches borrowed from the product-oriented, print-based economy. Those solutions are reactive and inappropriate.

Systematic approaches to knowledge management

Systematic approaches to knowledge management retain the traditional faith in rational analysis of the knowledge problem: the problem can be solved, but new thinking of many kinds is required. Some basic assumptions:

* A resource cannot be managed unless it is modeled, and many aspects of the organization's knowledge can be modeled as an explicit resource.
* Solutions can be found in a variety of disciplines and technologies, and traditional methods of analysis can be used to re-examine the nature of knowledge work and to solve the knowledge problem.
* Cultural issues are important, but they too must be evaluated systematically. Employees may or may not have to be "changed," but policies and work practices must certainly be changed, and technology can be applied successfully to business knowledge problems themselves.
* Knowledge management has an important management component, but it is not an activity or discipline that belongs exclusively to managers.

Conclusion

Digital Technology will clearly become more helpful in dealing with information overload. Techniques such as Digitization/summarization can reduce the load of persons attempting to find the right documents to use in some task. There is some promise, as yet unfulfilled, that intelligent agents may in the future help persons to prioritize the messages they receive. And the meta-data stored by portals can be used to draw visualizations of large amounts of information, although, contrary to intuition, graphical visualizations seem not to be better than their text-based equivalents, at least for information retrieval tasks.

Economic environment and information environment is changing quickly today. Knowledge management has become a powerful tool for promoting innovation and realizing reengineering the various walks of life. It occupies very outstanding position in the creation of the knowledge innovation systems of a country. How for the library circles to meet the challenge of knowledge economy and to build the knowledge management systems of Digital Libraries is a subject that demands our urgent study and solution.

Where do we stand at the moment, and where do we go from here? I conclude with a thought, As attested to in numerous articles in the popular press, knowledge management has already been embraced as a source of solutions to the problems of today's business and academic organizations. Still it has not been easy for this "science" to construct for itself that royal road of self validation. On the contrary, I believe that it is still, at least for the majority of the practitioners and their customers, in the stage of blind groping after its true aims and destination.

References

1. Working knowledge: How organization manage what they know, Boston: Harvard Business School press, 1998, p.18-35
2. Wang Yunhua. Knowledge Economy and the Development of the Library, Library Work & Research. 1999(6), 17-19
3. Hand in hand, Context magazine, April-May 2000, p.31
4. James W.Michaels and Dirk Smillie, Putting more now into knowledge, Forbes, May 15, 2000, p.32
5. Tom Stewart, 'The Case against Knowledge Management', *Business 2.0*, February 2002
6. M. H. Zack, "An Information Infrastructure Model for Systems Planning", Journal of Systems Management, vol. 43, no. 8, August, 1998, pp. 16-19, 38-40
7. Managing Codified Knowledge Sloan Management Review, Volume 40, Number 4, Summer, 1999, pp. 45-58
8. What Future Knowledge Management Users May Expect." Journal of Knowledge Management, 1999, 3, No. 2, pp. 155-165.
9. "Knowledge Management in Society and the Enterprise" in Proceedings of KMS'98, Turin, Italy: AIESEC, 1998.
10. http://www.ariadne/issue25/mueller/
11. http://www.ifla.org/IV/ifla66/papers/057-110e.htm
12. http://www.research.ibm.com/journal/sj/404/marwick.html
13. http://web.cba.neu.edu/~mzack/articles/kmarch/kmarch.htm

24
Marketing of Library and Information Center's Products and Services: Planning, Techniques and Strategies

K.S.Sivakumaren
Asst. Univ. Librarian Library, MIT Campus Anna University Chennai-600 044

T.Elanchezhiyan
Librarian M.N.Dastur & Campany Chennai-600 032

B.Jeyapragash
Librarian IndiraGandhi College of Arts and Science Pondicherry-8

ABSTRACT

Marketing is an important tool used to bring out the resources available in the library. Its aim is to obtain the needs of library users, make the information available for the users by introducing various plans and techniques to satisfy the user community. Marketing of library products and services helps to achieve the organization's goals. This paper is focused on plans, techniques, promotion and library / information professionals' role in promoting the usage of library products and services.

1. Introduction

Marketing is an essential component of any organizational business plan. Marketing management is the analysis, planning, implementation and control of programs designed to create, build and maintain beneficial exchange with the target customers for the purpose of achieving organizational objectives (Mandal Poddar&Choudhurys, 1998). Therefore, in coming days library and information services would not be available free to all particularly in highly specialized and technical libraries and information centres. So, it is essential for librarian or information specialists to know the practical aspect of marketing techniques, strategies and their application to library and information services. Thus, marketing has become an essential component in library and information centre.

2. Definition

The means of products, services and the whole cluster of things associated with creating, delivering and consuming their products/services concern marketing with satisfying the needs of the client.

According to Kotler "Marketing is a societal process by which individual and groups obtain what they need and want through creating, offering, and freely exchanging products and services of value with others"

3. Need for marketing

* Information explosion
* High demand for new services
* Effect of free economy
* Less usage
* In most of the cases there is a little involvement of users in the design of information services and products.
* To establish the value of information.

4. Why marketing?

Traditionally, libraries have not had the need to market aggressively but with the increased competition for funding and from bookstores, libraries need to attract the users by its products and services. Allen Paschal, CEO, Gale Group, says " Prior to the electronic age, they were undisputed foundation for information in the communities and now there is competition from AOL and Yahoo"

5. Marketing Mix

Marketers use number of tools to elicit desired responses from their target markets. These tools constitute a marketing mix .It is the set of marketing tools that the firm uses to pursue its marketing objectives in the target market.

McCarthy classified these tools into four broad groups that he called the four Ps of marketing Product, Price, Place and Promotion. Robert Lauterborn suggested that the seller's four Ps corresponds to the customer" four Cs

FOUR Ps	FOUR Cs
Product	Customer solution
Price	Customer cost
Price	Convenient
Promotion	Communication

5.1. Product (and services)

Product is the heart of the system. It may be associated with materials. What do we offer our clients? What are the benefits of the products and services for our clients. For example: Books Journals, Databases, Document delivery, Knowledgeable staff, Information literacy, Web sites, Study facilities.

5.2.Price (cost of services and resources to the clients of the organization)

Pricing of information services and products relatively

are new concepts. It has not considered seriously since library services were being provided "free". But, with the increased emphasis on accountability and self-sufficiency in relation to resources, it has become necessary to cost the various activities and to recover costs as much as possible. What does it cost? Should this service be free or funded by grant? Should the price be charged to cover the costs only? Should the price allow for profit? For example: Photocopying, Books, Laser printing, Fines Fee for service workshop etc.

5.3. *Place (availability, responsiveness, access and environment)*

This is component of the marketing mix that links product and customer. What is available? What can be done to make this product and service more accessible and available? For example: Personal visits, Staff consultation, E-mail, Phone, Library Websites, E-mail a librarian, Library buildings.

5.4. *Promotion (communicating with customers using various media)*

It involves mechanisms by which the target groups are informed about the resources available, services and products offered by the library and information centres.

How do you promote your products/services? What can be done to increase the visibility of the products and services. What can be done to increase its usage or exposure? For example: New letters, Advertising, Direct mail, Open days, Promotional evenings, Client consultations.

6. Application of 4Ps in library and information centres

In addition to the above 4Ps, Patricia G Olyer, in her two day workshop on "Library marketing" at the SMDT Women's University, Mumbai (7-8 Sep, 1992) added two more P's and these are Prelude and Postlude. Yes, for every activity preludes in the form of preparations and postludes in the form of follow-ups and evaluation are necessary. No activity can be successful without these two P's.

Product or Service	Price	Place	Promotion
Reference collection	No transaction fee to clients	Print collection available in the Library during the opening hours of Library ; Electronic access via the web available 24 hours a day	Library catalogue, Library Web pages, Information Literacy classes.
General Library workshop	No transaction fee to clients	Teaching Lab, Main Library, Web tutorials	E-mails, Brochures and Newsletters, Student diary, Notice boards.
Research workshop	Fees towards per day Tuition books, Special service etc.	Within Library	Web, E-mail, Notice Board, Information Desk posters.

Fig. 1.Application of 4Ps in Library and Information centres

7. Prerequisite for marketing

For marketing any commodity including the information commodity certain information are needed. In the case of information commodity the following conditions may be taken into consideration.

* A well-developed store or collection of data or information.
* Repackaging of the data of information into a marketable commodity.
* Marketing is managerial process involving analyzing, planning, implementation and control.
* Marketing is concerned with carefully formulated programs/ plans.
* A target community.
* Creating awareness about the commodity.
* Marketing of the commodity.
* Satisfaction of the consumer with the commodity.
* Continuous supply of the commodity without breaks or delays.

* Feed back from customers in the commodity, conducting of research with regard to the changing needs of the customers and improve the quality of the commodity

8. Marketing Plan

The most critical step to develop a comprehensive, strategic, focused marketing is the development of the marketing plan. It allows a planned rather than adhoc approach to your marketing plan.

8.1. Prepare a mission statement

The mission statement clearly and succinctly describes the nature of business, service offered.

8.2. List and describe target or niche markets

In this section, list and describe potential groups of users or clients. After you create the list, identify various segments of a market. Segments can include specific types of people in a company by role for e.g. CEO, Chief Financial Officer or Marketing Director, Heads of the Department.

8.3. Describe your services

It is necessary to conduct market research to understand your market and to identify the services they require. At same time inventory the services you currently offer and identify new services you wish to provide. Determine what it will take to provide these services in terms of staff, expertise and costs.

8.4. Spell out marketing and promotional strategies

The key for successful marketing is understanding what makes someone want to use or buy services and what type of marketing strategy they respond to. This requires you to learn needs, problems, industry trends etc.

8.5. Knowing your competitors

In developing your marketing strategy you must identify your competitors and learn how to position yourself in relation to them. Once you have identified both your direct and indirect competitors, you can determine how and why your services are special and benefits users in a particular way.

9. Strategic Marketing of Library and Information Centres

Successful marketing includes the art deciding that strategy/technique is used in different situation .As non-profit-making organizations; library and information centres cannot avoid marketing practices. Although libraries and information centres as non-profit organizations have three constituencies e.g. client's to whom they provide services, the parent institution from whom they receive funds and donor agencies; but they should market their services for the following reasons:

* Acquire (products) resources for use
* Make available in a suitable location saving the time of the reader (place) either by decentralization or mobile types of information vehicles
* Publicize its products to create demand and satisfy needs of majority of its users by exhibiting its resources and providing a conducive atmosphere for use
* At no cost (price) or at minimal price, thereby, in the ultimate analysis, providing every book its reader and every reader his/her book (TAHER, 1997).
* Marketing helps librarian or information managers to understand the real needs of users for taking good management decisions, which enable to give information services to the user more satisfactorily
* Librarian and information manager are not only interested for people who utilize the library services regularly. They are also interested on non-user groups. Marketing plays a vital role to identify the information needs of non-users and helps to provide them with necessary information.

* Librarians and information managers need to present their services as an indispensable part of the organization and try to justify the claim that users cannot do their job efficiently or effectively without a library services.
* Marketing may help to improve the image of the library and information profession through collection of revenue performing different services to users.

10. Marketing techniques in library and Information centres

The following marketing techniques can be applied in the library and information centres

10.1. Knowledge of purpose and resources

The librarian or information manager should know the purpose and resources/products of library and information centres and identify the goals, particularly for effective marketing program. He must know the products/resources well for serving the information needs of his patron.

10.2. Knowledge about competitors

Libraries and information centre are in competition with several non-profit and profit making organizations in providing information. They should identify those organizations with which they are in competition. They should evaluate their roles in terms of their services, products, distinctive competency and markets; and provide or create new services, which are not performed by their competitors.

10.3. Identification of users

Librarian and information managers should identify the users for marketing information services and take necessary steps for complete analysis of the marketing situation. They have to identify the various groups of users and update information services according to their needs by applying marketing techniques. Further, librarian has to identify the non- users of the library and provide them the required information services to them. They are very much important to library and information centres.

10.4 Establishment of marketing strategy

Establishment of marketing strategy is an essential ingredient of modern library / information services. Next step is to identify particular goals for the marketing program and develop specific marketing strategy.

10.5 Using marketing mix method

This includes advertising and public relations, channels of distribution and product policies. These are all communication with the library /information centres segments. It also makes to get feedback from the users.

11. What is User Expectation from the library &Information centres

Library and information managers should strive hard to gain a vision of who are our customers, what they want, what are their social character, values, desires, aspirations etc. The advancement in the technologies has phenomenally increased the self-help and do-it- you activities in the libraries. It comes to occupy more of our time and energy. At present, customer will definitely stress upon what he owns but he will also place high value on what he can do. Hence, new service delivery systems in libraries will require more specialized workers who are efficient in one-to-one service to customers.

11. 1. Individuality

The new generation customer is a global citizen who is more exacting and individualistic, change seeking and value conscious.

11. 2. Responsiveness

It is the willingness to help customers and to provide prompt services. This dimension emphasizes, attentiveness and promptness in dealing with customer's request, complaints, queries, and attention to problems. It also captures notion of flexibility and ability to customize the service to customer's needs.

11. 3 Relationship

To measure customer's satisfaction, the relationship between customer and the library must be understood. Customer relationship comprises of a hierarchy of encounters through facilities, resources, services etc.

12. Challenges for Librarian/Information Managers

The challenge of coping with the changes in social, technological, economical environment has forced the library and information centers to change their old practices. The library and information mangers will have to think of producing an information product, which is useful for revenue generation. Availability of right information for right user at right time and right cost has become most vital. This posed major challenges to the information sectors whose prime function is to satisfy the complex and increasing demands for information products and services. Library and information managers need to understand that just having information and storing it will serve no purpose, unless those who need it put it to an effective use.

Library and information centers will have to bring user and information together. However, increasing technological advancements is still putting more and more pressure on dynamic managers. As new technology is taking place every day, it is possible for the library and information managers to give more and accurate information than how it was earlier. Information network plays a vital role to break time and space barriers and user's expectations are also changing and increasing. Hence, librarian/information managers should give high quality information products and services.

13. Needs Assessment

Need assessment activities are regular part of library/ Information centres. SDI is a technique often used in libraries and Information centres to obtain the user needs. By developing and maintaining user interest profiles, library can continually monitor the information needs and interests of its services, population, allowing more effective collection building.

* The information needs assessment process is a well-planned, systematic approach to determining the information needs of each distinct customer group.
* The purpose of the information needs assessment is to highlight areas where improved information (content, technology and management support) is needed to achieve the organizations strategic objectives.
* It is an attempt on the part of the librarian/ information manager to understand not only what information is needed, but why, how will it be used?
* The information professionals must make an effort to understand where the information each department use comes from, what is done with it (additional analysis and processing) and to whom it is sent (usually in a repackaged value – added formal).
* It allows the librarian/information manager to gain a better understanding of the activities of other departments within the organization and where they fit into the whole.

Professional marketing researchers use many tools and methods, which include census, other demographic data, interviews, surveys, focus groups, direct observation and product/usage data. Analyzing market segment to determine what they need and how to deliver library services to them is really part of the planning process. One of the most useful ways to learn what information is required by organization is to conduct a survey of market, including both current and potential customers.

14. Professional skills for marketing

Librarian /information officer require the following professional knowledge and skills to market the Library Information and Services.

* Perception of the information requirements of users.
* Knowledge of the ways of accessories of information.
* Promotion of information by applying various marketing strategies, distribution, advertising and user satisfaction.
* Skills to obtaining feed back from users.
* Coupling of new information with the already existing information sources.
* Consumer interest analysis.
* Understanding the reasons for potential from users of information not seeking service from the system meant for them.
* Skilled and trained manpower
* Product design, its currency, quality and standards, access system, presentation and delivery
* Pricing of services/products
* Sales forecasting about the market environment

15. Awareness of Library Resources and services

The Librarian/Information professionals have to exhibit the existing library resources to the user in the following forms:

* Flowcharts related with resources and collections.
* Display arrangement guides
* Special material guides.
* Classification schemes adopted.

* Publicity of Library resources.
* Systematic and attractive arrangements of Library Collections.
* Electronic resources.
* Library Catalogue.
* Bibliographies.
* Indexing services, abstracting.
* Reprographic Service,
* Document supplies services.
* SDI, CAS, ILL.
* Internet access services E-mail, electronic collection based services.

16. Promotional activities of Library and Information products and services

Library and Information centres should engage in activities that help to promote the services to the specific individuals who can get benefit from them. This should include identification of user groups, finding their information needs, sending them the promotional materials/information. A systematic marketing plan will raise the image of library and information centres. The library will gain reputation and status among users. Promotion of its products and services can be made through various promotional activities as shown in the below fig. 2.

17. Role of Information Librarian/Information Manager

Library and information professionals must customize his products, information, according to the particular needs of each client, whether in strategic planning, accounting, sales or any other areas of the business. Information specialists should serve as

* Educators of the many types of information available on a particular subject.

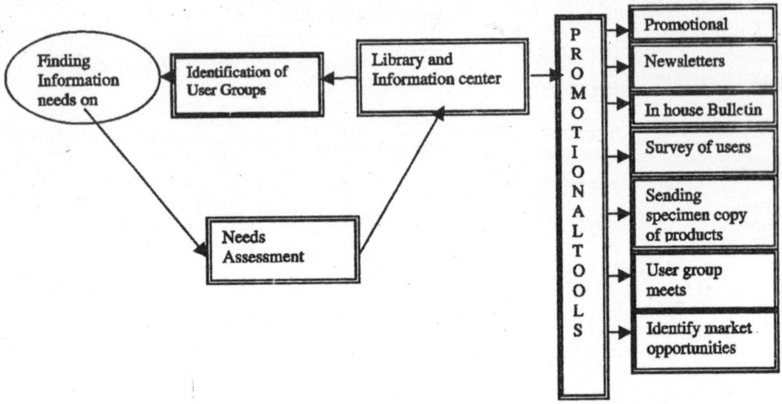

Fig. 2.Promotional activities of library and information centres

* Trainer who can use a variety of manufacturing tools and technologies.
* Internal consultants who can find and obtain the services of experts, either from within or outside the organization.

The main task of the information professional is to recommend the appropriate resources, help them to access and provide sufficient training in accessing or using various information media like CD-ROM. This will help the future users also to obtain information.

* Profile the information and requirements of the whole organization.
* Develop a strategy for acquiring sources to meet these requirements.
* Implement the tactics to delivery the data.
* The information specialists must have highly – developed communication skills and able to work at levels of the organization.
* He/she should be good decision-maker and able to tackle various problems at difficult situations.
* He or she should be able to develop and manage sub-ordinates as well as outside contacts and resources.

18. Benefits /advantages of marketing

The marketing of information products and services shall be beneficial in the following ways:

* Increase visibility of the Library and Information Centres.
* Improve the quality of Library services.
* Gain management support and commitment.
* Expand the professional role of the Library and Information scientists.
* Manage the affairs more effectively.
* Gives general information to the users about the Library information services and products.
* Encourage general awareness and appreciation of services of the Library and Information Centres.
* Ensures economic use of major resources.

19. Conclusion

User satisfaction is most important in library and information centers. It is the duty and responsibility of librarian / information officer to provide the required information to the users .The reputation of library and information centres is based on the usage of library services, products and resources. In the present situation, librarian / information professional have to play a n important role to identify the user groups and provide them the necessary information not only within or outside the library / information centre. They have to adopt the various marketing plans, strategies, techniques in the marketing of library products and services.

20. References

1. Desidoc Bulletin of Information Technology, vol.22 (3), May, 2002,
2. Kawatra, P.S. Text book of information science, A.P.H.Publishing corporation, New Delhi, 2000,p 81-104

3. http://www.infotoday.com/cil2003/
4. http: www.nafizu.netfirms.com/index.html
5. Kotler, Philip, Marketing Management, Prentice -Hall of India Private Ltd, New Delhi, 2000, p 7-19

25

Knowledge Management and Knowledge Repositories: Role of Management Libraries

Kaladhar Arnepalli
GITAM Central Library
Visakhapatnam-530 045
(gitamlib@yahoo.co.in)

ABSTRACT

The efficient management of knowledge has become imperative for almost all types of organizations. Many approaches exist for dealing with knowledge management. In the field of digital libraries advanced personalization and customization concepts exist. The development of knowledge management in recent years has become the key concern for librarians and libraries. Librarians in the digital and knowledge age should be in charge of knowledge management in their respective organizations in order to leverage the intellectual assets and to facilitate knowledge creation.

The management of knowledge is being regarded as the domain of librarians and libraries. Librarians and information professionals are trained to be experts in information searching, selecting, acquiring, organizing, preserving, repackaging, disseminating, and serving. With the growing interest in knowledge management, many questions have been raised in the minds of librarians regarding: the difference between information management and knowledge management; would librarians and information professionals with appropriate education and training in library and information science be fit in organizing knowledge repositories in their organizations; and what libraries can do in implementing knowledge management. This paper attempts to disclose the critical part being played by librarians, in Knowledge management and Management of Knowledge repositories.

What is Knowledge Management?

Knowledge management is a new concept and viewed differently by different writers from different focuses, its definitions vary accordingly. 'Jennifer Rowley' in her article, "What is knowledge management?" offers her definition below (2):

"Knowledge management is concerned with the exploitation and development of the knowledge assets of an organization with a view to furthering the organization's objectives. The knowledge to be managed includes both explicit, documented knowledge, and tacit, subjective knowledge. Management entails all of those processes associated with the identification, sharing and creation of knowledge. This requires systems for the creation and maintenance of knowledge repositories, and to cultivate and facilitate the sharing of knowledge and organizational learning. Organizations that succeed in knowledge management are likely to view knowledge as an asset and to develop organizational norms and values, which support the creation and sharing of knowledge".

What are the perspectives of Knowledge management (3)?

From the analysis of the objectives of the institutions of any kind, 'Davenport' et al were able to categorize them into four broad types of perspectives:

1. To create knowledge repositories: Knowledge repositories store both knowledge and information, often in documentary form. These repositories can fall into three categories:

Those, which include external knowledge, such as competitive intelligence. Those that include structured internal knowledge, such as research reports and product oriented marketing materials, such as techniques and methods. Those that embrace informal, internal or tacit knowledge, such as discussion databases that store "know how".

2. To improve knowledge access and transfer: Here the emphasis is on

Connectivity, access and transfer. Technologies such as video conferencing systems, document scanning and sharing tools and telecommunications networks are central.

3. To enhance the knowledge environment: It facilitates the environment is conductive to more effective knowledge creation, transfer and use. This involves tackling organizational norms and values as they relate to knowledge. Increase awareness on sharing knowledge embedded in client relationship and engagements. Provide awards for contributions to the organization's structured knowledge base. Implement decision audit programs in order to assess whether and how employees were applying knowledge in key decisions. Recognize that successful knowledge management is dependent upon structures and cultures.

4. To manage knowledge as an asset: It helps to recognize the value of knowledge to an organization. Others, however, sought to take a process view to define knowledge management.

Primary resources of Knowledge Management (1):

The management of explicit knowledge utilizes four primary resources

* Repositories of explicit knowledge;
* Refineries for accumulating, refining, managing, and distributing that knowledge;
* Organization roles to execute and manage the refining process; and
* Information technologies to support those repositories and processes.

The Knowledge Repository (Structure) (4)

For knowledge repositories to be meaningful, their structure must reflect the structure of shared mental models or contextual knowledge tacitly held by the organization. In most organizations, those structures are neither well defined nor widely shared. Yet their explication is essential for effectively managing explicitly encoded organizational knowledge. This requires defining what is meant by a knowledge-unit and how that collection of knowledge units should be meaningfully indexed and categorized for ease of access, retrieval, exchange and integration.

The design of a knowledge repository reflects the two basic components of knowledge as an object: *structure* and *content*. Knowledge structures provide the context for interpreting accumulated content. If the repository is conceived as a "knowledge platform", then many different views of the content may be derived from a particular repository structure. A high degree of viewing flexibility enables users to alter and combine views dynamically and interactively and to more easily apply the knowledge to new contexts and circumstances. At this point, knowledge-as-object becomes knowledge-as-process.

The basic structural element is the *knowledge unit*, a formally defined, atomic packet of knowledge content that can be labeled, indexed, stored, retrieved and manipulated. The format, size and content of knowledge units may vary depending on the type of explicit knowledge being stored and the context of their use. The repository structure also includes the schemes for linking and cross-referencing knowledge units. These links may represent conceptual associations, ordered sequences, causality or other relationships depending on the type of knowledge being stored.

To reflect the full range of explicit organizational knowledge, repositories should strive to record significant and meaningful concepts, categories, and definitions, (declarative knowledge), processes, actions and sequences of events (procedural knowledge), rationale for actions or conclusions (causal knowledge), circumstances and intentions under which the knowledge was developed and is to be applied (specific contextual knowledge), and the linkages among them. The repository should be indexed according to those concepts and categories, providing access paths that are meaningful to the organization. It should accommodate changes or additions to that knowledge (e.g., by linking annotations) as subsequent authors and creators adapt the knowledge for use in additional contexts.

A knowledge platform may actually consist of several repositories, each with a structure appropriate to a particular type of knowledge or content. These repositories may be logically linked to form a composite or "virtual" repository, the content of each providing context for interpreting the content of the others. For example, product literature, best sales practices, and competitor intelligence for a particular market might be stored separately but viewed as though contained in one repository.

The Knowledge Refinery

The refinery represents the process for creating and distributing the knowledge contained in the repository. This process includes five stages:

* *Acquisition:* Information and knowledge is either

created within the organization or can be acquired from many different internal and external sources.

* *Refining:* Captured knowledge, before being added to the repository, is subjected to value-adding processes (refining) such as cleansing, labeling, indexing, sorting, abstracting, standardizing, integrating, and re-categorizing.
* *Storage and Retrieval:* This stage bridges upstream repository creation to downstream knowledge distribution.
* *Distribution:* This stage represents the mechanisms used to make repository content accessible.
* *Presentation:* The value of knowledge is pervasively influenced by the context of its use. Capabilities should be provided for flexibly arranging, selecting, and integrating the knowledge content.

Knowledge Management Roles

A common weakness in knowledge management programs is the overemphasis on information technology at the expense of well-defined knowledge management roles and responsibilities. Traditional organizational roles typically do not address either knowledge management or the cross-functional, cross-organizational process by which knowledge is created, shared and applied. The architecture presented here suggests a set of organizational roles that should be explicitly defined. First, knowledge management, as a cross-organizational process, should be comprehensively "owned" and managed, and full-time responsibility assigned for an organization's knowledge management architecture. Organizations are creating a Chief Knowledge Officer role to handle this responsibility. Many organizations also cluster those responsible for knowledge management into knowledge or expertise centers, each being responsible for a particular body of knowledge. Their responsibilities typically include championing knowledge management, educating the organization, knowledge mapping, and integrating the organizational and technological resources comprising the knowledge management architecture. Additionally, explicit responsibility should be assigned for each stage of the refinery and the interfaces between them. Assigning responsibility for the seamless movement of knowledge from acquisition through use, as well as the interfaces between these stages, will help ensure that knowledge repositories will be meaningfully created and effectively used.

Management of Knowledge Repositories:

Knowledge repositories have a lifecycle that must be managed. Once created, they tend to grow, reaching a point where they begin to collapse under their own weight, requiring major reorganization. Their rejuvenation requires deleting obsolete content, archiving less active but potentially useful content, and reorganizing what is left. Content or topic areas may become fragmented or redundant. Reorganizing requires eliminating those redundancies, combining similar contributions, generalizing content for easier reapplication, and restructuring categories as needed. Successful knowledge management organizations proactively manage and reorganize their repositories as an ongoing activity rather than waiting for decline to set in before acting.

Influence of Digital Technology on Knowledge management and knowledge repositories (5):

The digital technology infrastructure should provide a seamless "pipeline" for the flow of explicit knowledge through the 5 stages of the refining process to enable

* Capturing knowledge,
* Defining, storing, categorizing, indexing and linking digital objects corresponding to knowledge units,
* Searching for ("pulling") and subscribing tc ("pushing") relevant content.

* Presenting content with sufficient flexibility to render it meaningful and applicable across multiple contexts of use.

In studies of information seeking habits of library users it has been fairly well established that convenience is what governs the choice of where users go for information. Desktop delivery of information, desktop access to library assistance, and more importantly, on-site personal assistance, is what the user community favors. In a recent study conducted in UK by a Higher Education Research Institute nearly 400,000 students at almost 700 institutions, it was revealed that 82.9% of first year students are using the Internet for research and homework. Potentially, the library faces the danger of losing touch with these students unless it can make the library and its services more conveniently accessible. The new digital tools and resources now make this possible.

The library professionals must begin to explore and use the new technologies, which will enable them to provide this on-site direct type of service. The services the library delivers must become more convenient so that users do not lose sight of what librarians and libraries have to offer — their ability to help users understand their information problem; the ability to put them in touch with the most critical electronic and print resources to answer their queries. The libraries' / librarian's task will be to make the web increasingly friendly and useful to scholarly endeavors and to assist in developing it, along with the university's digital information network, into the primary source for the institution's information needs. The creation of e-text centers, an explosion of electronic journal publications, new search engines and digital convergence of all media, suggest that this is both possible and desirable. Librarians will take a greater hand in designing tools and increasing ease of access. As the information experts, they will use their skills to provide in depth information and resources when and where required.

6. Conclusion

In the era of digital technology, knowledge management has became important and essential for Libraries to gain greater satisfaction from their users. In fact, libraries have had a long and rich experience in the management of information. Many of such knowledge and skills of librarianship can be applied to knowledge management. For any library to succeed in implementing knowledge management will require a strong leadership and vision from the top administration, which can influence the organization's knowledge sharing efforts in a positive way. As libraries enter the knowledge age of the 21st century, we should not take a back seat in the development of knowledge management. Instead, armed with our professional knowledge and experiences, we should be in the driver's seat.

Information technology and systems can provide effective support in implementing knowledge management. Library professionals should work together to develop the appropriate knowledge management systems. Furthermore, knowledge management should never be viewed as a way to control the process of knowledge creation.

In his book, *Enabling Knowledge Creation,* Georg Von Krogh et al made a strong argument for supporting knowledge creation rather than controlling it. In the process of knowledge creation, every library should strive to be an enabler and facilitator by mobilizing all its efforts and resources. The best knowledge creators are academics. Universities best perform knowledge creation. As a learning and knowledge organization, universities should empower their libraries to develop campus-wide knowledge management systems. It is now time for libraries to reposition themselves in the central stage of and as a leading player in knowledge management and management of knowledge repositories.

References

1. *Sloan Management Review*, Volume 40, Number 4, summer, 1999, pp. 45-582.
2. Jennifer Rowley, "What is Knowledge Management?" *Library Management* 20, no. 8 (1999): 416-419.
3. Thomas H. Davenport, DeLong, D.W., and Beers, M.C. "Successful Knowledge Management Projects," *Sloan Management Review* 39, no.2 (1998): 43-57.
4. "An Information Infrastructure Model for Systems Planning", Journal of Systems Management, vol. 43, no. 8, August, 1992, pp. 16-19, 38-40
5. 5. M. H. Zack, "Electronic Messaging and Communication Effectiveness in an Ongoing Work Group", Information & Management, vol. 26, no. 4, April, 1994, pp. 231-241

26
Emerging Confront for Library and Information Professionals in Knowledge Management Era

K.Vinitha
Research Scholar) Librarian,
National Engineering College, Kovilaptti-TN

S.Kanthimathi
Librarian, Rani Anna Government
College for women, Tirunelvelli-TN,

K.Tharani Devi
M.Phil., Student

ABSTRACT

The paper speaks about Knowledge management, its process, concept and importance in Knowledge management era. Various modules of Knowledge management are discussed. Human resource management and its application in Library and information centers is noted. Information technology its impact on library and IT as a tool for knowledge management is analyzed. Emerging roles and challenges of Library and information professionals, barrier & requisites for successful implication of Knowledge management is highlighted.

Introduction

Librarians had till recently been the "back room" staff-invisible to clients, unknown to top management, irrelevant to business development/marketing groups & insignificant to projects/business groups in typical corporate organization. Categorized as 'support staff' by personnel departments, the librarians were underused, undervalued & of course, underpaid. Not any longer: The emerging business environments coupled with the explosive technological capabilities of the information era have brought the library profession to an increasingly visible & a more team oriented platform in progressive corporate organization.

Knowledge management is now emerging trend of leading organization with transformation from manufacturing- oriented economy to service-oriented economy, the role of information & knowledge has become more prominent for all organizations. A knowledge resource is no longer just a factor of corporate status or image-It is now an issue for survival itself. What does this mean to library and information service professionals? Were librarians not organizing & providing access to knowledge earlier?

Is it a shift from the data-oriented approach? Now it is Knowledge management, discipline initiating the metamorphosis in the librarians role in corporate organizations, of knowledge-based companies call for an integration of librarian's role with business strategies?

Library and Information professionals need to be proactive team player in the emerging area of Knowledge management through various perspectives of

1) Librarians should view this emerging phenomenon through focused attention on the process of Knowledge management.
2) Librarians should keep on eye on how other interactive communities perceive Knowledge management.
3) Librarians should stimulate thinking about the role of library and information service professionals in

Knowledge management.

4) Librarian should visualize the role of library management knowledge.

Knowledge management needs to be taken seriously as an issue for Library and Information professionals because it is perceived to offer a substantial enhancement to their role. The leading organizations today are getting aware of the value of knowledge in various forms. Information professionals can play an important role in Knowledge management that will definitely enhance the professional image and their role.

What is knowledge management?

Knowledge is the business asset of any progressive organizations that get ahead. The implementation of knowledge management helps the information flows in the organization and in implementing organization-learning practices. Knowledge management is not just managing or organizing books or journals, searching the Internet for users or arranging for the circulation of materials. Each of these can of course, be an isolated part of knowledge management.

Knowledge Management is enhancing the use of organizational knowledge through information management and organizational learning. The purpose is to deliver direct value to the business. The knowledge is embedded in the processes and experiences, skills, wisdom and capabilities of people. Knowledge management rests on two foundations, i.e., utilizing the organizations information and application of people's competencies, skills, talents, thoughts, ideas, imaginations, etc.,

Knowledge Management aims to draw out the tacit knowledge people have, what they carry around with them, what they observe and learn from experience, rather than what is usually explicitly stated. Managing knowledge goes much further than capturing data and manipulating it to obtain information. The aim of knowledge management is for businesses to become more competitive through the capacities of their people.

Definition

According to Kalseth "Knowledge Management is about putting information and people's competence to work together."

According to Murry, "Knowledge Management transferred into capabilities for effective action."

University of Texas: The systematic process of finding, selecting, organizing, distilling and presenting information in a way that improves an employee's comprehension in a specific area of interest. Knowledge Management helps an organization to gain insight and understanding from its own experience helps focus the organism to gain insight and understanding from its own experience. Specific Knowledge Management activities help focus the organization on acquiring ,storing and utilizing knowledge fro such things as problems solving ,dynamic learning, strategic planning and decision-making. It also protects intellectual assets from decay, adds to firm intelligence and provides increased flexibility.

Knowledge management process, concept and importance

The term "Knowledge Management (K M)" has been borrowed from the corporate world which was used as a strategy to seek as well as capture the knowledge residing in people's heads and consciousness to help the business remain on the progressive path standing in a keen competitive environment. The main target of application of Knowledge Management in profit-seeking organizations is to gain competitive advantage and increases turnover to make a profit by enhancing and improving operations systems.

The strategically perspective, today's practice in KM still has some significant demerits. The reasons for this are manifold. Firstly the existing knowledge is capture and capitalized only to a low degree because knowledge is messy in character. Secondly, time factor- many employees are willing to document and use existing knowledge but pressure of work in enterprise should be allowed to participate in management but not in real practice and as a result , that un captured knowledge can't be utilized for Knowledge Management purposes.

"Knowledge Management is a conscious strategy of getting the right knowledge to the right people at the right time and helping people share and put information into action in ways that strive to improve organization performance. "Knowledge Management is nothing but cupping knowledge". Knowledge Management is used in LIC's for communicating knowledge between levels of management and who are directly involved to work processes as well as in service sectors.

According to Davenport Knowledge Management process is about acquisition, creation packaging and applications or reuse of knowledge. Whereas according to Probst it consists of identifications acquisition, developing, sharing and distributing, using and preservation of knowledge. The Knowledge Management process basically consists of four steps. These steps include all the terms and terminology described below:

Tacit Knowledge: includes the individual employee's expertise, memories, values and beliefs, view points and values.

Explicit Knowledge: is the process of communication from one place to another in a systematic way through documents and is more formal and codified.

Corporate memory: is the connection of know-how of an organization. This know-how relates to problems solving, project experiences, and human resources management.

Intellectual assets/ knowledge assets/capital: similar terms, which comprises knowledge assets regarding products, technologies, and market that a business owns.

Information economics: a study of the clear value of information to an organization.

Data mining: is the exploration and analysis, automatic and semiautomatic means of large quantities of data in order to discover meaningful patterns and rules.

Knowledge representation is the process of describing and presenting usable way of knowledge that is known by a person.

Knowledge mapping is finding existing knowledge in an organization and creating a detailed picture of skills. Maps can be simple directories of names to search online databases of human expertise, research materials and prerecorded information.

Concept mapping: is the visual summary of ideas or topics and these ideas or topics are related to each other.

Knowledge engineer is a person responsible of acquiring knowledge and developing data and rules for expert systems.

Steps in Knowledge Management

1. Knowledge capture: systematic procedure for organizing, structuring knowledge to make it accessible and usable to people.
2. Knowledge organization: An organization that values and uses its own knowledge in reflective ways that lead to profound shifts in directions, values, beliefs and operating assumptions.
3. Knowledge preservation: once the knowledge is collected, and codified it has to be stored in a suitable form in the organization's knowledge base. The knowledge can be stored in three forms: with individual employees, and by computer knowledge base. The advantage with the computer is its unlimited memory

and instant access. Intranets and the knowledge bases are the tools, which store the organizational knowledge.

Modules of knowledge management

The Knowledge Management system is primarily based on eight vital modules

1. INFORMATION: the most important bezel acts as an instant access to update and customize information
2. EXPERTISE: connects in real-time experts in an organizations to members who yearn assistance and even the tacit knowledge can made explicit
3. COLLABORATION: plays an important role to facilitate on-line brain storming sessions and preserves information
4. TEAM: ensures efficient and systematic management among shares skills
5. LEARNING: abridges skill gap with the help of on-line sessions
6. INTELLIGENCE: deals mainly with the explicit knowledge among shares skills
7. KNOWLEDGE TRANSFER: in a structure electronic form according to William Saffady relates to (a) Machine-readable data files (b)various on-line databases and CD-Rom information resides in the shape of optical disks, juke boxes or magnetic tape autoloaders and (d) Computerized networked systems
8. KNOWLEDGE MAPPING: identifies the body of knowledge within the organizations, which is primarily concerned with mute knowledge base and makes a repository of all skills and expertise in the organization.

Human resources management in libraries

Human resources management takes it as its basic starting point to train high quality specialized talents and to revitalize the library undertaking. In practice, we should pay full attention to diversity and variation of library staff's requirements, strengthened management of different library staff by applying contingency management approach. That is, to some people, rigid management method is applied, rigorous supervision and control imposed, and quality and quality requirements of work according to regulations and procedures are made clear, and to the rest of the people, more flexible management method is applied to let them participate in decision –making and consultation and undertake more jobs so as to bring their management abilities into full play and realize organizational and personal objectives.

Application of knowledge management in library and information centre

Libraries and information centers (LIC) are best by fractionalized systems and services (e.g., integrated library systems, disparate commercial online databases and CD-ROM products) that ".... Create ... problems for knowledge workers... faced with integrating information delivery systems in order to do their work". Knowledge Management systems comprising commercial news feeds, numbers of generic, open ended discussion databases and passive document libraries threaten to simply compound our problems. At great cost, companies and organizations build these systems only to become disenchanted when they fail to deliver the productivity gains touted in the literature. They fail because they do not provide information in a work-centered context that magnifies its utility several folds.

Successful KM systems are those that" package knowledge" in the process of doing real work. Packaging knowledge involves the "... filtering, editing and organizing pieces of knowledge...in such a way that it's insightful, relevant and useful" such actionable knowledge however, isn't cheap.

The topic(or request) itself

* Key constraints influencing resource selection and use(e.g. urgency, chronological and geographical coverage, purpose),
* Analytical notes on the resources used in the course of the research,
* All exchange between the researcher and his/her client or client group, and
* All supporting and working documentation up to and including the finished products.

End-to-end support for the research process requires an extensible standards-complaint platform; (not a single application) but what Watson and Harty call an "infrastructure". Groupware was the clear choice. Within a groupware infrastructure, the value of case histories as a form of KM is markedly increased through the capability to add integrated access to directory and messaging services, external information resources and services, corporate applications and local file systems. Given the innovative nature of RIM- r ,it was essential that librarians be capable of actively participating in the application development process. Accordingly, we chose a mature groupware infrastructure with significant end-user development capability.

Characteristics of knowledge in libraries

Human resource management is the core of Knowledge Management in libraries. In the knowledge economy era, the libraries will attach importance to vocational training and lifelong education of library staff to raise their scientific knowledge level and ability of acquiring and innovating knowledge. An all-round improvement of library staff's quality and positioning of human value will become important objectives of Knowledge Management in libraries. The objectives of Knowledge Management in libraries is to promote knowledge innovation, to promote relationships in and between libraries, between library and user, to strengthen knowledge internetworking and quicken knowledge flow. In the knowledge economy era, libraries will carry out researches on development and application of information resources, construction of virtual libraries, protection of intellectual property rights in the electronic era, etc. thus founding the base for knowledge innovation.

Information technology as a tool for knowledge management

It is impossible to accomplish such important tasks by using man's brains only in the modern society in which the knowledge changes with each passing day. It will be possible to link closely knowledge sources and knowledge workers by computer networks, thus constructing knowledge networks in libraries based on realization of single-point information.

Contents of Knowledge Management in libraries: as a completely new method of management, Knowledge Management in libraries leaves much to be desired in its theoretical system. In general, Knowledge Management in libraries should include such aspects as follows:

* Knowledge innovation management: Knowledge innovation management in libraries refers to the management of the production, diffusion and transfer of knowledge as well as of the network systems constructed by related institutions and organizations. It includes three aspects, namely, theoretical innovation management and organizational innovation management.
* Knowledge dissemination management: Knowledge management is of equal importance as compared to knowledge innovation .knowledge creators do not have much time and energy to look for knowledge users, Though there are a multitude of knowledge users, it is

very difficult to acquire knowledge that already exists in the minds of knowledge creators as restricted by various objective and subjective conditions. Therefore, libraries may play the part of knowledge leader diverse media and channels to disseminate new knowledge. In the 21st century, the internet, with its mass information and extensive contents, will provide people with the main approach to searching knowledge and acquiring information

* Knowledge Application Management: In the 21st century libraries should also attach importance to provision of services for people to acquire knowledge and achieve maximum functions and efficiency of knowledge information. Therefore, knowledge services based on high-speed information networks should be carried out by:
* Setting up virtual libraries or information centers for enterprise, governments, public organizations and scientific research institutions. It is difficult for an enterprise or a social organization to put sufficient manpower, material and financial resources on information gathering, organizing and developing. It is also impossible and unnecessary to spend a large amount of funds on information resources for their own use. Libraries can create virtual libraries or information centers for these organs separately according to their respective information requirements by using abundant information resources on the high-speed information networks.
* Settings up digitized knowledge services, which is actually a development trend of libraries in the 21st century. This presupposes: creating step the users-oriented information.
* Service systems such as information dissemination,

information search and special supply of information; quickening the creation of digitized libraries; studying the methods, means and techniques of information distribution and search with the internet as the base and web techniques as the core.

* 'Digitizing libraries resources'. the electronic libraries or digitized libraries are the technical modes and development trends of libraries in the knowledge economy era. The knowledge services of Libraries in the future will start with creation of databases comprising electronic journals and books in different languages that have discipline features and can operate on high-speed information networks. Great efforts should be made to transform all existing large non-electronic information resources into electronic information and integrate them into electronic libraries.

Emerging role of librarians and information professional

Traditionally, library professionals are assigned to take care of direct roles such as catalogue cards, classified tools help to find right books needed. The tools for thesaurus construction and controlled vocabulary are already helping us mange knowledge. Document management such as content management and accessibility of images play role in knowledge management activities. However with emergence of knowledge management in almost all services organizations, librarians and information professionals have to take on additional participative roles in expert systems, artificial intelligence and knowledge base management system (KBMS) lessons learnt through these technologies are directly applicable to knowledge to knowledge management. By helping knowledge workers in the performance of cognitive tasks. Decision support systems is like the knowledge management systems. Information professional need to broad base their expertise I the library to include communication ,facilitation, training and management skills.

They also require a basic understanding of computing and network architecture. All knowledge –based organizations today survive and grow on the strength of their knowledge workers, rather than floor workers or administrative staff. Where are the librarians placed in theirs segments? Are they being treated as-till recently- just support staff in administrative workers category, or do they too qualify as knowledge workers? The answer depends on who is seen as a knowledge worker? Almost everyone is, because either you are using the knowledge or contributing in gathering knowledge in the organization's business. There is hardly any hierarchy among the knowledge workers. The knowledge work is about the acquisition, creation, packaging or application or reuse of knowledge.

Barriers to implement proper km systems

Knowledge management is in reality a difficult process to implement particularly for an organization whose employees have been conditioned to the idea that knowledge equates power. In such an organizational culture little or not at all sharing of knowledge and information takes place between departments or even among colleagues within the same section. The staff in this organization would tend to hoard information, practice, and hence the "superiority" of their enlightened position, form being taken away from them. It is clear that the employees of different organizations require adjusting in values, culture and behaviors. These adjustments take time-often years and require commitment from the top ,clear focus, and persistent application within library units. However, there are some barriers to the implementation of KM in organization cited by O'Dell and Grayson include:

* Ignorance- not knowing who has the right information required for the job;
* Lack of time to find out and absorb the best practices recommended;

* Lack of a relationship between the sources and recipient of knowledge;
* Time lag taken to implement best practices recommended across departments.

To overcome the above barriers in connection with the implementation of KM in organizations need some changes according to organizational structure, co-operation with each other for sharing knowledge, elimination of bossism, mutual understanding among colleagues, eradication of superiority minded attitude, expertise to new information technology and ultimately involve the employees in participative management. Some other important factors in favors of the implementation factors of KM are:

* Set up the right people in the right job at the right time without any biases.
* Tackling personnel to solve the complex as and when they arise in the organization by cultivating their tacit knowledge.
* Authority and responsibility should be delegated as per level of position to professionals by which they can react immediately according to the situation with their professional experiences and efficiencies.
* Developing professionals by training, introduction of new technologies and know-how who try to keep up with them as a knowledge person.
* Develop sharing of knowledge system between units as well as among organizations as a whole through cooperation of the professionals.

Requisites for successful knowledge management

The last five years have seen a rapidly growing interest in the topic of knowledge management. Several articles and books are published on the subject that provides strategies for knowledge management like sharing best practices, improved customer services, faster problem solving and more rapid adoption to market changes etc., The recurring success factors for knowledge management like sharing best practices, improved customer services, faster problem solving and more rapid adoption to market changes, etc. The recurring success factors for knowledge management include:

* Support from top management, who recognizes the value of information or knowledge as a resource;
* Identification of the link between knowledge and the new measures of performance;
* A knowledge leader who can actively drive the knowledge agenda forward with commitment;
* Polices that drive the agenda forward;
* Creation of an environment or work culture that supports innovation, learning and knowledge-sharing.

Conclusion

Economic environment and information environment are changing quickly today. Knowledge management has become a powerful tool for promoting innovation and realizing reengineering the various walks of life. It occupies an outstanding position in the creation of the Knowledge innovation systems of a country. How far the library circles meet the challenge of knowledge economy and build the knowledge management systems of libraries is a subject that demands our urgent study and solution.

27

Establishing an Integrated & Interactive Video-conferencing Facility at the Library of IIM Lucknow

Roshan Lal Raina

Professor-In-Charge (Library), IIM Lucknow

ABSTRACT

Outlining the need, objectives and the use of establishing a video-conferencing facility at the library of a leading management school, the paper gives an idea of the equipment and other infrastructure facilities needed to establish the set-up. Cost implications are also highlighted.

1. Introduction

The Indian Institute of Management, Lucknow is a national level management education institute set up by the Government of India. The Institute strives "to help improve the management systems with regard to business, industry, and public services through pursuit of excellence in management education, research, consulting and training". To help excel in all its academic activities and interventions, the Institute is supported by a state-of-the art learning resource center, the Library.

2. Library: The Learning Resource Center of IIML

The library s housed in a spacious 30,000 sq. feet, two storied, air-conditioned, centrally located and functionally designed building with a seating capacity of 250 readers in five halls and equipped with ergonomically designed furniture and fittings. Its fast growing collection includes an up-to-date and well-balanced collection of over 62,000 select documents in the field of management and related areas including about 5000 volumes of important reference sources.

Besides currently subscribing to over 564 learned periodicals, the library has developed a strong collection of 11,875-microfilms/ fiche of all the core periodicals in microforms. 18 comprehensive databases and 891 journals subscribed to by the library in e-format form the nucleus of its electronic library. The library also stocks a collection of about 1538 reports of select corporations of the country and 2613 other important and similar documents. Recently, the library has started building its collection of audio-visual (AV) materials and presently stocks about 414 documents in AV form. The library provides a range of online as well as offline services that include electronic document delivery to its highly demanding clientele, both in internal (numbering over 1000) as well as external (numbering annually on an average over 250) environments. Using state-of-the art IT, and after working closely with the clientele, a number of 'client-directed' current awareness (CA) and select dissemination of information (SDI) services are made available to its clients through its electronic interface as shown in Appendix 1.

3. Proposal for Setting-up the Facility

Encouraged with the success of applying IT in building its learning resources, organizing them and then serving the same to its clientele, the library took a step forward in 2000 by getting involved in putting up a proposal to the MHRD (GOI) for setting up an integrated and interactive global videoconferencing facility.

4. Justification for Establishing the Facility

In the current business scenario, it is important to take

management education beyond the realm of classroom teaching as well as to reach out to great management educators and academicians throughout the world. As an interactive communication medium, videoconferencing gives us an affordable and cost effective option through which we can deliver and hear lectures and exchange ideas and thoughts, information and views to and from any corner of the globe, any time. This goes beyond building relationships and supporting collaboration among traditionally and geographically isolated but great institutions in a way that no other communication technology does. It has a wide spread appeal with the efficient use of key resource personnel and particularly in the context of education it appeals to a variety of teaching styles. As reported by educators from around the world, it impacts students and increases their depth of learning by heightened motivation, improved communication and increased connectivity – a value addition that the industry would most welcome, given their requirements.

Given the way, the world is shaping up today, it would be an understatement to say that education and its spread would form the core point from where the wealth of a nation would be built-up. Indeed, prioritizing education, in our national programs has been felt to be one of the core issues of concern where we don't spend that level of GDP to the cause of education.

The stock of effective 'Communicators' i.e. teachers being limited and that too in an area like 'Management', the wealth that such people have remains underutilized. If the world is going to be 'knowledge driven', then maximum usage of such people is critical.

And if the technology is available, then their contribution does not necessarily have to be limited to national boundaries only. It should reach far and wide. This will further aid in removing the sub-standard teaching, prevalent in the management education system of the country.

It is in this context that video conferencing as an effective tool becomes that much more relevant in the spread of education to a large number of people spread over wide spread geographical areas. The added advantage of it is the quickness of this mechanism and its impact. The lesser advantaged sections of the society, who can not access 'quality' education will have a chance to fall in the mainstream that such a process may usher in. This will, of course, call for government assistance – the NASA project experimented some time ago, only for a temporary period, is a reminder that video conferencing could indeed bring in vast fortunes to the society in terms of learning.

5. Primary Objectives of the Facility

Videoconferencing put simply, is a telephone call with pictures. More importantly it's a fast, flexible and highly affordable way to quickly exchange information between colleagues, to share expertise with partners, audiences, clients or suppliers without the need for the participants to be present at the same location. You can hold conferences with as few as 2 locations to as many as 80 through bridging facilities.

Videoconferencing, as explained above, has become an established tool for the spread of management education today. In view of the growing need and importance, highlighted by improved communication standards, audiovisual quality, and reduced costs, the broad objectives of the project were summarized as follows:

* Access of impactful and quality management education cutting across global and cultural boundaries.
* To take management education to countries where it is not easily available at an affordable cost.
* Increased depth of learning experience with increased on-line accessibility to management experts from all over the world.
* To shorten the time horizon of creating efficient

managers with the flexibility provided by a system like this, giving them a special edge over other management students.

* Facilitate recruitment process – a key concern – in a business school, particularly when one is looking at placements from the global perspective.
* Facilitate meetings, seminars, conferences, and other such interactions.

6. Equipment Procurement, Cost, Installation and Training

The Ministry cleared the project in March 2001 for rupees 15 lakh (as against Rs. 18 lakh proposed) for its completion in two years. Work on the project started with site visits to successful installations during 2001-2002. Based on the know-how and experience gained during the site visits, and keeping the above objectives in mind, a sub-committee, including technical experts, to firm-up the equipment requirements with appropriate specifications for procurement was constituted in January 2003. The sub-committee deliberated on the issue and finalised its recommendations for procurement of the equipment as shown in Table 1.

Table 1

Sl.No.	Equipment	Cost in Rupees	Quantity
1.	Group Video-Conferencing Unit (Main System Tanberg 800 NPP)	5,34,844.00	1
2	Polycom FX with 2 Microphones POD	5,00,000.00	1
3	T.V (Sony)	1,08,000.00	2
4	Quad BRI module for Polycom FX	51,879.00	1
5	Polycom Conferencing Unit VS-128	1,67,584.00	1
6	Smart Board Mimio XI & white Board	58,860.00	1
7	Document Camera TPL 781(Toshiba)	2,06,073.00	1
8	Desktop Video Conferencing unit Polycom Via-Video	1,04,370.00	3
9	Additional Camera Sony Ptz	52,320.00	1
10	Additional Microphone Pod (Polycom)	6540.00	1
11	Lap-Top Computers (Toshiba)	2,08,134.00	2

Purchase order was placed in March 2003 and supply was effected in May 2003. In parallel, efforts were on to organize the ISDN connectivity, which was through only in July 2004. By this time the installation had been completed. Successful installation, complete in all respects, and backed by training of staff was over by July 2004. First live demonstration of the facility was organized on August 6, 2004.

All this involved an expenditure of Rs. 15,31,004 (Rs. 14, 98, 604.00 for equipment and Rs. 32, 400 for installation and training). It however, does not include the cost of the item as mentioned at 2 above, as the Institute, under a different project, had already procured the same at a cost of rupees five lakh.

The lab has also been connected to one of the classrooms in the class room cluster.

This important phase of the project was undertaken completely by the Assistant Librarian, Mr. M K Singh, under the overall guidance of the Project Team.

7. Use of the Facility

Use of the facility started with organizing an industry-interaction talk on 'Careers in Finance', for students with the President of the IIM Lucknow Association, Mr. Vinit Singh Chauhan, who is currently working as *Global Manager* with J P Morgan, UK. This has been followed by several such talks with leading management professionals in the academia as well as industry. Trend is fast catching up to use the facility for placement purposes as well. Efforts are on to use the facility for student-teacher interaction with Institute's academic partners abroad. Similarly, the facility will come handy in facilitating student-teacher interaction with Institute's satellite campus at NOIDA. An experimental use of the facility in management development programmes (MDPs) was also encouraging. Resource persons from IIM Bangalore were used for interaction with the participants of an MDP on 'Information Technology Applications in LIS'. In all, and as of now, seven interactive videoconferences have already been organized during a short span of six months. Imagine the benefits and the savings. Each conference session running, on an average, for two to three hours meant a nominal expenditure of rupees 500.00 or so on communication link.

8. Acknowledgement

Guidance extended by Prof. P R Banerjee, Chief Project Coordinator, and Prof. Neerja Pande, Member of the Project Team, in firming up the project proposal as well as seeing it through is gratefully acknowledged. Help extended by all the members of the sub-committee, constituted to firm up the specifications of the equipment, is also sincerely acknowledged. The project would not have seen its successful fruition but for keen interest and involvement shown by Shri M K Singh, Assistant Librarian, IIML, who is now the Lab. Coordinator. Useful data inputs provided by him have helped me to send this contribution for sharing this experience with the participants of the MANLIBNET Convention 2005.

28

Digital Libraries in Knowledge Management : Opportunities for Management Libraries

V. Sivaraman
Professor & Nodal Officer,
Rajagiri College of Social Sciences, Cochin, Kerala

ABSTRACT

As we are at the threshold of information age, the Knowledge Managers (KMs) must assess and reassess the constantly changing library and information environment. There is a bright future for knowledge managers and it is not very far. Knowledge Managers individually and collectively cannot afford to ignore the changing shape of library and information services that are emerging in the globalization. The primary objective of libraries is to organize and provide access to information. This objective will never change, but the format and methods that are used will change dramatically, providing new opportunities and challenges. In the information age, the librarians are known as Knowledge Managers, as they are handling information and knowledge management. They will play a key role in facing challenges and to explore new ways to accomplish their goals with better quality of services. Automation will help in wider use of users services. New technology helps knowledge managers to merge the functions of technical and public services. It will enable personnel in the technical services to devote more time to provide sophisticated Users services such as specialized bibliographic services and other more personalized services. The reference Librarians will be relieved of their routine jobs and allowed to devote more time to challenging tasks. Knowledge managers have to make difficult decisions such as what activities to relinquish in order to provide new and more effective services. The Librarians/ Knowledge Managers of management libraries will emerge with special skills and abilities of information specialists in the dissemination of information of the management subjects like Financial Management, Marketing Management, Human Resources Management, Operations Research and Operations Management, Management Information Systems, Marketing Research, Business Ethics, Environment Management, Strategic Management, Business Communication, etc. In future, Knowledge Managers may have to function more like consulting information engineers than as traditional, passive information resource custodians and dispensers of documents.

This paper mainly emphasis the importance of Digital Library Technology and its applications and opportunities for management libraries. The author strongly advocates in the paper that computers and advanced Information Technology can simplify many a task for the Knowledge Managers/Librarians, but that special human touch is still required to manage Library and Information Service – LIS System.

Introduction

Digital libraries (DLs) are viewed as systems providing a community of users with coherent access to a large, organized repository of information and knowledge. The ability of the user to access, reorganize and utilize this repository is enriched by the capabilities of digital technology.; Digital libraries would, for the foreseeable future need to span both print and digital materials and that the central issue was to provide a coherent view of a very large collection of information. In this sense, an emphasis on content solely in digital format, i.e. to develop information systems providing access to a coherent collection of material, more and more of which will be in digital format and to fully exploit the opportunities that are offered by the materials. Recently Digital Libraries have emerged as one of the central and most compelling applications enabled by the National Information Infrastructure; numerous digital library research projects are underway.

The comprehensiveness and value of the collection accessible through a digital library system can be strengthened by the ability to integrate materials in digital formats that have not been well represented easy to access, or effectively usable in traditional library collection, such as multimedia, geo-spatial data, or numerical datasets. There is, in reality, a very strong continuity between traditional library roles and missions and the objectives of digital library systems.

Digital resources are available on some basis, to a wide population via the medium of the Internet. Library users will thus be able to read and refer to these digital holdings from their own desktops, without needing to visit a library reading room.

The status of Knowledge Managers/Librarians and Knowledge Management

We know that the library is known as knowledge industry. It is mostly related to knowledge and information. Knowledge is what consists of truth & beliefs, perspectives & concepts, judgments & expectations, methodologies & know-how. Knowledge is accumulated, organized, integrated and held over long periods, where as information consists of facts, figures and data that are organized to describe a particular situation or a problem. It is evident from the above that knowledge and information, though related are different things. No knowledge, except intellect can be acquired without resources of information. Information is storage of knowledge as well as its foundation stone. Libraries are charged with the responsibility of collection, storage, processing and marketing of recorded knowledge in the form of various kinds of conventional and non-conventional documents. Therefore, they are known as knowledge industry. They are able to generate income through their valuable resources of information in addition to their services to the users. Libraries are no longer considered as a non-profit making organization. Library and information services like most other services generally can be evaluated in terms of time, cost and quality factors.

The present society is characterized by the presence of ever-growing technology and information explosion. There has been a tremendous increase of library users due to the utility of information in their concerned disciplines as a means to enrich their knowledge. For users, quality information is considered as the lifeblood of strong and vibrant markets. As the quality of information increases exponentially through the Internet and other technologies, the quality of that information will be given a signal priority. Information will be a way of life for the users community. In this context, Library and information centers owe a responsibility to satisfy information needs of the users community.

The traditional functions and services of the library or knowledge industry are going dramatic changes and a new concept of library and librarians is emerging. Some of the changes that are clearly seen are the shift from a production to a managerial role for librarians where the traditional librarian tasks are handled by the supporting staff. This change is evidently seen in technical work like classification, cataloguing, and indexing. In future, librarians will provide reference services and research support through electronic means such as bulletin boards and electronic mail, etc. as part of selective dissemination of information- SDI and current awareness services- GAS. The knowledge managers will be teaching/guiding researchers to access database independently at the same time developing databases to provide access to materials otherwise not organized.

The Importance of Digital Library and Information Service to Librarians / Knowledge Managers

The Digital information resources and services are going to play a most vital role in the 21st century. Internet is the gateway for libraries and information centres to the electronic information era and different organisations, institution, research centres and individuals all over the world generate information in digital form on the Internet. Creation of digital resources with the establishment of the digital library is the need of the day. It would be a unique resource for library professionals to provide such digital information services like journals, statistics, government documents, electronic images and indexes. Simultaneously there are also Internet public libraries and virtual libraries on different disciplines that are providing such digital information services.

Digital refers to any resource, which is in digitised form. This can be read and scanned with the means of electronic media. Like conventional forms digitised resources do not require separate space in a library as this can be read and scanned with the means of electronic media. Like conventional forms digitised resources do not require separate space in a library, as this can be stored in a computer locally and remotely. Due to the emergence of information technology individuals, organisations and institutions are publishing scholarly papers, creating digital libraries using scanning technology and other software publishers are also publishing huge documents on the internet. But all the libraries and information centres are not in a position to spend an exorbitant amount to subscribe or to procure the same within their financial limit. In addition to the changeable resources, a lot of digital resources are available free of cost.

In the age of information technology and information explosion librarians / knowledge managers of management libraries must equip themselves drastically if they want to retain their identity in a rapidly developing information society. On the other hand the source of information is unlimited and the budget of the institution is limited for providing information to the users. The knowledge mangers have already started the compilation work under different heading like virtual library, digital library etc.

The Need to Digitize

The growing impact of Information and Communication Technologies (ICT), web technologies and database technologies has compelled library and information centres to use these technologies effectively to render services. With the growing number of E-sources, it has become imperative for information professionals to redefine their role in disseminating information to the users.

Advantages

Digitization brings together research information on topics, which are available in various formats and in various locations. These digital materials/sources may be widely scattered. Thus, digitization allows easy access allowing to build collections and compare items which can be viewed/ examined side by side solely by virtue of digital representation and access to digital reference materials, especially images that provide a great deal of information to researchers. Thus, digital conversion has added value in that:

* It can be saved digitally;
* It has enhanced intellectual control along with new finding tools;
* It has provided links to bibliographic records;

* There is an increased usage of library resources and web resources;
* There is an increased manipulation of text and images;
* There is encouragement of use by providing enhanced resources in the form of widespread dissemination of unique collections;
* There is an integration and synthesis of a variety of formats;
* There is an integration of related materials that are scattered among many locations;
* Duplication of digital resources is easy;
* Resources can be used simultaneously by more than one user;
* Provide timely access
* Support searching capabilities
* Save physical storage space
* Contain multimedia information
* Can be easily merged with alerting services
* No mutilation of pages because of high use
* Accessibility of resources (locally, Intranet/Internet)
* Resource sharing among libraries
* Easy to transfer to any place on Internet instantly
* Archival of resources
* Facility to create multi-media resources
* Easy to port on the Internet so that the same can be immediately accessed by others worldwide;
* Several libraries can form a consortium and access bibliographical databases/full-text journals online by spending only a nominal amount.

It is possible to acquire databases/full-text journals in digital form that can be made available in a local machine so that the participating institutions can access these with a nominal amount.

Disadvantages

The main drawback is the cost of digitization arid preservation of files. In this aspect one can justify the cost of digitizing of a unique collection such as the collection of SERC library especially when it leads to increased access and usage (of under-utilized collections). The disadvantages of digitization are:

* Acquire special skills to set up and maintain the DL
* Require special training
* User has to accept the media
* Bandwidth problem in accessing multimedia resources and full-text journals
* Scanning the original documents of the entire collections
* IPR issues
* Authenticity and credibility acceptance of the digitized resource
* Initial HW/SW cost
* Librarians are wary of the new technology

Types of digital Resources

Digital refers to any resources, which is in digitised form i.e. which can be read and scanned with the means of electronic media. Like conventional forms digitised resources do not require separate space in a library, as this can be stored in a computer locally and remotely. Digital resources include a wide range of material such as:

a. Collection in which complete contents of documents are created or converted into machine-readable form for online access.

b. Scanned images, images of photographic or printed text, etc.

c. Scientific data sets such as protein sequences.

d. Online databases and CD–ROM information products, particularly those with multimedia and interactive video components.

e. Computer storage device such as optical disk, juke boxes, CD ROM / DVD – ROM.

f. Databases accessible through Internet and other networks.

g. Digital audio, video clips or full length movies.

How to acquire Digital collection?

a. Digitising existing important and useful print material

b. Link and pointers, resources that are freely available on the Internet and are freely available on the Internet and are of significant scholarly value can be added to library catalogues and network resources.

c. Purchased or licensed material such as electronic journals or databases.

Setting up a Digital Library

Metadata and Dublin Core

Providing access to the internally created digital resources is very important. Therefore, a suitable software and format Has to be chosen and adopted in order to access the resources using various data elements. It is necessary to catalogue these digital resources using suitable software, which supports Dublin Core (DC) Standard that is being adopted internationally to create metadata of digital resources. Metadata is data about the data and objects. This may be a catalogue record, or web page or digital resource. Metadata record consists of a set of attributes, which are necessary to describe a resource. It is used to describe the digital and non-digital resources located in a distributed system, in a networked environment.

Dublin Core standard consists of a set of 15 elements for describing a wide range of networked resources. It is an exchange format for sharing records among multiple collections. DC was originated at a workshop, which was held in Dublin Core, Ohio in 1995, and DC recommends a minimal of 15 data elements to describe any documents. They are: Title, Subject, Description, Type, Source, Relation, Coverage, Creator, Publisher, Contributor, Rights, Date, Format, Identifier and Language.

Requirements

Hardware / software requirements for a medium level DL are indicated below. These are only indicative and not exhaustive.

HW Server: A Pentium (IBM, etc) IV server, RAID, 1.2 Ghz, 1 512MB RAM, 256 cache, 21" SVGA Monitor, SCSI 500 I GB HD, CD-writer, CD-Rom, FDD, SNAP server, 10/100 Mbps Ethernet card, and other accessories with Multimedia kit.

Back up device: Optical disk, CD/DVD -ROM, Mirror

Server / CD Juke box / DAT Drive

Scanner: Intelligent/High density flat bed scanner - (HP (ScanJet 6300C)/

Fujitsu 3097Getc, Minolta PS3000, Ricob IS420

Sheet Feed Scanners - Kodak, 500S, Drum Scanners

(Juno CP-4000,ScanMate 5000, ColorGetter

Digital camera (Minolta PS 3000, OmniScan 3000, Canon)

Laser / Ink Jet Printer

Fax

OS Windows 2000 server or Linux

SW Publishing: Adobe acrobat including Adobe capturing, MS-Word

Multimedia tools -Photoshop, Flash, Imaging, Library software with cataloguing and searching digital resources - VTLS, AutoLib, etc Searching documents created in various file formats -Dtsearch

WEB Server: Microsoft IIS, Java, Apache OCR software- TextBridge, Omnipage Imaging Capturing/Scanning Software - Itris, Optix, Power Office, FileNet, Data Data Scan, OmniDoc, data compression software

Database: MS-SQL server, Oracle, MS-Access

Formats: Files: txt, doc, html, xml, sgml, pdf. Postscript

Images: tiff, .bmp, jpg

Network: high speed LAN/Intranet/Internet connectivity Protocol: TCP/IP

The Challenges and Opportunities for Knowledge Managers / Librarians of Management Libraries

A vast amount of knowledge is scattered in a disorganised manner in our country. It requires professional managers to organise knowledge for any constructive purpose. Management of knowledge is therefore an indispensable imperative to make it useful and purposive. The knowledge managers are well trained for this purpose. However, they face many challenges in the managerial process of knowledge on fingertips, information explosion, increase in the cost of publications and shrinking budget, etc.

Though KMs face many challenges, the opportunities are greater for them. Accessing information has undergone revolutionary changes during the last three decades in the developed world. Laborious manual sifting of documentation for information is rapidly becoming a thing of the past. In these countries a user can now, by typing out commands on his desk top pc, swiftly scan numerous databases scattered over the globe and get the information he needs much faster than through a manual search in a library. These technological milestones have enabled this on-line access to current information. One was the advent of the pc and consequent spread of computing power to a large section of the population. The second was the invention of magnetic data storage systems so that large volumes of data could be stored in a small space and in computer readable format. The third was the development of methods to transmit data in bulk, at high speed and at a very low error rate, through telecommunication networks

With the results, the opportunities have become greater to Knowledge Managers; opportunities are in E-publishing / E-book, E-reading, E-book market, etc.

Potential need for Traditional Knowledge Digital Library - TKDL for non-patent libraries

There is a great demand for TKDL. When the traditional knowledge digital library TKDL comes into existence, India will be the first country to respond to the challenge of creating an easily accessible non-patent literature database. The patent offices of the developed countries did not have non-patent databases on the traditional knowledge of the developing world. When patent examiners search for literature they miss out on literature on non-patent prior art, which are buried in diverse literature. To protect the rich traditional knowledge that India need to create a TKDL.

The TKDL would document the country's traditional knowledge electronically under the appropriate classification within the international patent classification systems. Eventually, the creation of TKDL will serve a bigger purpose in enhancing the country's innovation capability. It could act as a bridge between the traditional and modern knowledge systems and provide an impetus to modern research.

Conclusion

Setting up a Digital Library is very important in any institution to meet the present and future information requirements. According to Donald Waters, the "promise of digital technology is for libraries to extend the reach of research and education, improve the quality of learning, and reshape scholarly communication". No single institution can effectively manage and provide access to more than a small portion of the information universe. There is an increasingly diverse array of networked digital library products and services. In a digitised environment it is possible for the users to have access to a library's own digitised collections, CD-ROM databases, online databases, E-book, E-signs, digitised holdings of other libraries, Internet and its myriad resources. India, today is experiencing an I.T revolution. We are in an ICE age. Information Technology, Communications and Entertainment are the three legs of ICE age. These three would from the base for the next change in society and mankind had made rapid strides in these sectors – Library and information Services have to play a crucial role in Socio – economic development, The knowledge Managers should be better equipped to meet the new challenges and participate in the process of generating and distributing information and knowledge for attaining social well being, a better quality of life and education for all. We should remember that computers could simplify many a task for the Knowledge Managers, but that special human touch is still required to manage a Library and Information system. As Dr. S. Radhakrishnan had rightly pointed out that "Education must make our people the masters of technology and not its slaves", the knowledge managers should not become slaves of the Information Technology.

The whole New Economy of a Nation is based on information. But information without access to it by right users in right time is no good. Modern Library and Information Schools teach their students to process raw data to get information, information to get knowledge and knowledge to get wisdom.

In a fast developing economy, the need for technical and professional staff gradually increases, as compared with those specialising in manual skills. In advanced countries, people today live in an information society, where generation and dissemination ideas and information is as important as goods and services. Such a society, which is largely knowledgeable, based, is one where highly educated personnel are engaged for putting knowledge to work.

Basic requirement of knowledge-based services are mainly libraries, library and information professionals, right users and information technology. We can understand that library is an important element or component in knowledge based industry and without that component the industry and its products like right information cannot be possible.

We need to appreciate and congratulate the organization for putting their effort to have the Management Libraries Network [MANLIBNET] for sharing of resources and information among the libraries. This itself is an opportunity for the Librarians/Knowledge Managers of Management Libraries.

References

1. Drucker, Peter. F. "Performance in the service institution" *in Management cases*, Mumbai, Allied Publishers private limited, 1979.
2. Drucker, Peter. F. "Managing the Knowledge worker", Ibid.
3. Drucker, Peter. F. "The information explosion in the *changing world of the Executive*", New York, Times Book, 1909.
4. Drucker, Peter. F *"Management challenges for the 21st century"*, Mumbai, Butterworth Heinemann Oxford, 1999.
5. Vashisth, C.P.et all. *New Horizons in Library and Information Science*: Velaya Venkatappaiah Festschrift. Madras, T R Publication, 1994.
6. Ravi, N.ed. *The Hindu speaks on Information Technology*. Madras, Kasturi &sons Ltd., 1996.

7. Parthasarathy, Anand. "Towards a new era of paperless publishing", *The Hindu*, Nov.4(1999)

8. Balasubramanian, G. "Winds of change in Libraries", *TheHindu*, June2 (1998)

9. Davenport, Thomas.H. and Prusak, Laurence. "Knowledge Management :Real value in Action", *Dataquest*, Mar. 31(2000)

10. Karthikeyan, R. "It pays to read", *"The Indian Express"*, Sep. 10(2000)

11. Jayaraman, M.S. "E-Merging convergence", *Computers* today, Sep.30 (2000)

12. Kant, Krishna. 'Technology with a multi dimensional approach", *The Hindu*, Sep.26 (2000)

29

Multimedia Content Development for new Generation Libraries

Ashok Pathak
Indian Institute of Management Kozhikode
(ashok@iimk.ac.in)

ABSTRACT

Information Technology has dramatically affected all facets of our lives and Library Services in the new era are no exception. The conventional libraries confined within a physical space are slowly transforming into digital information resources centers through a thoughtful and effective deployment of the technology which is now being used beyond just automating library's routine administrative functions and is catalytic in efficient and effective delivery of library services. However, just the availability of power of IT and digital contents is not enough to effectively deliver the digital/multimedia content unless the content forming part of the library resources is properly planned and designed.

This article gives brief introduction about the use of multimedia in library services, characteristics, current technology trends, pros and cons in using various different types of digital object formats, tools for creating these objects with their merits and demerits and the popular tools for digital content integration.

1. Multimedia defined

The term 'multimedia' has a variety of meanings to

different people. *Multimedia*[1] can be defined as the technology engaging a variety of media, including text, audio, video graphics and animation either separately or in combination, using computers, to communicate ideas or to disseminate information. The applications of multimedia are various and include virtual reality and 3-D presentations. Multimedia has become a generic term for "multimedia computing" or "interactive multimedia".

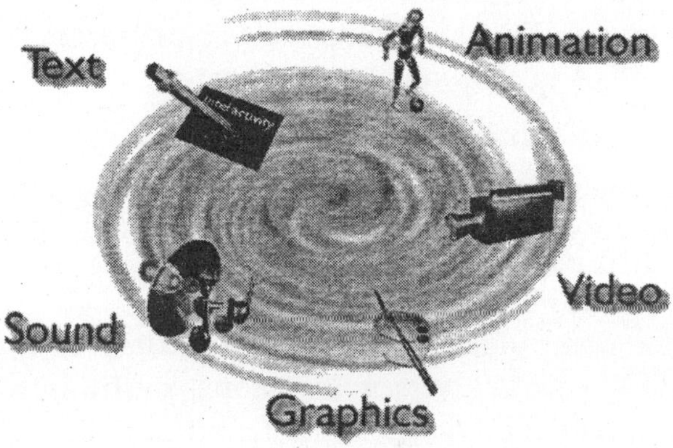

The computer and its software are used to control and navigate through the communications medium, not only one at the time, but several simultaneously which simulates the real-world and presents unique and innovative opportunities to captivate human senses.

The multimedia computer system

The essential capability of any multimedia computer[2] system is the ability to convert the analogue signal to a digital format and compress this information using standard algorithms. The power of the CPU determines whether this process can be carried out in real-time or whether it has to be done off-line. The compression process is necessary otherwise the quantity of data to be stored and transmitted would be excessive. It is now possible to digitize video and audio with desktop computers such as the PC or Macintosh, which makes possible the handling of multimedia material which can be used in support of teaching.

A multimedia computer system thus comprises of a powerful high speed central processor, relatively large memory, hard disk and floppy disk drives, CD-ROM, audio input and output devices, e.g. microphones and loudspeakers, video input and output devices, e.g. VCRs and video-cameras, still image input and output device, e.g. scanner, high graphics capability to handle both bitmap and vector graphics such as SVGA/XSVGA quality display and mouse.

2. Multimedia components/objects

One or more of the following media and/or their combination form part of any multimedia application[3]:

Text

Since computers can display a variety of fonts, in innumerable colors and combinations, multiple fonts in beautiful colors and backgrounds feature in almost all the multimedia applications and the ultimate result appears far better than the printed texts.

Graphics

This includes, pictures, photographs, graphs and charts and other art works. It is this media that makes up a visually fascinating material. The old proverb "A picture is worth a thousand words" still holds true.

Animation

This refers to the artificial movements of texts or other multimedia objects created in virtual environments, using specialized software packages. Animations are primarily used to demonstrate an idea or illustrate a concept. Video is usually taken from life, whereas animations are based on drawings. Animations are perhaps the most interesting part of multimedia computing but are extensively time consuming while creating and demand heavy artistic capabilities.

Audio

This includes speeches, music and other types of sounds. Audio element is generally used to enhance the usual multimedia environment.

Video

This includes the actual video clips that could be embedded right over the applications and can be played back without a hitch. The sizes of the clippings are usually much smaller than that from video cassette players.

3. Multimedia: Classifications[1]

Interactive multimedia

A multimedia application is called an interactive multimedia, if the user participates in every stage of the proceedings as the application advances. The degree of interactivity may vary from application to application. Most of the CD-ROM titles and Games-ware are of interactive nature.

Non-interactive multimedia

Non interactive multimedia is something; say a corporate presentation or a multimedia demo, in which the audience just watch the show as it proceeds from the beginning to the end in a sequential manner.

Entertainment multimedia

All games, multimedia books and novels and multimedia movies are examples of entertainment multimedia.

Edutainment multimedia

CD based self learning tutors, which try to educate the user in some specific curriculum, along with the entertainment, constitute edutainment multimedia.

4. Popular image formats

GIF (Graphics Interchange Format) [4]

Most computer color images and backgrounds are GIF files. This compact file format is ideal for graphics that use only a few colors, and it was once the most popular format for online color photos. The "GIF" format uses an 8 bit Color Look Up Table (CLUT) to identify its color values. If the original image is an 8 bit, gray-scale photo, then the "GIF" format produces a compressed *lossless* image file. (*Lossless* means that the image uncompressed from the file would be identical to the original.) A grey scale image typically has only 256 levels of gray. This is accomplished by the Run Length Encoding mechanism of compressing the information while saving a GIF file. If the original file were a 24 bit color graphic image, then it would first be mapped to an 8 bit CLUT and then compressed using RLE (Run Length Encoding). The loss would be in the remapping of the original 24 bit (16.7 million) colors to the limited 8 bit (256 colors) CLUT. RLE encoding would reproduce an uncompressed image that was identical to the remapped 8 bit image, but not the same as the original 24 bit image.

GIF has, however lost ground to the JPEG format when it comes to photos because GIF images are limited to only 256 colors but JPEGs can contain up to 16 million colors—and they can look almost as good as a photograph.

Interlaced GIF, A feature of the GIF89a graphics standard, displays images in two passes of alternating lines instead of loading them one line at a time. Depending on which graphics viewer or Web browser is being used, interlaced GIFs may produce a "venetian blind" effect or simply a blurry or blocky image that gradually sharpens. Pages using interlaced GIFs let people see at least the outline of an image sooner; thus the pages often appear to load faster than those with non-interlaced graphics. If a browser doesn't support interlaced images, an image will simply appear as a normal (non-interlaced) GIF.

A feature of the GIF89a graphics standard, a transparent GIF lets the background show through selected parts of an image. When creating the GIF, the designer can designate one color in the image's palette as transparent. When the GIF is displayed, areas using that color reveal whatever is underneath. Transparency is most often applied to a GIF's background color to let the page's own background show through, so that images appear to float on the page. Most modern Web browsers support transparent GIFs. Those that don't, simply display the images as normal GIFs.

JPEG[5]

JPEG is a standardized image compression mechanism. JPEG stands for Joint Photographic Experts Group, the original name of the committee that wrote the standard.

JPEG is designed for compressing either full-color or gray-scale images of natural, real-world scenes. It works well on photographs, naturalistic artwork, and similar material; not so well on lettering, simple cartoons, or line drawings. JPEG handles only still images, but there is a related standard called MPEG for motion pictures.

JPEG is "lossy," meaning that the decompressed image isn't quite the same as the one you started with. (There are lossless image compression algorithms, but JPEG achieves much greater compression than is possible with lossless methods.) JPEG is designed to exploit known limitations of the human eye, notably the fact that small color changes are perceived less accurately than small changes in brightness. Thus, JPEG is intended for compressing images that will be looked at by humans.

A useful property of JPEG is that adjusting compression parameters can vary the degree of looseness. This means that the image-maker can trade off file size against output image quality. You can make extremely small files if you don't mind poor quality; this is useful for applications such as indexing image archives. Conversely, if you aren't happy with the output quality at the default compression setting, you can jack up the quality until you are satisfied, and accept lesser compression.

Why use JPEG?

There are two good reasons:

1. to make your image files smaller, and
2. to store 24-bit-per-pixel color data instead of 8-bit-per-pixel data.

Making image files smaller is a win for transmitting files across networks and for archiving libraries of images. Being able to compress a 2 Mbyte full-color file down to, say, 100 Kbytes makes a big difference in disk space and transmission time! And JPEG can easily provide 20:1 compression of full-color data.

It takes longer to decode and view a JPEG image than to view an image of a simpler format such as GIF. Thus using JPEG is essentially a time/space tradeoff: you give up some time in order to store or transmit an image more cheaply. But it's worth noting that when network transmission is involved, the time savings from transferring a shorter file can be greater than the time needed to decompress the file.

The second fundamental advantage of JPEG is that it stores full color information: 24 bits/pixel (16 million colors). As compared to GIF, which stores 8 bits/pixel (256 or fewer colors)?

When should I use JPEG, and when should I stick with GIF?

JPEG is not going to displace GIF entirely; for some types of images, GIF is superior in image quality, file size, or both.

Generally speaking, JPEG is superior to GIF for storing full-color or gray-scale images of "realistic" scenes; that means scanned photographs, continuous-tone artwork, and similar material. Any smooth variation in color, such as occurs in highlighted or shaded areas, will be represented more faithfully and in less space by JPEG than by GIF.

GIF does significantly better on images with only a few distinct colors, such as line drawings and simple cartoons. Not only is GIF loss less for such images, but it often compresses them more than JPEG can. For example, large areas of pixels that are all exactly the same color are compressed very efficiently indeed by GIF. JPEG can't squeeze such data as much as GIF does without introducing visible defects. (One implication of this is that large single-color borders are quite cheap in GIF files, while they are best avoided in JPEG files.)

Plain black-and-white images should never be converted to JPEG. You need at least about 16 gray levels before JPEG is useful for gray-scale images. It should also be noted that GIF is loss less for gray-scale images of up to 256 levels, while JPEG is not.

PNG[6]

PNG is an extensible file format for the lossless, portable, well-compressed storage of raster images. PNG provides a patent-free replacement for GIF and can also replace many common uses of TIFF. Indexed-color, grayscale, and true color images are supported, plus an optional alpha channel for transparency. Sample depths range from 1 to 16 bits.

5. Tools for creating multimedia image objects

There are many tools available which one can use to create simple or elaborate drawings, images, manipulate pictures and photos. These objects can be either black-and-white or color and can be saved as a bitmap, JPG, GIF, Tiff or any other popular format. Example:

1. MS Paint
2. Microsoft Photo Editor
3. Painshop Pro
4. Adobe PhotoShop

6. Popular digital audio file formats[7]

Historically, almost every type of machine used its own file format for audio data, but some file formats are more generally applicable, and in general it is possible to define conversions between almost any pair of file formats — sometimes losing information, however.

File formats are a separate issue from device characteristics. There are two types of file formats: self-describing formats, where the device parameters and encoding are made explicit in some form of header, and "raw" formats, where the device parameters and encoding are fixed.

Self-describing file formats generally define a family of data encodings, where a header fields indicates the particular encoding variant used. Header-less formats define a single encoding and usually allows no variation in device parameters (except sometimes sampling rate, which can be a pain to figure out other than by listening to the sample).

Digital audio data is characterized by the following parameters, which correspond to settings of the Analog to Digital Converter when the data was recorded. Naturally, the same settings must be used to play the data.

* Sampling rate (in samples per second), e.g. 8000 or 44100
* Number of bits per sample, e.g. 8 or 16
* Number of channels (1 for mono, 2 for stereo, etc.)

Approximate sampling rates are often quoted in Hz or kHz ([kilo-] Hertz). Sampling rates are always measured per channel, so for stereo data recorded at 8000 samples / sec, there are actually 16000 samples in a second. The resultant audio files are huge in terms of file sizes as the data is uncompressed.

However, in order to effectively distribute audio over networks it has to be compressed to reduce the data size so that bandwidth doesn't become a bottleneck. There are many different Compression techniques available.

au[8], aiff[9], wave[10], mp3[11], WMA[12] etc are some of the popular audio file formats offering data compression and making them suitable for distribution of audio over the networks. Following graph shows the comparative file sizes after capturing an audio clip and converting it into MP3, MP3Pro, WMA and RA formats:

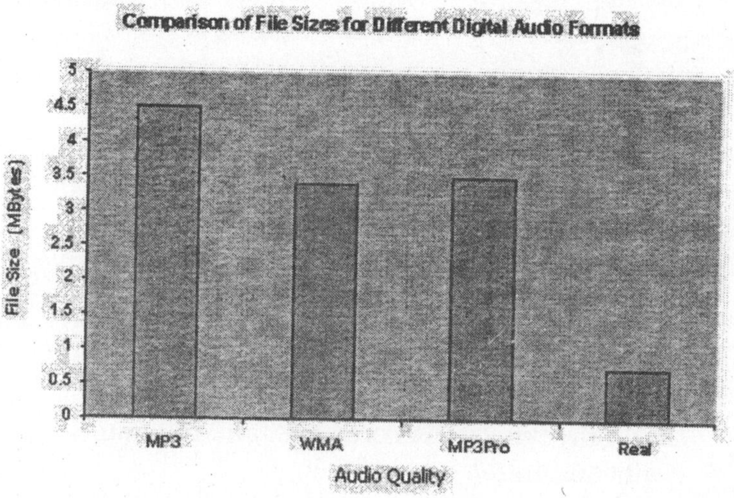

From the above graph, it is clear that the Real Audio format offers the best compression and is the most suitable format for distribution of audio over the Internet. However, this compression results in a loss in the quality of the audio. MP3 format offers the best quality with sufficient compression and is very suitable for distribution of audio on CDs and also over local area network (LAN).

In the table on the following page, I have tried to make a comparison of various features of three most popular digital audio storage formats:

Table: Comparison of various features of MP3, WMA and Real audio formats

Features	Audio File Format		
	MP3	WMA	Real
Quality	Excellent	Good	Very Good
Streamable	Yes	Yes	Yes
Bit Rates	128	64	96
Plug-ins	Winamp	Windows Media Player	Real One
Encoding Time	High	Medium	Low
Convertible back to WAV	Yes	Restricted	With Winamp
Availability of portable players	Widely	Available	Difficult to find
Price of portable players	Moderate	Expensive	Very Expensive
Popularity	Most Popular	Moderate	Moderate

7. Tools for creating audio files

1. Windows Sound Recorder - record sound/music clip limited to 60 seconds duration
2. MultitrackStudio - Mix, edit, and record music.
3. RecAll Sound Recorder (http://www.sagebrush.com)
4. Nero Burning Rom 5.5 - the latest versions includes an integrated wave file/sound editor
5. Cool Edit Pro 2.0 - Record, edit, and mix multi- track digital audio
6. LAVA burn - you can write MP3 files, wave files and Audio CD tracks on a audio CD. Convert Wave to mp3 with external encoder.
7. MP3 Encoder - lets you convert standard CD tracks and WAV files to constant-...
8. Winamp - MP3 player
9. MUSICMATCH Jukebox Plus - lets you Play MP3s, CDs, video, rip CD-quality MP3s, Burn CDs
10. AudioCD MP3-Studio - designed to burn your MP3s and WAV files to audio CD in one step directly to music CDs

8. Popular digital video file formats

A video file format is a standard for encoding digital video, audio and some auxiliary information into a file. In contrast to audio and image formats, most video file formats allow a variety of codecs, both audio and video, to be used.

Auxiliary information often includes:

* data required for correct synchronization between audio and video
* subtitles

Popular video file formats are:

AVI (Audio/Video Interleave) [13]

AVI is the file format used by Video for Windows, one of three video technologies used on personal computers. (The others are MPEG and QuickTime.) In AVI, picture and sound elements are stored in alternate interleaved chunks in the file.

AVI Tools

1. WINAVI 6.0
2. Windows Media Player

MPEG [14]

MPEG (Moving Pictures Experts Group) is a group of people that meet under ISO (the International Standards Organization) to generate standards for digital video (sequences of images in time) and audio compression. In particular, they define a compressed bit stream, which implicitly defines a decompressor. However, the compression algorithms are up to the individual manufacturers, and that is where proprietary advantage is obtained within the scope of a publicly available international standard.

Established in 1988, the group has produced MPEG-1, the standard on which such products as Video CD and MP3 are based, MPEG-2, the standard on which such products as Digital Television set top boxes and DVD are based, MPEG-

4, the standard for multimedia for the fixed and mobile web and MPEG-7, the standard for description and search of audio and visual content. Work on the new standard MPEG-21 "Multimedia Framework" has started in June 2000. So far a Technical Report and two standards have been produced and three more parts of the standard are at different stages of development. Several Calls for Proposals have already been issued.

Technically speaking MPEG is not a storage format but standards for digital video and audio compression.

MPEG Tools

1. DCM - a complete package of hardware and software tools for creating MPEG-2 and MPEG-1 content, including VideoCD 2.0 and DVD compliant video
2. Data Translations Broadway - Create quality video right on your PC.
3. Pinnacle Studio Software
4. Ulead Media Studio Pro
5. Fx MPEG Writer - Create VCDs or DVDs from AVI, MPEG, or Windows Media source files
6. Windows Media Player - MPEG Player for viewing MPEG video
7. Xing - VCD player for viewing VCD and MPEG video
8. Nero Burning Rom 5.5 - the latest versions includes an integrated MPEG encoder for creating VCDs

QuickTime[15]

Developed by Apple Computer, QuickTime is a method of storing sound, graphics, and movie files. If you see a MOV file on the Web or on a CD-ROM, you'll know it's a QuickTime file. Although QuickTime was originally developed for the Macintosh, player software is now available for Windows and other platforms and can always be downloaded from Apple's Web site.

QuickTime Tools

1. QuickTime Player: FREE premier multimedia player.
2. QuickTime Pro: Powerhouse media authoring.
3. QuickTime Streaming Server: License free server for streaming digital media over the Internet.
4. Darwin Streaming Server: Open-source streaming server for Linux, Solaris and Windows.
5. QuickTime Broadcaster: FREE live encoder to easily webcast live events over the Internet.

Real[16]

Tools from RealNetworks provide the universal platform for the delivery of any digital media from any point of origin across virtually any network to any person on any Internet-enabled device anywhere in the world.

Real Player Tools

1. RealOne Player: A tool necessary for media content to be experienced on the client PC. (Downloadable from http://www.real.com)
2. RealOne Enterprise Desktop: A configurable version of the RealOne Player that has been optimized for enterprise deployments.
3. Sound Forge Studio XP 5.0: Streamlined Audio Editor for the Web.
4. Helix Universal Server: The Helix Universal Server is streaming media server software. Able to run on multiple operating systems, RealSystem Server distributes audio, video, and other media to client computers via unicast or multicast delivery. RealSystem Servers are the cornerstone of RealSystem iQ, an integrated media-delivery platform designed for rich media delivery.
5. Helix Universal Gateway: Offers Universal media

delivery and caching capabilities in one integrated solution. Containing all the functionality of the Internet server, plus an integrated universal media cache to reduce bandwidth usage, this server is the ideal edge solution for Service Provider distributed deployments.

Windows Media Video

Windows Media Video (WMV) is a generic name for the set of proprietary streaming video technologies developed by Microsoft. It is part of the Windows Media framework. WMV is not built solely on Microsoft in-house technology. From version 7 (WMV7), Microsoft has used its own non-standard version of MPEG-4. The video stream is often combined with an audio stream of Windows Media Audio.

WMV files are customarily played by Windows Media Player on Microsoft Windows and Macintosh systems. Some third-party players also exist. Raw WMV video is packed into an AVI or Advanced Streaming Format (ASF) container. The resulting files may be named .avi if it is an AVI-contained file, or .wmv or .asf if it is an ASF file, but .wmv files are to be ASF files with audio/video content only.

WMV is usually found in the AVI file container when encoded with Microsoft's Windows Media Video 9 VCM software for Windows. Microsoft's Windows Media Player for the Mac does not support all WMV encoded files since it supports only the ASF file container.

WMV also features digital rights management facilities.

In the table on the following page, I have tried to make a comparison of various features of three popular digital video storage formats:

Table: Comparison of various features of WMV, QuickTime and Real Media formats

Features	Digital Video File Format		
	WMV	Quick Time	Real Media
Resolution	640x480	640x480	320x240
Video Compression	MPEG4	Sorenson, Cinepak, MPEG4	RM
Video bit rate	1000kbps	1000kbps	350kbps
Audio Compression	MP3, WMA, OGG, AAC, AC3	Sorenson, Cinepak, MP3	RM
Audio bit rate	128kbps	128kbps	64kbps
Size/min	4-10MB/min	4-20MB/min	2-5MB/min
Min/74min CD	60-180min	30-180min	120-300min
Hours/DVD	7-18hrs	3-18hrs	14-35hrs
Hours/Dual Layer DVD	13-30hrs	6-30hrs	25-65hrs
DVD Player Compatibility	Few	None	None
Computer CPU Usage	Very High	High	Low
Quality	Excellent	Excellent	Good

9. Popular tools for multimedia content integration

1. Common Word Processing Tools

The most common tools used for computer-generated documents is the native application tools such as:

1. Microsoft Word
2. WordPerfect
3. Microsoft PowerPoint etc
4. PageMaker

2. *Postscript*[17]

PostScript is a programming language optimized for printing graphics and text (whether on paper, film, or CRT is immaterial). In the jargon of the day, it is a page description language. It was introduced by Adobe in 1985 and first (to my knowledge) appeared in the Apple LaserWriter. The main purpose of PostScript was to provide a convenient language in which to describe images in a device independent manner. This device independence means that the image is described without reference to any specific device features (e.g. printer resolution) so that the same description could be used on any PostScript printer (say, a LaserWriter) without modification. In practice, some PostScript files do make assumptions about the target device (such as its resolution or the number of paper trays it has), but this is bad practice and limits portability.

3. *HTML*[18]

To publish information for global distribution, one needs a universally understood language, a kind of publishing mother tongue that all computers may potentially understand. The publishing language used by the World Wide Web is HTML (from HyperText Markup Language).

HTML is the lingua franca for publishing hypertext on the World Wide Web. It is a non-proprietary format based upon SGML, and can be created and processed by a wide range of tools, from simple plain text editors - you type it in from scratch- to sophisticated WYSIWYG authoring tools. HTML uses tags such as <h1> and </h1> to structure text into headings, paragraphs, lists, hypertext links etc.

HTML gives authors the means to:

* Publish online documents with headings, text, tables, lists, photos, etc.
* Retrieve online information via hypertext links, at the click of a button.
* Design forms for conducting transactions with remote services, for use in searching for information, making reservations, ordering products, etc.
* Include spreadsheets, video clips, sound clips, and other applications directly in their documents.

Tool for Creating HTML Documents

1. Any popular text editor such as Windows Notepad can be used to create HTML documents

2. Visual Tools such as FrontPage for creating HTML pages

5. Macromedia Tools[20]

One can create everything from web-based tutorials to sophisticated simulations incorporating audio and video with Macromedia Authorware, the leading rich-media authoring solution for e-learning, deliver applications on the web, corporate networks or CD-ROM, and easily track student results and return on investment.

1. Macromedia Authorware (a complete e-learning solution)
2. Macromedia Studio MX (for rapid development of rich Internet applications with approachable, integrated tools that leverage leading web server technologies and device platforms.)
3. Macromedia Flash MX (Create rich Internet content and applications)
4. Dreamweaver MX (for Build websites and web applications)
5. Fireworks MX (Design and optimize interactive web graphics)

6. Adobe Acrobat - Portable Document Format (PDF) [21]

(PDF) is the open de facto standard for electronic document distribution worldwide. Adobe PDF is a universal file format that preserves all the fonts, formatting, graphics, and color of any source document, regardless of the application and platform used to create it. PDF files are compact and can be shared, viewed, navigated, and printed exactly as intended by anyone with free Adobe Acrobat Reader software. You can convert any document to PDF using Adobe Acrobat software.

PDF is the emerging workflow standard in the multimedia and publishing industry. It also plays a key role in financial services, regulated industries, and government.

PDF offers the following benefits:

* PDF files can be published and distributed anywhere: in print, attached to e-mail, on corporate servers, posted on Web sites, or on CD-ROM.
* Platform independent: Whether your PC runs on MS-DOS, Windows, OS-2, MAC, or Sun/UNIX, you can distribute your PDF documents among them all, retaining all of your content, format, fonts, and graphics ... and more!
* Compact PDF files are smaller than their source files, can be downloaded a page at a time for fast display on the Web, and don't slow down your network.
* Web Friendly: PDF documents can be viewed directly within Web browser windows that are fully compatible with Netscape Navigator V.3.0 or Internet Explorer V.3.0
* Acrobat Reader software required for reading PFD documents is easy to download from the Adobe Web site free.
* Using Acrobat 5.0 software, you can easily add bookmarks, set security options, and generate miniature Adobe PDF previews. Acrobat 5.0 also lets you comment on and approve Adobe PDF documents with digital signatures, all within a Web browser.

Tagged Adobe PDF

Adobe Acrobat 5.0 software introduces tagged Adobe PDF, an enhancement to the PDF specification that allows PDF files to contain logical document structure. Logical structure refers to the organization of a document, such as the title page, chapters, sections, and subsections. Tagged Adobe PDF documents can be re-flowed to fit small-screen devices and offer better support for re-purposing content. They also are more accessible to the visually impaired.

Tool for Creating PDF Documents

1. Adobe Acrobat 5.0
2. Neevia docuPrinter
3. Jaws PDF Creator & Editor
4. PDF995 (downloadable from http://site4.pdf995.com/download.html)
5. PDFEDIT995 (downloadable from http://site4.pdf995.com/pdfedit.html)

PDF is one of the key technologies for multimedia publishing. PDF is becoming the 'defacto' standard for publishing on the Internet. By converting every existing or new document into PDF, any document can be published for viewing, navigation and printing by anyone, anywhere, anytime. The look and feel will be exactly the same, regardless of the hardware (computers and printers) or software being used.

7. Microsoft Publisher[22]

Microsoft Publisher 2002 business desktop publishing program is designed for business users who are serious about creating professional-looking marketing and business materials without the assistance of a professional designer. A flexible wizard model integrated into the new Task Pane allows users to quickly and easily apply design options to create high-quality newsletters, flyers, brochures, Web sites, and more. With increased support of commercial printing functionality, first introduced in Publisher 2000, and the creation of the Publisher Service Provider Program, business users can easily locate commercial printers, service bureaus, and copy shops to output Publisher files.

Benefits

Work faster with familiar Office tools. Publisher 2002 simplifies the way people work by incorporating popular productivity tools from current and prior versions of Office, further reducing learning between Office applications. New features include Headers and Footers, Print Preview, customizable toolbars, Office Clipboard, OfficeArt, AutoShapes, thesaurus, Auto Recover, multiple documents, and more.

Powerful design tools for business users. Publisher 2002 offers more than 8500 template options to start creating and customizing common business publications, including newsletters, postcards, brochures, Web sites, and catalogs. Publisher smartly integrates the Office XP task pane to give users thumbnail previews and single click access to important design tasks – Color Schemes, Font Schemes, layouts, and publication designs.

New commercial printing options. These features include a 4-color process and spot color printing, giving you additional options for professional printing. You can search online for a Publisher printer at www.microsoft.com/publisher/printers.

Publish online. Export print-ready Publisher files for viewing on the Web, AutoConvert an existing brochure or newsletter to a Web site, or create a new Web site with the Web Site Wizard. Or, distribute your single page Publisher file as an e-mail message or an e-mail attachment.

8. Adobe Content Server[23]

Adobe Content Server is a digital publishing system for protecting, managing, and distributing eBooks and electronic documents. A powerful foundation for creating secure digital publishing systems, Adobe Content Server software helps publishers, libraries, enterprises, government agencies, and application service providers (ASPs) produce, manage, distribute, and protect digital content. Built around Adobe Portable Document Format (PDF), Adobe Content Server ensures the highest standard of security and rights management while delivering full-fidelity eBooks and other digital content to customers and patrons around the world.

Adobe Content Server 3.0 is available with an English user interface. Documentation is in English and Japanese.

Adobe Content Server packages and distributes digital content in universally accessible Adobe PDF format. Anyone with free Adobe Acrobat eBook Reader software can acquire the content with ease, regardless of operating system. And because millions of publications are created with the aid of Adobe tools such as Adobe FrameMaker, Adobe InDesign, Adobe Photoshop, Adobe Illustrator, and Adobe Acrobat software, they are often eBook-ready, ensuring a huge source of content to satisfy readers' tastes and interests the world over.

8. eBOOK CREATOR[24]

ebook creator is incredibly easy to use. If you can work a mouse, you can create eBooks with eBOOK CREATOR in a snap. It is a complete, ready-to-use system that any information publisher can use to create his own contemporary-style eBooks. It is equipped with a detailed, easy-to-understand instruction manual that walks you through every step of the creation process. eBOOK CREATOR is so simple, you'll use the manual once and never have need of it again!

Designed to work on computers with Windows 95 / 98, Windows NT or Windows 2000 operating systems. (Requires Internet Explorer 4.0 or later) is available for immediate download so you may test all of the features below before you spend a penny of your money.

Just a few of the amazing features of eBOOK CREATOR that you will enjoy are:

* ***Unlimited eBooks:*** You may create as many eBooks as you like with no maximum limits set on the number of eBooks you may produce.

* *Royalty Free:* You never have to pay a penny in royalties or other fees for the eBooks you create. Once you have registered eBOOK CREATOR, there is nothing additional to buy.
* *Easy Distribution:* Each eBook is a self-contained .exe application program. You may distribute them in a variety of media: internet download, e-mail, diskette, CD-ROM, ZIP disks, networks, etc.
* *Amazing Simple Interface:* Easy-to-use buttons and menus makes creating eBooks a breeze for even the beginner.
* *Complete Help Documentation:* A step-by-step tutorial explains every menu option, every command, every feature, and every button in an easy-to-understand language.
* *Popular Compatibility:* eBooks created using eBOOK CREATOR use the exact same format as Internet Explorer, making them compatible with the world's most popular web browser. Supported are HTML, DHTML, Gif images and animations, JPEG and PNG graphics, JavaScript, VBScript, Java applets, and all I.E. plug-ins including the ever popular Flash.
* *Internet Linking:* Create web links within your eBooks to connect your readers to the internet...especially important for links to YOUR website and affiliate programs!
* *Password Protection:* eBOOK CREATOR has tremendous security features to protect your information product from "prying eyes." You may select to password protect your entire eBook, or just protect certain pages and allow your readers a preview of a portion of your eBook before they register for a password.

* Customize your own security message when the reader accesses a password protected portion of your eBook.
* Input up to 1,000 different passwords per eBook to prevent users from "sharing" passwords with their friends. (Each time your eBook is downloaded or copied, it will require a UNIQUE password to unlock the protected pages)
* Link directly to a form or webpage from your website for that specific user to get the password that will work for her.
* *Save Your* Projects: Most eBook compilers miss the mark here. Instead of re-entering all of your settings each time you want to create a new version of your eBook, eBOOK CREATOR's system allows you to save your settings and access them anytime you need them.
* ***HTML Protection:*** No longer can thieves steal your HTML source code and swipe your page designs. With eBOOK CREATOR's HTML security protection feature, you can select to disable right-mouse clicking!
* ***Branding:*** Every eBook created with this software includes your name, company name, your copyright message, your email address (or autoresponder, if you choose) and a link to your website.
* ***Unique Serial Numbers:*** A unique serial number is generated for each eBook that you create with eBOOK CREATOR.
* ***Unique Icons:*** Bored by the "same old" icons that every user of the other eBook software displays on their eBooks? Not to worry. With eBOOK CREATOR, you may your own icons. eBOOK CREATOR supports 99% of 32X32 pixel .ico files.
* ***Menu Customization:*** You may choose to turn on or off the various buttons and features in the eBook menu

bar. Toolbars, buttons, screen position, startup screens and more are all at your creative discretion.

* *Shareware-Style eBooks:* With this powerful feature, you may set your eBooks to expire in either of two ways: (1) After a set number of days has passed since the eBook was downloaded, (2) After a set number of uses of the eBook. This will allow you to offer free trial versions of your eBooks. After expiration, the user will need a password to use the eBook again.
* *Splash Screens and Start-Up Messages:* You can add your own splash screen graphic that appears when the eBook is launched. Additionally, you may choose to include a message box that appears as the eBook opens.
* *Built-In Search Engine:* With this powerful tool, the user inputs a keyword and the search engine lists every page within your eBook that the keyword appears on. Each listing is clickable for instant access to the page.
* *Custom Pages:* This feature allows you to set up special message boxes when your customers attempt to access a locked page in your trial version.

9. E-book reader software for windows

1. Ghostscript - Postscript Documents Viewer[25]

Ghostscript is an interpreter for the PostScript language. A PostScript interpreter usually takes as input a set of graphics commands. The output is usually a page bitmap, which is then sent to an output device such as a printer or display. PostScript is embedded in many printers.

Ghostscript has several main uses:

1. Display a PostScript file
2. Display a PostScript file to decide if you really need to print it
3. Print a PostScript file to a non-PostScript printer

Microsoft Reader[26]

Microsoft Reader 2.0 is a free software application downloadable from http://www.microsoft.com/reader/dowoloads/pc.asp. It is designed to deliver an on-screen reading experience that approaches the convenience and quality of paper. Microsoft Reader is the first product to include patented ClearType display technology, which improves resolution on LCD screens by up to 300 percent to deliver a print-like display. Microsoft Reader also pays strict attention to the traditions and benefits of good typography. It offers a clean, uncluttered layout; ample margins; proper spacing, leading, and kerning; plus powerful tools for marking, highlighting, and annotating your eBooks.

Benefits

Microsoft Reader is setting a new standard for electronic reading. With the new Microsoft Reader 2.0, you get:

* Best-of-breed content support, so you can now enjoy premium, Owner Exclusive content on any Windows-based PC, laptop, or Pocket PC 2002 device
* Greater convenience: Now you can Activate Microsoft Reader on up to four devices and read your eBooks where you want, when you want. New and improved user interface with easier navigation, Web linking, and custom dictionary support.

2. *Adobe Acrobat eBook Reader*[27]

Software for the ultimate eBook reading experience making you enjoy the portability, versatility, and interactivity of electronic books. The free Adobe Acrobat eBook Reader software enables you to read high-fidelity eBooks on your notebook or desktop computer – no special hardware is needed! Only this reader software displays eBooks with the pictures, graphics, and rich fonts you've come to expect from printed books. Combining a vivid, elegant reading experience with an intuitive interface, Acrobat eBook Reader gives you all that eBooks have to offer.

3. TK3 Reader[28]

The TK3 Reader allows anyone to read a TK3 book that has been made with the TK3 Author. The Reader enables a wide range of user functions, including a notebook, highlighter, "stickie" notes, powerful search options, and more.

It is free and has helpful user features, like:

* a notebook where you can write notes, save short passages (with source and page number automatically noted), or store audio and video clips
* searchable "stick-on" notes to place directly on the page
* a highlighter to mark any text you choose
* the ability to "dog-ear", or turn down the corners of any number of pages
* a find button to search both the TK3 book and any added notes. You can also search according to category (for instance, all dog-eared pages and margin notes, annotations only, etc.)
* enables you to distribute TK3 books through the internet or on a CD-ROM, DVD-ROM, or zip-disk

10. Different popular multimedia formats compared

Text/ASCII Files

Pros:

* Widely Supported - Text files can be opened on any platform, in any operating system. The only requirement for opening text files is that you must own a computer!
* Very Small - Text files can be compressed up to 90%, and they're not very big to start with! This means that they will download very quickly.

Cons:

* Very Plain - Text files are extremely plain and boring. There is absolutely no way to spruce them up to keep your reader's attention. You cannot change the font and you certainly cannot use bold or italics! The only way to emphasize anything is by using capital letters. Unfortunately, it's common knowledge that writing in capital letters will slow down the average reader by 70%!
* Very Unprofessional - If you send your information product out as a text file, you can expect to lose credibility with your customer before they have even read it! If you paid good money for an information package on the Internet and it arrived as a text file, would you be impressed? I think not!
* Very Insecure - The word "security" should not even be used in the same sentence as "text file"! There is absolutely no way of securing a text file. If you send your information out like this, expect it to be stolen.

DOC Files - "Microsoft Word Documents"

Pros:

* Flexible Layout – DOC files offer you the flexibility to layout your documents in an easy-to-use, attractive manner.
* Images – You are able to insert Bitmap images throughout a DOC file, giving it a little more pizzazz.
* Password Protected – You can password protect a word document so that it cannot be viewed until the password is entered.

Cons:

* Very Large File Size – DOC files become very big, very quickly. It takes absolutely no time at all for a DOC file to grow to 10 – 15 megs when you add any kind of

special formatting. Could you imagine having to download a 30 megabyte DOC file with a 28.8kbps modem? It would take forever!

* Compatibility Risk – It is true that most computers out there have some type of word processor on them that can support a DOC file, but each one displays it differently. So what may appear to be a beautiful presentation on your end could actually show up as jumbled mess of images and text on your consumer's end. If this turns out to be the case, you will have just lost all your credibility with your customer!
* Poor Security – Above I mentioned that you could password protect a DOC file with Microsoft Word. Unfortunately, that is about as far as the security goes. A password might be better than nothing, but in reality it is only going to keep the honest people honest. Anyone who decides to redistribute or pirate your information can simply hand out the password along with the file. You need to keep in mind that you have no way of limiting how many times the password can be used.
* No Copy Protection – This feature makes a Word document very dangerous to use. Anyone with a word processor is capable of copying your information and pasting it into other documents in infinite quantities! Even if the file is marked "Read Only", you can still copy and paste into other documents!

PDF Files

Pros:

* Flexible Layout – PDF files offer you the flexibility to design your documents in an easy-to-use, attractive manner. In fact, you can import your information directly from your word processor so that it is quick and easy to setup.

* Images – PDF files support the use of most common image formats so you can add a little more glamour with some flashy images.
* Password Protected – You can password protect a PDF file so that it cannot be viewed until the password is entered.
* Small File Size – PDF files have a very good compression ratio so they can be downloaded over the Internet quickly and easily.

Cons:

* Poor Compatibility – If your customer does not have the Adobe Acrobat PDF viewer installed on their computer they will be required to download it before they can access your information package.
* Poor Security – The security on the PDF file is equal to that of the DOC file; it allows a password to be placed on the PDF file so that you must have the password to open it. Like I mentioned before, a password might be better than nothing, but in reality it is only going to keep the honest people honest. Anyone who decides to redistribute or pirate your information can simply hand out the password along with the file. You need to keep in mind that you have no way of limiting how many times the password can be used.

Custom Built Files - "Macromedia Director"

Pros:

* Very Flashy - Custom built files can be very appealing, as they are custom designed to your specifications. They are also easy to navigate when designed properly.
* Interactive - Custom built presentations can be very interactive depending on the capabilities of your designer.

* Password Protected - Custom built presentations can be designed to include password protection similar to that of PDF files.

Cons:

* Very Expensive - This is by far the most expensive way to create publish your information online. Unless you are a professional programmer yourself, you will need to hire someone to design and build it for you. Good programmers do not come cheap!
* Difficult to Edit or make Additions to - Making changes to your eBook will be a hassle because you will need to contact the programmer each time. Again - this gets expensive very quickly.
* Insecure - the security in custom built software is equivalent to that of the PDF files. Although you may be able to password protect the eBook, you still have no way of controlling whether or not people share their file and password.

HTML Documents

Pros:

* Extensive Multimedia Support - If you decide to distribute your information in HTML files you can use any Internet technologies that you see on a web page. You can also spice up your presentations with multimedia technologies like Shockwave and Flash. HTML documents allow for extensive image support!
* Widely Supported – This is probably the most widely supported option so far. All your customer needs is a web browser to read your information and, since they found you on the Internet, they must have a web browser, right?
* Internal and External Linking – A big advantage to using HTML is the ability to link not only throughout your

documents, but also to external sites on the Internet. This gives you the option of using other web sites as a reference with just the click of a button.

* High Compress – HTML is a very compressed format and, since it was designed for the Internet, may be downloaded with relative speed and ease!

Cons:

* Very Insecure - Sending your information out in a plain HTML file for people to open up in their browsers is one of the most insecure ways of distributing your product. If someone is so inclined, all they need to do is upload your files to the Internet and Voila !! They would have their very own informative web site!
* Confusing to Distribute – If you did decide to package your information in HTML format, unless you had one page of straight text, your end user would be forced to deal with multiple files and images files on their hard drive. This would be a technical support nightmare! Just getting the end user to find the right file to click open your information package in the beginning can be tough enough!

11. Popular ebook formats compared

Following are some of the features, requirements, advantages and disadvantages of some of the major ebook formats:

1. Microsoft Reader (LIT) Format[25]

Platforms: Windows 95, 98, 2000, ME, XP, or Windows NT 4, Pocket PC.

Requirements: MS Reader software, Pentium 75 or higher microprocessor, 16 MB RAM and approximately 19 MB free hard drive space, Internet Explorer 4.0 with Service Pack 1 or higher.

Features: ClearTypeTM display technology improves

on-screen reading, external HTML linking, audiobook interface, adjustable font size, full text search, bookmark and highlighting capabilities.

Advantages: MS Reader formatted eBooks are easy to create with Overdrive's software packages, have relatively small files sizes, look fantastic and offer a very nice on-screen reading experience.

Disadvantages: MS Reader eBooks can only be read on computers using a Microsoft Windows operating system. The software is tied in with Microsoft's Passport features. Losing your Passport information can keep you from reading books you've paid for. Text is not printable under any conditions.

2. *Adobe Portable Document (PDF) Format*[20]

Platforms: Software for reading PDF files is available for all computer platforms and operating systems, including Palm Pilots and Pocket PCs.

Requirements: Requires Acrobat Reader or other PDF reading software. Versions available for PCs with 386 processors and greater, or Mac 68K and greater.

Features: Full text search, variable font sizes, zoom options, external HTML linking, internal hyperlinks, bookmarking.

Advantages: Broad consumer adoption, cross-platform compatibility, great format for printing.

Disadvantages: Although it is the perfect format for document printing, PDF documents are sometimes difficult to read onscreen. The security features offered by PDF writing software is easily circumvented.

3. *Adobe eBook Reader (EBX) Format*[26]

Platforms: Windows 95, 98, 2000, ME, XP, NT 4, Mac OS 9.0-9.1.

Requirements: Windows Pentium class computer with Internet Explorer 4 or greater. Mac with a PowerPC processor and Mac OS software 9.0 or 9.1 with Internet Explorer version 4.5 or Netscape Communicator 4.75 or greater.

Features: Bookmarking, full-text searching, notes and highlighting, two-page view, read out-loud (with publisher's permission), display rotation.

Advantages: Improved on-screen readability over regular PDF documents. eBook library page makes books easily accessible.

Disadvantages: Adobe has eliminated all the positive aspects of PDF in its ebook format. Documents are no longer cross platform, the eBook Reader software is buggy and requires a powerful computer to run efficiently.

4. TK3 Format[27]

Platforms: Windows 95, 98, 2000, ME. Mac OS 8.6 or later.

Requirements: TK3 Reader on Power Mac or Pentium PC with a minimum of 64 MB RAM

Features: Highlighting, bookmarks, sticky-notes, copy text or other materials to a built-in notepad, and more.

Advantages: TK3 Author creates very nice eBooks, which work with both the Mac and Windows version of the reader. Can include text, images, audio and video.

Disadvantages: TK3 Reader uses a great deal of processing power, and can be very slow to load on older computers. Very few people have the reader application already installed.

References

1. Multimedia Information Retrieval and Management Technological Fundamentals and Applications, by David Feng, W. C. Siu, Hong Jiang Zhang
2. Multimedia in practice : Technology and applications/Jeffcoate, Judith / 681.324 JEF
3. Multimedia on the web by McGloughlin, Stephen

4. http://tronche.com/computer-graphics/gif/
5. http://www.w3.org/Graphics/JPEG/jfif.txt
6. http://www.w3.org/Graphics/PNG/
7. http://sox.sourceforge.net/AudioFormats.html
8. http://astronomy.swin.edu.au/~pbourke/dataformats/au/
9. http://astronomy.swin.edu.au/~pbourke/dataformats/aiff/
10. http://astronomy.swin.edu.au/~pbourke/dataformats/wave/
11. http://mpgedit.org/mpgedit/mpeg_format/MP3Format.html
12. http://www.digitalpreservation.gov/formats/fdd/fdd000027.shtml
13. http://www.the-labs.com/Video/odmlff2-avidef.pdf
14. http://www.chiariglione.org/mpeg/
15. http://www.apple.com/quicktime
16. http://www.real.com
17. http://partners.adobe.com/public/developer/en/ps/5002.EPSF_Spec.pdf
18. http://www.w3.org/MarkUp/
19. http://www.microsoft.com/products/info
20. http://www.macromedia.com/
21. http://www.adobe.com/products/acrobat/acro_ad.html
22. http://office.microsoft.com/en-us/FX010857941033.aspx
23. http://www.adobe.com/products/contentserver/main.html
24. http://www.ebookcreator.com/
25. http://www.cs.wisc.edu/~ghost/
26. http://www.microsoft.com/reader
27. http://www.adobe.com/products/acrobat/readermain.html
28. http://www.nightkitchen.com

30

Digital Collection Development in J.R.D. Tata Memorial Library at Indian Institute of Science

M. Surulinathi
Gangadharesha
T.Tejaswini
Library Trainees
Indian Institute of Science Library, Bangalore-12

ABSTRACT

We are living in the age of information society and most of the user population like soft copy of information. Because of each and every library and information center digital collection should be established for a definite purpose and research library setting, the digital collection may be developed primarily for research and development etc. The effective and efficient information services provide only through digital collection development and network support. In the digital environment, a single copy of a work can be loaded on to a server and made accessible to unlimited number of users. This paper highlights the digital collection resources like subscribing e-journals, e-books, Online databases (full text and Bibliographic databases) and reveals that various digital collection resources and services that meets the appropriate needs of Indian Institute of Science client population.

Introduction

Digital Collection development, as a library activity, is designed with the specific purpose and aim according to the needs of the user communities. In order to reach this goal, each segment of the collection must be developed with an application of resources consistent with its relative importance to the mission of the library.

The following five elements represent the specific activities involved in the process of digital collection development: collection development policies, budgeting, type of materials for collection, selection and acquisition, and collection evaluation.

World Wide Web is a new medium of information delivery, coupled with the availability of powerful hardware, software and networking technology. Most of the publishers are using the Internet as a global way to offer their publications to the international community of scientists and technologists. The Internet and web technologies provide an unparalleled medium for delivery of information with greater speed and economy. Moreover, the web-based electronic information products not only eliminate paper, physical storage and transportation costs, they also offer a host of other possibilities for incorporating multimedia and hyperlink features in electronic documents hitherto impossible on paper media. The libraries and information centres, as consumers of electronic journals and online databases, are benefiting greatly from this technology-driven revolution. During the past decade, great progress has been made in both theoretical and practical research in the digital library. Besides acquiring and buying access to digital collections, academic and research libraries are exerting efforts to initiate digital library projects in their respective institutions to build their own digital collections.

Digital Collection Development in IISc Library

J R D TATA Library has a vast collection of books and journals. Some of the journal collections include those published in year 1820 and before. So there is no wrong in saying that IISC library is a packed collection of knowledge covering a broad area of subjects. The primary mission of the library is to support the educational and research programmes of the institute by providing physical and intellectual access to information, consistent with the present and the anticipated educational and research functions of the institute. In accordance with the objectives of the institute, the library aims to develop a comprehensive collection of documents useful for the faculty and the research community of the institute.

The secondary mission is, to serve as a resource center for the scholars and scientific community of the country. The collection of the library, which includes books, journals, reports, standards and patents, is regarded one of the richest collections in the country, in the field of science and technology. This rich and valuable collection built over nine decades has some of the rare reference materials and several important journals. This vast reservoir of knowledge, on a conservative estimate, is worth over Rs. 300 crores. The annual budget of the library is over Rs. 10.00 crores of which subscription towards periodicals alone is about 9.00 crores. The library currently receives over 1734 periodical titles of which 1381 are subscribed while the remaining titles are received as gratis and on exchange basis. About 600 titles are accessible online against the print subscription. The total holdings of the library exceeds 4,11,676 documents

Electronic Journals

Digital Collection built up through the MHRD INDEST Consortium, IISc users now have online access to a very large number of journals through the Internet. These include:

Elsevier's Science Direct, Springer's Link, IEEE/IEE journals, ACM digital library, and ABI/Inform.

User can access all these INDEST consortia journals, as well as IISc library's free against print journals, online subscription journals and completely free online access journals through E-Journals Information Service (E-JIS), the NCSI E-Journal gateway. Using E-JIS, you can select and access from over 10,000 online fulltext journals

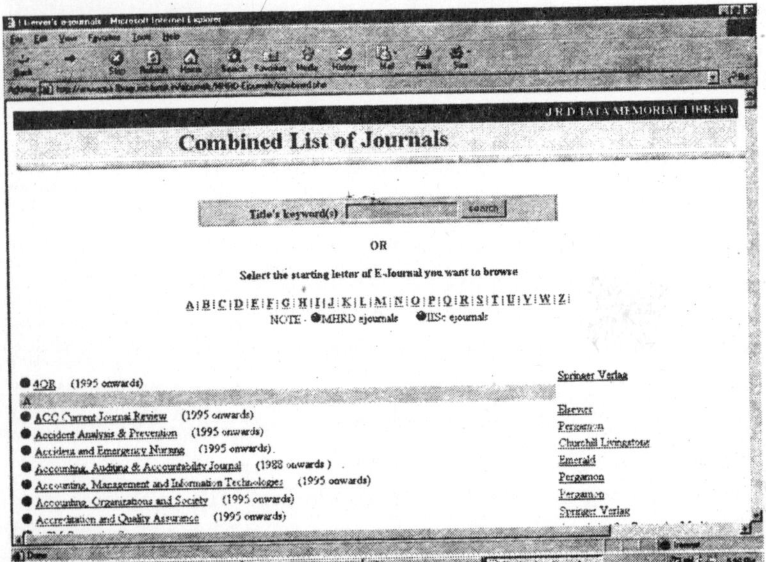

http://anuroopa.library.iisc.ernet.in/ejournals/MHRD-Ejournals/combined.php

Electronic Books

Online access to more than 10,600 books from e-book service providers like Knovel offering interactive access to over 600 Science and Technology Reference Books; Ebrary with 9449+ e-books on Computers, Technology, Engineering, Life & Physical Sciences; ENGnetBASE with access to 200+ Engineering Handbooks and Reference Engineering offering access to 300+ Reference Handbooks in Engineering. JRD Tata Memorial Library has subscribed to the e-books collection for the year 2005 and is made available to all IISC faculty, researchers and students. Electronic books available to the user in electronic form and its large structured collection bits transported on a storage media or delivered over a network connection.

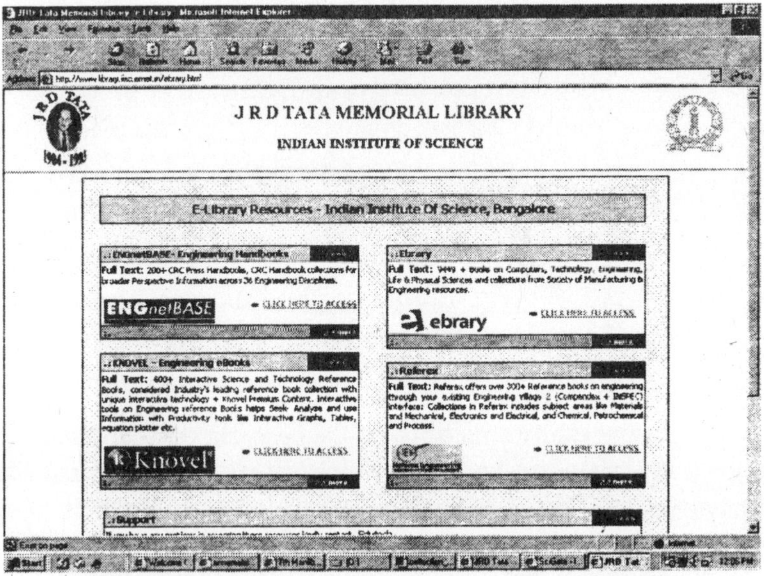

http://www.library.iisc.ernet.in/ebrary.html

CD-ROM Collection development in IISc Digital Library

The Library CD-ROM Collection include ProQuest Applied Science and Technology Plus (ASTP) fulltext Image database, Institute Theses full text (pdf) Image database creation (in progress), CD-ROM databases of few Journals, Books received with the Journal issues and Books respectively. Sizeable numbers of stand alone CD-ROMs in various fields like Art, Music, Science and Technology etc.

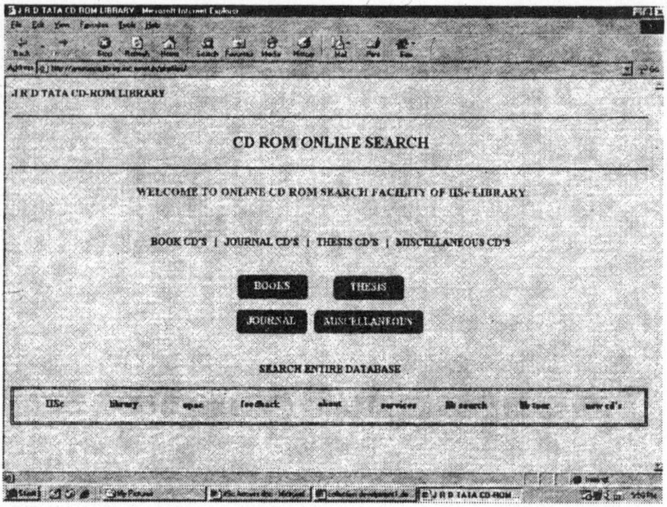

http://anuroopa.library.iisc.ernet.in/phpfiles/

Web OPAC

Library maintains network accessible databases such as Online Catalogue, i.e. books holdings available in the main library (over 1,28,000 records searchable by author, title and subject of the book) periodicals holdings, library user database etc. Library Online Catalogue, Periodical holdings Weekly list of additions are accessible on web as well.

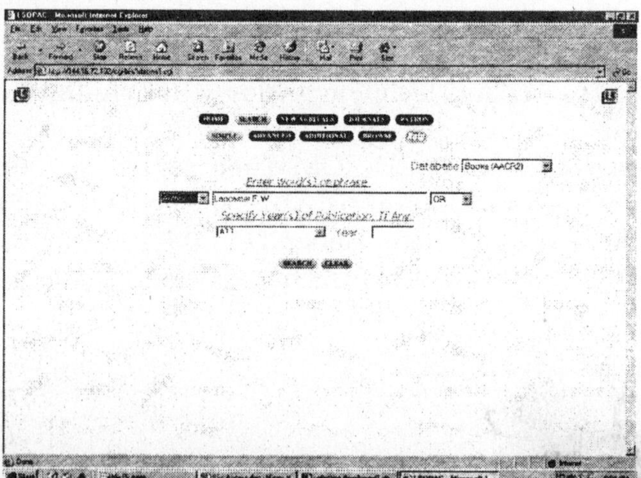

Digital library

The mission is to create a portal for the Digital Library of India, which will foster creativity and free access to all human knowledge. As a first step in realizing this mission, it is proposed to create the Digital Library with a free-to-read, searchable collection of one million books, predominantly in Indian languages, available to everyone over the Internet. This portal will also become an aggregator of all the knowledge and digital contents created by other digital library initiatives in India. Very soon we expect that this portal would provide a gateway to Indian Digital Libraries in science, arts, culture, music, movies, traditional medicine, palm leaves and many more. The result will be a unique resource accessible to anyone in the world 24x7, without regard to socioeconomic background or nationality.

Typical large high-school libraries house fewer than 30,000 volumes. Most libraries in the world have less than a million volumes. The total number of different titles indexed in OCLC's WorldCat is about 48 million. One million books, therefore, is more than the holdings of most high schools, and is equivalent to the libraries at many universities and represents a useful fraction of all available books.

One of the goals of the Digital Library of India is to provide support for full text indexing and searching based on OCR (optical character recognition) technologies where available. The availability of online search allows users to locate relevant information quickly and reliably thus enhancing student's success in their research endeavors. This 24x7 resource would also provide an excellent test bed for language processing research in areas such as machine translation, optical character recognition, summarization, speech and hand writing recognition, intelligent indexing, and information retrieval in Indian languages.

It is our expectation that the Digital Library of India will be mirrored at several locations worldwide so as to protect the integrity and availability of the data. The DLI will also partner with other country specific Digital Libraries initiatives as part of the Universal Library Project (www.ulib.org) spearheaded by Prof. Raj Reddy and Carnegie Mellon University.

In J.R.D.Tata Memorial Digital Library, the existing sources of information may be in print media. These sources can be converted into digital media by scanning the materials. This is the most popular method of converting the existing sources of information. Scanned documents are stored in different form like OTIFF, PTIFF, etc or graphics and this should be converted HTML, TXT and RTF etc. Further following software used for scanning process like Scan fix , SV Infosys Image Cropper and ABBY Fine Reader 7.0.

2. Non-copyrighted materials

Materials published before 1920 are in the public domain and may be scanned for this project. To reduce the costs of selection, the project will probably develop a strategy of selecting key topics and then removing large runs of books and journals from a selected repository. Having a reasonable turn-around time will be essential to the success of the project. A strategy has been devised to understand the logistics of shipping the materials and the impact of their absence from the home library

Conclusion

The primary long-term objective is to capture all books in digital format. It is believed that such a task is impossible and could take hundreds of years, and never is completed. Thus, as a first step we are planning to demonstrate the feasibility by undertaking to digitize 1 million books (less than 1% of all books in all languages ever published) by 2005. We believe such a project has the potential to change how education is conducted in much of the world.

A secondary objective of this project will be to provide a test bed that will support other researchers who are working on improved scanning techniques, improved optical character recognition, and improved indexing. The corpus this project creates will be one to three orders of magnitude larger than any existing free resource.

The major reasons to go digital collection is to broadening access to resources of Information –needy customers and survival. It provides user community no matter their location, with immediate, ubiquitous access to tremendous amount of information. Further several Research and Development Laboratories and academic institutions depended upon journal collection of the IISc. Moreover our library identified by INFLIBNET center of UGC as resource center for Science and Technology Journal, to cater to the need of academicians/researchers of the southern region through Document Delivery Services. The technological advances today make it possible to think in terms of storing all the knowledge of the human race in digital form by the year 2008.

Reference

1. Gorman. G.E., Miller, R.H., 1999, Collection Management for the 21st Century: A Handbook for Librarians, Greenwood Press, Westport, CT.
2. Hamaker, C.A, 1996, "*Redesigning research libraries: first step toward the 21st century*", Journal of Librarianship, 22, 4, 33-48.
3. Harloe, B, Budd, J.M, 1994, "Collection development and scholarly communication in the era of electronic access", Journal of Academic Librarianship, 20, 2, 83-7.
4. Jenkins, C., Morley, M., 1991, Collection Management in Academic Libraries, Gower, Brookfield.
5. Martin, K.F, Rose, R.F, 1996, "*Managing the CD-ROM collection development process: issues and alternatives*", Collection Management, 21, 2, 77-101.
6. Rioux, M.A, 1997, "*Order out of chaos: collection development and management of Internet resources*", Serials Librarian, 30, 3 and 4, 129-47.

31
Web Mining for Knowledge Resource Centers (Libraries)

B.Sivakumar
Head – Learning Resource Center,
PSG Institute of Management

R.Sujatha
System Administrator,
PSG Institute of Management

R.Solaimalai
Students, Post Graduate Diploma in Management,
PSG Institute of Management

K.Rajkumar
Students, Post Graduate Diploma in Management,
PSG Institute of Management

ABSTRACT

This paper creates an intelligent agent for automated collection development in a digital library setting. It uses a predictive model based on facets of each Web page to select scholarly works. A program has been designed to analyze the Web page for each criterion and applied to a large collection of academic and non-academic Web pages. It provides a global view of the data generated in libraries and the variety of decisions that those data can inform. It describes ways in which library and users can use web data mining in their libraries, i.e. web mining, to understand patterns of behavior among library users and staff members and patterns of information resource use throughout the institution. Addition to that, a set of problematic pages that becomes difficult to classify because of their similarity to scholarly works is gathered and classified using the models.

The resulting models can be used in the selection process to automatically create a library of Web-based academic works. In addition, the technique can be extended to create a digital library of any type of structured electronic information. Today, there are many more tools available for discovering similar patterns in complex datasets from data mining and statistics. In addition, tools from management science such as Online Analytical Processing [OLAP] can be used to explore the data for patterns.

1. Introduction

'Thirty years ago most people thought that change would mean more of the same, only better. That was incremental change and to be welcomed. Today we know that in many areas of life we cannot guarantee more of the same... [We] cannot even predict with confidence what will be happening in our own lives.' (*Handy 1991*)[1]

Web Data Mining is an analytic process designed to explore data (usually large amounts of data) in search of consistent patterns and/or systematic relationships between variables, and then to validate the findings by applying the detected patterns to new subsets of data. The ultimate goal of data mining is prediction - and predictive data mining is the most common type of data mining and one that has the most direct applications. Web sites contain information that ranges from the highly significant through to the trivial and obscene, and because there are no quality controls or any guide to quality, it is difficult for searchers to take information retrieved from the Internet at face value. The Internet will not become a serious tool for professional searchers until the quality issues are resolved.

1.1 Problem Statement

A library consists of enormous amounts of academic works due to the rapidly growing academic research works by the faculty and students. This paper publishes the academic works on the Web. The general search tools overwhelm the researcher with non-academic documents, and the subject-specific academic search tools may not meet the needs of those in other disciplines. An automated collection development agent is one way to quickly discover online academic research works.

In order to create a tool for Web-based academic research, a decision-making model for selecting academic research must first be designed. Therefore, the goal of the present study is to develop a decision-making model to assist the librarians and that can also be used as a Web search tool to automatically select the pages that contain academic research works which the common users can use.

2.2 Academic Research Works

To specify the types of resources that this predictive model will identify, the term "scholarly research works" must be defined. For this study, scholarly research is limited to research written by students or faculty of an academic institution, works produced by a non-profit research institution, or works published in a scholarly peer-reviewed journal. A research work is defined as a Web page (a single HTML or text file) that contains the full text of a research report (*Scott Nicholson, 2003*)[3]. As the Web page has become the standard unit for indexing and reference by search tools and style manuals, the Web page is used here as the information container.

2. Knowledge Discovery in Databases (KDD Process) for Library:

2.1 Introduction to KDD Process:

Once the criteria have been operationalized and collected with program for a large sample of pages that are linked to academic library Web sites and for another sample of sites that are not academic, patterns must be found to help classify a page as scholarly. Data mining will be useful for this, as it is defined as "the basic process employed to analyze patterns in data and extract information" (*Trybula 1997, pg.199*)[3].Data mining is actually the core of a larger process, known as knowledge discovery in databases (KDD). KDD is the process of taking low-level data and turning it into another form that is more useful, such as a summarization or a model (*Fayyad, Piatetsky-shapiro and Smith, 1996*)[6].

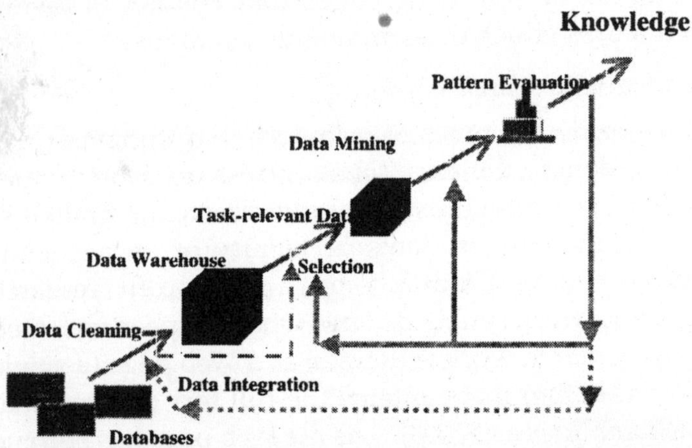

Fig 1. Data mining: the core of knowledge discovery process

Knowledge Discovery Process:

The Knowledge Discovery in Databases process (Fig 2.1) comprises of a few steps leading from raw data collections to some form of new knowledge. The iterative process consists of the following steps:

* *Data cleaning:* also known as data cleansing, it is a phase in which noise data and irrelevant data are removed from the collection.
* *Data integration*: at this stage, multiple data sources, often heterogeneous, may be combined in a common source.
* *Data selection:* at this step, the data relevant to the analysis is decided on and retrieved from the data collection.
* *Data transformation:* also known as data consolidation, it is a phase in which the selected data is transformed into forms appropriate for the mining procedure.
* *Data mining:* it is the crucial step in which clever techniques are applied to extract patterns potentially useful.
* *Pattern evaluation:* in this step, strictly interesting patterns representing knowledge are identified based on given measures.
* *Knowledge representation:* is the final phase in which the discovered knowledge is visually represented to the user. This essential step uses visualization techniques to help users understand and interpret the data mining results.

It is common to combine some of these steps together. For instance, data cleaning and data integration can be performed together as a pre-processing phase to generate a data warehouse. Data selection and data transformation can also be combined where the consolidation of the data is the result of the selection, or, as for the case of data warehouses, the selection is done on transformed data.

The KDD is an iterative process. Once the discovered knowledge is presented to the user, the evaluation measures can be enhanced, the mining can be further refined, new data can be selected or further transformed, or new data sources can be integrated, in order to get different, more appropriate results.

Data mining derives its name from the similarities between searching for valuable information in a large database and mining rocks for a vein of valuable ore (*Osmar R. Zaiane, 1999*). Both imply either sifting through a large amount of material or ingeniously probing the material to exactly pinpoint where the values reside. It is, however, a misnomer, since mining for gold in rocks is usually called "gold mining" and not "rock mining", thus by analogy, data mining should have been called "knowledge mining" instead[6]. Nevertheless, data mining became the accepted customary term, and very rapidly a trend that even overshadowed more general terms such as knowledge discovery in databases (KDD) that describe a more complete process. Other similar terms referring to data mining are: data dredging, knowledge extraction and pattern discovery.

2.2 *Data Mining Process:*

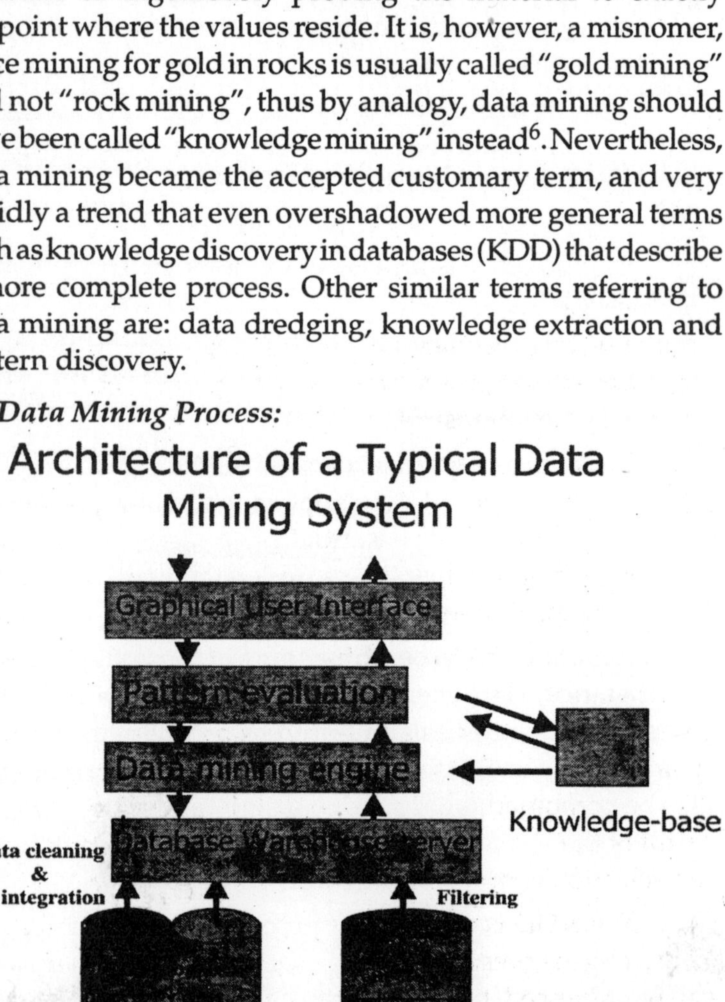

Fig 2. A typical Data Mining System

From the above Fig 2.2.shows how a data is retrieved from the database warehouse server and then sends to Graphical User Interface. Data cleaning, data integration, filtering are the process involved in retrieving the data from database warehouse server. After that it sends to the data mining engine. In the data mining engine it extracts the particular data for the user and then it sends to Graphical User Interface.

2.3 Data Mining in Library and Information services:

With the increasing use of the Internet and the World Wide Web, digital libraries have burgeoned, and these serve a huge variety of different user audiences, e.g., people interested in health and medicine, industry and world news, law, and business (*Nicholson, S. & Stanton, J. 2003*)[2]. With this expanded view of libraries, two key insights arise. First, libraries are typically embedded within larger institutions. Corporate libraries serve their corporations, academic libraries serve their universities, and public libraries serve taxpaying communities who elect overseeing representatives. Second, libraries play a pivotal role within their institutions as repositories and providers of information resources. In the provider role, libraries represent in microcosm the intellectual and learning activities of the people who comprise the institution. This fact provides the basis for the strategic importance of library data mining: By ascertaining what users need to know and how well those needs are served, Web mining can reveal insights that have meaning in the context of the library's host institution.

Because some readers may not have a detailed sense of the behind-the-scenes activities in contemporary libraries, we begin by providing a data-focused overview of the internal workings of libraries. Workflow in a traditional "bricks and mortar" library creates a number of data sources appropriate for Web mining. Before a library obtains new information resources (e.g., books, databases, reference tools, electronic access, etc.), a librarian assesses the needs of the existing collection in light of available and upcoming publications. Next, acquisitions personnel obtain the information resources specified from this needs assessment. Once the library obtains requested new resources, cataloging personnel either create or purchase a catalog record for the new resource. The circulation department then makes the resource available to end-users. Depending upon the size of the library and the scope of its operations, these activities fall within the purview of one, a dozen, or possibly hundreds of different employees organized into specialized departments.

After an information resource appears in the library's collection, users can locate it using catalog search systems and bibliographic databases. Although there is little uniformity with regard to the specifics of the user interfaces for these systems, most catalogs and bibliographic databases do support the use of a standard Web browser client as the front end of the system. Increasingly, catalogs and databases are all cross-linked, and each user's search record and traversal of links can appear in log files. When users find resources that they wish to borrow, the circulation department records their selection in a database that tracks the location of each resource owned by the library.

As this overview suggests, all functional processes of the library – collection assessment, acquisition, cataloging, end user searching, and circulation – generate large reserves of available data that document information resource acquisition and use. Library information systems frequently use large relational databases to store user information, resource information, circulation information, and possibly bibliographic search logs.

Although the processes outlined above adequately describe the traditional library with its physical infrastructure and tangible resources (e.g., books, maps, etc.), an increasing proportion of libraries offer many or most of their information resources in digital form over local or wide area networks. These "digital libraries" do, however, employ many similar techniques for selecting and acquiring information as those described above. While the personnel involved may have different titles and slightly different roles, the activities remain the same: identify resources needed for the collection, acquire the resources, make the resource available to users, and assist users in locating the resource through electronic and virtual reference aids. Most digital libraries do not have a circulation function; if users need something, they just save it or print it with to their own equipment. Unlike the traditional library, the information systems of a digital library can track and log the entire visit of a user to a digital library.

The vast data stored in the databases of traditional and digital libraries represent the behavioral patterns of two important constituencies: library staff and library users. In the case of library staff, mining available acquisitions and bibliographic data could provide important clues to understanding and enhancing the effectiveness of the library's own internal functions.

As a note, many companies have information services that are not explicitly called digital libraries, but can nonetheless be analyzed. These sources may be called knowledge bases, and are commonly associated with online help applications.

3. Data warehousing and OLAP Technology for Data Mining

A decision support database is maintained separately from the organization's operational database. It can support information processing by providing a solid platform of consolidated, historical data for analysis. "A data warehouse is a subject-oriented, integrated, time-variant, and nonvolatile collection of data in support of management's decision-making process." (*Jiawei Han and Micheline Kamber*)[7]

3.1 Data warehousing

The process of constructing and using data warehouses is called as data warehousing. It also focuses on the modeling and analysis of data for decision makers, not on daily operations or transaction processing. It provides a simple and concise view around particular subject issues by excluding data that are not useful in the decision-support process. Integrated data warehouse is constructed by integrating multiple, heterogeneous data sources such as relational databases, flat files, on-line transaction records. Data cleaning and data integration techniques are applied. It ensure consistency in naming conventions, encoding structures, attribute measures, etc. among different data sources. A time-Variant data warehouse is significantly longer than that of operational systems. It provides information from a historical perspective. Every key structure in the data warehouse contains an element of time, explicitly or implicitly. But the key of operational data may or may not contain "time element". A Non-volatile data warehouse does not require transaction processing, recovery, and concurrency control mechanisms. But it requires only two operations in data accessing: *initial loading of data* and *access of data(Nicholson, 2003)*[3]..

3.2 Data warehousing Process

There are two kind of process in Data Warehousing namely, OLTP and OLAP.

* *OLTP (On-line Transaction Processing)*

It is a major task of traditional relational DBMS. It is very much useful for Day-to-day operations.

* *OLAP (On-line Analytical Processing)*

It is a major task of data warehouse system. It is mainly used for data analysis and decision making process.

Comparison between OLTP and OLAP:

Table 3.1: Comparison between OLTP and OLAP

	OLTP	OLAP
Users	IT professional, clerk	Knowledge worker
Function	Day-to-day operation	Decision support
DB design	Application-oriented	Subject-oriented
Data	Current, up-to-date, detailed, flat relational isolated	Historical, summarized, multidimensional integrated
Usage	Repetitive	Ad-hoc
Access	Read/write	Lot of scans
Unit of work	Short, simple transaction	Complex query
#record accessed	Tens	millions
# users	Hundreds	Thousands
DB size	100MB-GB	100GB-TB
Metric	Transaction throughput	Query throughput, response

3.2 *Data warehouse Architecture:*

There are three views regarding the design of data warehouse namely top-down view, data source view and data warehouse view.

* *Top-down view:*

It allows selection of the relevant information necessary for the data warehouse.

* *Data source view:*

It exposes the information being captured, stored, and managed by operational systems.

* *Data warehouse view:*

It consists of selection tables and dimension tables.

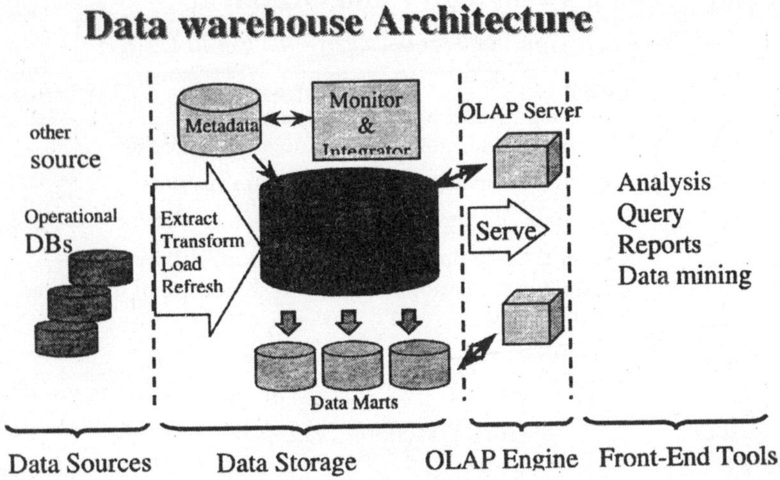

Fig 3. Data warehouse Architecture

From the above Fig 3.1: it shows the architecture of the Data warehouse. It extracts the information from the operational database and loads it in the data warehouse. Once the loading process is over, then it checks that data is correct or not with the help of the data marts. After this process is completed, then the data is send to OLAP server. In the OLAP server, it analysis the query reports which are taken from the data mining.

3.3.1 Determining Areas of Focus

The first step in the Web mining process is to determine the area of focus. This area might come from a specific problem in the library or may be a general area requiring exploration and decision-making. The first decision is to do *directed* or *undirected* data mining. Directed data mining is problem-focused: there is a specific problem that drives the exploration, e.g., "Budget cuts have reduced the staff time for contacting patrons about delinquent materials. Is there a way to predict the chance patrons will return material once it is one week late in order to prioritize our calling lists? " Undirected data mining is used when a library manager wants to get a better idea of a general topical area; one possible area of focus would be: "How are different departments and types of patrons using the electronic journals?"

There are several dangers with undirected data mining, as this type of exploration involves the use of many tools repeatedly to locate any available patterns. Many data mining techniques are based on probability, and therefore there is a small chance that each pattern found is incorrect: the more times this type of tool is used, the greater the chance of finding an invalid pattern. Another problem arises with data mining tools that locate the most frequently occurring patterns: in a complex data set, the most frequent pattern may only occur a few times. Therefore, all patterns that are found will need to be explored to make sure they are valid, make sense to the librarians involved, and are not trivial. Undirected data mining may produce an overwhelming number of patterns to explore. Given the time it takes to collect and clean the data, undirected data mining should be considered only when a strong data warehouse is in place.

3.2.2 Identifying Data Sources

After determining the areas of focus, the next step is to identify appropriate data sources. There are two types of data sources that should be considered. Internal data sources are those already within the library system. As most library systems have their data stored in different data silos around the organization (patron database, transactional data, Web server logs), discovering and extracting the internal data might be challenging.

External data sources are those that are not located within the library system. In an academic setting, these might include demographic information related to a specific ID number that is located in the computer center or personnel management system. For a public library setting, this might include demographic information for zip codes from census data.

3.2.3 Creating the Data Warehouse

Assuming that the data do exist, the challenge remains of combining different data sources into a single data warehouse that does not contain publicly identifiable information. A data warehouse is a database that is separate from the operational systems and contains a cleaned and anonymized version of the operational data reformatted for analysis. To create the warehouse, the librarian writes queries to extract the data from the identified sources, combines those data using common fields, cleans the data, and writes the resulting records into either a flat file or a relational database designed specifically for analysis[8]. Once this procedure has been tested, it can be automated to pull data from the operational systems into the data warehouse on a regular basis.

3.2.4 Building the Data Warehouse

Building the data warehouse takes much more time than mining the data(*Barry and Linoff, 1997*)[3]. This can make the process seem never-ending. It is essential that all involved realize that this portion of the process is an investment; once the programs for collection and cleaning are written, they will require only minor maintenance in the future as long as the library uses the same system. Because of this initial time investment, it is suggested to start with a narrowly defined web mining topic and work through the entire process. This iterative process also has the advantage of allowing those developing the data warehouse to improve their collection and cleaning algorithms early in the life of the web mining project (*Nicholson, 2003*)[3].

Table 3.2 Original Circulation Records

Original Circulation Records		
Book ID	**Subject**	**Patron**
QA76.9	Computer Science	392-398
PS159.G8	American Literature	524-589
HF5415.125	Marketing	333-335

Table 3.3. Original Patron Records

Original Patron Records		
Patron	**Name**	**Dept.**
333-335	Abby Lavender	English
392-398	Kenneth Moore	Computer sci.
524-589	Sophie Richards	Marketing research

Table 3.4. Data warehouse combined circulation records

Data Warehouse—Combined Circulation Records			
Book ID	**Subject**	**Name**	**Dept.**
QA76.9	Computer Science	Kenneth Moore	Computer sci.
PS159.G8	American Literature	Abby Lavender	English
HF5415.125	Marketing	Sophie Richards	Marketing research

Here the example of how to build a data warehouse that maintains important information for without-keeping personally identifiable information. When an item is returned, many libraries delete all information about that transaction. However, there is valuable decision-making information that is lost. While the operational system is a user-focused data source, the data warehouse is an item-focused data source. Therefore, before deleting the transactional information, a record should be created in the data warehouse that combines information about the item with demographic information about the patron. This will capture the important information about the transaction without identifying the patron involved, and will still allow the discovery of patterns about patrons without compromising personally identifiable information.

Once the data warehouse is set up, it can be used for not only traditional SQL-based question-answering, but also online analytical processing (OLAP) and data mining. Fig 3.1. It provides a schematic overview of the complete process from the collection of the data, through creation of the data warehouse, to the application of various analysis techniques. Multidimensional analysis tools for OLAP would allow library managers to explore their traditional frequency-based data in new ways by looking at statistics along easily changeable dimensions. The same data warehouse that supports OLAP also sets the stage for data mining.

3.3.5 *Selecting appropriate analysis tools*

Once the data warehouse has been developed, the stage is set for analysis. As mentioned earlier, traditional aggregations and ratios can be easily calculated to create traditional reports. However, interesting and useful patterns may be hiding behind these aggregate measures; these patterns allow library managers to better understand their individual user groups. For example, use of Interlibrary Loan data for collection development can be problematic due to the short-term needs of some ILL users. Web mining could be used to look for patterns in ILL use in order to remove the short-term ILL needs from consistent collection deficiencies.

3.4 *Data warehouse usage:*

There are three different kinds of data warehousing applications such as information processing, analytical processing and data mining.

* *Information processing*

It supports querying, basic statistical analysis, and reporting using cross tabs, tables, charts and graphs

* *Analytical processing*

It supports multidimensional analysis of data, basic OLAP operations, slice-dice, drilling, pivoting.

* *Data mining*

It is a knowledge discovery from hidden patterns. It supports associations, constructing analytical models, performing classification and prediction, and presenting the mining results using visualization tools.

5. Exploring the Data sources:

Although the system used in most parts of the library is commonly known as an *Integrated* Library System (ILS), very few ILS vendors make it easy for the library to access the data generated by the system in an integrated fashion. Instead, most librarians conceptualize their system as a set of separate data sources. While a relational database stands at the heart of most ILS systems, few system vendors provide sophisticated analytical tools that would promote useful access to this raw data. Instead, vendors encourage library staff to use pre-built front ends to access their ILS databases. These front ends typically have no features that allow exploration of patterns or findings across multiple data sets.

The library data sources are divided in three groups for this discussion namely ILS data sources from the creation of the library information system, ILS data sources from the use of the collection, and external data sources not normally included in the ILS. In order to systematically explore these data sources, we define each source, explain current analysis techniques used in libraries, and describe applications of that source to a digital library environment.

4.1 ILS Data Sources from the Creators of the Library System

The process of developing a library information system creates several types of data that may be useful in understanding the activities of the library staff (*Nicholson and*

Stanton)[2]. One source of data is the collection of records that represent materials in the library, commonly known as the Online Public Access Catalog (OPAC). The OPAC is created by catalogers and used to locate materials in the library. This typically contains records in MARC (Machine-Readable Cataloging) format, which contains information about the title, authorship, publication, physical description, access method, unique call number, subject headings, and other bibliographic metadata about the work.

In order to understand the collection, librarians commonly analyze the bibliographic database for basic frequency information. The number of works in the collection is counted both overall and by classification groups (using the call number; e.g., literature, science, etc.). Librarians then compare these breakdowns to other libraries (either individual libraries or among a set of similar peer libraries) in order to evaluate the size and relative proportions of different areas of the collection. Libraries will compare individual items to some type of list — usually normed for a subject and age group — to evaluate the quality of the collection.

Acquisitions Information:

Another source of data for web mining comes from the process of acquisitions, in which items are ordered from suppliers and tracked until received and processed by the library. This data source contains information about the orders (e.g., the vendor or publisher), the acquisitions librarian who ordered the work, the cost of the work, the order date, problems with the order, and the delivery date. Sometimes it may also contain information about the person who selected and/or requested the work. Other than simple analyses to reveal problem vendors, libraries have rarely analyzed and/or shared these data for competitive advantage. Instead, these data mainly support logistics, e.g., to track missing or late orders. In general, because digital libraries do not order tangible, physical goods such as books, somewhat different acquisition methods and vendor relationships are the norm. Nonetheless, in both traditional and digital library environments, acquisition data have much untapped potential for examining, understanding, controlling, and forecasting information resource costs.

4.2 ILS Data Sources from Usage of the Library System

User Information:

In order to track users who wish to check out materials (and in some cases, even allow users to enter the institutions), libraries maintain user databases users. In libraries associated with institutions, e.g. academic, school, and corporate libraries, the user database is closely aligned with the organizational database, so user data may come from enrollment or personnel databases rather than directly from users. When library managers wish to understand their user population better, they often perform frequency analyses to explore the demographics of their user base. In public libraries, however, user databases often contain only sparse information (e.g., name, date, and contact information) gathered directly from the user by the library. In the public library environment, analysis of the user population often requires outside data, such as census data or user surveys, and is therefore more time-consuming and expensive. Sophisticated libraries link user records through zip codes with demographic information and learn more about their user population.

Digital libraries may or may not have any information about their users. If the library requires no login to use, then the users are only accesses to a Web page. Libraries that do require a login procedure can also collect demographic information about their user base and this may provide a better idea of different user groups that access the library.

Circulation Information:

One of the richest untapped sources of information about library user behavior is circulation records. Notably, however, important legal and ethical issues limit the uses of circulation data and make it the most protected information source in the library. When a user checks out a work, the checkout date, due date, call number, and user identification is recorded. When the work is returned, borrower information disappears from the librarian's perspectives, but the borrowing record may remain hidden in the database. A similar data source is a hold/request database, where requests for works either not in the library or already checked out are recorded. Again, once the hold/request has been dealt with, the user information is removed from the view of the librarian. In most cases, however, the user identifiers are still kept in the underlying database, locked away in inaccessible tables.

Librarians use this information to guide purchasing and removal of materials from the library. Items with a high number of circulations, holds, and/or requests help selectors choose new works to bring into the library. In addition, when collection personnel make decisions about which books to remove from the shelves, the circulation information gives them an idea of which works have rarely circulated.

With the exception of some "e-book" services, most digital library information resources do not provide circulation information for mining. Viewing a page by clicking a link does not necessarily carry the same message as checking a book out of the library, although it is easy to imagine capturing meaningful information in a database that records requests to print or save a full text information resource. Current information retrieval services, already implement server-side capture of such requests from their browser-based user interfaces.

Searching and Navigation Information:

The Online Public Access Catalog (OPAC) serves as the primary means of searching for works owned by the library. Additionally, because most OPACs use a browser interface, users may also access bibliographic databases, the World Wide Web, and other online resources during the same session. Search records and activity logs can be captured for the entire session for users at the library, or, for users outside of the library, for those elements of the session that uses the library's servers. Online searching has been an active area of research in Library and Information Science for studies in information seeking behavior and human-computer interaction.

Digital libraries typically capture logs from users searching their databases and can track, through "clickstream" analysis, the elements of Web-based services visited by users. Through the use of browser cookies, one can circumvent some of the difficulties in determining which set of searches constitutes a single session. In addition, the combination of a login procedure and cookies allow connecting specific users to the services and searches they used in a session.

4.3 External Data Sources

Reference Desk Interactions:

The reference librarian's primary responsibility is to assist users in defining information needs and locating resources to satisfy them. In the typical face-to-face or telephone interaction with a library user, the reference librarian records very little information about the interaction. Some libraries keep limited records about the interaction (e.g., the type of question; directional, factual, etc). If librarians wish to gain knowledge from reference transactions, they must capture more information from these types of transactions from not only the reference desk but from other areas of the library, because users direct questions toward most library staff. This process has recently become considerably easier because many reference librarians use a desktop computer as the first resource they consult to answer user inquiries.

Library managers can examine reference interaction

data to help make staffing decisions, both in what type of staff (librarians or paraprofessionals) and the amount of staffing needed Digital reference transactions occur through an electronic format such as e-mail, Web-based forms, message boards, instant messaging, or live chat. The text of the questions and answers can be captured for later analysis. Even digital reference work done through synchronous interfaces can be recorded. These data provides analysts a much richer record of transactions than is available in traditional reference work. Some traditional libraries are beginning to offer e-mail and other virtual reference services, and thus may also have the ability to capture and analyze these transactions. The utility of these data can be increased if demographic information about the user can be captured as well.

Item Use Information:

While circulation information and computer logs give two views of the user's borrowing and search behavior Web mining opportunities may provide the impetus to begin a regular tracking procedure when reshelving books and other materials. This task becomes much easier in a digital library, as Web logs can be analyzed to discover what sources users examined.

Interlibrary Loan:

Most physical libraries offer some type of Interlibrary Loan (ILL) service. This service is unique in that the resulting data source is a combination of information seeking behaviors from both library users and library staff. In most ILL situations, the user seeking an item contacts the ILL department, and the ILL staff members locate the material from another library and borrow the book. Once the requesting library receives the book, they lend it to their user. Therefore, there are two levels of seeking namely the user seeking the original material and the staff seeking a source for lending. The cost for lending and the time it takes for delivery vary by the source selected. Many libraries have a number of consortium agreements, each with different response times and costs, which makes this a complex data source. The information tracked varies by library, but usually contains information about the item requested, the user, the lending library, and the essential dates involved.

6. Web Data Mining:

The WWW is huge, distributed, global information service centre for information services, hyperlink information and access usage information. WWW provides rich sources for data mining. In WWW there is no standards and structure for complex data warehousing and data mining. There is abnormal growth in the WWW as shown in the graph below Fig 5.1

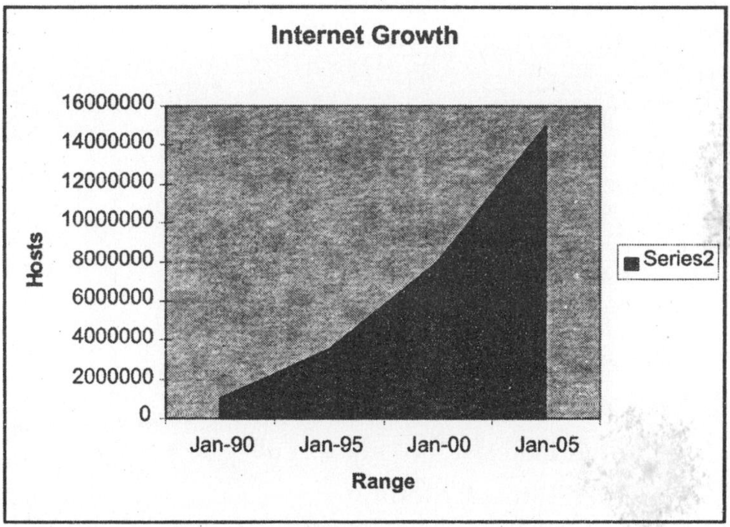

Fig 5.1. Internet Growth Graph

5.2 Web Selection methodology:

5.2.1 Criteria Creation:

A list of criteria used to select academic research was gathered from a literature review of criteria used in selecting print and electronic documents for academic libraries. The criteria were ranked and the librarians were allowed to suggest new criteria (*Nicholson*)[1]. The list was then changed to remove low-ranking criteria and add new suggested criteria. This process was repeated until consensus was reached. A summary of the final list of criteria follows.

Summary of Selection Criteria for Web Pages

Appropriate indexing and description

1. Author Criteria

   Author has written before

   Experience of the author

   Authenticity of author

2. Content Criteria

   Work is supported by other literature

   Scope and depth of coverage

   Work is a reference work

   Page is only an advertisement

   Pages are inward focused

   Hyperlinks to other pages

   Existence of advertising on the site

   Original material, not links or abstracts

3. Organizational Criteria

   There is an abstract for the work

   Pages are well-organized

   Currency of date/ systematically updated

4. Producer/Medium Criteria

Document is reproduced in other forms

Available on-line when needed

Does not require new hardware or software

Past success/failure of the publishing house

Produced by a reputable provider

Unbiased material

Stability of the Web server

Response time for the site

Site is durable

5. External Criteria

Indexed in standard sources

Favorable reviews

Linked to by other sites

These are the criterion are taken into an account for normal academic libraries. They are some more criterion are present in the libraries, if they needed they also takes part in summary of selection criteria for web pages.

5.3 Web Mining Architecture:

In the above Fig 5.2: it explains the functions of web mining architecture. Web log is filtered to generate a relational database with the help of data cleaning process. After the cleaning process, data cube is generated from database. From the database, data is passed to data cube. OLAP drills-down and rolls-up the data cube. After the process of OLAP, the searched data will be passed in the form of sliced and diced cubes. Finally OLAM mines the sliced and diced cubes, and then sends the mined results to the User.

On-Line Analytical Processing (OLAP):

OLAP puts an interactive view of the data on the decision-makers desktop. Under the surface, the OLAP tool has run thousands of database queries to combine all of the selected variables along with all of the selected measures. These reports are presented in an easy-to-understand menu-driven system. The user will pick one of many variables from a list to examine, such as use of e-journals. They can then select basic dimensions, such as time and subject. The OLAP system will then present a high-level view of this data in a tabular report, perhaps by year and general classification. The user can then click one of the dimensions to expand the report – in our example, if the user clicked on a year, the tool would expand the year into quarters, leaving the subject headings the same and recalculating the data. The user can then click on another field to "drill down" into the data.

OLAP tools are powered by a data warehouse. All of the fields are defined ahead of time, and the system runs many queries before anyone uses it. Therefore, response to the user using the OLAP front end for reports is instant, which encourages exploration. During exploration, the user can capture any view of the data and turn it into a regular report.

Analysis and Implementation

Once the results, either static reports or decision-making models and aids, have been developed, they must be validated. The first step is to test the data on a sample of the data that was not used to build the model, in order to test the robustness of the model on different data. The most important validation, however, is to have a librarian who is familiar with that library context examine the models. The librarian should concur with the results found. The patterns can be the data-based validation of the tacit knowledge gained from working in a library situation. If the librarian disagrees with a pattern, it is essential to explore the data streams carefully. This type of disagreement usually stems from a flaw in the data or a misapplication of a tool.

The final step is to implement the report/model. It is essential to monitor the variables that power the models over time. If the mean of a variable strays too far because of changes in the library, the model may have to be reevaluated.

5.4 Web Mining to Improve Library Services

The users of library services are one of the most important constituencies in most library organizations. Most libraries exist to serve the information needs of users, and therefore, understanding those needs is crucial to a library's success. Examining the behaviors of a large group of users for patterns can then allow the library to have a better idea of the information needs of their user base, and therefore better customize the library services to meet those needs.

In order to locate works in the library, users rely on the OPAC. Librarians often examine user comments and surveys to assess user satisfaction with these tools. Librarians may wish to examine the artifacts of those searches for problem areas instead of relying on user comments and surveys in order to improve the user experience. When upgrading or changing library system interfaces, librarians can explore these patterns of common mistakes in order to make informed decisions about system improvements.

Web mining can also be used to predict future user needs. By looking for patterns in high-use items, librarians can better predict the demand for new items in order to determine how many copies of a work to order. Once these patterns have been discovered, appropriate policies can be put in place to reduce inventory losses.

Digital libraries, as well as libraries with Web-based services, can use different techniques and tools to examine common patterns in the path taken through their Web site. This could give the library ideas of problem areas of their Web site, good places to post important messages, areas where more guidance is needed, and opportunities to keep people from leaving the site. As library managers must observe a physical library for signage needs, digital libraries must also be examined for appropriate areas for guidance.

Web Data mining could be used to discover patterns for tools that will automatically assign questions to experts based upon past assignments. In addition, by mining the question/answer pairs for patterns, an expert system could be created that can provide users an immediate answer while they wait for a human to answer the question.

Web Mining Applications:

Each web mining analysis can reveal a pattern of activity within the library. Uncovering and reporting these patterns may have potential benefits at three nested levels: benefits for individuals through improved library services, benefits for library management through the provision of improved decision-making information, and benefits for the institution that the library serves through reporting of relevant patterns of user behavior. Additionally, by providing information on the performance and utility of the library as a unit, web mining can provide justification for continued financial and institutional support for library operations. These levels serve to structure our presentation of web mining opportunities and applications.

Data Flow diagram for Web Mining Applications

Input Data Sources	Selection Information	Acquisitions Information	Reference transactions
	Online catalog, bibliographic database, and Web search logs	Access history of works through circulation, download, print, or Interlibrary Loan	User information from library and external sources
	↓	↓	↓
Data Warehouse	Multiple compatible integrated tables; Common fields for joins: User identification, Bibliographic identification(either at an ISBN/ISSN or topical level), Library staff identifier		
	↓	↓	↓
Analysis and Visualization	Predictive modeling	Standard relational database queries	OLAP, multi-dimensional visualization

7. Conclusion

The process of using library data more effectively begins by discovering ways to connect the disparate sources of data. Connecting these disparate sources in data warehouses can facilitate systematic exploration with different tools to discover behavioral patterns of the libraries primary constituencies. These patterns can help enhance the library experience for the user, can assist library management in making decisions and setting policies, and can assist the library's parent organization or community in understanding the information needs of its members. Information discovered through the application of web mining techniques gives the library the potential to save money, provide more appropriate programs, meet more of the user's information needs, become aware of gaps and strengths of their collection, and serve as a more effective information source for its users. Web mining can provide the data-based justifications for the difficult decisions and funding requests library managers must make. Finally, web mining can inform the processes and products of knowledge management that have grown in importance within contemporary organizations.

8. Future Enhancements

Libraries have gathered data about their collections and users for years, but have not often used those data for better decision-making. By taking a more active approach based on applications of data visualization and statistics, these information organizations can get a clearer picture of their information delivery and management needs. At the same time, libraries must continue to protect their users and employees from misuse of personally identifiable data records. Libraries must compete against downloadable audio books and the vast supply of "free" information of varying quality from the Internet, librarians must begin to take the initiative in using their systems and data for competitive advantage and to justify continued support and funding of libraries.

9. References

1. Nicholson, S. (2003) The Web mining Process: Data Warehousing and Data Mining for Library Decision-Making. Information Technology and Libraries 22 (4). 146-151.
2. Nicholson, S. & Stanton, J. (2003). Libraries. In Nemati, H. & Barko, C. (Eds.). Organizational data mining: Leveraging enterprise data resources for optimal performance. Hershey, PA: Idea Group Publishing. 247-262.
3. Nicholson, S. (2003). Bibliomining for automated collection development in a digital library setting: Using data mining to discover Web-based scholarly research works. Journal of the American Society for Information Science and Technology 54(12). 1081-1090.
4. Nicholson, s. (2003) Data Mining Techniques. Third Edition.
5. http://www.bibliomining.com/
6. Fayyad U.M., Piatetsky G, Smyth R and Uthurusamy R, Advances in Knowledge Discovery and Data Mining, AAAI/MIT Press, 1996
7. www.cs.sfu.ca
8. Dunham M H, Data Mining: Introductory and Advanced Topics, Prentice Hall, 2002

32

Knowledge Organization in Digital Libraries Using Rough Set Theory

B. Kannan
Lecturer, Dept. of Computer Applications

Veerankutty Chelatayakkot
Junior Librarian,
Cochin University of Science and Technology
(bkannan@cusat.ac.in)

ABSTRACT

Unlike the search engines, Digital Libraries have to present the Internet resources in a organized way. Knowledge organization is a challenge in Digital Libraries. This paper describes how Internet resources can be classified by using Rough Set Theory.

Introduction

Knowledge is a broad and abstract notion that has sparkled epistemological debates in Western philosophy since classical era. The term 'knowledge' is defined as " a justified personal belief that increases an individuals capacity to take effective action"(Nonaka, 1994). Action, in this context, refers to physical skills and competencies, cognitive/intellectual activity or both cognitive elements in the form of knowledge(Alavi ,2002)

Similar definitions and difference of knowledge, information and data can be found in Information Science literature. Data is raw numbers and facts, information is processed data and knowledge is information made actionable. "Knowledge is information possessed in the mind of a individual; it is personalized or subjective information related to facts, procedure, concepts, interpretations, ideas, observations and judgment " (Alavi , 2002)

Since knowledge is personalized, for one persons' knowledge to be useful for another individual, it must be communicated in such a manner as to be interpretable and accessible to the other individuals. Knowledge management is the process of making more efficient use of human knowledge that exits within an organization.

Knowledge management refers to a systematic and organizationally specified process for acquiring, organizing and communicating both tacit and explicit knowledge of incumbents. The major focus of knowledge management is to identify and gather content from documents, reports and other sources and to be able to search that content for meaningful relationships.

Digital library

Digital library is the collection of information objects that support users in dealing with information, organization and presentation of these objects available directly or indirectly via electronic or digital means. A digital library should provide powerful and efficient functionalities for content management (acquisition, storage, indexing, access, and maintenance), manifold metadata for content enrichment, and structuring, as well as services for effective content search, access, annotation, filtering, and dissemination. Earlier, digital libraries were, like traditional libraries, a collection of books and reference materials in digital format. Now information sources available over the World Wide Web is also a part of digital library. The true benefit of a digital library comes from its ability to hyper-textual linking or related texts, full text searching of holdings, and the integration of knowledge management, and data visualization. The collection and organization of Internet resources is a challenge to digital libraries. In this paper we analyses the possibilities/ application of Rough sets theory in knowledge classification in a digital library.

Rough set Theory

Rough Set Theory was developed by Zdzis Law Pawlak in the early 1980's. It deals with the classificatory analysis of data tables. The data can be acquired from measurement or from human experts. The main goal of the rough set analysis is to synthesize approximation of concepts from the acquired data.

Rough set theory is another approach to vagueness. Suppose we are given a set of objects 'U' called Universe and in indiscernibility relation R Íð U ´ð U, representing our lack of knowledge about elements of U. For example, take a set of documents and classification. We assume that R is an equivalence relation. Let X be a subset of U. We want to characterize the set X with respect to R The lower approximation of a set X with respect to R is the set of all objects, which can be for certain classified as X with respect to R. The upper approximation of a set X with respect to R is the set of all objects which can be possibly classified as X with respect to R The boundary region of a set X with respect to R is the set of all objects, which can be classified neither as X nor as non-X with respect to R. Now, Set X is crisp (exact with respect to R), if the boundary region of X is empty and Set X is rough (inexact with respect to R), if the boundary region of X is nonempty. Thus a set is rough (imprecise) if it has nonempty boundary region, otherwise the set is crisp (precise).

Obviously, each rough set has boundary line cases, i.e., objects which cannot be with certainty classified by employing the available knowledge, as a member of the set or its complement. Therefore, in a rough set approach, with any rough set a pair of crisp set - called lower and upper approximation of the rough set is associated. The lower approximation consists all objects which possibly belongs to the set. The difference between the upper and lower approximation constitute the boundary region of the set.(Pawlak 1982). This can be illustrated as follows.

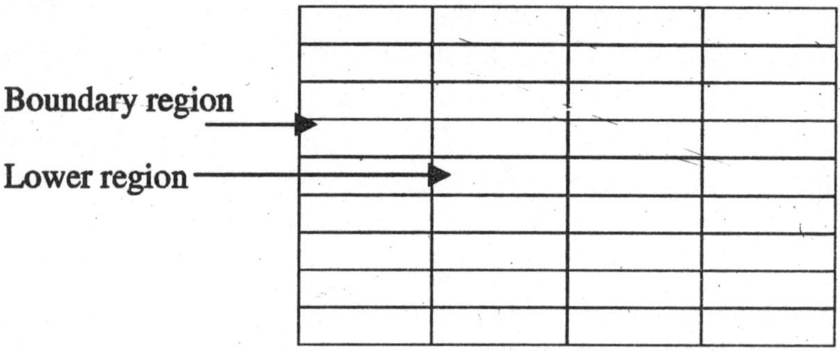

For example, let 'U' be the Set of all documents under consideration. Let R denotes the relation 'having the same classification'. Let X be the subset of all documents classified under Medicine. A lower approximation of X would be the set of all documents 'having the keywords 'Dieses', 'Cancer', 'Patient', and 'Diagnosis', since these keywords would be surely classified under Medicine. An upper approximation will be the set of all documents having any medicine related keywords. The difference between this two will be the boundary.

Application of Rough Sets Theory in Knowledge Classification

In our approach, each document is searched for keywords, which are obtained by filtering out usually found words such as proposition, adjective, common words etc. Each keyword is given a relevance score ($r_{cw)}$ in the range 0 to 1 for each classification. The relevance score can be calculated either manually or by using automated system. In the manual method, the relevance score is fixed by a classifier according to relevance and relationship of keywords among different disciplines. For example, the key word 'Cancer' has high relevance in Medicine (0.9) while less relevant in Philosophy (0).

Keyword	Discipline	Relevance Score
Cancer	Medicine	0.9
	Social Science	0.4
	Philosophy	0
Genetics	Medicine	0.5
	Social Science	0
	Life Science	0.8
Alcohol	Medicine	0.3
	Social Science	0.2
	Psychology	0.1

One way to automating this process is by using data from already classified documents and finding the relative frequency of these keywords in each classification. For example, if in a 1,00,000 classified documents containing the word 'Cancer', 75,000 documents are related to medicine, then we can say that the relevance score of Cancer is 75,000/ 1,00,000 = .75.

Now the documents rough set membership for each classification is calculated by multiplying the relevance score of each word by its relative frequency and summing up: i.e.,

$$fc\,(D) = \Sigma_w\, r_{cw} * f_w$$

where fc (D) is the relevance score or rough set membership of document D for classification and f_w is the relative frequency of the word W in D.

We can include the documents in a particular classification if $fc\,(D) > a$, where the value of a is fixed by the user. If user wants high precision, he should fix the value of a as above.5, then the system will include all documents with relevance score above .5 and vice versa.

References

1. Alavi, M and D.E. Leidner (2002) '*Knowledge management systems: issues, challenges and benefits* in Knowledge Management Systems: Theory and Practice ed. by Stuart Barnes, Thomson Learning :United States. pp. 15-35.
2. Nonaka,I (1994) 'A dynamic theory of organizational knowledge creation , *Organization Science* 5(1),14-37.
3. Pawlak,Z (1982) Rough Sets International Journal of Computer and Information
4. Sciences, 11(5), 341-356.

33

An Integrated Model for Digitization of Information Resources

Kapil Mohan Garg
Mahesh Singh Rana
A M Sherry
IMT Ghaziabad

ABSTRACT

Information technology has emerged as the most potent tool to collect organize and disseminate information to the people on a large scale through communication network. It is one of the fastest spreading technologies in the world in terms of use and production. It is diffusing rapidly into all industrial and service sectors and is seen as one of the most crucial technologies for managing the information resources. Members of the information profession have become acutely aware from the words like "we are working and living in tomorrow's 'virtual world', and we must begin to look to the future and prepare ourselves for what networked technology is making possible". As a consequence, much of the recent literature in the field has been devoted to discussing and exploring the shape of future library and information services.

One area receiving significant attention is the development of access to information through digital libraries. This paper focuses on the existing research on the digitization of library and information resources and is concerned with the practical application or implementation of digital libraries.

There are thousands of digital library projects currently underway, in all sectors of the library community. These projects have taken widely varying approaches, dependent on the needs of the different libraries, the sector in which they are based and in part, the definition of digital library that has been applied. This has led to a variety of digital libraries being developed, with no common model being available. This paper deals with key aspect of digital library and prepares a model for the digital library herewith discussing the components, categories and environment of digital library.

Introduction - The Digital Library

The basic concept underlying the digital library is not new. At initial stages, digital library projects were started by universities and museums in USA and UK to digitize selected rare and special collections. It was envisioned that this concept will be used by individuals as "a sort of mechanized private file and library". It would be able to store large amounts of books, pictures, periodicals, newspapers, correspondence, and so on, with material being indexed for easy retrieval. The digital library seems a revolutionary development, the concepts and technologies involved are more accurately described as evolutionary.

Terminology and Definitions

Although not a recent concept, in terms of actual development, digital libraries are still relatively new. Because of this, there is as yet no universally agreed terminology in place. In the literature, the *digital library* may also be called the *library without walls, virtual library, electronic library, e-library, desktop library, online library, future library, library of the future, logical library, networked library, hybrid library, gateway library, extended library* or *information superhighway*. Among these terms, *digital library, virtual library, hybrid library* and *electronic library* are the most common. Just as there is no universally agreed upon terminology for digital libraries, neither is there a common definition for this concept. In the 1990s, terms such as *digital library, virtual library* and *electronic library* became widely used, but considerable uncertainty remains about what they actually mean. Few authors distinguish between the various terms, defining each one differently. However, such distinctions are relatively rare, with the various terms usually being used to refer to essentially the same thing, i.e., shared access to networked information.

The term *digital library* has been defined both broadly and narrowly. In the narrower form, a digital library is construed as a mainly, if not wholly, digital entity, although this fully digital scenario is dependent on the necessary materials being available in an appropriate format. In the broader construction, the digital library is defined as a hybrid of traditional library services and new electronic sources and methods. One of the more comprehensive definitions termed the digital libraries as the concept of remote access to services of libraries and other information resources, combining an on-site collection of current and heavily used materials in both print and electronic form, with an electronic network providing access to the external worldwide library and commercial information. In essence, the user is being provided with the effect of a library, which is a synergy created by bringing together the resources of many libraries and information services.

Components of the Digital Library

Regardless of the wide variety of terms used to describe the digital library concept, it is clear from the literature that there are certain common elements, regardless of the terminology applied. There must be, in some sense, a *collection*, to which clients must be linked in an efficient and satisfying manner. There is also a set of *services*, either human or electronic, which link clients to the collections. The *technologies* involved in providing digital library services should support document creation, retrieval, transfer, dissemination, manipulation and management. Finally, there must be an *institution* in which the digital library collections and services are embedded. These include:

* The use or development of electronic document delivery services;
* Policies, services, reallocations that emphasize access to information over ownership;
* Participation in cooperative development or purchase of electronic files;
* Participation in the development of a campus-wide information system;
* A written plan stating its goal as access to information from a single workstation;
* Enhancement of the online public access catalogue (OPAC) to include the holdings of other libraries besides those held locally;
* Providing gateway from the OPAC to other databases or networks, like Internet;
* End-user access to online files from on or off campus,
* Internet Connectivity.
* Training faculty and students for using the Internet sources;
* Subscribing to electronic journals;
* Digitization of text for electronic storage, retrieval and/ or dissemination;
* Access to electronic full-text;
* An e-mail front-end that allows users to initiate interlibrary loan and document delivery requests, suggest purchases, or ask reference questions from within the OPAC;

When grouped together logically, these activities fall

into eight basic categories:

1. The Internet and Intranets

Development of library Internet and/or Intranet sites;

2. Integrated access to resources

Single workstation access to resources, use of OPAC as a gateway and Inclusion of external holdings on local OPAC.

3. Digitization of materials

Digitization of project reports.

4. Electronic publications

Journals and full-texts;

5. Electronic document delivery

Commercial and library-to-library electronic document delivery;

6. Resource sharing

Access to resources over ownership;

7. Cooperative activities

Cooperative purchasing or development of resources;

8. End-user services

End-user access to online resources;

Internet training for clients;

Searching training for clients;

End-user electronic requesting;

These elements then may be considered as the basic building blocks of the digital library. Although the exact nature and extent of the application of each component will depend upon the circumstances and needs of the library and/or the organization to which the digital library is attached.

The Digital Library Environment

Just as the literature identifies a number of activities

that together make up digital libraries, it also shows that the development of digital libraries is heavily dependent on a number of inter-related enabling (or hindering) factors. These includes issues such as copyright, client attitudes, changes to financial structures, need for new organizational structures, technological issues, staff training, and so on. When grouped together, these factors fall within nine inter-linked subject categories:

1. *Legal issues*

Copyright, Contracts and Privacy.

2. *Financial issues*

Financial resources.

Changes to funding allocation.

3. *Client issues*

Client needs and Client attitudes;

Resistance to introduction of new technologies.

4. *Personnel issues*

Staff commitment to new systems and services.

Changed staff training and competencies.

Effect of automation on staff skills and Professionalism.

5. *Organizational issues*

Need for new organizational structures.

Reorganization of hierarchies and work divisions.

Organizational size.

Balance between professional and para-professional staff.

Appropriate position levels.

6. *Management issues*

Strategic planning.

Need for new or different performance measures.

Organizational support and leadership.

Need for champions within the organization.

Appropriate statistical measurement.

7. Technological issues

Security.

Infrastructure development.

Use of appropriate technologies.

Standards.

8. Collaboration issues

Resource sharing.

Cooperative purchasing of information resources.

Cooperative purchase or development of Hardware and infrastructure.

9. Subject discipline issues

Availability of content for different disciplines.

Appropriateness of delivery method.

Although writers in the field differ on the relative importance of these individual issues, it is widely agreed that the continued progress and ultimate success of digital libraries is dependent on their resolution. If this is the case, then these issues can be said to make up an environment that surrounds the digital library itself. The digital library and its environment may then be modeled as shown in *Figure*.

Conclusion

Based on the literature in the field, a model for digital libraries is suggested as shown in *Figure*. The model comprises the components that made the digital library and factors that impacted on its environment. It is being considered that all components are equally applicable to all libraries. Besides, the elements suggested by the authors in the form of a integrated model are open for debate as it may vary due to

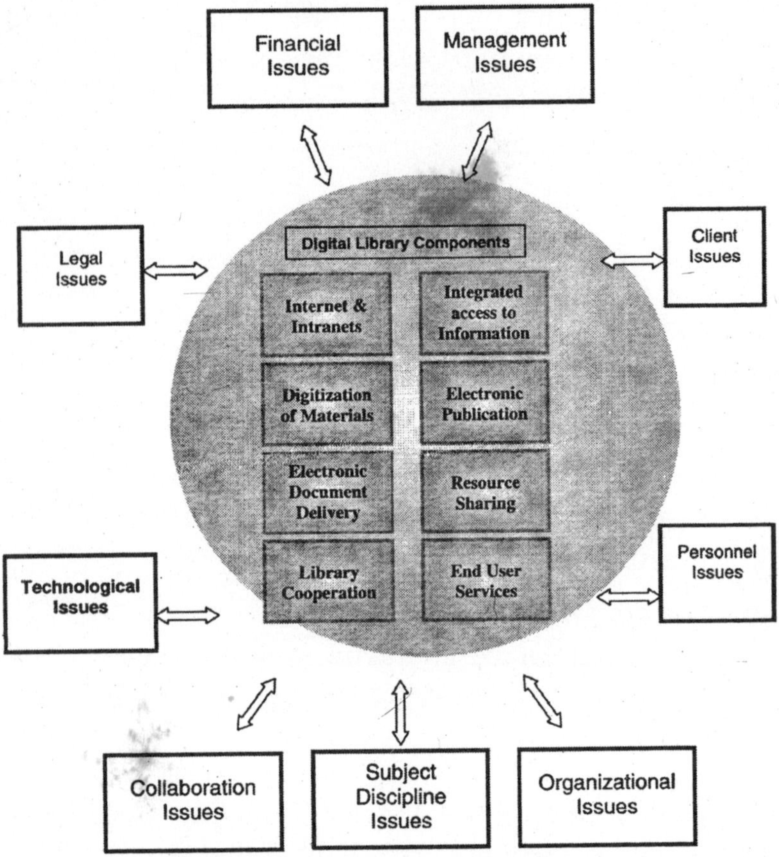

INTEGRATED MODEL OF DIGITAL LIBRARY

reasons such as ever changing advancements of technologies. It is that the integrated model in the digital library may serve as the basis and guidance for the practitioner as well as the theorist of digital libraries

References

* Andrews, Judith, "Digital Libraries: Policy, Planning and Practice", Hampshire: Ashgate, 2004, ISBN 0-7546-3448-5.
* Brophy, Peter, "Libraries without walls: The distributed delivery of library and information Services", London: Facet Publishing, 2004, ISBN 1-85604-511-0.

* Dhiman, Anil Kumar, "Internet based library services: in electronic information environment and library services: A contemporary paradigm", ILA, p.99-106, 2003.
* Digital Library Federation, "A Working Definition of Digital Library", http://www.clir.org/diglib/dldefinition.htm, 1998.
* Garg, Kapil Mohan and Rana, Mahesh Singh, et. al., "An Empirical Study of Instigating RFID Technology for Adept Management of Libraries", ICIM2005, p.587-595, vol. I, 2005, ISBN 81-7764-770-9
* Kaul, H.K., "Resource Sharing: ILL technology for libraries", NACLIN, 2001.
* Roberti, Mark, "The 5-Cent Challenge", www.rfidjournal.com/article/view/1100, Aug. 30, 2004
* Soundararajan, E., et. Al., "Digital Library: The integrated Search System", International Conference on Digital Libraries, New Delhi. TERI, p912-916, 2004.
* Witten, Ian H. and Bainbridge, David, "How to build a digital library", San Francisco: Elsevier Science, 2003.
* http://www.ala.org/acrl/guides/rarethic.html/
* http://www.lib.uchicago.edu/

34
Managing Digital Library

Babita Garg
Librarian
PGIMS, Rohtak
(babita_khusi1@yahoo.co.in)

ABSTRACT

With the advent of digital libraries and wide area networks, enormous amount of textual information are made available all over the world. A digital library is a special kind of library. One of the main goal in developing digital libraries is to provide access to coherent collection of materials more and more of which will be in digital format time goes on. The information technology and digital technology has brought about a sea change in the functioning of Libraries with the help of digital information system large amount of data can be stored in a retrievable form. Recent advances in information technology as well as exponential growth of data in digital form have created as intensive interest in techniques to assist the users in locating different data.

Introduction

Making the right information available to the right person. At the right time is the aim of any modern library service today. Digital library is the electronic library in which information are stored in the digital form organized transmitted and displayed without any intervening conversion process with the availability of computer capable of computing at high speed and having large disc storage space, it is possible to store information in form of high quality graphics colored images, voice signals and video clips at very affordable coast. Digital library does not mean library in classical sense. It is a group of distributed repositories that users see as a single repository in a digital form.

There is an increasingly wide range of digital resources from formally published electronic journals and electronic books through databases and databases in many formats I,e bibliographic, full text images, audio, video statistical and numeric datasets. Further, a digital library is not a single entity although it may have digital contents created in house or acquired in digital formats stored locally or servers. A digital library may also act a portal site providing access to digital collection held elsewhere through networks.

To adopt the change of digital library, the conventional libraries must convent their documents to digital formats. It may be done through processes like retrospective conversion, scanning, compression, indexing etc.

Digital libraries will come realities only after all the books likely to be in demand are available on optical disk. It will take a long time and involve a massive investment. It will also be necessary to produce electronic readers locally at affordable prices.

Thus it is now imperative for the library and information professionals to embrace information technology and facilitate in getting every reader his / her book and every book its reader and while doing so save the time of the reader. Computer based information storage and retrieval system have now made feasible the exchange of information and further sharing of resources with minimal efforts via various upcoming networking programmes. It is now possible to interact with fellow professionals without the boundaries of geography and times zones and especially in India where they are frequently isolated from one another because many work in one-person libraries decentralized branches of small groups.

Large library networking programme such as Inflibnet,

Calibnet, Delnet, Bonnet, Puneet etc. have been announced. The libraries that participate in such programme will be better placed to derive the benefits of the application of information technology to libraries

What is digital library

Digital libraries are organizations that provides the resources include of the specialized staff, to select, structure, other intellectual access, interpret, distribute, preserve the integrity of and ensure the persistence over time of collection of digital works so that they are ready readily and economically available for use by a defined community or set of communities (water 98). As discussed in more depth else where (Borgman 1999, 2000), researches are focusing on digital libraries as networked information system and as content collected on behalf of user communities while librarians are focusing more on digital libraries as institution or services. Those communities are not mutually exclusive of course and most large digital library research projects involve libraries as well as scholars from information and computer science.

Digital libraries are a set of Electronic resources and associated technical capabilities for creating, researching and using information. In this sense, they are an extension and enhancement of information storage and retrieval system that manipulate digital data in nay medium (text, images, sounds) static dynamic image and exist in distributed networks. The content of digital libraries includes data, meta data that consist of links or relationships to other data or metadata whether internal or external to the digital library.

Digital libraries are constructed, collected and organized- by a community of users and their functional capabilities support the information needs and use of that community. They are a component of communities in which individuals and groups interact with each other using data, information and knowledge resources and system. In this sense they are an extension, enhancement and integrâtion of a variety of information institutions as physical places where resources are selected, collected, arranged, preserved and accessed in support of user community. These information institutions include among others, libraries, museums, archives and school but digital libraries also extend and serve other community, setting, including classroom, offices, laboratories, home and public spaces.

Assumption of digital libraries

In the context of digital library four assumptions can be identified

a) Digital library is totally a paperless system with computer network and communication facilities.

b) It is suppose monetary facility to traditional library for faster retrieval and better communication.

c) Any individual can have a direct link to electronic publishers their agents/through computer communication facilities with or without knowledge of librarianship.

d) Any commercially interested organization or an electronic publisher can become local promotional trade agent in information service like one of the IST/STD centers electronic typing center reprography centers etc.

Transmission from traditional to digital library

Information technology has brought about a phenomenal change in the process of collection storage and distribution of information especially with the advent of digital libraries. The information explosion computer technology and the development of telecommunication have left a major impact on acquisition organization and dissemination of information. In the new scenario a library is no longer the central place where users come and seek the information. In the past a library has been a place for centrally stored information researchers and scholars coming for information on a wide range of subjects were available under one institutional roof. The generation of information was not as speedy as perhaps there was no need to apply the new technologies for exhaustive and pinpointed provision of information. But now with the rapid growth in the production of documents and specialization in the various fields or knowledge, the traditional libraries are not able to deal with the new order.

Components of a digital library

Internet and web are thought to be two important components of the digital library. The internet provides the distributed environment for accessing the information in the digital library while the internet services are the carriers which provide content delivery mechanism (TCP/IP and associated protocols) the web provides tools and techniques for the content publishing, hooting and access of information. Therefore the digital library which is supposed to access to the digital information, is a combination of structured unstructured text no., data, scan, image, graphic, audio and video recording etc.

For establishment of a digital library a great deal of new infrastructure, which is not available of the shelf as packaged solution, is essential use of open architecture and standard protocols, however, make it possible that pieces of required infrastructure, be it hardware, software or accessories, are gathered from different vendors or resources.

The digital librarv is used to denote one or more of the following

* Collection in which complete content of documents are created or converted to Computer-Processible forms are online access.
* Providing electronic access to the material that already

exists in the traditional library collect online. Libraries of images, scanned text, image in photograph, digital audio, video clipping or full length movies.

* Online data bases and CD Rom information products.
* Computer storage devices on which information embedded in the digital format like CDs, DVD's etc.
* Databases including library catalogue accessible to internet.

Design and management of digital resources

The following steps involved in the design and management of digital resources: -

1. Infrastructure Planning: It needs IT components, furniture, space etc.
2. Information resource planning
3. Information accessing method/techniques
4. Method to be adopted for information resource development
5. Man power
6. Financial needs

Rusbridge has divided the digital libraries resource in to four categories:

1. **Legal Resources:** These are major resources of existing libraries. This includes manuscript, slides, maps, audio, video records.
2. **Transmission Resources:** These include print form. These resources are converted into digital form for increased access and to reduced reliance on physical libraries.
3. **New Digital Resources:** These resources are design with a particular use in mind. Internet and Web technologies may be considered in these categories.

4. **Future Digital Resources:** It includes published electronics books through databases.

Digital library resources can be built by adopting the following methods:

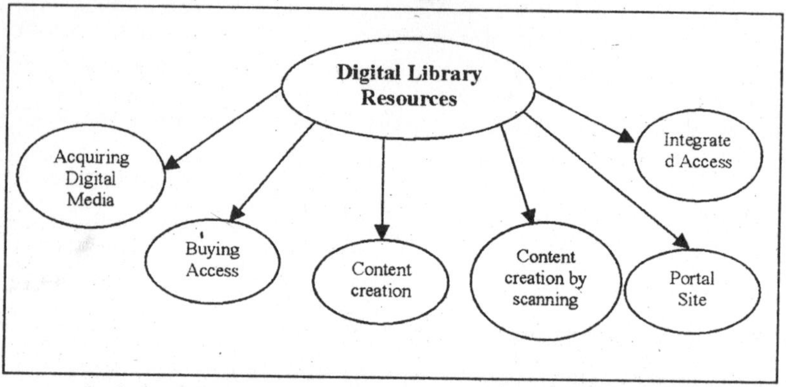

1. Acquiring Digital Media: A digital media contain a vast ocean of knowledge. These sources of information can be procured according to our needs. Today a number of commercial agencies like McGraw-Hill Multimedia Encyclopedia of science and technology, silver platter systems produce more than 250 information products on CD-Rom.

2. Buying Access: - Now a good number of technical journal published in electronic form. Libraries can subscribe these sources of digital information.

3. Content Creations: - In academic institution, many faculty members of research scholars published articles regularly. Authors may be requested to provide a soft copy of their articles to the library and this information can be added to our collection. This is called born digital.

4. Content Creations by Scanning: - These sources of information can be converted into digital media by scanning the materials. Scanned documents are stored like pictures or graphs and this should be converted as text documents. Much software's are available for this purpose.

5. ***Portal Site:*** - It includes addresses of websites, which are of interest to our readers in the library. If the users are interest to visit a site, he can directly click the address and he will be connected to that site. In this way our library can act as a portal site.

6. ***Integrated Access:*** - Digital collection can also be delivered by combining one or more method discussed above.

Means: -It includes finances and hardware and software IT components. P-IV with UNIX based machine are more reliable and user and multi tasking.

Storage: -Storage of the digitized information is very important. Two options are available (1) Using a data base or creating a special directory (2) File structure. We have number of databases to choose from e.g. Oracle, MSQL, Microsoft Access, etc. Oracle is a good choice for a data base on a UNIX based machine.

Accessibility of information: Accessibility of information to users is much important. This involves deciding on the target audience. It must be decided whether the resources can be accessible to everyone irrespective of system specification or only to those with more advance hardware and software.

Search Engine: -Search engine is an important part of a digital library. We could create our own search engine or download a free search engine from the Internet i.e., www.greenstone.org.com. etc. If we develop of our own search engine, we have to spend money and time.

Security: -Security of the information stored in the digital library is an important issue and a lot of attention to be given to protect the same. Each user can be allotted a user name and password so that unauthorized access can be avoided. Another option is to secure certain areas of the site. When a user tries to access these areas a user login and password box appears. Only a correct login and password will allow the users to access that section of the site.

Quality of Information: - Quality data is to be only added in the digital library. Data may be examined by a editor critically before adding it to the collection. If the data is useful to the readers it is added otherwise it is discarded.

Key measures towards digital preservation in india

To provide guidance in formulating policies which are appropriate for the purposes of data creation, management and long-term preservation.

Assist agencies in designing digitization programmes, which maximize their cost effectiveness and fitness for purpose over the life cycle of the resources.

Inform strategic planning amongst institutions and information's centers, which invest in the creation and/or collection of digital information resources and seek in some way to ensure the long- term viability of those resources.

To help raise awareness of the strategic issues, dependencies, and need for cooperation between the different stakeholders and agencies identified in the study.

To select and bring together case studies and literature on standards, current research and ongoing projects which will provide further guidance on specific sectors, media, and issues relevant to the effective implementation of the policy and of supporting digitization and preservation programmers.

Digital information needs active management from its inception if it is to survive and be kept accessible across different technological regimes. Computerization is changing forever the way information is being created, managed and accessed. The ability to generate, easily amend and copy information in digital form; to search text and databases; and transmit information rapidly via networks world-wide, has led to a dramatic growth in the application of digital technologies to all areas of life. The preservation community is only beginning to explore possible alternatives to storing digital information in software-independent form Rothenberg (1955) proposed an approach for maintaining the content of digital materials intact without loosing the ability to retrieve meaning rich sources. He recommended retaining the original document in its original format encapsulated in a virtual "envelope" that contains software instructions for retrieval, display, and processing of the message in the envelope. The envelopes would contain contextual information and the transformational history of each subject. Execution of the instructions would rely on an archive of hardware and software emulators or on instructions in the envelope with specification to construct emulates

Advantages of digital library

Some of the key advantages digital libraries provided as follows

a) Universal accessibility of data

b) Data can be access by all type of uses at all level retrieving all kind of information

c) Information is provided in a large amount than it possible to physically acquired and maintained is compares to traditional and automated library

d) The E-books and journals provide keywords, subject and various other searches

e) Facility for downloading and printing

f) Saving cost-manpower for publishing and bringing out new edition

g) One copy of document could be viewed by many number of person simultaneously

h) Saving space which is required for physical documents

i) A tool for the presentation of the heritage

j) Preservation: Digital information can be copied without

error, As a result preservation in a digital world does not depend on having a permanent object and keeping it under guard but on the ability to a multiple copies assuming that at least on will survive

k) Access current information.

Advantages of digital library

a) Lack of portability in contrast with books

b) Failure of hardware and software would affect the functioning of the library

c) Users must be acquainted with tools and techniques used for searching and retrieving the information available in the digital library

Challenges faced by digital library

1) Protecting the intellectual property right: Major administrative challenge is in copying with copyright and intellectual property rights issues. The library authority has to discuss seriously with publishers on this aspect to have profit to both uses, publishers as well as authors users may be charged for each access, downloading from servers and each kind of digital library collection

2) Security aspects : Security aspects is one of the most pressing challenge of digital affairs piracy of data-base, viral invasions, parallel satellite networking stress are some of the issues for digital libraries are confronted as a way of routine

3) Lack of expertise: Due to lack of expertise in the country and abroad overseas venors change too much and also reluctant to important techniques/ technology

4) Technophobia: Some people in India have fear for upcoming technology hence are nit still ready for using it

5) Problems with electronic publications faced by libraries are:

1 Issues/Return of CDs

2 Life of CDs

3 Checking out CDs content

4 Criteria of use of CDs

Conclusion

With the changes and development in the field of Information Technology, the scenario of information science is changing at a very fast pace. Information, nascent today may become absolute tomorrow. The access to right time is very essential and in the new scenario also. The extent of maintenance of library collection is a manageable problem. The willingness among librarians, information scientist or documentation officers for adopting multimedia technology, is must for preservation of important and regularly used documents. In India and World wide, much remains to be done in research, development and implementation before we can assume that even a small portion of our digital heritage. Now the Government and many institutes are gradually realizing the needs of digital reserving are UGC – INFONENT and other lives programs are the innovative step towards digitization and digital preservation.

References

1. Digital library by Babita Garg : Society for information science 2003.
2. Digital Preservation by Amrita A Pandey: International conference of Information Management - vol. 2, 2005.
3. www.google.com.
4 Managing Digital Library Resources in Health Services by S.K.Pandey National Convention MLAI- 2004

35

Friend Agent: A Novel Scheme for Information Retrieval

R. Bhaskaran
M.E. (CSE) final year,
Raja College of Engineering and Technology,
Veerapanjan, Madurai-20, Tamil Nadu

K. Vinitha
[2] *Librarian, National Engineering College,*
KovilPatti, Tamil Nadu - 628 503

Keywords: Information Retrieval, Friend Agents, Mobile Agents, Friend Network, Mobile computing.

ABSTRACT

This paper presents a Novel Scheme for Information Retrieval in Mobile Computing. The Proposed concept of this paper "FRIEND AGENT" is to enhance the need for Effective Information Retrieval. It helps in gathering the required information Independent of the location. Friend Agent offers Network Bandwidth Consumptions, Optimal routing, Security, Effective Data Transfer.

Introduction

The advances in Computing Technology have produced Miniaturization. The rapid deployment of wireless Communication Technologies such as Cellular Network, Wireless Ad-hoc Networks support the universal connectivity.

Overcoming the challenges facing the network can access the Global network easily and efficiently. The most important problem concerning with mobile networking is Quick Access to Information independent of its Location.

The other concern to be considered in the network security as constant location changes of mobile station occurs. Authentication is needed between mobile and base station. It also requires immediate update of the changes in the location.

In this Paper, We Propose a Novel and Noble scheme for Retrieval of Information and Routing Information Update based on mobile traffic pattern. We begin Section 2 with Mobile Agent Concept. In Section 3, we present the concept of Friend Network. In Section 4, we introduce the concept of "Friend Agent". In Section 5, Performance analysis and other related issues. In Section 6, concludes the Paper.

2.0 Mobile Agents and its Challenges

[2][3][7]Mobile agents are computational software processes capable of roaming wide area networks (WANs) such as the WWW, interacting with foreign hosts, gathering information on behalf of its owner and coming 'back home' having performed the duties set by its user. These duties may range from a flight reservation to managing a telecommunications network. However, *mobility is neither a necessary nor sufficient condition for agent-hood.*

Challenges:[3]

Transportation

Authentication

Low Bandwidth or Busy Network

Dynamically Re-plan Migration path to adapt circumstance

3.0 Friend Network

[1]The Static Network is inadequate to support Mobile Networking. We require the combined function of Mobile Host (MH), Base Station (BS), and Mobility Support Router

(MSR) to be a part of Mobile Networking. Friend Network forms a "Ad-hoc Network" whenever required. It does not require any Fixed infrastructure to work. It provides greatest possible Flexibility. It forms Instant Infrastructure for Disaster Relief and Remote area Communication.

A network is considered as Friend Network of mobile host if the following conditions occur

- Substantial network traffic exists between the network and the mobile host
- The network is trusted network of the mobile host and equipped with Mobility support router.
- Prohibiting the routing information into unfriendly networks can also provide the network security.

3.0 Friend Agent [8][9]

The proposed concept "FRIEND AGENT" has the advantages of friend network and overcome the challenges facing the mobile agents.

It is the combination of Friend network concept and the Mobile agent Technology.

Overcoming the barriers of Mobile agents

Friend Agent provides the solutions for overcoming the challenges faced by the mobile agents. The challenges mentioned above can be solved by providing a optimal solution through the Friend Agent.

Network-Bandwidth Problem

Friend Agent solves the network bandwidth problem. Network bandwidth in a distributed application is a valuable (and sometimes scarce) resource. A transaction or query between a client and the server may require many round trips over the wire to complete. Each trip creates network traffic and consumes bandwidth. In a system with many clients and/or many transactions, the total bandwidth requirements may exceed available bandwidth, resulting in poor performance for the application as a whole. By creating an agent to handle the query or transaction, and sending the agent from the client to the server, network bandwidth consumption is reduced. So instead of intermediate results and information passing over the wire, only the agent need be sent.

The Network Bandwidth used for routing information update can be greatly reduced by achieving Optimal Traffic Routing. Information should be propagated

Only to those routers or hosts who needs to communicate with the mobile host, instead of Broadcasting. This assumption is very general in mobile traffic scenarios.

Dynamic Re-plan Migration:

Case (i):

When the encapsulated packet destined for mobile host arrives to mobility support router, it is de-capsulated and finds whether the mobile host is available within the Home Location Register (HLR). If yes, it is delivered to mobile host via its own mechanism, through Base station.

Case (ii):

If mobile host is out of HLR, and MSR updates the information of the location of the MH. In the mean time, the MH on reaching the other location registers in the corresponding Visiting location Register (VLR), which is updated in the HLR, the packet is re-encapsulated and routed through the MSR and VLR for serving the MH. In this way, the Migration is re-planned dynamically.

5.0 Performance Analysis of Friend Agent:[3]

Many factors needed to be considered in Network routing, and the information retrieval. In Ad-hoc networks each node must be able to forward data for other nodes. The routing table must somehow reflect these changes in topology have to be adapted. It takes very minimum time for the routing table to be updated. The topology changes during distribution, [4]LIR- (Least Interference Routing) can be used to avoid the wastage of Bandwidth, and while Topology changes occur during distribution.

Comparison between Traditional Information Retrieval and Friend Agent Information Retrieval [2]

Traditional Information Retrieval:

Transfer Information	: 100KB*1S/KB= 100S
Transfer Back Results	: 1KB*1S=1S
Total Time spent in communicating	: 100S+1S=101S

Friend Agent Information Retrieval :

Transfer Agent	: 1KB* 1S =1S
Carry Information Locally	: 100KB*0.1S/KB=10S
Transfer Back result	: 1S
Total Time spent in communicating	: 1S+10S+1S=12S

As a result of the Performance Analysis, Time for retrieving information is reduced approximately EIGHT times by using Friend Agents on comparison with Traditional Retrieval Systems.

6.0 Conclusion [4][5]

We have proposed a novel concept called "Friend Agent" which overcome the challenges in mobile agents using the advantages of Friend Network, and it provides Secured and Faster Information Retrieval .It also offers the following advantages reduced Network resource consumption, by provides Optimal routing, Authentication only to Friend Networks and paves a way for the Network Security. In addition to this, it also offers greatly reduced time for Data transfer when compared with traditional Information Retrieval System. This Concept can be deployed to a wide range of Mobile Computing Applications.

References

1. Ruixi Yuan - An Adaptive Routing Scheme for wireless Mobile Computing – Wireless and Mobile Communications by Kluwer Academic Publishers
2. www.csc.ncsu.edu/faculty/ mpsingh/papers/positions/maas-97.pdf
3. agent.cs.dartmouth.edu/workshop/1997/slides/jorstad.ppt
4. Mobile Communication – Jochen Schiller
5. Computer Networks - Andrew S.Tanenbaum
6. http://www.computer.org/concurrency/pd1999/pdf/p3080.pdf
7. www.objs.com/agent/00-12-05.ppt
8. R.Bhaskaran – "Friend Agent – A Novel Scheme for Information Retrieval " Proceedings of Asia Pacific Conference on Parallel & Distributed Computing technologies – 2004 VIT Vellore.
9. R.Bhaskaran- "Enhanced Information Retrieval" Proceedings of 3rd international CALIBER-2005 Cochin University & Inflibnet centre

36
Digital Archives: Design and Development

K. R. Mulla
HKBK College of Engineering, Nagavara, Bangalore

Shivakumar A. S
Librarian, Indian Institute of Management, Bangalore

Chikkamallaiah,
M. Chandrashekara
Sr. Lecturer, DOSLISc. Manasagangothri,
University of Mysore, Mysore-570 006.

ABSTRACT

All over the world libraries are undergoing a major transformation. The need of the society is forcing the libraries to undergo such a change. The emerging technology of digital libraries (DL), an offshoot of information revolution, can drastically improve the efficiency and effectiveness of management of physical and financial resources of libraries. The advantages of having a DL are now well understood by librarians, technologists, managers and others. The library has to equip to meet with global trends for the ultimate benefit of information seekers. Several factors play major role in the process of digitization. This paper discusses the transformation of a library from traditional type to the automated to digital form. It also highlights some of the issues involved in such process. Eventually coupled with digital technology, the DL becomes reality for anybody, anytime and anywhere.

1. Introduction

The movement towards the electronic information society is pushing libraries to automation, CD ROM networking and digital based movement. Digital Libraries (DLs) provide access to digital information collections. DL includes a combination of structured/unstructured text/ numeric data, scanned images, graphics, audio and video recordings etc. DL are required to select acquire, organize, make accessible, and preserve digital collections.

The conventional libraries of books were integrated together with the newly developed non-print learning resources or information resources. Because of the complex media technologies, difficult classification of information resources/artifacts/ media elements, lack of proper storage systems and fast obsolescence of media technologies, the stock and content of learning resources centers/ media centers, could not be sustained. One simple reason from the point of view of providers and users was, the requirement of learning of the skills of operating a variety of hardware, for proper use of software for teaching and learning.

The evolution of affordable technologies of computer based networking (Intranet and Internet) and Interaction Television Networking (ITN) by the Space Applications Centers (SAC) and INFLIBNET etc., are compelling us to adopt the digital information resources each in day to day instructional work using various modes contact, offline distance and online distance education. Looking to the theses needs and the revolution in digital technology, a DL with large number of artifacts/information resources is immediately required. By doing so, for the first time, a long awaited dream will possibly be concretized in the form of an effective, interactive and proactive DL, that can be accessed by anyone who requires knowledge.

2. Digital revolution and library evolution

In the present era of Information Technology (IT), digital media seems to have overshadowed the print and analog media. The accumulated knowledge of mankind in the form of books in the library and instructional audio and video broadcasting, are unfortunately losing their appeal among the masses. Books, becoming costlier and less affordable for many, access to the instructional radio and television being less flexible, at the same time the need of intellectual society to have access to the knowledge at a distance, demands revolutionary changes in traditional library.

Thus conventional print and non print material (including analog based materials) can be transformed in form of e-books, digital texts, graphics, audio, animation, digital video and also computer assisted learning and training materials and transmitted directly in the users hands globally rather than selected bands of users locally. This has become possible because of the emergence of computer technology to manage and administer the knowledge base (digital resources) and the communication and multimedia technologies to deliver information at a distance.

3. Objectives of digital library & archives (dlaa)

* Analyze and design computerized information systems for DLAA that can be accessed on both intranet and Internet.
* Develop the computerized information system for the DLAA to effectively and efficiently manage different forms of learning resources of all curriculum areas, other general resources and also web-based resources available in the institution and on the Internet.
* Identify and address issues related to data security, copyright and subscription/licensing.
* Acquire, transform and preserve the existing learning and general resources (physical and analog artifacts) in

form of print material, analog audio and video, into digital artifacts/archives.

* Implemented and provide access to the DLAA information system to the library users over Internet and Intranet.
* Preserve the digital artifacts/archives.
* Maintain the digital archives information system.

4. Advantages of DLs Vs traditional libraries

* Resources can be easily accessed on the net from anywhere, at anytime and according to individual choice. Faster access to all forms (text, graphics, audio, animation and video) of information on-site and off-site resources, at the desktop.
* Simultaneous access to the same resources and facilitating storing and printing the resources at users end. Resources in digital format can be managed and administered easily as compared to traditional management system.
* Preservation of Intellectual property.

Based on the objectives stated above, the establishment of 'DLAA' was carried out in different phases as described below:

5. Phase 1: design aspects

5.1. Output query & interface design

In the process of development of any information system, 'output query and interface design' and 'input data and interface design' are the initial and primary step. The design aspects that was considered in each of the above two steps are detailed below:

* What are the different resources available in a curriculum area of a subject by a author and or a particular publication?

* What are the general resources available that are accessible on-site and off-site by a digital library member?

The different features of this web based interface that were identifiable is stated below:

(i) The web-based interface should facilitate the DL members/visitors search resources stored on the DL server.

(ii) Facilitate feature to access the learning resources to registered user through login identification and a password.

(iii) The interest of the casual visitors interacting with the DL web site is sustained by providing them access to some general resources of interest available on-site or on Internet in the public domain.

(iv) Facilitate users/visitors to download necessary plug in necessary to access resources.

(v) A link that will enable visitors to visit web site to get more information about institution profile.

5.2 Input data design

The available resources that could be part of DL were identified and these resources are divided into two broad classes or four categories. The classification/categorization was based on 'Learning' and 'General' resources, the types of available resources and the different users who will access the resources. These details are given in a tabular form in table [1]

5.3 input interface design -(at server end) (Application Interface Design)

The feature of the application interface (front end) to administer and manage these resources at the server end by the DL administrator was identified and the layout designed.

The different features of input data interface that were identified was as follows:

I. The interface should facilitate addition, deletion, and modification, listing and saving of resources, to and from the resource database (Oralce8i).

II. Only authorized administrator through login identification and a password may be allowed to administer and manage the DLAA resource from the server system.

III. Facilitate creation, deletion, and modification of data/information of a member.

IV. Facilitate navigation and search options in the application interface.

6. Phase 2: DLAA architecture

6.1 System architecture

There are different ways an application can be developed. The design of a system or the system architecture will depend on a lot of factors like the design specifications, user requirements, the number of users, the performance requirements, reliability and maintainability, the scalability requirements and so on. Based on these factors, an application of three-tier architecture in a client server environment was proposed to design for using the latest technology tools. The technology tools that were identified for storing and managing the knowledge base (resource database- 2nd tier) was Oracle8i, Visual Basic (VB) for developing front end Graphic User Interface (GUI) application (1st tier-which can help to administer and manage the digital library resources) and Active Server Pagers (ASP) ASP-3rd tier to fetch/accessing resources from Oralce8i data based at server end as per the users need through Java Script coding and web browser. The first and the third layers or tiers interact with the second layer and in the best of circumstances that are independent of the individual compositions. The proposed three-tier architecture of the information system is shown in figure [1]

6.1.1. Technology standards

Based on the technology tools selected to develop DL, the technology standards for transforming different forms of resources available in the institute such as physical/analog artifacts (print and non-print) into digital format were prescribed, as shown in the table [2]

6.1.2. Data coding scheme

To uniquely identify the resource data in the database table, it is necessary to use consistent data coding scheme, which will distinguish data of one entity set from another. Some of the sample data coding scheme adopted is as given in the table [3]

6.2 *Infrastructure facilities*

The basic infrastructure that was setup for the DLAA is small computer room with dedicated computer server to administer and manage and software to design and develop/transform digital artifacts. Dedicated manpower like librarians, programmer and specialized manpower to acquire, digitize, develop and manage the digital artifacts for implementing the DL were also identified. The basic infrastructure facilities in terms of hardware/software and manpower required.

a). Hardware:

* Dedicated server, Juke Boxes, Hard Disk with Terabyte capacity, Professional Scanner, Digital Camera Workstations

b). Software:

* Windows NT Server with Internet Information Server (liS) installed, Oracle 8i, VB, Microsoft Front Page/Interdev, Adobe PhotoShop, Paint Shop Pro,

Macromedia Flash, VRML, Audio-Video Processing tools etc.

7. Phase 3: system-developmental aspects

An application interface to administer and manage the digital library by the administrator at server end and a data retrieval system (at client end) that will be used by the library users/visitors was developed, based on the design considerations defined earlier.

7.1 input interface-development (Application Interface-Server End)

As per the three-tier design architecture and the identified features, an application interface using VB was developed to administer and manage digital resources. Some other important features incorporated in the application are to create/manage resource database, member entry, media management, cataloguing, searching a resource from the knowledge base etc. JavaScript and ASP were used to access resources from the data based. The resource database was created with thirteen different data tables, to ensure data integrity, avoid data redundancy and to eliminate the data inconsistency due to data insertion, deletion, and modification. The data normalization up-to three level was considered. Similarly, forms and source codes for administrating login identification cataloging the resources, creating members, curriculum area, subjects, author, publisher, currency, country, media type, source, supplier, resource category, general resource category and general resources were designed and created for manipulating data related to the resources.

7.2 Output interface- development (Web Based Interface-Client End)

As per the features desired during the designing phase, a web-based interface was developed for the DL user to access

'General Resources' as well as 'Learning Resource & Institute Archives (LRIA)'. Home page, login page, learning resource page and general resource page using Hyper Text Markup Language (HTML) were developed. Java script coding was also used at client end to create select condition for the searching the resource, which was then processed by triggering ASP at computer server, special features to download 'Plug in' such as 'Internet Explorer' and 'Acrobat Reader' are also provided to the library members to access the resources. Using this web interface the user can access any learning resources of a particular curriculum area, in a subject, written by a author and published by a particular publisher. Features are also provided for having access to the classified resources such as external DLs, e-journal, virtual library etc., on the Internet, access to these Internet web sites will be made available to the users after the institute taken a policy decision and subscribes and takes license for the external resources. A user can also have access to the general resources, which are developed and made available onsite and offsite (Internet public domain) such as institute newsletter e-dictionary, encyclopedia, e-journal, etc.

8. Phase 4: maintenance

Maintenance of 'DLAA' is another important phase. A well-organized system was developed to acquire the digital born archives as and when it is developed in the institution. These resources are then made available through the digital system over the Intranet. Time to time, the feedback provided by the members of the DL through e-mail is helping the administrator himself to updates the resources, ensures availability of the resource content and also repairs any broken links of the resources.

9. Management issues

The DL has come into existence and use, recently. To

sustain the library, there are certain management issues, which needs to be tackled.

1. Establish a clearinghouse team which will scrutinize new information resources before they get admitted to the DL, the scrutiny / editing need well defined criteria / norms / standards to be established by the institute in near future.
2. Policy decision concerning norms for compensation to the authors needs to be developed.
3. Norms and conditions for partnership with distributed DL of other institutions need to be formulated.
4. The norms for deciding the membership fees by the users of the institute and other potential users of the country, needs to be established.
5. Procedure for registration and collection of membership fees / subscription amount has to be formulated.
6. Exclusive funds needs to be made available for transforming existing printed and analog information resources into digital resources as well as for acquiring digital born resources, developing new digital barn information resources and maintaining and updating the resource and technology standards

10. Future developmental issues

It is sure that the establishments of DL will speedup at much faster rate in educational establishments. With the increase in number of DL and their beneficiaries, different developmental issues may hinder the progress of the library. To take care of such managerial, operational, administrative and academic issues, it is highly desirable that a cross-country forum to address issues related to DL needs to be established for India and Asia Pacific region. India is not an exception in this race of DL revolution; digital library of India (DLI) initiative was launched in September 2003 by president of

India. DLI portal (http://www.dli.ernet.in) DLI is being implemented in close collaboration with universal DL project (http://www.ulib.org) at Carnegie Mellon University. DLAA evolution for the Education system, made a well beginning implementing using contemporary web based technologies that are used world over.

The forum shall take policy decisions; evolve ways and means for prescribing norms and standards including technology standards and also for ensuring that all the member libraries follow these norms/ standards. These are many other avenues/issues for future developments of DLs are:

i. Confirming that no violation of copyright by the DL does occur before any information resources becomes integral part of the library. At the same time, ensuring that the copyright of the intellectual property of DL are also protected.

ii. Increasing cooperation amongst distributed libraries.

iii. The networking of the DL will normally occur within the fraternity of institutions pertaining to a particular category such as technical education, management education, science & technology and medical science education etc.

iv. The forum should also develop a system of deep classification of digital information resources to ensure cross referencing/ searching/using the concept of key words.

v. The forum should also concentrate upon integration of DL with several instructional/educational endeavors, in contact, offline distance/online distance modes so that ultimately the students acquire competencies implying skills pertaining to all the four domains: cognitive, affective, psychomotor and interactive.

11. Conclusion

After a long gap, and era of evolution of electronic media, DL technology will initiate and sustain the effective development, dissemination, classification, and storage/ preservation of digital resources, to promote utilization of all kinds of media resources, old and new digital-born ones, for effective life-long learning. The synergy of networking, quick cross-referencing and mouse-click away accessibility of learning resources will change drastically the teaching-learning models in all modes of education and training: contact, off-line distance and on-line distance. The institutions learners using DL can possibly and quickly transform their organizations into an effective learning organization.

References

1. Er. S.K. Soni, 'Multi-media Archival for Technical Education in Indian Ocean Region Countries An Indian Proaction', XXVII, Annual Convention of ISTE, MACT, Dec. 1997
2. George Koch and Kevin Loney, 'Oracle 8i - The Complete Reference', 3rd ed., TMH, New Delhi, 1997.
3. Mathew Strebe, Charles Perkins, 'Internet Information Server', 1st ed., BPS Publication, New Delhi, 1998.
4. Evangelos Petroutsos, 'Mastering Visual Basic 6', BPB Publications, New Delhi, 1998.
5. Colombo Plan Staff College for Technician Education, Manila, Philippines, 'Leading Change in TET', October, 1999.
6. A Keyton Weissinger, 'ASP in a Nutshell', O'Reilly, Shroff Publisher & Distributors Private Limited, Mumbai, 1999.
7. R. Allen Wyke, 'Pure JavaScript', 1st ed., SAMS, Techmedia Publication, New Delhi, 1999.
8. Sybex Authors Team, 'HTML Complete', 1st ed., BPB Publication, New Delhi, 1999.
9. Nicholas Chase, 'Active Server Pages 3.0 from scratch', QUE, Prentice Hall of India Private Ltd. New Delhi - 110001, 2000.
10. Mike Gundearloy, 'Visual Basic Developer's Guide to ADO', BPB Publications, New Delhi, 2000.

11. Witten Ian. H and Bainbridge David, 'How to Build a Digital Library' Murgan Kaufmann Publishers, San Francisco, 2003.

12. Talawar V G and Biradar B S, "Digital Resources and Services in Libraries" : Organized by Kuvempu University and ASSIST, 4th ASSIST National Seminar April 30th –May 1st 2004.

13. Murthy. T A V and et all., "Multilingual Computing and Information Management in Networked Digital Environment: organized by CUST and INFLIBNET, 3rd International CALIBER February 2-4, 2005.

ANNEXURE

Table [1]. Classification/Categorization of Resources

SI.No.	Classification Resource Category	Available Resources	Users
1.0	Learning Resources	Instructional Materials, Audio-Video Tapes, CBTs, Curriculum documents, Journals/ conferences-papers, dissertation, project reports, thesis, Power points etc.	Authorized/ Registered Users.
1.1	Classified Resources	External libraries, Online Journals, virtual libraries for which institution subscriptions are required.	Authorized/ Registered Users
1.2	Institute Archives	Are the resources that are in particular related to the Institutions properties/ archives that can be assessed by selected identified users in the governing body of the Institution such as Annual report, board resolutions etc.	Identified Members of Institutes Governing Body.
2.0	General Resources	Internet based resources that were available on public domain such as e-dictionaries, e-encyclopedias, e-Institute News Letters, e-Reports, e-magazine, e-newspaper, e-online journals, virtual Universities, e-virtual Library etc.	All users

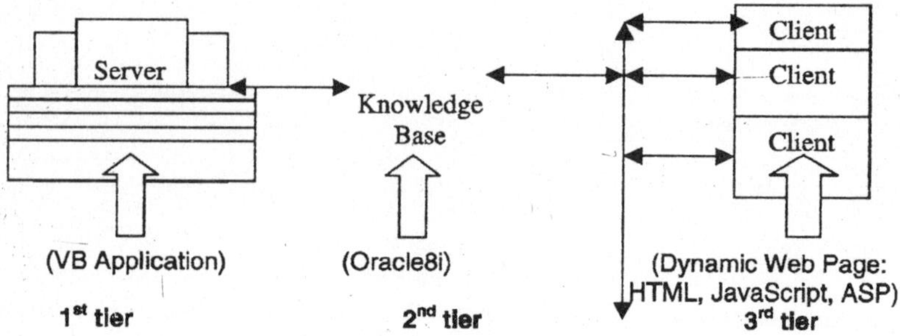

Fig. 1 - DLAA: A Three Tier Architecture Technology Table [2].
Technology Standards for Data/Resource Transformation

Table 2. Technology Standards for Data/Resource Transformation

S.No.	Media Resource	Digital Media Format
1.	Textual	PDF (PDF Writer)
2.	Graphical	GIF, JPEG Format
3.	Audio	MP3 Format
4.	Animation	GIF, Macromedia Shockwave, Macromedia Flash, VRML
5.	Video	MPEG format
6.	Computer Assisted Learning	Authored in a Web Authoring Tool

Table 3. Data Coding Scheme

Entity (Table Name)	Data Coding Scheme (First two characters after removing vowels)
Author	AT
Country	CN
Curriculum	CR
General Category	GC
Media (Learning Resources	MDL
Media (General Resource)	MDG
Publisher	PB
Source	SR
Subject	SB
Supplier	SP

37
Text Mining for Information Retrieval

Jyothiprakash
Librarian, Amrita School of Business
Coimbatore – 641 105

ABSTRACT

Hundreds of megabytes of data are distributed around the world every day and it is no longer possible to monitor this increasingly rapid development. This growth is exponential. We are confronted with the new paradox about the growth of data that more data means less information. In future, the ability to read and interpret alone will not be enough to survive as a professional or as a scientist of a commercial organization. The mechanical production and reproduction of data force us to adapt our strategies and develop methods for filtering, selecting, and interpreting data. More than eighty percent of the data are in the form of text. Text mining technology extracts information from mountains of information.

Introduction

Text Mining is the discovery of computer of new, previously unknown, information; by automatically extracting information form different written resources. A key element is the linking of the extracted information together to form new facts or new hypotheses to be explored further by more conventional means of experimentation. Text mining is different from what we are familiar with in web search. In search, the users are typically looking for something that is already known and has been written by someone else. In text mining, the goal is to discover unknown information, something that no one yet knows and so could not have yet written down. Text mining is a variation on a field called data mining that tries to find interesting patterns from large databases. The difference between regular data mining and text mining is that in text mining the patterns are extracted from natural language text rather than from structured databases..

Since a textual format is a very flexible way to describe and store various types of information, large amounts of information are stored and distributed as text. Moreover, the amount of accessible textual data has been increasing rapidly. Such data may potentially contain a great wealth of knowledge. However, analyzing huge amounts of textual data requires a tremendous amount of work in reading all of the text and organizing the content. Thus, the increase in accessible textual data has caused an information flood in spite of hope of becoming knowledgeable about various topics.

The most important issue for this text mining technology is how to represent the contents of textual data in order to apply statistical analysis. Since any information that cannot be retained within the representation cannot appear in the final output, we should carefully examine the expressive power of the representation system. Then, once the appropriate information is extracted from the text, the next issue is how to provide statistical analysis. We should then apply appropriate mining functions adapted to the representation of the original content of the text. Finally since the content of the text varies greatly, it is essential to visualize the results and allow an interactive analysis to meet the requirements of analysis working from multiple points of view.

Text Mining Definition

Text mining, also known as intelligent text analysis, text data mining or knowledge discovery in text (KDT), refers generally to the process of extracting interesting and non-trivial information and knowledge from the unstructured text. Text mining is a young interdisciplinary field, which draws on information retrieval, data mining, machine learning, statistics and computational linguistics. As most information (over 80%) is stored as text, text mining is believed to have a high commercial potential value (from Wikipedia encyclopedia).

Kostoff and DeMacro (2001) define science and technology text mining as "the extraction of information from technical literature. It has three components: information retrieval (gathering relevant documents), information processing and information integration. Information processing is the extraction of patterns from the retrieved records by bibliometrics, computation linguistics and clustering. Information integration is the synergistic combination of the information processing output with the (human) reading of the retrieved relevant records. The information processing output serves as a framework for the analysis, and the insights from reading the records enhance the skeleton structure to provide a logical integrated product. Again, substantial manual labor is noted, and technical details are not given, leaving doubt as to what kind of and how much computational linguistics and clustering were actually implemented.

Text retrieval is a branch of computerized information retrieval where the information is stored primarily in the form of text. In short it is the study of techniques of retrieving textual documents relevant to the needs of a searcher (from Wikipedia encyclopedia).

Data Mining

Most organizations have large databases that contain a wealth of potentially accessible information. However, it is usually very difficult to access this information. The unbridled growth of data will inevitably lead to a situation in which it is increasingly difficult to access the desired information. Data Mining or KDD (knowledge discovery in databases) mines data from large databases. There are many differences between data mining and SQL. It is important to realize that query tools and data mining tools are complementary. A data-mining tool does not replace a query tool, but it does give the user a lot of additional possibilities. Suppose that you have a large file containing millions of records that describe your customer's purchase over the last ten years. There is a wealth of potentially useful knowledge in such file, most of which can be found by firing normal queries at the databases. But what is an optimal segmentation of my clients? Or what are the important trends in customer behavior could not be found out from normal query. Through the application of Data Mining techniques we will get these types of answers.

Text mining technology

Text mining technology mainly deals with document-handling technologies and related areas like natural language processing for extraction of information, statistical analysis to find interesting patterns among the concepts and visualization to allow interactive analysis.

The term "text mining" is sometimes used to indicate document handling technology because it detects and extracts documents and it allows us to select data related to some specific topics that we are interested in so that the amount of data we have to handle is reduced without losing the information we want. However, we have to specify what we want in the form of a query in order to use this technology. Thus, the use of this technology is limited when we do not have a clear intention about what to search for and knowledge of what can be retrieved from the database we are searching.

In terms of knowledge extraction, many kinds of knowledge can be extracted from textual data, such as linguistics knowledge for natural Language Processing (NLP) and domain-specific lexical and semantic information that may be stored in a database. The technology of Information Extraction is also related in terms of extracting meaningful items from textual data. Thus text mining is a text version of generalized data mining, and it consists of NLP to extract concepts from each piece of text, statistical analysis to find interesting patterns among the concepts and visualization to allow interactive analysis.

Natural Language Processing

Natural language processing (NLP) is the branch of linguistics, which deals with computational models of language. Its motivations are both scientific and practical. NLP has several levels of analysis: phonological (speech), morphological (word structure), syntactic (grammar), semantic (meaning of multiword structures, especially sentences), Pragmatic (sentence interpretation), discourse (meaning of multi-sentence structures), and world (how general knowledge affects language usage). When applied to IR, NLP could in principle combine the computational (Boolean, vector space, and probabilistic) models practicality with the cognitive models willingness to wrestle with meaning. NLP can differentiate how words are used such as by statistical text analysis. Clearly, NLP could be a powerful tool for text mining.

Text Categorization

Once appropriate concepts are extracted from each piece of text, we can apply various statistical analysis methods in data mining to the set of concepts as well as to structured data. As a result, even a simple function that examines the increase and decrease of occurrences of each concept in a certain period may allow us to trends in topics. Moreover, the semantic classification of concepts enables us to analyze the content of text from the viewpoints of various semantic categories.

The semantic classification also enables us to find significant features for some topics by analyzing associations among concepts. Although finding association rules is one of the most attractive functions in data mining in terms of discovering novel facts, analysis of association rules in very large text samples does not provide much useful information if we simply treat each piece of text as a set of items consisting of content words within the text. Because of the large number of variations in items extracted from the text, the number of association rules is usually too large to verify. In addition, most of them are elements of compound words that naturally occur together. However, by using the semantic categories, we can detect the significant associations based on the assumptions that concepts in the same semantic category have a similar distribution of associations in comparison to other concepts.

Text Visualization

Visualization techniques are a very useful method of discovering patterns in data sets. In order to deal with requirements from various viewpoints and to compensate for the low accuracy of linguistic analysis, it is indispensable to provide functions to visualize the results for intuitive understanding and to allow interactive analysis. Text mining implies homing in on "precious nuggets" whereas text visualization seems to be concerned with the big picture.

An Example of Text Mining Software

IBM launched a product named "Intelligent Miner for Text in 1998. It is a software development toolkit, not a ready to run application for building text-mining applications. It addresses system integrators, solution providers, and application developers. The toolkit contains the necessary components for" "real text mining", feature extraction, clustering, categorization, and more.

Text Mining Applications

* *Information Retrieval* : It comprises (1) Retrieve documents based on various sorts of information about the documents content (2) Indexing and retrieval of textual documents and (3) Finding a set of documents that are relevant to the query
* *Information Extraction*: Extraction of relevant information from a document (summarization, feature extraction etc.)
* *Web Mining*: It indexing and retrieval of textual documents and extraction of partial knowledge using the web
* *Classification*: Classifying and organizing of documents according to their content, Products and class for each text document
* Organize repositories of document related Meta information for search and retrieval

Conclusions

This paper tries to shed light on text mining, the various components of text mining technology, difference between text mining and data mining, the application of text mining in libraries and an example of text mining software. Text mining supports the creation of knowledge by preparing and organizing unstructured textual data and by supporting the extraction of relevant information from large amount of unstructured textual data through automatic pre-selection based on user-defied criteria. Using automatic mining process to organize and scan huge repositories of textual data can significantly enhance both efficiency and quality of a routine task.

References

1. Sullivan, Dan, "Exploring Text with Qualitative Data Analysis", DM Review, May 2004, Vol.14, No.5.
2. Saravanan, M (et al), "Summarization and categorization of text data in high-level data cleaning for information retrieval", Applied Artificial Intelligence, May-Jyly 2003, Vol.17 No.5/6.
3. Mena, Jesus, "Data Mining your websote", Boston: Digital Press, 1999
4. http://en.wikipedia.org
5. http://www.twocrows.com/glossary.htm

38

Institutional Repositories - A New Paradigm to Sharing Information

Gayatri Doctor

Faculty Member

ICFAI Business School, Ahmedabad

(gayatridoctor@ibsindia.org)

ABSTRACT

Repositories are "collections of digital objects", which are valuable tools to enable sharing and reuse of resources. There is a need for repository development within learning & teaching communities to ensure the availability of content, improve quality of the learning experience and cater to different learning styles.

The paper discusses the typology of repositories. Institutional Repositories (IR) are collections of digital material (pre-prints, post prints, theses, technical reports, grey literature and other digital material) hosted, owned or controlled by a college or a University. The paper also states that the research output created by the faculty, research staff, and students of an institution and accessible over the Internet to end-users both within and outside of the institution, with few if any barriers to access is also called as an e-prints archive. The content in these repositories can be shared at the metadata level by using the Open Archives Initiative (OAI) interoperability protocol, OAI Protocol for Metadata Harvesting (OAI-PMH)

The paper also throws light on open–source software packages that enable people to set up institutional repositories and to encourage authors to self-archive. The Eprints.org software from University of Southampton; and the D-Space software from Massachusetts Institute of Technology are finding a growing number of users throughout the world as implementing this technology is relatively simple.

The paper elaborates on the functions & benefits of Institutional Repositories and a few the Search Enablers of the Global Institutional Repositories.

Repositories and Need for Information Sharing

A Repository is defined as a managed storage system with content deposited on a personal, departmental, institutional, national, regional, or consortial basis, providing services to designated communities, with content drawn from the range of digital resources that support learning, teaching and research.

Repositories are 'collections of digital objects'. An increasing range of activity areas within the information environment refer to their deposited content collections as 'repositories'.

In order to encourage communication across activity areas, and promote interoperability, we need to be able to define the characteristics of 'repositories' and seek the coherence of a common approach.

The repository can be managed as an *institutional repository* or a *subject repository*. The content of the repository could be an *e-prints repository* or a *data repository* or a *learning object repository*.

The primary need of repository development within teaching and learning is to ensure

* The availability of content,
* To improve the quality of the learning experience,

* To cater to different learning styles.
* To share and re-use digital objects.

Even the wealthiest institutes cannot purchase access to all the information that all their researchers require. New technology, in particular the coming of the internet allows us to revise or to reinvent scholarly communication.

There is a need for development of institutional repositories and open access journals so that the way they interact could result in a future where the world's research is available to all.

The Digital Repository & Library

It might be argued that a digital repository is simply a digital library and the terms can be applied interchangeably. Over time, one term may become dominant but at present there is a subtle distinction to be made.

A library is a place where resources are stored but librarians have control over what is to be placed in the library.

Repositories, on the other hand, place a little more emphasis on the fact that they are places where people can contribute resources. It does not simply ensure safe storage and delivery but sharing and reuse.

The term repository is used to emphasize the fact that many people may contribute *learning objects* to be shared among a community.

It has the following characteristics:

* content is *deposited* in a repository, whether by the content creator, owner or third party on their behalf
* The repository architecture manages content as well as metadata
* The repository offers a minimum set of basic services e.g. put, get, search, access control
* The repository must be sustainable and trusted, well-supported and well-managed

Digital repositories, unlike most of the other forms of educational technology, do not force the participants into one particular approach but that many different people can support many different forms of teaching and learning using a single digital repository. In short – digital repositories are pedagogy-neutral. It is as likely that a lecturer preparing a classic lecture and handouts will find useful, and reusable, resources in a digital repository as it is that an educational technologist will find key resources for online courses to be taken by students in many different locations.

Repositories are valuable tools to enable sharing of resources - Sharing supports learning, teaching and research.

Digital repositories can benefit all teachers throughout an organisation no matter how much or how little they adopt other forms of educational technology.

A few terminologies.

Content: Information captured digitally and imparted to learners. Formats for e-learning content include text, audio, video, animation, simulation, and more.

Learning object. Basically, it's a self-contained, small chunk of *learning* that accomplishes a specific *learning* objective. A *learning* object is also self-describing. In other words, in addition to the content, it contains a description of itself that includes such information as the nature of the content, *learning* objectives, author, language, and version. Information that describes the object is typically referred to as metadata.

Metadata (The content about content): Information about content that enables it to be stored in and retrieved from a database.

Typology of Repositories

To give teachers easy online access to a wide range of digital learning materials, which they can use to support their teaching across the curriculum and to aid communication it would be useful to develop a typology of repositories.

By target user group

- Learners
- Teachers
- Researchers

By Content type:

- Raw research data
- Derived research data
- Full text pre-print scholarly papers
- Full text peer-reviewed final drafts of journal/ conference proceedings papers
- E-theses
- Full text original publications (institutional or departmental technical reports)
- Learning objects
- Corporate records (staff and student records, licences etc)

By Coverage:

- Personal (author's personal archive)
- Journal (output of a single journal or group of journals)
- Departmental
- Institutional
- Inter-institutional (regional)
- National
- International

By primary Functionality of repository:

- Enhanced access to resources (resource discovery and location)

- Subject access to resources (resource discovery and location)
- Preservation of digital resources
- New modes of dissemination (new modes of publication)
- Institutional asset management
- Sharing and re-use of resources

Institutional repository (IR)

"A Institutional Repository could be any collection of digital material hosted, owned or controlled, or disseminated by a college or university, irrespective of purpose or provenance."

An institutional repository or a digital archive of the research output created by the faculty, research staff, and students of an institution and accessible over the Internet to end-users both within and outside of the institution, with few if any barriers to access is also called as an *e-prints archive*. As a facility it consists of hardware, software and procedures to capture, organize, archive, disseminate and manage digital research resources of the institution.

Institutional repositories – the contents

* Pre-prints
* Post-prints
    * Author post-prints
    * Publisher PDFs
* Technical reports, Working Papers
* Theses & dissertations
* Books or chapters of books
* Research databases
* Conference proceedings
    * Text

* Video recordings
* Teaching materials
* Digital research materials, e.g. simulations, code

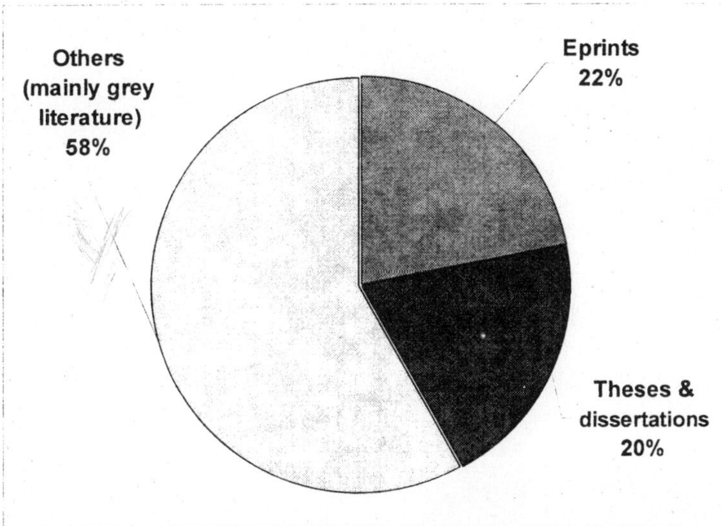

Fig. 1 : Types of Documents in Institutional Repositories

Source : "The State of Play" Mark Ware, Director, Mark Ware Consulting Ltd presentation at PALS Conference 04 – "Institutional Repositories and Their Impact on Publishing"

Further, by using the Open Archives Initiative (OAI) interoperability protocol, OAI Protocol for Metadata Harvesting (OAI-PMH) content in these repositories can be easily shared at metadata level to establish a single point cross-indexing and search service at national level. The same protocol enables integration of content in these repositories with worldwide cross-archive search

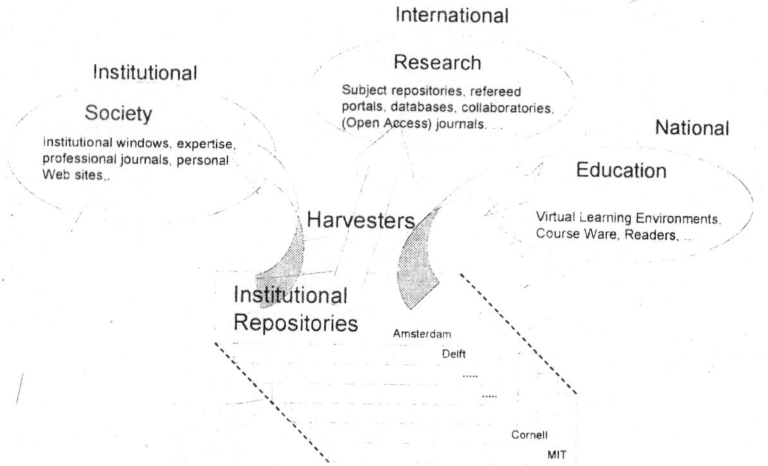

Fig. 2. An Institutional Repository Concept

Source : " Institutional Repositories and Open Access " - *Leo Waaijers, Project Director, DARE.* (DARE, Digital Academic Repositories) presentation at PALS Conference 04 - Institutional Repositories and Their Impact on Publishing"

A number of significant developments, such as the launch of MIT's DSpace in the autumn of 2002, as well as the University of California's eScholarship and the growth of repositories based on the University of Southampton's EPrint software, have brought the issue of institutional repositories increasingly to the fore.

The two open –source software packages that enable people to set up institutional repositories and to encourage authors to self-archive: the Eprints.org software from Southampton; and the D-Space software from MIT. are finding a growing number of users throughout the world as implementing this technology is relatively simple

Some Institutional Repository Initiatives

While many universities are pondering whether or how to implement an institutional repository, a growing number of institutions and consortia are actively engaged in setting up and running repositories. The practical experiences gained by these initiatives— organizational, technical, and legal— should prove instructive to other institutions, and the technical infrastructures that several of the projects are developing might provide turnkey systems that speed repository implementation by others.

California Digital Library eScholarship Repository

The California Digital Library (CDL) eScholarship Repository, announced in April 2002, illustrates the continuum between digital libraries broadly conceived and institutional repositories. The CDL launched the eScholarship repository, a web site and a suite of digital support services, to distribute academic research and working papers of University of California faculty. The CDL service adopted the OAI metadata harvesting protocol in order to participate in the global network of shared repository contents.

DSpace

DSpace, a collaborative project of the MIT Libraries and the Hewlett-Packard Company, is creating a stable, long-term digital repository to preserve the significant body of articles and other research materials generated by MIT researchers each year. Significantly, it also seeks to build a repository system that can support a federation of institutional repositories that adopt the system. To support this goal, the DSpace project is exploring related issues including access control, rights management, versioning, retrieval, faculty receptivity, community feedback, and flexible publishing capabilities. Because of its focus on the specific requirements of the institutional repository, DSpace design and functionality is paying particular attention to the content input side of the process, which should ease and encourage author participation.

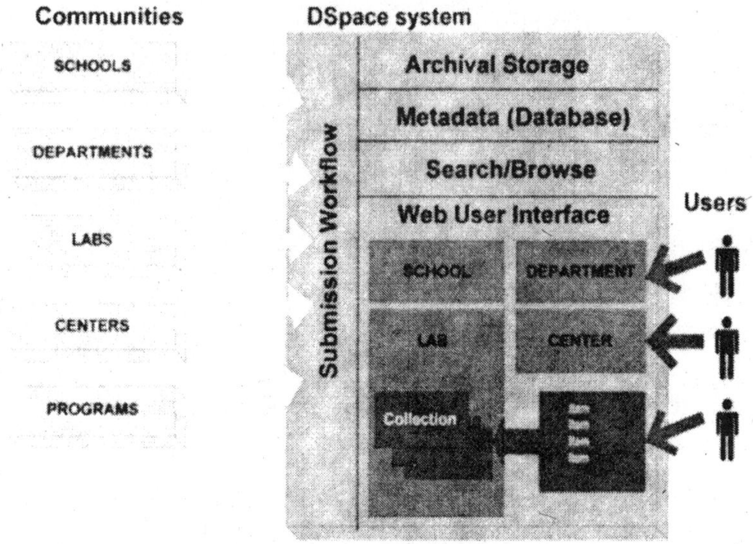

Fig. 3. DSpace information model

Source : " DSpace - An Open Source Dynamic Digital Repository " Mackenzie Smith, D-Lib Magazine , January 2003 Volume 9 Number 1

GNU EPrints

Developed at the University of Southampton, the open source EPrints self-archiving software (GNU EPrints) now comes configured to run an institutional preprints archive. The generic version of e-prints is fully interoperable with all the *OAI Metadata Harvesting Protocol.*

Universities that have implemented e-prints solutions include Cal Tech, the University of Nottingham, University of Glasgow, and the Australian National University.

The Indian Scenario

MHRD (Ministry of Human Resources Development, Govt. of India) has advised all the consortium members of INDEST (Indian National Digital Library in Engineering Sciences and Technology – http://paniit.iitd.ac.in/indest/

to set up e-print archives using appropriate OAI-compliant e-print software.

MHRD has also recommended that a central server may be deployed to harvest metadata from all such eprint archives. It is strongly felt that if the submission of research publications is followed conscientiously at all participating member institutions, the combined collection developed in the process would significantly complement and supplement the traditional publishing approach.

In a Workshop on Institutional Repositories at the Indian Institute of Science, Bangalore, India 27-29 July 2004, participants from 21 leading Indian academic research institutions received training in setting up institutional e-print archives using the GNU EPrints open source software to fulfill the recommendation of the INDEST consortium to its member institutions to set up OAI-compliant Open Access Eprint Archives for their research publications, on the model of the Indian Institute of Science.

Institutional Repositories-Search Enablers

OAIster is a project of the University of Michigan Digital Library Production Service. Its goal is to create a collection of freely available, previously difficult-to-access, academically-oriented digital resources that are easily searchable by anyone.

OAIster offers information that links to hidden digital resources such as the complete contents of books and articles, technical reports, preprints (unpublished works that have not yet been peer reviewed), white papers, images of paintings, movies, and audio files of speeches . OAIster retrieves these elusive resources by tapping directly into the collections of a variety of institutions using harvesting technology based on the Open Archives Initiative (OAI) Protocol. U-M's OAIster service provides access to more than 5 million harvested records describing and pointing to these resources. Currently, the resources are created and hosted by 444 research libraries and institutions from around the world. http://oaister.umdl.umich.edu/o/oaister/

ARC - A Cross Archive Search Service is an experimental research service of Digital Library Research group at Old Dominion University. Arc is used to investigate issues in harvesting OAI compliant repositories and making them accessible through a unified search interface. It is not a production service and may be subject to unscheduled service interruptions and anomalies. http://arc.cs.odu.edu/

Yahoo searches OAIster A repository of information that provides links to previously difficult-to-locate electronic scholarly resources will be widely available under a new agreement between U-M and Yahoo! Inc. The repository—developed through the University Library's OAIster Project—is available through Yahoo's Content Acquisition Program (CAP) and accessible through Yahoo! Search.

Google searches DSpace

In a pilot project with Google, DSpace, and OCLC .... OCLC will use the OAI protocol for metadata harvesting to collect eligible metadata records from participating institutions, resolve the DSpace Handles (or other persistent IDs) to the standard form of URLs that Google prefers, and Google can then use the URLs in OCLC's registry to index the relevant content from participating institutions.

Functions of Institutional Repositories

They are institutionally defined, although some countries may have national repositories.

They contain a wide range of materials, including preprints, working papers, published articles, enduring teaching materials, student theses, data-sets, etc. All together, this material represents the intellectual wealth of an institution.

They are cumulative and perpetual, and thus act as an

archive. Material is not deleted after a certain amount of time, but is built upon and always available.

Most importantly, they are inter-operable and have open access. That is, different search engines are able to view the content of the institutional repository so that it is available to people outside the institution.

Benefits of Institutional Repositories

The institutional repository provides a means for institutions to create archives and make available their wealth of knowledge.

It allows individuals (scientists and researchers) to self-archive their own material.

For the individuals, the institutional repository acts as a central archive for their work, representing a CV that provides a complete list of their research over the years. Because it is open access, it increases the dissemination and impact of their work.

For institutions, it acts to preserve their intellectual wealth. It increases their visibility and prestige, and can act as an advertisement for funding sources and industrial sponsors.

Since the archive is freely accessible on the Internet, more researchers can consult and cite your research publications

For society, it provides access to the world's research and ensures the long term preservation of research.

E-prints archive provide a simple, web-based mechanism to researchers to deposit ('self-archive') and access their research publications. They have the potential to bring significant benefits to educational and research institutions:

Institutional Repositories help in establishing priority to your research findings, long-term preservation of research papers, improved research knowledge management, integrated view of your institutional research which is otherwise distributed over a large number of external sources.

Conclusion

As even the wealthiest institutes cannot purchase access to all the information that all their researchers require. New technology, in particular the coming of the internet allows us to revise or to reinvent scholarly communication. There is a need for development of institutional repositories and open access journals so that the way they interact could result in a future where the world's research is available to all.

Repositories are valuable tools to enable sharing and reuse of resources. Institutional Repositories (IR) are collections of digital material (pre-prints, post prints, theses, technical reports, grey literature and other digital material) hosted, owned or controlled by a college or a University. They are the research output created by the faculty, research staff, and students of an institution and accessible over the Internet to end-users both within and outside of the institution.

Open–source software packages that enable people to set up institutional repositories and to encourage authors to self-archive: the Eprints.org software from University of Southampton; and the D-Space software from Massachusetts Institute of Technology are finding a growing number of users throughout the world as implementing this technology is relatively simple.

With the growth of Institutional Repositories on the global arena , the biggest issue is of persuading faculty to participate and self archive. Archiving in a repository goes against established practice of publishing and this has to be dealt with.

Technical Skills have to be developed for maintaining the repository and metadata Organisational and administrative matters like establishing Institutional Repositories, their funding and growing storage requirements for long-term preservation are some issues to be looked into.

Certification, Peer review, Quality control and Legal Issues of who owns the copyright are important areas that have to be sorted out with growing Institutional Repositories & Open Access Journals.

The advent of Search Enablers such as OAIster, ARC and Yahoo's Content Acquisition Program (CAP) accessible through Yahoo! Search. are important developments towards Institutional Repositories and a new paradigm of sharing information.

References

1. Crow, R. "The Case for Institutional Repositories: A SPARC Position Paper."
2. SPARC,2002. http://www.arl.org/sparc/IR/IR_Final_Release_102.pdf
3. Duncan, Charles, "Why Digital Repositories? " An Intrallect white paper, November 2002, http://www.intralect.com/papers/
4. Duncan, Charles ,"Digital Repositories: e-Learning for Everyone", eLearn International, Feb 2003, elearninternational_edin_feb2003.doc
5. Lynch Clifford, "Institutional Repositories: Essential Infrastructure for Scholarship in the Digital Age," ARL Bimonthly Report 226 (February 2003), 1-7.
6. Peters, Thomas A. "Digital Repositories: Individual, Discipline-based, Institutional, Consortial, or National?" Journal of Academic Librarianship 28/6 (2002) : 414-417.
7. Prosser, David, 'Institutional repositories and Open Access: The future of scholarly communication', "Information Services and Use" vol. 23 (2003), issue 2-3, p. 167-170.
8. Smith , MacKenzie, " DSpace - An Open Source Dynamic Digital Repository " D-Lib Magazine , January 2003 Volume 9 Number 1
9. http://www.dlib.org/dlib/january03/smith/01smith.html
10. Waaijers, Leo "Institutional Repositories and Open Access"
11. Presentation at PALS Conference 2004
12. http://www.palsgroup.org.uk/palsweb/palsweb.nsf/pubframe
13. Ware, Mark "The State of Play" A presentation based on his

pathfinder research for PALS on Institutional Repositories.

14. http://www.palsgroup.org.uk/palsweb/palsweb.nsf/pubframe

Weblography

1. Learning Circuits Glossary
   http://www.learningcircuits.org/glossary.html
2. DSpace Open Source Community
   http://www.dspace.org/
3. EPrints.org - Self-Archiving and Open Access (OA) Eprint Archives
   http://www.eprints.org/
4. Archives using GNU EPrints
   http://software.eprints.org/archives.php
5. eprints@IISC ...Open Access Repository of IISC publications.
   http://eprints.iisc.ernet.in/
6. Joint Information Systems Committee (JISC) , Digital Repository Programme http://www.jisc.ac.uk/index.cfm?name=programme_digital_repositories
7. OAIster 5,195,319 records from 444 institutions (updated 4 March 2005) http://oaister.umdl.umich.edu/o/oaister/
8. ARC - A Cross Archive Search Service http://arc.cs.odu.edu/

39

Organizing for Digital Archiving: A Network Model at SDMIMD

Harinarayana N.S.
Faculty, Department of Library and Information Science, University of Mysore, Mysore

Sunil M.V.
Librarian, SDM Institute for Management Development, Mysore

Keywords: Institutional Repositories; Greenstone; Digital Libraries; e-library; Archiving.

ABSTRACT

Acquisition, organization, preservation, retrieval and dissemination of scholarly information are the fundamental functions of libraries over the centuries. The ICTs have had impacted the way in which these functions are carried out from time to time. The role of libraries in archiving has seen a paradigm shift. With the publishers are marching forward to grab the archiving function from the libraries, libraries have found new avenues for using their skills in archiving. This situation has lead to the mushroom growth of localized digital libraries, institutional repositories, OAIs etc. The availability of Open Source Software such as GSDL, dSpace, ePrints etc., has augmented the interests of librarians to experiment with the development of institutional based full-text retrieval systems.

Sri Dharmasthala Manjunatha Institute for

Management Development (SDMIMD) has developed an e-library portal which serves as a long-term archive as well as an information system for providing distributed network services to its patrons. The e-library has been designed to cover five collections, viz., Contemporary Issues; Faculty Publications; Summer Projects; Articles (Frequently used e-resources); and A/V Materials. The e-library portal has been welcomed with lot of enthusiasm from students and faculty alike. This pilot project would be expanded to cover the entire sister institutions coming under the umbrella of SDM Educational Trust.

Introduction

Libraries have been using the technology for a long time now. Libraries are always in forefront when it comes to the adoption of new technologies as and when they are available. Right from the typewriter technology till the web enabled OPACs, the libraries are the first among many institutions to experiment with new technologies. MARC is a living example, which tells the success story of libraries in effective implementation of the technology. MARC was conceived and implemented as early as the first part of 1960s itself. At that time very few professions were talking about the implementation of technologies for their professional work.

Though the technology might have changed the way the libraries function, the fundamental philosophy of librarianship has remained the same over the centuries. Libraries have always been perceived by the society as a social organization aiming at identifying, acquiring, storing, organizing, retrieving, disseminating and archiving of information. The technologies have provided new means for carrying out these functions. Much has been written about the all the functions mentioned except the last one. Archival function is probably one of the important but unsung functions of the libraries.

Traditionally, libraries have had the important role of archiving the information for the posterity. National libraries for example, have been assigned the task of preserving the cultural heritage of their nations by archiving the information. Thus, the society recognizes the national libraries as the sole agency for archiving nation's intellectual output. To be fair, even the other types of libraries like University libraries, Public libraries etc., have had this role though archiving was not their paramount importance. Thus one can say that all kinds libraries have the responsibility of archiving information. For this reason, libraries were some time called "memory organizations" and have similar role to play as that of museums.

The overall role of traditional libraries in the communication chain can be best described in the figure 1 given below:

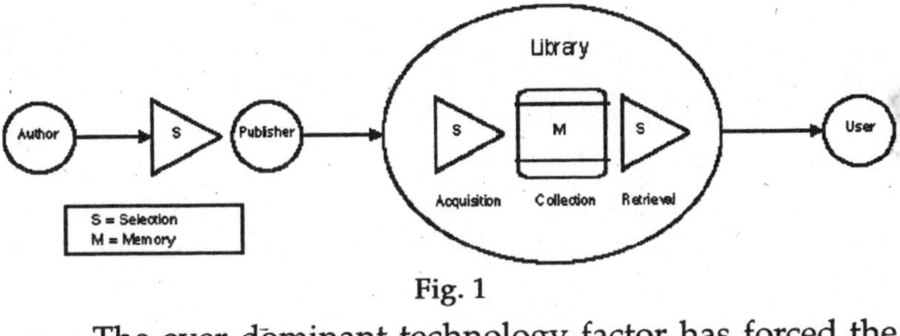

Fig. 1

The ever dominant technology factor has forced the libraries to shift from the traditional role of the library as a "clearing house" and "ware house" for printed publications, to a role as a supplier of networked services for digital information resources. It is vivid that the technology has encouraged the publishers for taking away the archiving role of libraries to themselves. The technology is so simple and effective that publishers can now afford to take-up this role. This has twin advantages for the publisher; they can have more control over the data and use libraries only as means in the communication chain. Secondly, they can make some more profit by providing additional services from the archived data with minimal or no extra cost. However, some authors are not comfortable with this kind of new role grabbed by the publishers. They argue that relying on the publisher to perform the archiving role may be costly and quite unprofitable activity. However, if one scans through the literature one would find that the archival functions of the libraries are fading away. Figure 2 shows the digital distribution model carried out by the present day libraries.

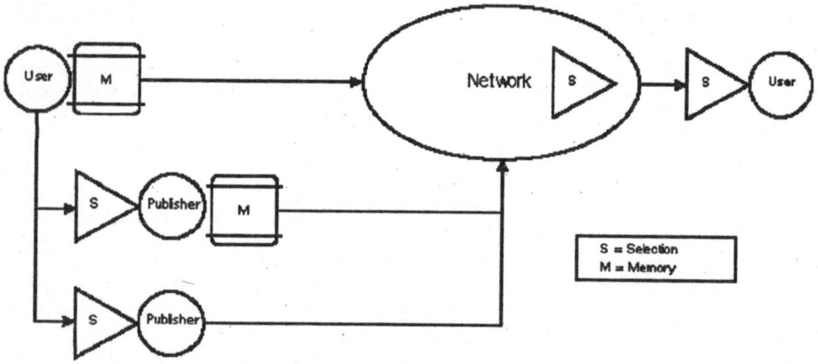

Fig. 2

What this means to the libraries in general? Now that they have very less responsibility of archiving the third party published information, they are now turning towards the archiving their own institutions intellectual output. One cannot say that this is all together new activity of the libraries. They were doing this kind of activity earlier also. However, what has changed is the vigour and intensity with which they are attempting for archiving institutional outputs. The following are some of the reasons for the paradigm shift:

* With the upcoming of electronic journals and e-books the archival function of the libraries have reduced. The skills acquired by them over the years are now being productively used to archive the once own (institutions) intellectual activity.
* The technology - storage and software - for digital archiving is available in economically feasible proportion. This has encouraged even the small libraries

to take-up the archiving function in way of building Institutional Repositories, OAIs, etc.,

* Another factor that has contributed a lot towards the growth of localized digital libraries is the Open Source Movement. Open Source Software such as - Dspace, eprints, GSDL, etc., have become so popular among the library community that they are now willing to take up the archiving responsibility.

This trend is perhaps a blessing in disguise for the society at large. Earlier there were instances when intellectual output of an organization was not available to itself, because of lack of control over its output. This has led to a situation where an institution was not able to assess its own strengths and weaknesses. Now with the growth in the interest among librarians to develop institutional repositories, the institutions are now capable of having more control over their production. Thus, if each organization engages itself in organizing its intellectual output, the long-term benefit to the society could be tremendous.

With this intention, SDMIMD has started developing e-library portal. This portal has been developed with the following twin objectives

* To develop institutional repository of the intellectual output of the academia of SDMIMD. This repository should serve as a long-term digital archive for the institution.
* To provide distributed network information services through the e-library portal.

The effort at SDMIMD, Mysore is taken up as a pilot project for developing the digital library for the host of institutions coming under SDM Educational Trust. After gaining required expertise, the experiment would be expanded to include all institutions under the Trust.

SDMIMD, Mysore

SDM Institute for Management Development, Mysore was established in 1993 under the chairmanship of Dr. D. Veerendra Heggade, Dharmadhikari of Dharmasthala. Driven by his vision to create global business leaders, SDMIMD is today a nationally renowned institute. The institute offers the Post Graduate Diploma in Business Administration (PGDBA), Management Development Programmes (MDP), Certificate Programme in Business Management (CPBM) and consultancy.

The specialization courses offered at present are in the areas of Marketing, Finance, Systems and HRM.

SDMIMD Library has an fairly good collection of books, journals, research documentation and micro-documents. An e-Library appended with latest electronic databases has made SDMIMD proud of having the best management library in educational capital of Karnataka state. The library is designed in a split layered structure with different sections for periodicals, books, reference, e-learning with multimedia and audio-visual center.

SDMIMD is managed by the SDM Educational Trust, which runs over forty premium educational institutions. SDM Educational Trust is also deeply involved in charity and social uplift.

E-library: a model for management digital library

The SDMIMD e-library portal, hence after called just e-Library, is a local area network based information system developed using GSDL software. The e-Library has been designed to have the following collections:

* Contemporary Issues
* Faculty Publications
* Summer Projects
* Articles (Frequently used articles)

* A/V Materials

Of the above the first four have already been implemented and described in the subsequent paragraphs. However, the fifth collection, viz., A/V materials, is under development. It is proposed to include hyperlinks for CD Mirror Servers which contain A/V items and other educational databases from within GSDL.

The homepage of the SDMIMD e-Library is shown below in Figure 3

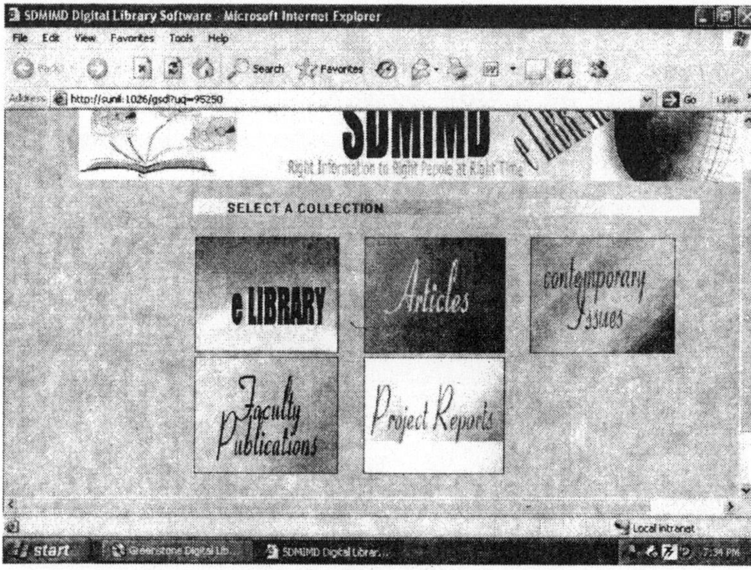

Fig. 3

Contemporary issues

This collection aims at capturing the academic output of the students of SDMIMD during their study in the institute in the form of assignments and seminars. The collection has been named 'Contemporary Issues' because most of the assignments submitted by the students are on the current issues during their study. The assignments will be prepared under the guidance of a faculty member and will be presented in the form of seminar by the student. The assignment so prepared will be included in this collection.

After we started archiving the assignments it has been found that there is a slight improvement in their quality. This is basically because the students will take up the task of preparing the assignment little more seriously than before. This is for the obvious reason that their peers in the institutes will view the same and the faculty will be keen to maintain some standard. If an assignment is not up to the mark, it will not be included in the collection. Only on the recommendation of the concerned faculty members the assignment will find a place in the collection. This has again motivated the students to work hard and improve the quality of the assignment. The screen shot of the contemporary issues is shown in figure 4.

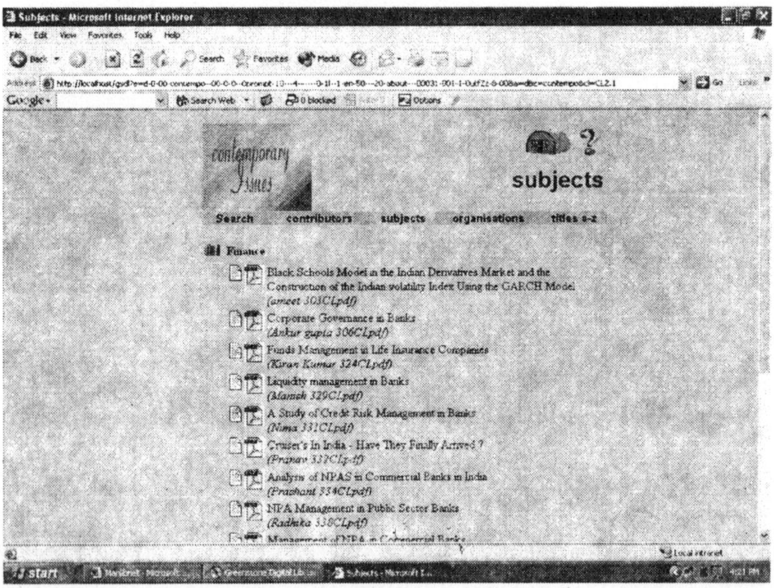

Fig. 4

Apart from the general search, the collection can be browsed through Contributors (the Faculty), Subjects, Organizations (Companies) and Titles. All the assignments are converted into pdf format before inputting to GSDL. At the time of writing this article, the collection contained 1232 papers. The collection was developed since 2001. For the assignments submitted before 2001, we are contemplating to add only the bibliographical details, as we don't have the full-text of the assignments submitted. Some of the interesting topics one can find in this collection are Credit Risk Management in Banks, Business Process Reengineering in Manufacturing Industry, Business Trends in Software Industry, Behavioral Aspects in Marketing, Challenges faced in Internet Marketing, Mutual Funds, Interim Financial Reports, Stock Market Analysis for respective periods, etc.,

The students have found this collection useful. Before the collection was developed the students were finding it difficult to consult the hard copies of documents, as they were not been issued out of the library. But now as the assignment papers are available on the network most of the students have expressed that the collection is being used for verities of purposes. Students use this collection for identifying the topics, to understand the method of presentation, to get the background information about a particular topic, and so on. There has been a demand for consulting this collection from the visitors from other colleges and institutions in and around Mysore City.

Faculty publications

SDMIMD Library volunteered to maintain the archive of the faculty publications. The data was collected from each faculty. Most of the papers were in printed form and softcopies were not available. The SDMIMD Library scanned all these papers using hp 3820 scanners and converted the documents into pdf form. The screen shot of faculty publication is given below as figure 5.

Fig. 5

The faculty publication collection can be browsed through author, title and source. The collection includes the publications of 15 faculty members accounting to 147 titles. This includes 63 international publications, 84 national publications. As this collection is available only locally we are not violating any copyright law. It has been perceived that the development of this collection has made the faculty more visible among their peers.

Summer projects

To have a close interaction with industries the PGDBA program is designed to have a summer internship in reputed companies. At the end of the first year they undertake this three-month internship in an organization of their choice. These summer project reports will be prepared under the guidance of a faculty member and the executive incharge of the project in the respective organization. The student will present the report of their summer internship before the evaluation committee. On recommendation of evaluation committee the summer project reports will find a place in the collection. The screen shot of the summer project report is shown in figure 6.

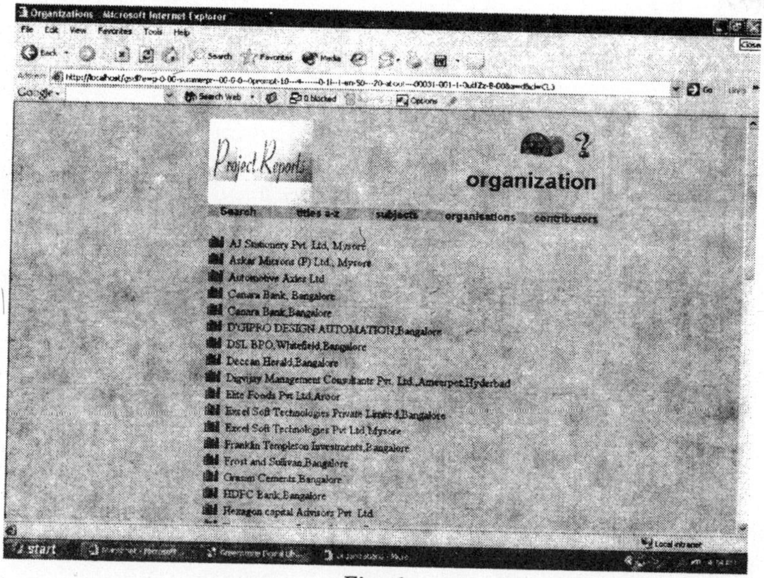

Fig. 6

Apart from the general search, the collection can be browsed through Contributors (the Faculty), Subjects, Organizations (Companies) and Titles. The softcopy of the summer projects submitted are converted into pdf format before inputting to GSDL. There 236 summer reports were placed in the e-Library at present. Each of these projects, on an average will contain 60 pages which include tables, illustrations, figures, drawings etc.

As summer project reports are considered as the reference materials, these reports were not issued to the students and the visitors. The technology has helped us to overcome this barrier and helped us to reach out these reports to our patrons. This very concept was very much appreciated and found useful by the students. e-Library portal has helped the new students to have an idea about the aspect of summer projects, the presentation technique, areas of project, etc.,

Articles

This collection basically contains those e-resources visited on the Internet by the faculty of the institution. If they perceive that a resource is of importance to others in the institution and to the teaching learning process, they will send the resource along with the URL to the librarian through email. Then it will be stored locally in GSDL collection, provided if the resource is copyright free. At this juncture, it is not out of context to mention a policy decision regarding this. The reason for downloading the e-resources completely instead of just hyper linking is that locally a word-by-word index can be generated for the resources. This would increase the access points for the users. It has been a matter of experience that indexing the resource locally increases the usability of the resource rather than by just providing the hyperlink to the e-resource. Already, more than 4000 articles have been collected under this collection. The screen shot of the article collection in e-Library is shown in Figure 7

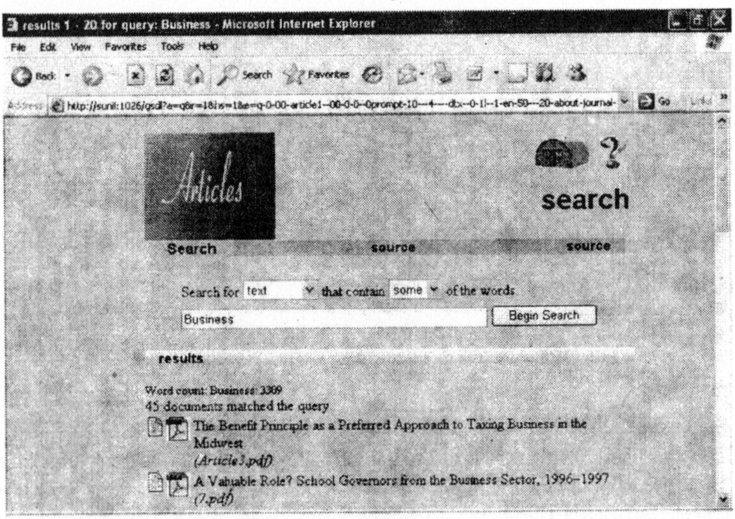

Fig. 7

As can be seen from Figure 7, the collection can be browsed through source.

Conclusion

The ongoing move towards the digital distribution through the global network infrastructure has major consequences for the traditional archival function. The need for the libraries to archive the third party publications is on the downward trend. So the libraries can now concentrate more on developing a digital archiving mechanism for their own locally developed resources. This would strengthen their parent institution. The archive so developed can also be successfully used for providing a distributed service for the local users. An attempt in this direction has been made at SDMIMD Library by way of developing e-Library Portal. This experiment will be expanded in the near future to include all the institutions, which come under the umbrella of SDM Educational Trust.

Reference

1. Lynch, Clifford A., *Institutional Repositories: Essential infrastructure for scholarship in the Digital Age*. ARL Bimonthly Report 226, February 2003.
2. Johnson, Richard K. *Institutional Repositories: Partnering with faculty to enhance scholarly communication*. D-Lib Magazine, 8 (11), November 2002.
3. http://www.greenstone.org

40

Institutional Digital Repositories/E-archives: Inflibnet Initiative in India

Yatrik Patel
Scientist-B (Software R&D Group)

J K Vijayakumar
Scientific Technical Officer-I
(Database Management R&D Group)

T A V Murthy
Director
INFLIBNET Centre Ahmedabad

Keywords: Institutional Repositories, Digital Repositories, E-Archives, DSpace, INFLIBNET, dArchive-India

ABSTRACT

The technological advances today make it possible to think in terms of storing all the knowledge of the human race in digital form and several organizations worldwide are experimenting with less-expensive ways to create Institutional Repositories. For long-term preservation of our knowledge base and cultures, we have to find out an economical way to save digital content for future generations. INFLIBNET (Information and Library Network Centre) decided to opt DSpace for its Institutional Repository and archive its publications, conference proceedings, lecture notes etc. D-Space, jointly designed by MIT and HP, is a groundbreaking digital library system that captures, stores, indexes, preserves and redistributes the intellectual output of a university's research faculty in digital formats. This paper narrates the practical experiences and provides an overview of INFLIBNET's institutional repository and dArchive-India developed for Indian academic and research community to archive their intellectual work.

0. Introduction

The technological advances today make it possible to think in terms of storing all the knowledge of the human race in digital form and several organizations worldwide are experimenting with less-expensive ways to archive and disseminate scholarly information and in-house knowledge as Institutional Repositories. In India also leading institutions started creating of Digital Libraries in different disciplines by utilizing open sources and provide open access to their scholarly literature. For long-term preservation of our knowledge base and cultures, we have to find out an economical way to save digital content for future generations. Institutions in India started using variety of open source archiving solutions like Green Stone, E-Print, DSpace etc since 2000. After experimenting all popular solutions, INFLIBNET decided to opt DSpace for its Institutional Repository and archive its publications, conference proceedings, lecture notes etc. The capability of DSpace to handle multilingual content, even at Metadata level using globally accepted UNICODE standard was the important issue for selecting this solution, especially a country like India with its mullti-lingual dilemma in digital content creation and storage.

1. About D-Space

D-Space is a groundbreaking digital library system that captures, stores, indexes, preserves and redistributes the intellectual output of a university's research faculty in digital formats.[http://dspace.org/]. In March 2000, Hewlett-Packard Company (HP) awarded $1.8 million to the MIT Libraries for an 18-month collaboration to build DSpace™ a dynamic repository for the intellectual output in digital formats of multi-disciplinary research organizations. HP Labs and MIT Libraries released the system worldwide on November 4, 2002, under the terms of the BSD open source license, one month after its introduction as a new service of the MIT Libraries. As an open source system, DSpace is now freely available to other institutions to run as-is, or to modify and extend as they require to meet local needs. From the outset, HP and MIT designed the system to be run by institutions other than MIT, and to support federation among its adopters, in both the technical and the social sense. The DSpace Federation will be explored in a later section [http://www.dlib.org/dlib/january03/smith/01smith.html].

2. DSpace@INFLIBNET

At INFLIBNET we have downloaded Dspace from http://dspace.org/. It has been installed in test-bed and experimented its capabilities and performance. After all sorts of testing required, Dspace was customized according to our requirements and it was installed on one of the WWW Server on Linux (RedHat 9) platform. Then we have requested Corporation for National Research Initiatives (CNRI) site for providing *Persistent Identifiers (CNRI Handles)* which promotes interoperability among open archives through Open Archives Initiative Protocol for Metadata Harvesting (OAI-PMH). The Handle System® covers assignment, management, and resolution of these persistent identifiers and are compliant with the IETF's Uniform Resource Name (URN) specification. The customized Dspace Archive is accessable through Web at http://dspace.inflibnet.ac.in (Fig. 1). This site is listed by DSpace at their "DSpace Live Sites".

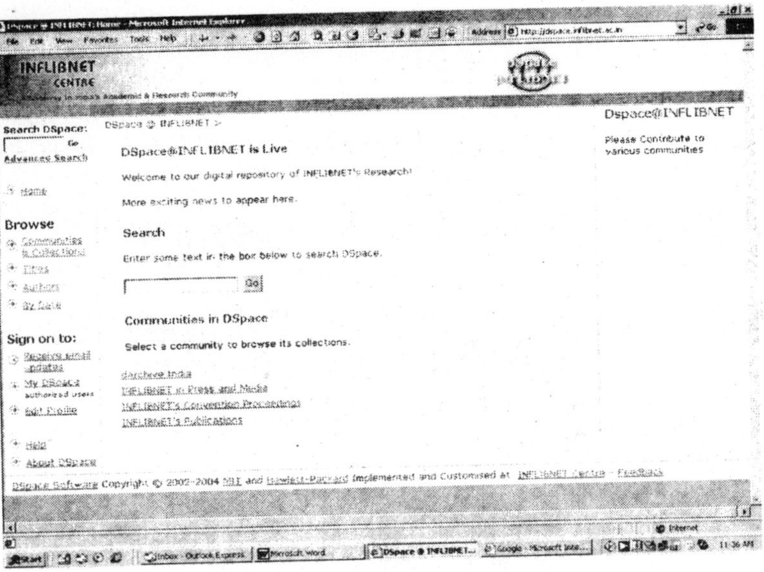

Fig. 1: Snapshot of Dspace@INFLIBNET

2.1 Communities in Dspace@INFLIBNET

Each DSpace site is divided into *communities*; these typically correspond to a department or laboratory or research center of an organisation, which can be organized into a hierarchy. "Communities" of DSpace contain *collections*, which are groupings of related content. At INFLIBNET we have extended this definition and categorized communities according to types of collections or area of interest. These are further divided into Sub- communities/Collections collections. The following table will provide you the details.

Comunities	Description
INFLIBNET's Convention Proceedings	INFLIBNET Centre has been organizing two conventions called CALIBER and PLANNER every year in different parts of the country in collaboration with different universities. These Conventions

	provide a unique forum to the library professionals, information providers and users involved in automation and networking of libraries to come together and interact on the subjects of mutual interest. The convention proceedings published in print form is digitized and archived under this community, under each collection separately named as different conventions.
INFLIBNET in Press and Media	Coverage of INFLIBNET activities appeared in different media is being collected and archived here
INFLIBNET 's Publications	INFLIBNET has been bringing out the various publications on regular basis, like Newsletter, various course materials etc. Lecture notes, presentations etc made by INFLIBNET staff will also be available here.
dArchive-India(Digital Academic and Research Content Hosted By INFLIBNET. for Value Education- India)Promotion of Indian content creation and archiving of Indian scholarly out put are the basic objectives of this initiative. Any faculty member or researcher in India can made submissions under the ten sub-communities created according to Main Classes at Dewey Decimal Classification (DDC) Scheme.	Sub-communities are created according to Dewey Decimal Classification (DDC) Scheme as follows; 000:Computer Science, Information and General Works 100:Philosophy & psychology 200:Religion 300:Social Sciences 400:Language 500:Science 600:Technology 700:Arts & Recreation 800:Literature 900:History & Geography

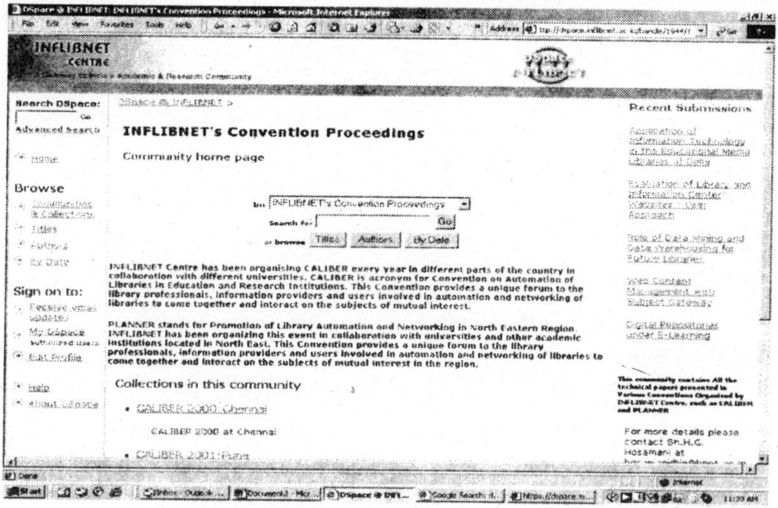

Fig. 2. Screenshot of INFLIBNET Convention Proceedings Community

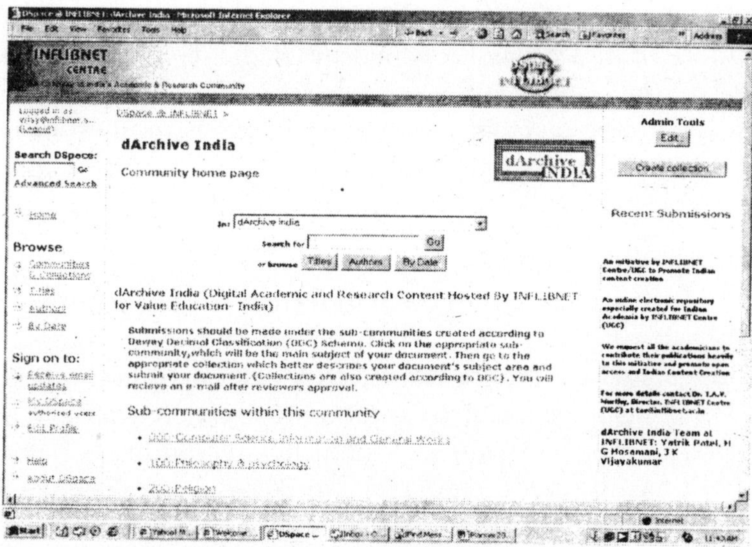

Fig. 3. Screenshot of dArchive-India Community

3. Creation of Metadata

DSpace holds three types of metadata about archived content, and during creation of *Communities* we can define the default metadata, who will evaluate the metadata etc.

3.1 Descriptive Metadata

Each *Item* has one qualified Dublin Core metadata record. The set of elements and qualifiers used by MIT Libraries is the default configuration included in the DSpace source code. These are loosely based on the Library Application Profile set of elements and qualifiers, though there are some differences. Other descriptive metadata about items may be held in serialized bit-streams. *Communities* and *collections* have some simple descriptive metadata (a name, and some descriptive prose), held in the DBMS.

3.2 Administrative Metadata

This includes preservation metadata, provenance and authorization policy data. Most of this is held within DSpace's relation DBMS schema. Provenance metadata (prose) is stored in Dublin Core records. Additionally, some other administrative metadata (for example, bitstream byte sizes and MIME types) is replicated in Dublin Core records so that it is easily accessible outside of DSpace.

3.3 Structural Metadata

This includes information about how to present an item, or bit-streams within an item, to an end-user, and the relationships between constituent parts of the item. In addition to some basic technical metadata, bit-streams also have a 'sequence ID' that uniquely identifies it within an item. Additional structural metadata can be stored in serialized bit-streams, but DSpace does not currently understand this natively.

4. Search and Browse in DSpace

DSpace allows end-users to discover content in a

number of ways, including:

* Via external reference, such as a Handle
* Searching for one or more keywords
* Browsing though title, date and author indices

Search is an essential component of discovery in DSpace. Users' expectations from a search engine are quite high, so a goal for DSpace is to supply as many search features as possible. DSpace's indexing and search module has a very simple API which allows for indexing new content, regenerating the index, and performing searches on the entire corpus, a community, or collection. Behind the API is the Java freeware search engine. Fielded searching, stop word removal, stemming, and the ability to incrementally add new indexed content without regenerating the entire index are also available.

Another important mechanism for discovery in DSpace is the browse. This is the process whereby the user views a particular index, such as the title index, and navigates around it in search of interesting items. The browse subsystem provides a simple API for achieving this by allowing a caller to specify an index, and a subsection of that index. The browse subsystem then discloses the portion of the index of interest. Indices that may be browsed are item title, item issue date and authors. Additionally, the browse can be limited to items within a particular collection or community.

5. DSpace@INFLIBNET is OAI-PMH Compliant

The Open Archives Initiative develops and promotes interoperability standards that aim to facilitate the efficient dissemination of content. The Open Archives Initiative Protocol for Metadata Harvesting (OAI-PMH) provides an application-independent interoperability framework based on *metadata harvesting*. DSpace@INFLIBNET server acts as a *repository,* which is network accessible and can process the OAI-PMH requests as described by OAI-PMH. The *Items* submitted in this *repository* will have a *unique identifier*, which unambiguously identifies an *item* within a *repository*, i.e., *CNRI Handles*. Thus based on request, a record will be represented, which is the metadata expressed in a single format in an XML-encoded byte stream. Here we are providing an example for one metadata record generated for an *item*, which is having CNRI handle as 1944/429;


```
xml version="1.0" encoding="UTF-8" ?>
- <OAI-PMH xmlns="http://www.openarchives.org/
  OAI/2.0/" xmlns:xsi="http://www.w3.org/2001/
  XMLSchema-instance" xsi:schemaLocation="http://
  www.openarchives.org/OAI/2.0/ http://
  www.openarchives.org/OAI/2.0/OAI-PMH.xsd">
<responseDate>2005-04-06T07:25:46Z</responseDate>
<request identifier="hdl:1944/429" metadataPrefix="
  oai_dc" verb=" GetRecord">http://dspace.inflibnet.
  ac.in/dspace-oai/request</request>
<GetRecord>
<record>
<header>
<identifier>hdl:1944/429</identifier>
<datestamp>2005-04-05T20:41:17Z</datestamp>
<setSpec>hdl_1944_414</setSpec>
</header>
<metadata>
<oai_dc:dc xmlns:oai_dc="http://www.openarchives.org
  /OAI/2.0/oai_dc/" xmlns:dc="http://purl.org/dc/
  elements/1.1/" xmlns:xsi="http://www.w3.org/2001
  /XMLSchema-instance" xsi:schemaLocation="http:/
  /www.openarchives.org/OAI/2.0/oai_dc/ http://
  www.openarchives.org/OAI/2.0/oai_dc.xsd">
<dc:creator>Vijayakumar, J K</dc:creator>
```

<dc:creator>Murthy, T A V</dc:creator>

<dc:creator>Khan, M T M</dc:creator>

<dc:date>2005-01-10T12:06:27Z</dc:date>

<dc:date>2005-01-10T12:06:27Z</dc:date>

<dc:date>2004-11</dc:date>

<dc:identifier>81-900825-8-2</dc:identifier>

<dc:identifier>http://hdl.handle.net/1944/429</dc:identifier>

<dc:description>Digital libraries of electronic theses and dissertations (ETDs) offer an alternative to this waste of valuable academic scholarship and offer researchers and University Libraries in India opportunities to explore the possibilities electronic publishing trend in academic sector. The emergence of UGC Infonet, the aspiring and dream project of University Grants Commission, which also aims at Content Creation by Indian Academic Sector, will definitely boost this idea The idea of E-Theses and Dissertations (ETD) is coming up in International scenario, which can be easily located, readily accessible and delivered over the web. While describing a framework for Indian Universities to go zbout with creating their own Institutional Repositories of Theses and Dissertations, the paper also high lighten the Formats, Software and copyright issues related to ETD archiving. It suggests DSpace as the software.</dc:description>

<dc:format>48532 bytes</dc:format>

<dc:format>application/pdf</dc:format>

<dc:language>en</dc:language>

<dc:publisher>INFLIBNET Center</dc:publisher>

<dc:subject>Digitization</dc:subject>

<dc:subject>Electronic Theses</dc:subject>

<dc:subject>ETD</dc:subject>

<dc:subject>INFLIBNET</dc:subject>
<dc:title>Electronic Theses and Dissertations for Indian Universities : A Framework</dc:title>
<dc:type>Article</dc:type>
</oai_dc:dc>
</metadata>
</record>
</GetRecord>
</OAI-PMH>

6. Conclusion

We in India always will come out with long lists of problems and issues, instead of considering several available strategies to comply with the latest technological developments and availability of free solutions for a better and effective implementation of ICT. We have to develop and support new models of scholarly publishing that cut the costs of distributing and retrieving information. If academic Institutions continue to operate as we do now, our library collections will grow, but their scope and depth will diminish day by day. INFLIBNET believes that it is our responsibility to strengthen the change for a realistic outlook in Indian scholarship Awareness building in Open Archives and Institutional Repositories in Indian academic Institutions is the main focus of INFLIBNET. There are several workshops on DSpace arranged across the country with financial support from INFLIBNET, which is going to repeat in more places for the benefit of Indian academic and librarian community.

7. References

1. MacKenzie Smith and others (2003). DSpace: An Open Source Dynamic Digital Repository, D-Lib Magazine, 9(1), Available at http://www.dlib.org/dlib/january03/smith/01smith.html
2. http://dspace.inflibnet.ac.in
3. http://www.dlib.org

4. http://dspace.library.cornell.edu
5. http://dspace.mit.edu
6. http://www.dspace.org
7. http://www.openarchives.org/OAI/openarchivesprotocol.html

41
Metadata: Automatic Generation and Extraction

Noufal P.P
Indian Institute of Technology Kanpur
(noufal@iitk.ac.in)

ABSTRACT

Today, library technical services departments have a new imperative: to carry forward their role to organize the world's information and apply it in the digital age. At the heart of the necessary transition is envisioning the future of technical services as a future with millions and millions of digital objects and e-resources in it. It is therefore a future with metadata in it. The world of information technology is awash in talk of metadata. Metadata can be thought of as a lubricant for information flow- easing the difficulty of discovery and organization of resources. It can also serve as a nozzle — directing, channeling, and focusing information flow to make it more manageable and effective. Producing metadata has long been the task of professionals such as librarians and indexers. Nowadays metadata is also being produced by non-specialists (e.g., ordinary users), publishers, commercial agents, and even software systems. Creating metadata is often labour-intensive. Though automated procedures and new types of tools for creating and managing metadata are evolving and will continue to become more sophisticated. Some word processors, editors, and format filters generate embedded metadata tags when a document is first created. Other tools automatically extract metadata values from the documents themselves. This paper explores the features of Dublin core metadata and tools for automatic metadata extraction from electronic resources.

Metadata defined

First, let us define metadata. The common definition of metadata is "data about data." The notion of metadata is relative. It is only really meaningful in a context that makes clear what the data itself is. Metadata describes the attributes of an information-bearing object (IBO) - document, data set, database, image, artifact, collection, etc.; metadata acts as a surrogate representation of the IBO. A metadata record can include representations of the content, context, structure, quality, provenance, condition, and other characteristics of an IBO for the purposes of representing the IBO to a potential user - for discovery, evaluation for fitness for use, access, transfer, and citation. According to W3C, metadata is data that provides information about, or documentation of, other data managed within an application or environment. Metadata is also machine understandable information for the web. In the digital environment, the surrogate role of metadata is key because many resources are not easily browsable and others do not carry clear data about themselves. The rise of interest in metadata is part of the effort to organize messy world of digital resources and to provide access and services for users at the right time. It is also a way to exchange data between disparate stores of resources and to allow searching across digital warehouses.

Metadata: - Types

All of these perspectives on metadata become important in the development of Digital Information System. But they lead to a very broad conception of metadata. Different kinds of metadata are designed for different purposes: - *Administrative metadata* - this is to use to manage and administer information resources, as acquisition information, documentation of legal access information etc. *Descriptive metadata* - this is to describe or identify information resources as cataloguing records, annotation by users, finding aids and specialized index etc. *Preservation metadata* –This is related to the preservation management of information resources as documentation of physical condition of resources, documentation of actions taken to preserve physical and digital versions of resources, e.g., data refreshing and migration. *Technical metadata* - Metadata related to how a system functions or behave, hardware and software documentation, Digitization information, authentication and security data, e.g., encryption keys, passwords.

Metadata – Why?

Metadata serves many important purposes like data description, data browsing and data transfer. It provides additional context that makes a document or record more meaningful, accessible, and useful. Discussions of metadata in the library community have largely centered on issues of resource description and discovery. There is, however, a growing awareness that metadata has an important role in digital resource management, including preservation. Regardless of whether emulation-based or migration-based preservation strategies are adopted, the long-term preservation of digital information will involve the creation and maintenance of metadata. Properly used metadata can identify the name of the resource, the creator, who reformatted it, and other descriptive information. We can discuss the various roles of metadata in digital information system as follows: -

Increased accessibility: Effectiveness of searching can be significantly enhanced through the existence of rich and consistent metadata. Metadata can also makes possible to search across multiple collections or to create virtual collections from materials that are distributed across several repositories, but only if the descriptive metadata are the same or can be mapped across each site. Digital information systems and emerging metadata standards developed by different professional communities such as Encoded Archival Description (EAD), Text Encoding Initiative (TEI), and the Dublin Core are making it easier for users to negotiate between descriptive surrogates of information objects and digital versions of the objects themselves, and to search at both the item and collection level within and across information systems.

Interoperability: Describing a resource with metadata allows it to be understood by both humans and machines. Interoperability is the ability of multiple systems with different hardware and software platforms, data structures, and interfaces to exchange data accurately. Using defined metadata schemes, shared transfer protocols, and crosswalks between schemes, resources across the network can be searched more seamlessly. Two approaches to interoperability are cross-system search and metadata harvesting. The Z39.50 protocol is commonly used for cross-system search. Z39.50 implementers do not share metadata but map their own search capabilities to a common set of search attributes. A contrasting approach taken by the Open Archives Initiative is for all data providers to translate their native metadata to a common core set of elements and expose this for harvesting. A search service provider then gathers the metadata into a consistent central index to allow cross-repository searching regardless of the metadata formats used by participating repositories.

Multi-versioning : Objects enter a digital information system by being created digitally or by being converted into digital format. Multiple versions of the same object may be created for preservation, research, dissemination, or even product development purposes. The creator may include some administrative and descriptive metadata for this purpose.

Legal issues: Metadata allows repositories to track the many layers of rights and reproduction information that exist for information objects and their multiple versions. Metadata also documents other legal or donor requirements that have been imposed on objects - for example, privacy concerns or proprietary interests.

Preservation: If digital information objects that are currently being created are to have a chance of surviving migrations through successive generations of computer hardware and software, or removal to entirely new delivery systems. They will need to have metadata that enables them to exist independently of the system that is currently being used to store and retrieve them. Technical, descriptive, and preservation metadata help to know how a digital information object was created and maintained, how it behaves, and how it relates to other information objects. It should be noted that for the information objects to remain accessible and intelligible over time, it would also be essential to preserve and migrate the metadata also.

System improvement and economics: Metadata is also helpful to evaluate and refine systems in order to make them more effective and efficient from a technical and economic standpoint. The data can also be used in planning for new systems.

Metadata Characteristics and standards

Some of the common characteristics of all metadata include semantics, syntax and structures. Semantics refer to type and content of metadata elements, syntax refer to the way in which content is structured according to a specifies grammar – metadata standard may range from simple syntax like Dublin core metadata element set to a complex coding systems such as mark up languages like SGML. While structures refer to the over all architecture that contain metadata content and syntax. Metadata may be embedded in the digital object and extracted as needed or they may reside in separately indexed databses.the data can be contained in a variety of architectural structures including Z39.50

compliant library catalogues, proprietary databases or Resource Description Frame work (RDF) standard [7].

Interoperability and extensibility are desirable characteristics of metadata standard systems. Interoperability refers to the ability to transfer metadata among different schemes and information systems. A core element set that is common to all will facilitate the exchange and use of metadata at a general level and description and retrieval. Extensibility allows expansion of the core element set to provide more precise description and retrieval. Element qualifiers are used to narrow the meaning of an element. Metadata schema or schemas should be applied in order to best meet the needs of the information creator, repository and users; At the time of planning of DL system, we should think carefully about which metadata attributes and format is going to use. If you do not, you may find yourself constrained by the absence of useful metadata, or have to add a new metadata field or convert an existing field to a different format when you already have several thousand resources in your database. Moreover, decisions about metadata will in turn affect the design of your interface especially the parts of it used for cataloguing and/or submitting new resources for consideration. Before selecting metadata standards we have to keep the following points in our mind.

* Deciding which aspects of metadata are essential for what they wish to achieve, and how granular they need each type of metadata to be - in other words, how much is enough and how much is too much. There will likely always be important tradeoffs between the costs of developing and managing metadata to meet current needs, and creating sufficient metadata that can be capitalized upon for future, often unanticipated uses;
* Ensuring that the metadata schemas being applied are the most current versions

Structuring Metadata

Metadata schemes (also called schema) are sets of metadata elements designed for a specific purpose, such as describing a particular type of information resource. The definition or meaning of of the elements themselves is known as the semantics of the scheme. The values given to metadata elements are the content. Metadata schemes generally specify names of elements and their semantics. Optionally, they may specify content rules for how content must be formulated (for example, how to identify the main title), representation rules for content (for example, capitalization rules), and allowable content values (for example, terms must be used from a specified controlled vocabulary). There may also be syntax rules for how the elements and their content should be encoded. A metadata scheme with no prescribed syntax rules is called syntax independent. Metadata can be encoded in any definable syntax. Many current metadata schemes use SGML (Standard Generalized Mark-up Language) or XML (Extensible Mark-up Language). XML, developed by the World Wide Web Consortium (W3C), is an extended form of HTML that allows for locally defined tag sets and the easy exchange of structured information. SGML is a superset of both HTML and XML and allows for the richest mark-up of a document. Useful XML tools are becoming widely available. XML plays an increasingly crucial role in the exchange of a variety of data on the Web.

Frameworks of Metadata

There are several metadata frame works. Most of web authors insert metadata through the use of "META"tags in HTML. A META tag can have a name and a content attribute with the value for the content determined by web authors. In the example below, the META tags provide a general description for this article.

<META name= "description" content= "This article describes about automatic metadata extraction">

<META name = "keywords" content = "Digital Libraries, Metadata, Metadata extraction, Dublin Core" >

Unlike a cataloguer, web authors who insert META tags into their documents often will not be conversant with controlled subject schemes. For this reason, there are tremendous interests in metadata formats that do not require special skills to create or maintain them. There are a number of metadata frameworks like Dublin Core, Warwick, EAD, IMS MODS, METS and MPEG -7

Dublin Core

Among the various metadata standards, it seems that Dublin Core Metadata Initiative (DC for short) has gained the special importance among the resource description communities. Within the diverse resource discovery activities of the mid 90s, ranging from unstructured indexing of full-text resources by search engines to richly structured data like MARC and TEI records, DC arose as a means to mediate these extremes [9]. DC developed in the *March 1995 Metadata Workshop* sponsored by the Online Computer Library Center (OCLC) and the National Center for Supercomputing Applications (NCSA), to advance the state of the art in the development of metadata records for networked information resources. One of the main goals of the workshop was to reach a consensus on a simple and core set of metadata elements to describe electronic resources. The result of the workshop was a set of 13-metadata elements, which was called Dublin Core Metadata Element Set (DCMES) for describing what called Document-Like Objects. By the third workshop the elements set was developed to 15 elements.

The Dublin Core Metadata Element Set includes: Title, Creator, Subject, Description, Publisher, Contributor, Date, Type, Format, Identifier, Source, Language, Relation, Coverage, and Rights (Dublin Core, 1999).

The characteristics of Dublin Core that distinguish it as

prominent candidate for description of electronic resources fall into several categories: simplicity, semantic interoperability, international consensus, and flexibility (Weibel, 1997). The Dublin Core is intended to be a maximum simplicity and flexibility. Simplicity of Dublin Core is its main feature and originates from this fact that the elements of Dublin Core designed to be used by the creators of the resources, who are not trained catalogers or have no knowledge of cataloging, to describe the resources. Since Dublin Core provides internationally agreed upon elements that are commonly understood among various communities and fields, it promotes some level of semantic interoperability. The interoperability of Dublin Core enables resource description records created using it to be implemented across disciplines and in different fields. On the other hand, Dublin Core can be qualified and extended to meet the requirements of a wide variety of communities. Though it concentrates on describing intrinsic properties of the information object, the extension mechanism will allow the inclusion of extrinsic data for objects that cannot be adequately described by the small and simple set of Dublin Core elements. It is possible to encode many controlled vocabularies and description standards such as LCSH, MeSH (Medical Subject Headings), DDC, and LC in Dublin Core elements through Dublin Core qualifiers (Dublin Core, 2000).

Among the current metadata standards, Dublin Core has the potential of being adapted as an international standard for resource description and discovery on the web and as a *lingua franca* for metadata, partly because of its simplicity. Its simplicity promotes general applicability but also suggests an important problem that is lack of consistency and trust. Regarding the importance of and the need to trust and provenance of data and metadata in the web (Lynch, 2001),

Why Dublin Core?

Dublin Core has received widespread acceptance amongst the resource discovery community and has become the defacto Internet metadata standard [3].

The Dublin Core metadata schema offers the following advantages:

* Its usability and its flexibility
* The semantics of these elements is designed to be clear enough to be understood by a wide range of customers, without the need for training
* The elements of Dublin Core are easily identifiable by having the work in hand, such as intellectual content and physical format
* It is not intended to supplant other resource descriptions, but rather to complement them. It is intended to describe the essential features of electronic documents that support resource discovery. Other important metadata such as accounting and archival data, were deliberately excluded to keep the schema as simple and useable as possible.
* It is mostly syntax independent, to support its use in the widest range of applications
* All elements are optional, but allows each site to define which elements are mandatory and which are optional
* All elements are repeatable
* The elements may be modified in limited and well-defined ways through the use of specific qualifiers, such as the name of the thesaurus used in the subject element
* It can be extended to meet the demands of more specialized communities. From the very beginning, the Dublin Core creators recognized that some resources could not be adequately described by a small set of elements. The Dublin Core creators came up with two

solutions. Firstly, by allowing the addition of elements for site-specific purposes or specialized fields. Secondly, by designing the Dublin Core schema so that it could be mapped into more complex and tightly controlled systems, such as MARC.

Below is an example for Dublin Core metadata elements created for this article.

<HTML>

<HEAD>

<TITLE>Automatic Metadata Extraction </TITLE>

<META NAME="DC.Title" CONTENT=" Automatic Metadata Extraction">

<METANAME="DC.Creator" CONTENT="Noufal">

<META NAME="DC.Type" CONTENT="text">

<META NAME="DC.Date" CONTENT="2005">

<META NAME="DC.Format" CONTENT="text/html">

</HEAD>

Automatic Metadata Creation and Extraction

Nowadays automatic metadata extraction is a hot research topic. Over the past several decades computer tecquniqes for text analysis have been developed that can achieve impressive result in constrained domains Structured markup languages such as XML help make as key aspects of documents accessible to computers and people alike. They encode certain kind of information in such a way that it can be extracted by parsing the document structure. Basic metadata about a document – its title, author, publisher, date of publication, keywords and abstract- is often present in the first page of publication for all to see. Moreover it is frequently presented in fairly uniform way. Automatic metadata extraction depends too much on the format and style of documents.

Metadata generation is the act of creating or producing metadata. Generating good quality metadata in an efficient manner is essential for organizing and making accessible the growing number of rich resources available on the Web. The success of digital libraries is mainly depends on interoperability. Metadata creation and management have become a very complex mix of manual and automatic processes and layers created by many different functions and individuals at different points in the life of an information object. This metadata can be contained within the same envelope as the information object - for example, in the form of header information for an image file, e.g. Dublin Core, or through some form of bundling, for example, with the Universal Preservation Format (UPF). [1] Metadata can also be attached to the information object through bi-directional pointers or hyperlinks, while the relationships between metadata and information objects, and can be documented by registering them with a metadata registry. As systems designers increasingly respond to the need to incorporate and manage metadata in information systems and to address how to move them forward through time, many additional mechanisms for associating metadata with information objects are likely to become available. Metadata registries and schema record keeping systems are also more likely to develop as it becomes increasingly necessary to document schema evolution and to alert implementers to version changes [4].

Major challenges for Digital Library projects and inititatives are the growing number of resources requiring metadata. Library cataloguers and indexers generate metadata are prohibitive due to the limited availability of both qualified persons and financial recourses. Author-generated metadata projects appear to be less popular in the organizational setting. The greatest problem of the author-generated metadata is the inability to relay on its accuracy. The rationale given for this predicament is that authors lack the metadata professional's expert skills, and they will therefore produce insufficient and poor quality metadata (Weinheimer 2000). In this context, automatic metadata extraction is becoming more popular and acceptable among Digital library communities. According to Anderson & Perez-Carballo, automatic metadata extraction is more efficient, less costly and more conversant than human oriented process. Researches indicate that automatic metadata generation can produce acceptable results for subject metadata (Liddy. Et al. 2001)[8]. Researchers have concluded that the most effective mean of metadata creation is to integrate to the human and automation methods (Schwartz, 2000).

Metadata may be generated or updated at various times in the life cycle of a resource, so workflows must be designed accordingly. Declarative rules or prescriptions can be used to explicitly describe how, when, and by whom a metadata element will be produced or updated. Research on metadata creation and management will enable systems to use document analysis to automate metadata capture, automatically extract subject classifications, trigger the update of metadata when a resource is modified, support the capture of temporal metadata, certify metadata at the time of publication, and remove metadata when a resource is obsolete. Such tools must become integrated into a variety of environments from Web site management utilities to databases, data warehouses, and legacy resources. If used on a wide scale, they could significantly improve the quality and cost-effectiveness of metadata in the networked environment. There are some commercial and open source tools are available for metadata creation and extraction.

Tools for metadata generation

This paper mainly concentrates on Dublin core metadata generation and extraction. Because Dublin core is widely accepted and popular among DL communities. It gives great flexibility, simplicity and ensures interoperability with others schemes. There are two types of tools that facilitate the creation of Dublin Core metadata.- Editors and generators

Templates are basic *crib* sheets that sketch a framework or provide an outline of schema elements without linking to supporting documentation. Templates have been predominant in metadata generation, probably because they are simple to produce and maintain. These tools guide metadata creation through the provision of a form without the bells and whistles. The MARC bibliographic form supporting cataloging in many second-generation online catalogs has functioned in much the same way, without any sort of automatic linking to authority files and content guidelines. This facility is fortunately changing as many catalogs become Web-based and hyperlink to cataloging documentation, thus functioning more like an *editor.*

Editors are similar to templates in that they require human input. They are more sophisticated in that they provide direct access to standards and documentation underlying metadata creation. These tools often assist with syntactical aspects of metadata creation via automatic means. One of most popular Dublin Core editors is the Nordic Dublin Core Metadata Template (www.lub.lu.se/cgi-bin/nmdc.pl). This editor supports the generation of metadata records with HTML META tags for embedding in the header of a Web resource. The Nordic Template has been adapted to many different Dublin Core projects. A partial list of them is at: http://dublincore.org/tools/. Another example is the Reggie Metadata Editor (http://metadata.net/dstc/), which allows for metadata to be generated within RDF. Editors can also include off-the-shelf software like Metabrowser (http://metabrowser.spirit.net.au/), which hyperlinks to documentation supporting metadata generation and automatically provides the correct syntactical encoding. People work with a wide variety of Web forms when joining an organization, posting information on an online communitv bulletin board or purchasing a product over the Internet. All of these forms function as metadata editors documenting transactions, activities, events and other types of objects beyond the traditional information resource.

Generators –This support automatic metadata production. Generators first require the submission of a uniform resource locator (URL), a persistent uniform resource identifier (PURL) or another Web address in order to *locate the object*. An algorithm is then used to comb an object's content, including its source code, and automatically assign metadata. There are some interesting tools are available. some of them are DC-dot,. Describthis and Klarity

DC-dot

DC-dot (http://www.ukoln.ac.uk/metadata/dcdot/) is a generator developed by UKOLN (UK Office for Library and Information Networking) based at the University of Bath. DC.dot is open source and can be redistributed or modified under the terms of the GNU General Public License as published by the Free Software Foundation. DC-dot produces Dublin Core metadata, and can format output-according to number of different metadata schemas (e.g., USMARC, SOIF, IAFA/ROADS, TEI headers, GILS, RDF, and IMS). Metadata creation with DC-dot is initiated by submitting a URL. DC.dot, copies resource "identifier" metadata from the Web browser's "address prompt," and harvests "title," "keywords," "description," and "type" metadata from resource META tags. If source code metadata is absent (meaning META tag are absent), DC-dot will automatically generate "keywords" by analyzing anchors (hyperlinked concepts) and presentation encoding, such as bolding and font size, but will not produce "description" metadata. DC.dot also automatically generates "type," "format" and "date" metadata, and can read source code programming that automatically tracks date. For example, "lastmodified" might be coded as: "Last Modified"

+ lm_day+' '+monthName[lm_month-1]+' "+lm_year" for last updated date. This example illustrates DC.dot's ability to partially conform with the recommended Dublin Core Qualifiers.

Describethis

DescribeThis (http://www.describethis.com), a service designed for the automatic extraction of metadata from online resources. The site offers an easy to use interface where you can indicate the resource to analyze and how to download the results as XML, XHTML or RDF files. In the current version, the site's engine is able to find the resources to process using keywords, full URLs or more complex queries with operators, like "ISBN", used to collect the bibliographic data for published documents (see http://www.describethis.com/help/search.html). In the first case it works as a meta search engine using other search engines to locate the best sites where the resource can be found. The results returned back contains all the recognized and generated Dublin Core elements for the requested resource and can be downloaded as RDF, XML or XHTML collections.

Describethis's main fields of applications are to support and extend the application and development of the Dublin Core format as one of most appropriate metadata standards to describe or catalog resources, digitals or not, to use the site as a tool to support the cataloguing of online resources, oriented to information specialists and Internet users in general. And To deliver services of automatic metadata management, designed for managers of bibliographic and content databases and to create an efficient way for administrators and website authors to dynamically provide metadata information about their sites to page crawlers, bots, spiders, agents, worms and other automatic indexing and site classification systems, with the aim of contributing to the improvement of the whole Internet content organization.

In the describethis.com front page you can find several samples to illustrate the normal operation of the service. In this version, DCS can automatically analyze and to generate metadata registers for the following formats:

- HTML and XHTML Documents
- Dublin Core/RDF
- Dublin Core/XML
- Dublin Core/HTML (META tags)
- GIF, JPG (EXIF) and other image formats
- RSS
- bibTex

Support for other well-known formats like PDF, MARC, stream formats (MP3,MPEG, etc), OAI directories, FOAF networks and others will be added in the near future

Klarity

Klarity is a commercial service that was produced by the Australian company tSA, now named Intology (Intelligent Technology) (http://www.intology.com.au/). The Klarity archive is found at: http://archive.klarity.com.au/. Dublin Core metadata is automatically generated when an identifier (e.g., URL) is submitted, and the metadata is converted into HTML META tags or eXtensible Markup Language (XML) within the Resource Description Framework (RDF) (Brickley and Guha, 2004). Klarity automatically generates metadata for the following five elements: Identifier, title, concepts, keywords, and description. "Identifier" metadata is copied from the Web browser's "address prompt," "title" metadata is harvested from the resource source code, and "keywords" and "description" metadata are extracted from resource text. Klarity's "concepts" element is a unifying concept representing keywords and functions more like a classificatory node. An algorithm based on term frequencies is matched against an underlying vocabulary to create this element.

Klarity's editor feature, where a human can manually enter additional metadata by answering a series of questions

Conclusion

There is an interesting study of features of DC dot and Klarity by Prof. Greenberg. He concluded that generators have the potential to create useful metadata. Major challenges for Digital Library projects and initiatives are the growing number of resources requiring metadata. Library cataloguers and indexers generated metadata are prohibitive due to the limited availability of both qualified persons and financial recourses. Author-generated metadata projects appear to be less popular in the organizational setting. The rationale given for this predicament is that authors lack the metadata professional's expert skills, and they will therefore produce insufficient and poor quality metadata. In this context, automatic metadata generation and extraction is the right option. It is more efficient and less costly than practicing involving human workforce. However the best metadata generation process is to integrate human and automatic process.

Acknowledgements

I would like to place on record my sincere gratitude to Shr. R.Mishra, Librarian, Indian Institute of Technology Kanpur for the encouragement and support received from him throughout.

References

1. Conway, Paul. Preservation in the Digital World. Washington, DC: Commission on preservation and access, 1996
2. Day, M. Metadata in nutshell. Information Europe 2001; 6(2) (Summer): 11
3. Dublin Core Metadata Element Set, Version 1.1: Reference description. (2005): http://dublincore.org/documents/2005/01/10/dcmi-terms/
4. Greenberg, J., Crystal, A., Robertson, D., & Leadem, E. (2003a)

Iterative Design of Metadata Creation Tools for Resource Authors. In Sutton, S., Greenberg, J., and Tennis, J. (Eds.). 2003 Dublin Core Conference: Supporting Communities of Discourse and Practice Metadata Research & Applications. September 28 - October 2, 2003, Seattle, Washington. New York: ERIC Clearinghouse on Information and Technology: http://www.siderean.com/dc2003/202_Paper82-color-NEW.pdf.

5. Greenberg, J. (2003). Metadata and the World Wide Web. In Encyclopedia of Library and Information Science, 2nd ed. vol. 3 (New York: Marcel Dekker, 2003): 1876-88

6. Hlava, M. (2002). Automatic indexing: A matter of degree. Bulletin of ASIS&T, 29(1):

7. Ian H, Witten , David Bainbridge, 2003, How to build a digital library, Morgan

8. Liddy, E. D., Sutton, S. A., Paik, W. Allen, E., Harwell, S. Monsour, M., Turner, A, & Liddy J. (2001). Breaking the metadata generation bottleneck: preliminary findings. JCDL 2001: 464.

9. Nangao, Katashi, 2003, Digital content annotation and transcoding, Artech house

10. http://www.intology.com.au

11. http://dublincore.org

12. http://www.describethis.com),

13. http://www.ukoln.ac.uk/metadata/dcdot/

42
Document Genre and Digital Libraries

Swati Bhattacharyya
Librarian, Indian Institute of Management Calcutta
(swati@iimcal.ac.in)

1. Document Genre – what it is

The lexical meaning of the term "Genre" is category, class, group etc. In the broad sense, the term signifies result of classification of a group of materials based on some characteristics. It can also be the result of subdividing a whole, based on some characteristics. Such typology / classification is associated with many domains of human knowledge. Consciously or unconsciously, human minds, can associate such typology with objects that they come across in their everyday life.

Document genre implies a result of classification of documents into various kinds by employing some characteristics. Classification is an act with which librarians are very much familiar over more than a century. However, predominantly, librarian's activity in classification implies grouping documents based on subject or topics, that are dealt with in the textual matter of the documents.

The concept of genre and practice of differentiating between various kinds of texts, based on some characteristics, can be traced back to the time of Aristotle, Thus identifying a piece of text with a specific genre has been a long practice in human civilization. This concept has ample usage in literature and art. Letter, memoir etc are example of document genres in language-based text. Fiction, essay, biography, bibliography are some of the established document genres. In fact, existing classification codes used by librarians accommodate several such genres.

Genre concept has also been extended to non-verbal mode of communication such as art, music etc. In the domain of art, painting, sculpture are some of the known genres. One can identifies the concept of genres in music too. This paper primarily focuses on concept of genres in language based texts.

Our genre literacy, with respect to language based texts, identifies three characteristics which can be applied to create or establish document genres. One of those characteristics is the content, another is the purpose of communication and the other is the format of presentation. Fiction differs from non-fiction in contents. Braille documents meant for communicating to a special group is another genre. Here the purpose is to communicate to a distinct group. Similarly, course list of a university is a type of document and its purpose is to intimate students on the syllabus. Format of presentation of such course lists may vary from one university to another but all such documents belong to one genre. The genres of letter, note etc. are created by form as characteristics. There are document instances, which have more than one of these characteristics and can be mapped with more than one genre.

How an individual associates an instance of a document to a certain genre is grounded in his/her social and cultural background and the discourse community to which he/she belongs to. One particular document instance may be placed in different genres, by members of different discourse communities. This opens up a scope for exploring whether or not there can be fixity in document genres. If there is no fixity, then how to associate one instance of text, in a collection with a specific genre and communicate the same to all users.

This obviously leads to a direction which ensues

developing a scheme for organization of document genres. An exhaustive list of all document genres is yet to be developed for several reasons. Lack of existence of fixity may be a hindrance. This entails establishment of a mapping scheme between two discourse communities who are placing same document to different genres. Though concept of genre is very old, newer genres, particularly in the current digital age, are emerging. That the genres can be unstable, changeable and divisible, make the problem for developing a classification scheme still complicated. As the genre identification involves classification, it requires to meet the condition of mutual exclusivity and joint exhaustively. As stated in the previous paragraph, these two conditions may not be satisfied simultaneously when a document has features of more than one genre.

1. Document Genre and Information Retrieval from Digital Libraries

Information seeking by individual is highly dynamic and varying in nature. Different people may seek different aspects of information on a same topic. How a particular piece of information becomes relevant to a user depends on (1) his/her cognitive level and (2) the situation from where the information is sought. Existing information systems, supported by researches in the area of Information Science, provide access to a piece of information in various ways by defining several access paths. Subject index is one of the important access paths.

Tague-Sutcliffe, in her definition of information stressed that information in a record embedding text and/or picture, is relative to a user. It is a transaction between the user and the record and hence user's motive in consulting the record cannot be ignored. User may have a need for particular kind of information to solve a problem. She also stressed that effect of records on the cognitive structures of the reader may not be independent of the order in which the records are read.

This underscores the importance of evaluation of a document from more than one perspective, for relevance judgement.

A complete solution to such complexities of matching between the information need and information available in a system, still remains elusive. The main reason is that access paths, as used traditionally by information systems, together do not always help the users to judge the relevance of the document retrieved, to the situation of the user, without going through the text. Researchers are trying to understand what other cues from document records can help user to assess the relevance of a record without going through the document itself. In this context, it is believed that the format or purpose of communication of information presented in a document may be as important clue as the topic, if not more.

But use of document genre as metadata, in information retrieval entails the users to recognize the genre and a shared understanding of a genre between the author, indexer and the user. This may not be a problem for printed documents. Recognition of a specific document genre, in printed format, is triggered by the long familiarity of users with the structure of such documents. Thus form of a printed document is a powerful metaphorical construct in document recognition. But in digital collection, such cue is not directly discernible.

Along with the development of internet, digital library has now become a permanent feature of society, though the connotation of the term varies from one community to the other. In everyday life, web is looked upon as a digital collection of a variety of documents, such as website, personal homepage, documents etc. Each type of documents can meet a certain kind of need. For example, if some one wants to know how a good resume looks like, the best retrieval set should contain a sample resume uploaded by someone as example. But a search on Internet may retrieve hundreds of documents which may include as diverse a document like sales advertisement of books on this topic or even a link to another site. Thus the actual document may be hidden under the deluge of entire retrieved set.

In an academic environment, digital library may be the one containing full text of documents such as books, journals etc. For example, a digital collection related to Social science may contain journal articles, reports etc. It may not be unlikely that in such a digital collection documents of several genres are organized together.

As mentioned earlier, formats of presentation, in printed documents, signal the typology of the documents. Thus it is easier for the user to decide, looking at the format, whether the document will be useful or not. Someone looking for a bibliography will easily identify a textbook and discard the same, without even skimming through the pages. But in digital collection, documents of all possible genres remains merged in one sequence and it makes difficult for the user to differentiate one genre from the other.

On the other hand, in the digital environment, users' expectations regarding extracting information that suits her needs best, is continuously increasing. Granularity of information sought by users also vary highly. Some users may be interested to have a look at the tables, recording data, embedded in a text. In this case, table can be considered as one genre of information, embedded in another genre of information, i.e. body of the text. This leads to the possibility of creating sub-genre or loops within a genre of documents.

In sum, a relevant information, for a user's point of view, is a combination of content and presentation. Hence information retrieval should facilitate access to relevant information from all possible perspectives and document genre is one of such perspectives.

2. Research Areas in Document Genres

Efforts have been initiated to understand if document genre, in digital environment, will be a sufficient clue to the users about the relevance of the document. Several related issues such as effectiveness of using document genre in web searching, what genres are used and sought by the users on web, the possibility of automatic definition of document genre, possibility of including genre metadata in searching, are also being addressed. Whether document genre can be used to rank a retrieved set, is also worth consideration. This has lead to the following areas of researches as below:

(1) Identification of web document genres from users' perspective and how such need is articulated by the users;

(2) Considering the possibility that a document may belong to two different genres, how to create a multidimensional classification scheme of the genres;

(3) How to incorporate genre metadata into search mechanism, evaluation and use of documents ;

(4) Evaluation of the degree to which incorporation of genre metadata in information retrieval systems makes searches more effective;

(5) Identification and evaluation of various features of interfaces for visualizing and presenting genre metadata.

Studying document genres demands that the same is done in real situation. This implies that there should be enough provision to incorporate new genres which may emerge in course of time. Range of document genres, used by various discourse communities, must be examined for this purpose. As genres are socially constructed, existing schemes may not be sufficient to capture dynamic nature of genres. It is most important to identify what clues people do use to identify genres, particularly in the digital environment. A multidimensional or facetted classification scheme has been stressed upon to organize the entire range of genres as a particular document instance may have more than one genre characteristics. It is also necessary to understand how a specific social group use the document genre to effectively extract information in digital situation say web. This will help to identify ways for integrating genre metada with other metadata used to describe a document, through query construction, organize resultant sets etc. Besides, establishing interoperability between genres identified by various knowledge domains also needs attention.

3. Treatment of Genres in Librarian's Tools

To have detailed information on genres, existing information organization and retrieval tools can be helpful. Such tools will provide enumeration of existing document genres in various knowledge domains and a scheme to organize those genres. Such tools like classification schedule, subject heading lists are used by Librarians. These tools give a fair idea about the genres identified in those tools and the limitation of those organizations.

Most of the prominent tools have treated genres in a mixed way. Universal Decimal Classification has included document genres through several auxiliary subdivisions. In auxiliary table, under common auxiliary subdivisions, a very detailed list of language based text genres has been enumerated in the range of (01) to (09).

For example under the common auxiliary subdivisions (04)

Pamphlets. Brochures

Lectures

Personal letters

Business letters

Similarly, under the subdivision (07)

Documents for instruction, teaching, study, training

Curricula. Syllabus

Most prominent treatment of genre is found under

literature, i.e., literary forms, genres under the class 82 in the range 82-1/-9.

For example:

1-1	Poetry. Poems. Verse
1-2	Drama. Plays
1-3	Fiction. Prose narrative
1-4	Essays
1-5	Oratory....
1-6	Letters. Art of letter-writing
1-7	Prose satire....
1-8	Various other genres....

On the other hand, various genres of non-verbal communications such as sculpture, drawing, painting have been treated as subdivision of respective broader subject areas.

For example:

73	Plastic Arts. Sculpture...
74	Drawing. Design...
75	Painting
76	Graphic Arts.
77	Photography and Similar Process
782/785	Kinds of Music

Dewey Decimal Classification and Relative Index has also similar kind of treatment for various document genres, i.e. the concept is found under subdivisions of subjects as well as under several tables.

Overall, these tools have captured the traditional genres, from subject point of view and that is the reason why in some places genre has been treated as subdivision of subjects and as subdivision of tables in other places. Though it serves the purpose of classification of homogeneous collection, the same may not be true in digital environment. For example, according to any of these schedules, a book on painting and a painting will get same class number. But in a digital collection, further differentiation between these two kinds of records is required. Moreover, a classification schedule is not helpful to understand how different social groups or discourse communities identify document genres within their respective knowledge domain and what is the degree of similarities/dissimilarities between the genres identified by different groups. Additionally, classification schedules also do not provide any clue on how to bring the multifaceted features while organizing genres. Thus, there remains a scope to examine the possibility of expanding existing schedules or developing a new organization scheme for document genres.

4. Conclusion

Document genre is likely to play an important role in digital environment. Incorporation of developer's and/or the users' genre literacy, domain knowledge and information expectations in the development of database search and retrieval technique needs to be given a serious view. For this purpose, a detailed study in more than one knowledge domain, to assess and capture genre literacy of the respective domains will be a good beginning.

5. References

1. Beghtol, Clare (2000): Concept of genre and its characteristics. Bulletin of the American Society for Information Science and Technology, 27(2), 17-19
2. Crowston, Kevin and Kwasnik, Barbara H (2003): Can document-genre metadata improve information access to large digital collections? Library Trends, 52 (2) .
3. Dewey Decimal Classification and relative Index. 4v. Ed 22. Ohio, OCLC, 2003
4. Kwasnik, Barbara H. *et al.*(2000): Identifying document genre to improve web search effectiveness. Bulletin of the American Society for Information Science and Technology, 27(2), 23-26
5. Tague-Sutcliffe, Jean (1995): Measuring information: an information service perspective. Academic Press.

6. Toms, Elaine G (2000): Recognizing digital genre. Bulletin of the American Society for Information Science and Technology, 27(2),20-22

7. Universal Decimal Classification. 2v. British Standards Institution. 1985

43

Establishing Digital Library in Higher Educational Institutions

A. Fazlur Rahman,
Librarian,
Dr. Mahalingam College of Engineering and Technology, Pollachi (fazrah@yahoo.com)

ABSTRACT

This paper aims at explaining what Digital Library is and its need in Higher Educational institutions. Everyone is having different opinion in Digital Libraries. Through this paper an effort has been made to know concept of Digital Libraries in a lucid way. A systematic manner and step by step method is adopted in explaining how digital libraries can be set up. Components of DL are narrated in a manner that everyone who reads the paper can easily understand the process. This paper includes role of librarians and management in establishing Digital Libraries. Apart from these, hardware requirements for setting up a DL are discussed.

Fortune knocks at every door once in life time. After having knocked the doors of Agriculture by Green Revolution, Sea resources by Blue Revolution, Milk products by White Revolution, Space Revolution by planning to send a satellite to moon, atomic revolution by explosive of nuclear bombs at Pokhran etc., now it is the time for bringing revolution in the field of Information Science, especially in the area of Library and Information science. This revolution may be called

"Digital Library Resources Revolution". This revolution has its own speciality, that it is not an indigenous revolution but the world itself revolves around it and get the benefits out of it. This revolution, in future, will lead to the emergence of revolutions in all other developing fields

Definition of Digital Library

According to IEEE CAIA Workshop on Intelligent Access to Online Digital Libraries 1994, "A Digital Library is an assemblage of digital computing, storage and communications machinery together with the content and software needed to reproduce, emulate, and extend the services provided by conventional libraries based on paper and other material means of collecting, cataloguing, finding, disseminating information".

A full service digital library must accomplish all the essential services of traditional libraries and also exploit the well known advantages of digital storage, searching and communication.

Concept of Digital Libraries

In general there are two concepts in establishing Digital Libraries.

i) Acquiring the resources in digital format and using equipment, softwares, networks etc. to disseminate the digital resource. Example: CDs, Floppies, DVDs, Database containing online, e-books etc.

ii) Digitize the available resource of the library without violation of copy right rules and sharing the resources among the users through latest technology.

When creating Digital Library it should clearly be planned whether the library should purchase digital resources or convert the printed resources into digital resources by employing appropriate hardware and software techniques.

Process of Digitalization

A library is said to be a Digital Library when it renders information services required by the users in a digital form. The following process are to be carried out when converting a library that follows traditional functions into a library that employs digital mode for all its activities:

1. Automation of Entire Library Activities
2. Implementation of Barcode Technology
3. Online Public Access Catalogue - OPAC
4. Internet Connectivity.
5. Resource dissemination through CD/DVD Mirror Server Network Technology
6. Online Journals Database Subscription
7. Online Database Subscription
8. Procurement of e-Books
9. Converting Printed Resources in to Digital Resources
10. Developing Library Information Portal
11. Multimedia Library Services
12. Library Web Page

1. Automation of entire library activities

The following activities of the library must be computerized. This is the preliminary step towards the digitalization process. Through this process, the library staff does his routine in a semi digital environment and the users get the required information on the resources like books and periodicals.

Acquisition, Circulation, Over Dues, Subscription of Journals, Periodicals, Maintenance of Journals, Non – receipt of books on the due date information, Back Volume, Binding, Reference section, Question Bank, Non Book materials, Student eligibility, Staff eligibility, Book transfer to department libraries, Borrowers status, On Line Public access Catalogue.

2. On line public access catalogue - OPAC

It is retrieval system in a very effective semi digital format. Under this system, a particular resource may be searched with the following search engines.

Title, Author, Publisher, Call Number, Accession Number wise searches and Book Borrowers status.

Web OPAC

The concept of Web OPAC is mounting the OPAC on the Library Information Portal on the Web to provide Online Public Access Catalogue facility not only within the library or with in the particular campus but to open the access even to remote users. The benefits of the web OPAC are:

* access to remote users
* due to access of resource of other institutions, Inter Library Loan facility is initiated
* access to resource of scientific institutions and organisations
* access to resource throughout the world
* dissemination of resource globally
* knowledge sharing becomes easy

The placement of resources and the availability are known. In case of a Web based OPAC service, it is possible to know the resources of other institutions. Online Reservation of Resources is also possible in this digital mode.

3. Internet connectivity

The Library should be connected to the Internet. The Internet is a network of networks. Net works are made up of computers to each other through cables. The Internet is a global network, which has internal networks of computers connected to each other for the purpose of sharing information. Internet connectivity is backbone of Digital Library activities. Without the Internet connectivity digital library concept will lose its importance. Resources could not be accessed and shared among people.

4. Dissemination of resources through cd/dvd mirror server network technology

A Library which moves digitalization should also utilise the technology of CD/DVD Mirror Server Network. As for as this concept is concerned Mirror images of the contents of CD/DVD are created and stored in the specialized Hardware Configurations using Networking facilities. These Mirror Images and Contents can be accessed throughout the campus. By introducing the OPAC Search Engines facility required Contents of CD/DVDs can be accessed as per priority of the users. The Hardware and Software specification for CD/DVD Technology is provided below.

Model 1

Data FORCE 1000R Enterprise- Strength, High-Speed Cross Platform CD/DVD-ROM Access

Combining embedding revolutionary storage management software with high capacity and accelerated performance, Procom delivers the enterprise-strength CD/DVD-ROM networking solution. The DataForce 1000R offers:

* Supports Windows 2000 with ADS (Active Directory Services)
* Seamless integration into heterogeneous network environments
* Accommodates up to 1000 CD/DVD- ROM titles
* 300GB protected storage
* 220x performance
* Hardware RAID 5 level protection
* Direct connection to the network
* Advanced security and metering
* Hot swappable power supplies, fans & drives

Model 2

Techfocuz Digital Library 3.01 capable of hosting around 1450 CDs of 400 MB Each (IBM X 226) with Expandability more than 2TB.

Configuration

* IBM X226 Xeon 3.0GHz with EM64T Technology/800 Mhz
* FSB/1GB ECC DDR2 SDRAM/Dual Channel U320 SCSI Controller/Gigabit Ethernet/Dual Redundant Power Supplies(Qty 1)
* 2*512MB DDR PC3200 ECC DDR2 SDRAM (Qty 1)
* 146.4 GB Ultra 320 SCSI HDD 10k rpm hotswap (Qty 4)
* Exp400 Storage expansion unit (Qty 1)
* 2 METER EXT CABLE, LVD OR ULTRA FOR PEDESTAL OR RACK, TIMPAN (Qty 1)
* 6M RAID (Redundant Array of Inexpensive Disk) Card (Qty 1)
* 36 GB 10K U320 HS (Qty 2)
* 15" Color Monitor, Key Board, Mouse (Qty 1)
* DVD R/W-(Qty 1)

Facilities

Content Search	: Search Engine Support
CD-Rom Format	: CD-DA (Audio CD), CD-ROM, CD-R, Video CD, DVD-ROM, DVD Video, UDF
CD-ROM File System	: ISO 9660 level 1 & 2(including Romino, Joilet and Rock-Ridge Extension) DVD-Video & Audio
Storage Models	: All Models of storages like DAS, SAN, NAS, ISCSI, etc.

5. Online journals subscription

The Digital Library should have access to online journals which are available freely or for a cost. It is more useful to the users to browse and get the information from the online journals than reading a printed form. Search keys are also available to get very relevant information within a short span of time. Lot of printed journals and periodicals publishers have now entered into the field of online journals publication. The following are a few and famous among the online journals publishers:

Institute of Electrical and Electronics Engineers, Elsevier Publisher, Springer verlog, ACM digital Library, American Society of Mechanical Engineers, American Society of Civil Engineers etc.

6. Online database subscription

In addition to online journals, the renowned print copy publishers and the online journals subscription providers are providing the facility of online database subscriptions. The databases will cover more number of web based publications like journals and magazines. Some online database subscription providers take an effort of bringing subject wise magazines published in the web free of cost and free of copyright problems. They give access to all these subject-wise free journals at some cost to the subscribers.

Some of the online database subscription providers

Provide information and learning, Elsevier Engineering Information Inc.

Engineering Village, Informatics (India) Limited

H W Wilson, A team

7. Procurement of e - books

e Books are web based resources available as a counterpart for printed books. These books are available in the web-based languages. These e Books have the unique facility of multiple access. Any person from any part of the world, at any time can access these resources. Access and retrieval time is very short e-books are available in the following media:

* CDs, DVDs and through e mail attachment

In general, for the purpose preventing easy accessing, copying, manipulating transferring, editing etc. by unauthorized sources, e books are available in PDF format.

The following are some of the famous e books publishers as per the website http://12.108.175.91/ebookweb/publishers, Amazon e-Bookstore, Amber Quill Press Bookmice.com BooksForABuck.com, Bookzone.com, Digital Literature Institute, Inc. eBooks.com, Hidden Knowledge, KBS Books, Kingfisher Books

8. Developing library information portal

Any individual or institution or library can develop its Digital Library Portal. The portal is the entrance through which subscribed and free subscribed online journals and online databases can be stored under the name of the own digital Library.

The library can develop its Information Portal by means of adopting the following techniques:

a. The Librarian should identify interested staff members who can voluntarily contribute for the development of digital library portal.

b. The selected staff members have to browse the net in search of free e-journals or e-magazines or e-databases or e books in their respective subject fields.

c. The staff members have to give the URL to the Librarian

d. The Librarian will take necessary steps with the web hosting people in the college to add the free e journals

This Library Information Portal can be used on the Digital Black Board of the college by way of digitizing lesson plans, study materials, lecture notes etc. and made them available on the Library Information Portal.

9. Multimedia library services

The creation of the digital library, should add the multimedia facilities inside it. Multimedia library services means, providing library services using various digital technologies. When the users get these multimedia library services he can feel more satisfied in addition to the normal satisfaction level he attains while reading a printed textual document or book or periodical etc.

Multimedia, in simple can be explained as a combination of text, graphic, art, sound, animation and video delivered by computers or other electronic means according to Tay Vaughan in his book entitled " Multimedia: Making it work" published by Tata McGraw Hill, 2002. Multimedia based library services can be provided as follows:

Hard copy of books, i.e. text form, information dissemination through library automation, i.e. semi digitized, Procurement of e-books, subscription of online journals and databases, i.e. graphic form, User education programs through animation format, providing required video cassettes by the users to have visual reference, other electronic library multimedia services means providing digitized resources through CD ROMs and DVD ROMs, providing issues returns and overnight issues through library automation, Web based OPAC.

10. Converting printed resources into digital resources

During the process of conversion of Printed Copies into Digital formats in order to develop the Digital Black Boards as digitized in the previous point Developing Library Information Portal. It may be periodical News letter, lesson plans, study materials, lecture notes, College Calendar and other published work of the institution. The librarian can add the published works of the staff members of the institution subject to their permission for digitizing their books or periodicals which are available in the library. He must take careful effort that the copyright act is not violated.

Hardware / Software requirements for Digital Library

According to Chitra M Hariharan, et al in their article "Developing of the Digital Library in Civil and Structural Engineering R & D Institutions" " Library and Information Networking NACLIN 2002" Published by DELNET the following requirements needed for a medium level Digital Library

Hardware:

Server:

A Pentium (IBM, etc) IV server, Raid, 1.2 Ghz, 512 MB RAM, 256 cache, 21"SVGA Monitor, SCSI 500 GB HD, CD writer, CD Rom, FDD, SNAP server, 10/100 Mbps Ethernet card and other accessories with multimedia Kit, Back up device: Optical , CD/DVD-ROM, Mirror Server/CD Juke Box/DAT Drive, Scanner Intelligent/high density flat bed scanner–(HPScanJet600C) Fujitsu 3097Getc, Minolta PS3000, Ricoh IS420 sheet Feed scanners–Kodak, 500S, Drum Scanners (Juno CP 4000, Scan Mate 5000, Color Getter, Digital Camera (Minolta Ps 3000, Omniscan 3000, Canon) Laser/Ink Jet Printer FAX.

OS:

Windows 2000 server or Linux

Software:

Publishing Adobe acrobat including Adobe capturing, MS Word, Multimedia tools – Photoshop, Flash, Imaging, Library software with cataloguing and searching digital resources – VTLS, Insproplus (any suitable Library software) etc., Searching documents created in various file formats – Dtsearch, WEB Server: Microsoft IIS, Java, Apache, OCR

Software – Textbridge, Omnipage, Imaging Capturing/ Scanning Software – ITRIS, OPTRIX, POWER OFFICE, FILE NET DATA SCAN, OMNDOC, Data Compression. Software Database: MS SQL server, Oracle, MS Access, Formats: Files: TXT,DOC,HTML,XML,SDML,PDF.POSTSCRIPT Images: TIFF, BMP, JPG Network: High speed LAN/Intranet/Internet connectivity, Protocol: TCP/IP

11. Library web page

In the process of Digitalization, it would be more appropriate to develop a library web page before starting subscription of digital resources and Digital Library Portal. The library web page should be viable to access Web OPAC, Digital Black Boards, Library Information Portal of the institution library resources and should collect all the e journals, e books e databases under the caption of the Digital Library. The Library web page can add the information of rules and regulations of the library, staff details, library committee details, list of new arrivals in book section and journal etc. So the user can get all the digitized informations in one place.

Though Librarian is instrumental in the creation of the Digital Library, it will be successful only when he is supported by the management with required fund, positive approach, provision of enthusiasm etc. He requires the support from the staff members in developing digital library portal and get their assistance in finding out right resource which will be useful in a particular subject field. The Librarian should conduct continuous education programs, where he motivates the students to utilize the Digital Library Resources to its full extent. When the librarian gets hundred percent utility from the side of the users, the digital library becomes successful.

References

Books

1. Chaudhary S.K, 2002, Modern Library Strategies, New Delhi: APH Publishers (305p)
2. Dorothy Issac etc, 1993, 'Academic Libraries: Role in the national development ' T.R Publications Chennai (304p)
3. Krishnan Gopal, 2001, Intellectual freedom in digital Libraries' New Delhi Author Press (287p)
4. Kumar P.S.G, 2001 ' Indian Encyclopedia of Library and Information Science', New Delhi : S.Chand Publisher (454p)

Journals

1. Anjali Gulati, November 1999, ' Knowledge Management: An Information Technology Prospective', Vol 19, No 6, 3-7, p36. Desidoc Bulletin of Information Technology, New Delhi.
2. Jagdish Arora, November 2001, ' Building Digital Libraries: an overview' vol 21 No 6.3-23, p55, Desidoc Bulletin of Information Technology, New Delhi.
3. Sreenivasalu V, July 1999, 'Role of Information Technologies in Electronic Information Transfer and in providing value added information services', vol 19, No 4&5, 35-38, p48, Desidoc Bulletin of Information Technology, New Delhi.

Author Index